THE POLITICAL ECONOMY OF
THE WORLD
TRADING SYSTEM

THE POLITICAL ECONOMY OF THE WORLD TRADING SYSTEM

From GATT to WTO

Bernard M. Hoekman and Michel M. Kostecki

OXFORD UNIVERSITY PRESS · OXFORD

Oxford University Press, Great Clarendon Street, Oxford OX2 6DP
Oxford New York
Athens Auckland Bangkok Bogota Bombay
Buenos Aires Calcutta Cape Town Dar es Salaam
Delhi Florence Hong Kong Istanbul Karachi
Kuala Lumpur Madras Madrid Melbourne
Mexico City Nairobi Paris Singapore
Taipei Tokyo Toronto Warsaw
and associated companies in
Berlin Ibadan

Oxford is a trade mark of Oxford University Press

Published in the United States by
Oxford University Press Inc., New York

British Library Cataloguing in Publication Data
Data available

Library of Congress Cataloging in Publication Data
Data available
ISBN 0-19-828955-3
ISBN 0-19-829017-9 (Pbk)

Printed in Great Britain by
Bookcraft (Bath) Ltd., Midsomer Norton, Somerset

To Anne and Patricia

PREFACE

Starting as an obscure trade agreement, unknown to most citizens of participating countries, by the early 1990s the General Agreement on Tariffs and Trade (GATT) had become a prominent institution. The most recent round of multilateral trade negotiations held under its auspices, the Uruguay round, was particularly important in this connection, catapulting the institution into the limelight for the first time in its history. With the creation of the World Trade Organization (WTO), the multilateral trading system was put on a firmer foundation, and its coverage was expanded to services and intellectual property rights, as well as trade in goods. Although popular interest in the subject has been increasing, no readily accessible, yet comprehensive, introduction to the institutional mechanics, economics, and politics of the trading system exists. This book aims to fill this gap.

What matters in understanding the operation of the trading system are not just the rules *per se*, but also the political and economic forces that sculpted them, and the incentives for countries to abide by them. This book not only provides a description of the main disciplines embodied in the WTO, but does so from a political economy point of view. The presumption is that governments are not necessarily the social welfare-maximizing entities found in introductory economics textbooks, but instead develop policy subject to the pressures of a variety of interest-groups. A political economy approach helps to understand how the WTO functions, why the GATT has been very successful in reducing tariffs, and why it has proved much more difficult to expand the reach of multilateral disciplines to domestic policies that have an impact on trade.

We owe a substantial intellectual debt to those who have written on various aspects of the multilateral trade regime, to many members of the WTO secretariat, both past and present, as well as to numerous trade negotiators, diplomats, and scholars. Parts of the discussions in Chapters 3 and 7 draw on papers written with Michael Leidy. A number of people have commented on various versions of parts or all of the manuscript. Our thanks go in particular to Patricia Crémoux, Anne Guimond, Patrick Low, Petros C. Mavroidis, Will Martin, Patrick Messerlin, David Palmeter, Carlos Primo-Braga, Richard Snape, Robert Stern, John Whalley, and Alan Winters, who read the entire manuscript and provided many helpful comments and suggestions. We are also grateful to Alice Enders, Richard Hughes, Mark Koulen, Serban Modaran, Adrian Otten, and Paul Shanahan for discussions and for providing us with information. However, none of the above is responsible for the views expressed in this volume or any inaccuracies. That responsibility is ours alone.

B.M.H.
M.M.K.

CONTENTS

Contents

LIST OF FIGURES

LIST OF TABLES

LIST OF BOXES

LIST OF ABBREVIATIONS

AD	Anti-dumping
AMS	Aggregate measure of support
APEC	Asian-Pacific Economic Co-operation
BOP	Balance of payments
CAP	Common Agricultural Policy (of the EU)
CEEC	Central and Eastern European country
c.i.f.	cost, insurance, and freight
CMEA	Council of Mutual Economic Assistance
CTH	Change in tariff heading
CVD	Countervailing duty
DSB	Dispute Settlement Body (of the WTO)
EEC	European Economic Community
EFTA	European Free Trade Association
EU	European Union
FDI	Foreign direct investment
f.o.b.	free on board
FTA	Free trade area
GATS	General Agreement on Trade in Services
GATT	General Agreement on Tariffs and Trade
GSP	Generalized System of Preferences
GPA	Government Procurement Agreement
GDP	Gross domestic product
HS	Harmonized Commodity Description and Coding System
ILO	International Labour Organization
IMF	International Monetary Fund
INR	Initial negotiating right
IP	Intellectual property
IPRs	Intellectual property rights
ISO	International Organization for Standardization
ITC	International Trade Center (UNCTAD/WTO)
ITO	International Trade Organization
MFA	Multifibre Arrangement
MFN	Most-favoured-nation
MTN	Multilateral trade negotiation
NTB	Non-tariff barrier
NTM	Non-tariff measure
NAFTA	North American Free Trade Agreement
OECD	Organization for Economic Co-operation and Development

OTC	Organization for Trade Co-operation
QR	Quantitative restriction
R&D	Research and development
RIA	Regional integration agreement
S&D	Special and differential treatment (for developing countries)
SDR	Special Drawing Right
SPM	Sanitary and phyto-sanitary measure
STE	State-trading enterprise
TPRB	Trade Policies Review Body (of the WTO)
TPRM	Trade Policies Review Mechanism (of the WTO)
TRIM	Trade-related investment measure
TRIPs	Trade-related intellectual property rights
UNCTAD	United Nations Conference on Trade and Development
VER	Voluntary export restraint
WCO	World Customs Organization
WIPO	World Intellectual Property Organization
WTO	World Trade Organization

Introduction

The World Trade Organization (WTO) is an international organization, established in 1995. It is responsible for administering multilateral trade agreements negotiated by its Members, in particular the General Agreement on Tariffs and Trade (GATT), the General Agreement on Trade in Services (GATS), and the Agreement on Trade-Related Intellectual Property Rights (TRIPs). Total world trade in goods, services, and intellectual property stood at US $5 trillion in 1995, of which services and intellectual property accounted for over $1 trillion. The WTO's rules and principles establish a set of disciplines regarding the regulatory framework in which this exchange takes place.

The WTO builds upon the organizational structure that existed under GATT auspices as of the early 1990s. After its creation in 1947, the GATT progressively developed into a system of great complexity. Its reach expanded steadily in response to developments in the world economy and the interests of its signatories. Initially largely limited to a tariff agreement, the GATT increasingly came to incorporate negotiated disciplines on non-tariff trade policies, which increased in relative importance as average tariff levels fell. Its success was reflected in a steady expansion in the number of contracting parties. During the Uruguay round (1986–94), some 25 countries joined—bringing the total to 128 as of early 1995. To a large extent the GATT managed to fill the gap created by the stillborn International Trade Organization (ITO) of 1948 and emerge as the world's *de facto* trade organization. With the 1994 agreement to establish the WTO, the institution was formally transformed into an international organization of equal standing to the International Monetary Fund (IMF) and the World Bank (as originally intended by the 1944 Bretton Woods conference where agreement was reached to create these bodies). The WTO itself does not embody substantive rules regarding government policies—it is simply a formal institutional structure under whose auspices Members negotiate and implement trade agreements. The rules are contained in the treaties it oversees (GATT, GATS, TRIPs). The GATT therefore continues to exist as a substantive agreement, establishing a set of disciplines on the trade policies of its Members. Indeed, its reach was greatly expanded by the Uruguay round. As trade in goods is by far the most important component of international trade, understanding what the GATT is and what it does (and does not do) is the key to understanding the WTO. Much of this volume therefore focuses on the GATT.

The basic underlying philosophy of the WTO is that open markets, non-discrimination, and global competition in international trade are conducive to the national welfare of all countries. The underpinnings of the GATT and the WTO go back to the 1930s, a period when many countries pursued beggar-thy-neighbour policies including competitive devaluations and the imposition of high, discriminatory trade barriers. Such short-sighted, non-cooperative behaviour was widely recognized to have constituted a very inferior policy in the aftermath of the Second World War. To a great extent the rationale for the creation of the GATT in 1947 was to prevent a repeat of the trade wars of the 1930s, not to mention the world war that followed. The collapse of world trade during the 1930s made a lasting impact on the generation that negotiated the GATT, as well as the International Monetary Fund and the World Bank. The GATT became a forum for consultations and for recurring negotiations to extend multilateral liberalization and co-operation on trade and related policies. It also acted as an institution that could act as a guarantor of domestic trade policy reform undertaken by governments desiring to dismantle barriers to imports.

The creation and success of the GATT constituted a striking example of international co-operation in an area where mercantilism was historically the norm. The basis of mercantilist policy was to maximise exports and minimize imports with a view to accumulating foreign exchange reserves (gold and silver). Mercantilism was driven by nationalism, the perception being that trade surpluses and political power were closely linked. Policy therefore tended to favour direct promotion of exports and restriction of imports through tariffs, taxes quotas, embargoes, and state monopolies. Despite arguments of major economists such as Adam Smith and David Ricardo that mercantilism constituted folly, few governments—Great Britain being a major exception—were convinced that free trade was a much preferable policy from a national welfare point of view. However, throughout much of the second half of the nineteenth century many countries negotiated bilateral trade agreements. The landmark that stands out in the commercial history of the nineteenth century is the Cobden–Chevalier Treaty of 1860, which liberalized trade between Great Britain and France, as well as throughout Europe. During 1862–7, France concluded a range of commercial treaties with every major trading nation in Europe (except Russia) and with the United States. As the treaties included a most-favoured-nation clause, and in each case the countries concerned also negotiated treaties with each other and with Great Britain, the trade concessions granted became general for all. As of the late 1860s, France was at the centre of an impressive network of trade agreements which substantially reduced protectionist trade barriers throughout Europe (Curzon, 1965).

A result was that the world economy became significantly more integrated during the second half of the nineteenth century, global trade expanding much faster than global output. After the First World War, however, countries reverted to protectionist policies. To a significant extent this reflected US trade policies, which were traditionally rather protectionist. The US was unwilling to participate in efforts during the 1920s to liberalize trade and re-establish a more open global economy following the disruption that occurred during the war. As the US economy moved from recession into depression following the 1929 stock market crash, the US Congress adopted the infamous Smoot–Hawley Tariff Act, leading to a rise in average US tariffs from 38 to 52 per cent. This led US trading partners to impose retaliatory trade restrictions and engage in rounds of competitive devaluations. A domino effect occurred, as trade flows were diverted to relatively unprotected markets, forcing down prices, giving rise to protectionist pressure, and thus inducing higher trade barriers. The negative consequences of the trade wars and beggar-thy-neighbour policies of the early 1930s were still very vivid at the end of the Second World War. To a very significant extent they inspired the US willingness to pursue the type of international co-operation on trade that it had rejected in the 1920s and actively support multilateral liberalization efforts (the GATT). The fear of a repeat also considerably hampered protectionist forces in the post-Second World War period.

While very successful in moving countries to liberalize trade and co-operate on trade policy-related matters, GATT rules and principles were often bent, if not broken, by its contracting parties. In instances where the choice was between risking serious conflict and attempting to enforce the letter of GATT disciplines—for example, on regional integration or on subsidies— the contracting parties generally 'blinked' (Finger, 1993*b*; Hudec, 1993). In large part this reflects the nature of the institution, which is basically a club. The club has rules, but its members can decide to waive them, or pretend not to see violations. With the WTO, the institution has been strengthened, especially with regard to dispute-settlement and surveillance mechanisms. The WTO may therefore be somewhat less 'flexible' than the GATT was, which may in turn lead to greater pressures being put on the organization if Members decide to pursue the implementation of its rules more vigorously than in the past. This possibility is tempered by the fact that the WTO is a negotiating forum as well as a code of conduct. As under the GATT, bargaining and deal-making will remain at the heart of the WTO, as the organization will continue to operate on the basis of consensus. Negotiating positions, the implementation of agreements, and the invocation of provisions allowing for the reimposition of protection are in turn all driven by internal political considerations in each WTO Member, tempered by multilateral rules and expectations regarding the actions of other members of the club. The role of bargaining is probably the most striking dimension of the world trading system and perhaps the one that is most difficult for an outsider to grasp.

This book is an introduction to the WTO as an institution and as a regime. Our goal is to provide a succinct description of the multilateral trading system's principles, rules, and procedures, as well as a political-economy-based discussion of its disciplines—or lack thereof. It is not a negotiating history of the recently concluded Uruguay round—although the results of this negotiation are discussed at some length. The focus is on the resulting rules of the game, not on the quantitative impact of the trade agreements (the effect on trade flows or the distribution of gains across countries). While such empirical issues are important, they are not particularly useful in understanding how the trading system functions. The subject of this book is the institution—the multilateral trading system—its rules, strengths, and weaknesses, and the challenges it will face in the coming decades. Being an introduction, this book cannot be more than a starting-point. Extensive references are made to the literature, and guides to further reading are provided at the end of every chapter. Readers interested in pursuing specific issues are invited to consult the listed works. We hope that this book will be a non-specialist's guide and companion to the multilateral trading system and will encourage the reader to learn more about this important and, in many respects, unique forum for international co-operation.

The book has four parts. Part I deals with the institution. After an introductory overview of the evolution of the trading system in Chapter 1, Chapter 2 describes the organizational structure of the WTO, its scope and functions. Chapter 3 turns to the role of the WTO as a forum for negotiations. Special attention is given to the concept of reciprocity, this being a central element of multilateral trade negotiations (MTNs) and the functioning of the system. Part II focuses on the disciplines of the GATT, the GATS, and the Agreement on TRIPs. Chapter 4 describes the GATT's basic rules and principles, and the political and economic rationale underlying them. Chapters 5 and 6 address trade in services and trade-related aspects of intellectual property rights, respectively. Part III turns to what we call the holes and loopholes in the WTO (Hoekman and Leidy, 1993). The various mechanisms in the GATT allowing for the (re-)imposition of trade barriers are discussed in Chapter 7, which summarizes the WTO's rules on—and the economics of—the use of instruments of 'contingent protection'. These loopholes have been a weak element of the GATT, often circumvented if too constraining, and abused if vaguely worded. Chapter 8 discusses sector-specific issues that have affected the trading system, in particular trade in agricultural products and in textiles and clothing. Uruguay-round negotiators succeeded in reintegrating both agricultural products and textiles and clothing into the GATT, one of the major achievements of the round. Chapter 9 deals with one of the most important exceptions to the most-favoured-nation rule allowed by the GATT and the GATS: regional integration agreements. Part IV looks to the future. Chapter 10 discusses the evolving role of developing countries in the multilateral trading system. Chapter 11 turns to the future of the WTO, and discusses the issues that are likely to be on the negotiating agenda for some time to come: competition (anti-trust) policy, labour standards, investment, and environmental policies. Chapter 12 presents a number of conclusions regarding the role of the WTO in maintaining international co-operation, its relevance to Member countries, and the challenges that are likely to confront the organization in the future.

PART I
The Institution

1

Overview of the Trading System

Although economic theory suggests that countries should pursue liberal trade policies and exchange goods and services on the basis of their comparative advantage, in practice most nations actively intervene in international trade. Since 1947 the GATT has played a major role in constraining trade policies, in the process creating an ever more complex network of rights and obligations regulating international trade relations. Progress has sometimes been fitful, often involving two steps forward and one step back. None the less, recurring MTNs and the positive demonstration effects of the success of outward-oriented development strategies led to very significant declines in average levels of protection. GATT principles and mechanisms helped countries to grow by allowing firms to specialize and thereby fostering ever greater integration through trade. The trade flows involved are very large. Global trade in goods and services equalled soms US $5 trillion (thousand billion) in the early 1990s. At $3.7 trillion, trade in goods accounted for the lion's share of global flows, followed by trade in services, which passed the $1 trillion mark in 1992. Much of the trade in merchandise involved OECD countries. As can be seen from Fig. 1.1, Western Europe dominates global

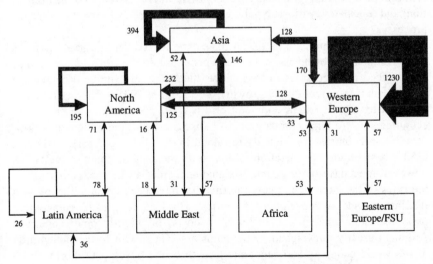

Note: Only flows greater than $15 billion (0.5 per cent of world trade) are recorded.
Source: GATT, *International Trade 1993* (Geneva: GATT, 1993).
Fɪɢ 1.1 Network of world merchandise trade, 1992 (US$ billion)

trade flows, intra-European trade accounting for over $1.2 trillion in 1992. Western European exchanges with the rest of the world accounted for another $450 billion. Fig. 1.1 illustrates the dominance of trade between and within the three major regions of the global economy: Europe, North America and Asia. Trade flows involving other parts of the globe are relatively small. Trade between these other regions is generally less than 0.5 per cent of world trade.

Although trade flows between developing country regions of the world are much smaller than those involving high-income regions, the volume and growth rate of global trade flows are important because international trade is an engine of growth. OECD markets provide developing countries with their most important export opportunities, while growth in developing countries generates imports of intermediate and capital goods as well as know-how. World trade growth has outstripped the growth of output consistently throughout most of the post-Second World War period, resulting in steadily increasing trade openness ratios for most countries (the sum of exports and imports relative to gross domestic output). In the 1985–95 period, the growth of world trade was more than twice as high as the growth of global output (World Bank, 1995). This implies that the world is becoming ever more integrated through trade. Rising trade openness ratios and integration in turn has significant positive impacts on total factor productivity—the portion of real output growth not accounted for by increasing inputs of labour and capital. This is because greater trade implies greater competition and therefore pressures to innovate and enhance productive efficiency, while at the same time allowing technological upgrading. By encouraging trade liberalization, non-discrimination, and transparency of trade policies, the GATT supported the globalization process.

Developing countries in particular have experienced very large increases in trade volumes and openness to the world economy. In the 1985–95 period they experienced real increases in trade flows that were on average 6 percentage points higher than real output growth (World Bank, 1995). This performance reflected to a great extent unilateral efforts by these countries to open their economies to foreign competition. As discussed at greater length below, developing countries traditionally refrained from full-fledged participation in GATT-based trade liberalization efforts. With the establishment of the WTO, however, most developing countries signalled a greater willingness to abide by the rules of the game. The many reforms that have been taken unilaterally in the last decade by developing countries will lead to greater competitive pressure and concomitant dislocation costs in high-income countries. Although greatly outweighed by the gains associated with further integration of the world economy and economic growth of the developing world, fuller participation of developing economies and former centrally planned economies in global trade is likely to lead to frictions. The creation of the WTO and the associated expansion of multilateral disciplines and strengthening of the institution therefore occurred at a propitious time. Indeed, the two developments were clearly linked. One of the major immediate challenges confronting the WTO will be to manage the process of integrating large economies such as China and Russia into the trading system. More generally, the system will be confronted with the continuing challenge of furthering the integration of the global economy.

This is truly a challenge, as past experience has amply demonstrated that pressures for protection and incentives to deviate from multilateral rules will arise. The creation of the WTO and the Uruguay round negotiations were a direct response to the managed trade and new protectionism that had proliferated during the 1970s and early 1980s. The recourse by OECD governments to non-tariff barriers in this period was driven in large part by exogenous shocks (the collapse of fixed exchange rates; successive oil price hikes by the OPEC cartel) and political developments (*détente*) that reduced the primacy of foreign policy considerations in maintaining co-operation in trade. Trade restrictions formed part of an inappropriate policy response to the resulting structural adjustment pressures, which were augmented by the emergence of competition from East Asian nations. The successful completion of the Uruguay round revealed that the major trading nations were willing to maintain multilateral co-operation and strengthen disciplines regarding the use of non-tariff measures. The fact remains that pressures for protection will continue to confront WTO Member governments as the business cycle changes and technological developments require industries to adjust.

WTO members face a different world from that existing in the immediate post-Second World War period. The US is no longer the hegemon of the world economy, willing to tolerate deviations from multilateral rules by trading partners. Many of the trade disputes and the recourse to NTBs in the 1980s were in part a reflection of what has been called the diminished giant syndrome of the USA (Bhagwati, 1991). The rising trade openness ratios alluded to earlier reflect the existence of a much more interdependent world than existed in the early 1950s. Instead of one hegemon (the US), there is a triad of powerful traders (the EU, Japan, and the USA). None of the three can be relied upon to take a leadership role. At the same time, the WTO as an international organization has very few powers and at the end of the day what matters is the willingness of WTO Members to invoke multilateral dispute-settlement procedures and play by the rules of the game. The absence of a hegemon can, in principle, prove beneficial in this regard, as all players have an interest in maintaining co-operation (or alternatively, enforcing the rules). Doubts can be and often have been expressed regarding the relevance of the rules for large players. The rise of creative forms of protectionism in the 1980s, such as voluntary export restraints, illustrates the difficulty of enforcing multilaterally negotiated rules. Time will tell how successful the WTO will be in maintaining and extending multilateral co-operation and preventing large countries such as the US from pursuing solutions to trade problems outside the system. The very act of creating the WTO gives some cause for optimism in this regard.

1.1. A HISTORICAL OVERVIEW: FROM GATT TO WTO

Formally the GATT was not an international organization (i.e. a legal entity in its own right), but an inter-governmental treaty. As a result, instead of member states, GATT had 'contracting parties'. The agreement reached at the end of the Uruguay round (April 1994) to establish the WTO changed matters. The WTO is an international organization that administers multilateral agreements pertaining to trade in goods (GATT), trade in services (GATS), and trade-related aspects of intellectual property rights (TRIPs). To reflect the fact that the WTO is an organization, in this book we will generally use the terms 'contracting parties' to refer to signatories of the old GATT, and 'Members' to refer to signatories of the WTO. We also make a distinction between GATT-1947 (the old GATT) and GATT-1994 that is embodied in the WTO. The GATT-1994 is much more far-reaching than the GATT-1947.

The various treaties overseen by the WTO are between nation-states and customs territories, and deal with government policies. The WTO is essentially not concerned with the behaviour of private businesses. It deals only with the actions of governments, establishing disciplines on trade-policy instruments such as tariffs, quotas, subsidies, or state-trading. Thus, the WTO is a regulator of the regulatory actions of governments that affect trade and the conditions of competition facing imported products on domestic markets. In this it is no different from the old GATT.

A fundamental perception of the founders of the GATT was that multilateral institutions facilitating co-operation between countries were important not only for straightforward economic reasons, but that the resulting increase in interdependence between countries would help to reduce the risk of war (Penrose, 1953; Hirschman, 1969). The expected beneficial impact on real incomes associated with trade liberalization and non-discriminatory access to markets was expected to reduce the scope for political conflicts, while the increase in transparency and the availability of a forum in which to discuss potential or actual trade conflicts was expected to reduce the probability of these spilling over into other domains.

The Preamble of the GATT-1947 states that the objectives of the contracting parties include 'raising standards of living, ensuring full employment and a large and steadily growing volume of real income and effective demand, developing the full use of the resources of the world and expanding the production and exchange of goods' (GATT, 1994a: 486). It goes on to say that reciprocal and mutually advantageous arrangements involving a substantial reduction of tariffs and other barriers to trade as well as the elimination of discriminatory treatment in international trade will contribute to the realization of these objectives. Nowhere is any mention made of free trade as an ultimate goal. Instead, the role of the GATT was (and is) to facilitate the reduction of barriers of trade and ensure greater equality with respect to conditions of market access for contracting parties.

The GATT emerged from the negotiations to create an International Trade Organization after World War II. The negotiations on the charter of such an organization, although concluded successfully in Havana in 1948, did not lead to the establishment of the ITO because the US Congress refused to ratify the agreement. The GATT had been negotiated in 1947, before the ITO negotiations were concluded. As the countries involved in the 1947 exchange of tariff reductions were anxious that their implementation not be conditional upon the conclusion of the ITO talks, the GATT was created as an interim agreement. As the ITO never came into being, the GATT was the only concrete result of the negotiations. Although the GATT incorporated many of the specific provisions of the ITO, having been conceived as a temporary trade agreement it lacked an institutional structure. In the first years of its operation it did not exist as an entity except once or twice a year when formal meetings of the contracting parties were held (Curzon and Curzon, 1973). Its organizational structure emerged only gradually. While major decisions were taken at the sessions of the CONTRACTING PARTIES,[1] it rapidly became obvious that a standing body was needed. An inter-sessional committee was formed in 1951 to organize voting by air mail or telegraphic ballot on issues relating to import restrictions justified for balance-of-payments reasons. This committee was replaced in 1960 by a Council of Representatives which was given broader powers and responsibilities for day-to-day management.

As of the early 1990s, a well-oiled GATT machine existed, allowing contracting parties to manage developments in the trading system, including a capacity for surveillance of trade policies and assisting conflict resolution through consultations, negotiations, mediation, and dispute settlement. The Secretariat that supported these interactions has always been relatively small—standing at some 450 staff in 1995. Much of the work was—and is—done by several thousand experts, diplomats, bureaucrats, and politicians, most of whom are based in capital cities of Member States. The GATT Secretariat was formally known as the Interim Commission for the International Trade Organization (ICITO), created during the negotiations on the ITO. It was technically a United Nations (UN) body, as the ITO negotiations occurred under UN auspices. But because the ITO never came into

---

[1] The term CONTRACTING PARTIES, in capital letters, was used to denote joint actions taken by all signatories to the agreement, i.e. to distinguish these from the actions of individual contracting parties. With the creation of the WTO, this potential source of confusion among the non-initiated has been eliminated, as the WTO is an organization.

TABLE 1.1 *From GATT to WTO: A chronology*

Date	Event
1947	The GATT is drawn up to record the results of tariff negotiations between 23 countries.
1948	GATT provisionally enters into force. Drafting of the ITO Charter (Havana Charter) which was to incorporate GATT is completed.
1949	Annecy round of tariff negotiations; eleven countries participate.
1950	China (Republic of) withdraws from GATT. The US Administration abandons efforts to seek Congressional ratification of the ITO.
1951	Torquay round of tariff negotiations. The Inter-sessional Committee is established to organize voting by air-mail ballot on issues concerning use of trade measures to safeguard the balance of payments. Germany (Federal Republic) accedes to the GATT.
1955	A review session modifies numerous provisions of the GATT. A move to transform GATT into a formal international organization by establishing an Organization for Trade Co-operation (OTC) fails. The USA is granted a waiver from GATT disciplines for certain agricultural policies. Japan accedes to the GATT.
1956	Fourth round of multilateral trade negotiations is held in Geneva.
1957	Creation of the European Economic Community.
1960	A Council of Representatives takes over GATT's 'housekeeping' duties. The Dillon round is started and is concluded in 1961.
1962	The Long Term Arrangement on Cotton Textiles is negotiated. It is renegotiated in 1967 and extended for three years in 1970.
1964	The United Nations Conference on Trade and Development (UNCTAD) is created to press for trade measures to benefit developing countries.
1964	The Kennedy round begins (concluded in 1967).
1965	Part IV, 'On Trade and Development' is added to the GATT, establishing new guidelines for trade policies of—and towards—developing countries.
1967	Poland becomes the first centrally planned country to accede to the GATT.
1973	The Tokyo round is initiated (concluded in 1979).
1974	The Agreement Regarding International Trade in Textiles, better known as the Multifibre Arrangement (MFA) enters into force, restricting import growth to 6 per cent per year. It is renegotiated in 1977 and 1982, and extended in 1986, 1991, and 1992.
1982	A GATT ministerial meeting—the first in almost a decade—fails to set the agenda for a new round. A GATT work programme is formulated with a view to establishing an agenda for a new MTN.
1986	Launching of the Uruguay round in Punta del Este, Uruguay.
1988	A GATT ministerial meeting to review progress in the Uruguay round is held in Montreal in December. The mid-term review is completed only in April 1989.
1990	Canada formally introduces a proposal to create an international organization ('Multilateral Trade Organization') that would cover the GATT, the GATS, and other multilateral instruments agreed to in the Uruguay round.

1990	A GATT ministerial meeting in Brussels fails to conclude the Uruguay round.
1993	In June the US Congress grants fast-track authority—under which it cannot propose amendments to the outcome of negotiations—with a 15 December deadline. On 1 July Peter Sutherland becomes Director-General of the GATT.
1994	In Marrakesh, on 15 April, Ministers sign the Final Act establishing the World Trade Organization (WTO) and embodying the results of the Uruguay round.

existence, the formal relationship between the GATT (a treaty) and the UN was always tenuous.

Over the more than four decades of its existence, the GATT system evolved into a *de facto* world trade organization. Its fairly complex basic legal text was extended or modified by numerous supplementary codes and arrangements, interpretations, waivers, reports by dispute-settlement panels, and Council decisions. Table 1.1 highlights some of the major milestones. GATT's early years were dominated by accession negotiations, a Review Session in the mid-1950s that led to modifications to the Agreement, and the creation of the European Economic Community (EEC) in 1957. In 1962 a multilaterally negotiated derogation from the GATT rules in the area of trade in cotton textiles was made. This developed into successive Multifibre Arrangements (MFA-I through MFA-IV; see Chapter 8). Starting in the mid-1960s, recurring rounds of multilateral trade negotiations (MTNs) were held that gradually expanded the scope of the GATT to a larger number of non-tariff policies, and eventually led to the creation of the WTO.

Eight rounds of multilateral trade negotiations have been held under GATT auspices: the Geneva round (1947), the Annecy round (1949), the Torquay round (1951), another Geneva round in 1956, the Dillon round (1960–1), the Kennedy round (1964–7), the Tokyo round (1973–9), and most recently the Uruguay round (1986–94). The outcome of these rounds and the modalities of negotiations are discussed in subsequent chapters. What follows gives a brief overview of the main elements of negotiations (Table 1.2). The first five rounds dealt exclusively with tariffs. Starting with the Kennedy round, attention began to shift towards non-tariff trade restrictions and to the problem of trade in agricultural products. Although the Kennedy round dealt only with non-tariff barriers (NTBs) that were already covered by the GATT, the Tokyo round addressed policies that were not subject to GATT disciplines (the foremost examples being product standards and government procurement). This trend was continued in the Uruguay round, which included trade in services, intellectual property, and rules of origin—all matters on which the GATT had very little to say.

TABLE 1.2 *Multilateral trade negotiations, 1947–1995*

Name	Period and number of contracting parties	Subjects and modalities	Outcome
Geneva round	1947 23 countries	Tariffs: item-by-item negotiations	Concessions on 45,000 tariff lines
Annecy round	1949 29 countries	Tariffs: item-by-item negotiations	Modest tariff reductions
Torquay round	1950–1 32 countries	Tariffs: item-by-item negotiations	8,700 tariff concessions
Geneva round	1955–6 33 countries	Tariffs: item-by-item negotiations	Modest tariff reductions
Dillon round	1960–1 39 countries	Tariffs: item-by-item negotiations; proposal by the EEC for a 20 per cent linear cut in duties on manufactures not adopted	Tariff adjustments following the creation of the EEC (1957); 4,400 tariff concessions exchanged.
Kennedy round	1963–7 74 countries	Tariffs: formula approach, supplemented by item-by-item negotiations; non-tariff measures: anti-dumping, customs valuation	Average tariff reduction of 35 per cent by developed countries; some 30,000 tariff lines bound; agreement on anti-dumping and customs valuation.
Tokyo round	1973–9 99 countries	Tariffs: formula approach; non-tariff measures: anti-dumping, subsidies, customs valuation, government procurement, import licensing, product standards, safeguards	Average tariffs of developed countries reduced by one-third (to reach 6 per cent on average for manufactures); so-called codes of conduct established for interested GATT members on specific non-tariff measures.

Uruguay round	1986–94 103 countries in 1986; 117 by end-1993; 128 as of early 1995	Tariffs: combination of item-by-item and formula negotiation; non-tariff measures: all Tokyo issues, plus pre-shipment inspection, trade-related investment measures, rules of origin; new issues: trade in services and intellectual property rights, dispute-settlement procedures, transparency and surveillance of trade policies.	Tariffs of developed countries reduced by about one-third on average. Agriculture and textiles and clothing brought into GATT; creation of the WTO, and agreements on services (GATS) and intellectual property (TRIPs); most Tokyo round codes enhanced and made a part of GATT-1994, i.e. apply to all Members of the WTO.

The Early Rounds

The first round of multilateral tariff negotiations was the Geneva round of 1947, which led to the creation of the General Agreement. Some 45,000 tariff concessions covering about half of world trade were exchanged. The twenty-three countries involved were also participants in the drafting of the Havana Charter (which involved a total of fifty-six nations), reflecting the fact that originally the GATT was supposed to be embedded in the ITO. Two MTNs were held relatively soon after the creation of the GATT, and largely consisted of accession negotiations. The first took place in Annecy (France) in 1949, at which time nine countries joined the GATT. A second followed in Torquay (UK) in 1951, with four more countries acceding. This brought GATT membership to a total of thirty-two, as four countries had ceased to participate in the Agreement by 1950. Three of these countries—China, Lebanon, and Syria—were original contracting parties, while the fourth—Liberia—had joined during the Annecy round. A third round followed in Geneva during 1955–6, by which time Japan had also acceded, bringing the total number of contracting parties to thirty-three. None of these rounds had as large an impact in terms of reductions in average tariffs as the 1947 meeting did. Indeed, the outcomes were rather minor. For example, for the United States, the average cut in its tariffs achieved in 1947 was 21.1 per cent, whereas cuts in the next three rounds were only 1.9, 3.0, and 3.5 per cent, respectively (Baldwin, 1986: 193). By the mid-1950s, the weighted average tariff of the main industrialized nations had been reduced to some 15 per cent.

The Dillon Round (1960-1)

Following the establishment of the EEC in 1957, a series of large-scale tariff negotiations were held under GATT auspices. As will be discussed at greater length in Chapter 9, the GATT stipulates that any customs union or free-trade area must be examined to ensure that its establishment does not result in a higher average level of protection against other GATT members. Non-member countries that are negatively affected by the formation of a customs union that involves a member country adopting higher tariffs have the right to compensation. The resulting bilateral negotiations with the EEC were supplemented by a round of multilateral tariff negotiations, with a total of thirty-four nations participating. The Dillon round—named after the US Under-Secretary of State who proposed the talks—yielded relatively modest results, with only 4,400 tariff concessions exchanged. No concessions were granted on agricultural and many other sensitive products, notwithstanding that these were the products where effective tariffs and trade barriers more generally were expected to rise as a result of the formation of the EEC (and more specifically the Common Agricultural Policy).

The Kennedy Round (1963-7)

Named after President Kennedy, some forty-six nations participated in the Kennedy round, although membership of the GATT had reached seventy-four by the end of the round. A new tariff negotiating method (an across-the-board formula approach) for industrial products was adopted by major OECD countries, resulting in an average tariff reduction of 35 per cent for their trade in such products. Product-by-product negotiations on agricultural trade were less successful. The Kennedy round was the first MTN to go beyond tariffs and deal with certain non-tariff measures (NTMs). It resulted, in particular, in the conclusion of an Anti-Dumping Code (see Chapter 7), and an agreement on US customs valuation procedures for certain products (see Chapter 4). The Kennedy round also included efforts that led to the formal inclusion of preferential treatment in favour of the developing countries. This was embodied in a new Part IV of the General Agreement in 1965 (see Chapter 10).

The Tokyo Round (1973-9)

Ninety-nine countries, representing nine-tenths of world trade, participated in this MTN, named after the city where the negotiations were launched. Tariffs were reduced on thousands of industrial and agricultural products, and some 33,000 tariff lines were bound. The total value of trade affected by tariff commitments was in the range of US $300 billion, measured in 1981 imports. As a result, the average import weighted tariff on manufactured products maintained by industrialized nations declined to about 6 per cent. This represented a reduction of 34 per cent (measured in terms of tariff revenue), comparable with the magnitude of tariff reduction achieved in the Kennedy round. The Tokyo round also led to the adoption of a range of specific agreements. These included the legalization of preferential tariff and non-tariff treatment in favour of developing countries and among developing countries (the so-called Enabling Clause—see Chapter 10) and a number of codes dealing with NTMs or specific products. Codes addressed: (*a*) subsidies and countervailing measures (*b*) technical barriers to trade (product standards) (*c*) government procurement (*d*) customs valuation (*e*) import licensing procedures, and (*f*) a revision of the Kennedy round anti-dumping code. In addition, arrangements on bovine meat and dairy products, as well as an agreement on civil aircraft, were negotiated. The use of codes was partly driven by the fact that developing countries objected to the expansion of GATT disciplines, so that the two-thirds majority required for amending the GATT was unlikely to be attained. By negotiating a code, like-minded countries were able to co-operate without having all GATT members on board. At the same time, this weakened the system, as it allowed countries to pick and choose among disciplines (the term GATT à la carte was often used to describe the code approach).

The Uruguay Round (1986–94)

This most recently concluded MTN—named after the country that hosted the Ministerial meeting that established its agenda in 1986—continued the trend of widening the negotiating agenda, increasing the number of participating countries, and taking longer to conclude. In addition to policies affecting trade in goods, measures affecting investment, trade in services, and intellectual property were also put on the table. The Uruguay round led to a further liberalization of international trade, including not only tariff reductions but also the elimination of tariffs for certain product groups, the reintegration of agricultural trade and textiles and clothing into the GATT, and the expansion of GATT disciplines. The new GATT-1994 embodies a series of Agreements on specific issues—many of them renegotiations of Tokyo round codes. The creation of a new GATT allowed contracting parties to bypass the need to formally amend the GATT-1947, and to ensure at the same time that the results of the round were a Single Undertaking that applied to all. The WTO was established to oversee the functioning of the GATT, the GATS, and the Agreement on TRIPS. The average tariff on the manufactured products of industrial countries, weighted by the volume of trade in the products concerned, fell from 6.4 per cent to 4.0 per cent, a cut of almost 40 per cent. This compares to a weighted average duty of 35 per cent before the creation of GATT (1947), and around 15 per cent at the time of the Dillon round (the early 1960s).

In the period leading up to the establishment of the WTO, the GATT was already a quasi-universal institution, with 128 signatories as of early 1995, and another twenty potential members in the queue for accession (a list of WTO Members is included in Annex 1). With the notable exception of the Russian Federation, China, and Taiwan, all major trading nations are WTO Members. All three of these countries were engaged in accession negotiations at the time of writing. Once concluded, all of the world's important trading nations will be WTO Members. Suggestions made during the Uruguay round negotiations that 'GATT is dead' sit oddly with these signs of popularity.

1.2. FUNCTIONS OF THE MULTILATERAL TRADING SYSTEM

Multilateral co-operation among sovereign nations often occurs through the creation of institutions or regimes. Because a central authority is absent in international relations, political scientists have developed the concept of a regime, defined as 'sets of implicit or explicit principles, norms, rules, and decision-making procedures around which actors' expectations converge in a given area of international relations' (Krasner, 1983: 2). The principles and procedures imply obligations, even though these are not enforceable through a hierarchical legal system. Although regimes are arrangements motivated by self-interest, they reflect patterns of co-operation over time among members that are based on the existence of shared interests. The GATT-1947 and the WTO that suceeded it can be regarded as a major building-block of the multilateral trade regime.

Two viewpoints are particularly helpful in understanding the role of the WTO. The first is to regard the institution as a code of conduct; the second is to view it as a market. The WTO is a market. Trade negotiations are conducted to reduce barriers to trade, agree to rules of behaviour, and resolve disputes. They can be regarded as market through which nations attempt to create and alter rules governing the trade policies of Members (the code of conduct), and engage in the reciprocal exchange of liberalization commitments. Two fundamental elements can be identified in this context: achieving an agreement, and enforcing it. Basic international trade theory suggests that whether there is an economic rationale from a national welfare point of view for trade restrictions depends largely on the market power of a country. A small country that cannot influence prices on world markets will generally lose from imposing trade barriers, and therefore has little to lose and much to gain from a multilateral agreement to lower trade barriers. Indeed, such countries should pursue such liberalization unilaterally (see Box 1.1). In contrast, large countries may be able to change the terms of trade—the price of their exports relative to the price of imports—in their favour by restricting trade. However, for the world as a whole the imposition of trade restrictions by one or more countries can only reduce welfare. Large countries may thus find themselves in a so-called Prisoners' Dilemma situation: it may be in each country's interest to impose restrictions, but the result of such individually rational behaviour is that all countries end up in a situation where their welfare is lower than if all countries followed free-trade policies (see Chapter 3). Both small and large countries therefore have an incentive to co-operate and agree not to impose trade barriers. Liberal trade is a positive-sum game.

Box 1.1. Why trade liberalization?

The central concept underlying trade is opportunity cost. Producing (consuming) something comes at the cost of not producing (consuming) something else. An important economic theorem based on the concept of opportunity cost states that there are gains from trade associated with specialization. That is, aggregate production and consumption of a group of people, a group of countries, or the world as a whole can be larger if the people or countries concerned specialize in the production of goods and services in which they have a comparative advantage and are permitted to freely exchange their products for those of other people or countries (see e.g. Caves and Jones, 1985). It is largely due to such specialization and international trade that, on average, the level of consumption (real incomes) has increased by about four times over the last eight decades.

Consider a simple example. If the people of Plains, who are good at raising animals (say cows), must also spend time growing food (at which they are less good than in raising cows), they will be able to keep fewer cows. Each hour spent growing food has a high opportunity cost in terms of cows foregone. Suppose the people of Agria are good at farming, but do not have much aptitude for raising cows. Agria will then have a high opportunity cost in terms of time not spent farming. If these two countries or groups of people could trade with each other, they could concentrate on what each one does best. Economists say that they would specialize according to their comparative advantage. This will ensure that total output produced is maximized, and that each party ends up being able to consume more vegetables and cows than would be possible otherwise.

The decision what to specialize in depends on what one does best compared with the other things that could (or would have to) be done. The people of Plains might actually be better farmers than those of Agria, in that for every hour invested in farming they get a bigger harvest than Agria does. However, as long as an hour spent by the people in Plains on farming has a higher cost in terms of foregone cows than does an hour spent on farming in Agria, Plains should specialize in cows. What matters is not absolute, but comparative advantage. International trade provides nations with the opportunity to specialize in production according to their comparative advantage. Trade liberalization, which is a major objective of the GATT, thus helps nations to realize a more efficient utilization of their resources (production capacities). Trade liberalization has two essential effects. First, it brings about a reallocation of resources towards those activities in which the country has comparative advantage. Secondly, trade liberalization expands the consumption opportunities of countries, as more efficient production generates greater income and increased opportunities to buy goods and services from other countries. No matter how poorly endowed a country is, it will always have a comparative advantage in something.

This suggests that countries interested in maximizing their wealth should not impose trade barriers. This is certainly the case for small countries which are price-takers on world markets. However, as explained at greater length below, there are often political difficulties in liberalizing access to markets. In part this is because some people will always lose. While these can be compensated in principle, in practice this is not always easy. It is also the case that even though a country will benefit from liberalizing its trade, it is even better that trading partners do the same. This is one of the rationales for engaging in multilateral liberalization attempts. Large countries can benefit from trade restrictions if they have the power to affect world prices (an import barrier—by reducing demand—can lead to a fall in world prices). A problem is that if all countries follow this policy, all will end up being worse off than if free trade was pursued. Another problem is that if tariffs are not set at the optimal level, the country may lose—even if other countries pursue free trade. Large countries therefore will usually also benefit from the reciprocal reduction of trade barriers.

Maintaining or achieving a liberal trade policy is no trivial matter. In most countries numerous groups will exist that have different preferences with respect to trade measures. The structure of protection at any point in time is the result of the interaction between the demand expressed by various interest groups and the supply offered by governments. Attempts to alter this equilibrium, i.e. to move towards a welfare-increasing reduction in protection, will result in opposition by those groups that expect to lose from liberalization. The losses associated with liberalization are usually concentrated on import-competing industries, while the gainers tend to be much more diffuse: the consumers of the product. A political economy problem therefore arises. Those facing large losses have a much greater individual incentive to organize and invest in lobbying against liberalization than those that gain from liberalization, as individual gains are relatively small and dispersed among a large number of issues. This, indeed, is the main reason why trade restrictions are imposed in the first place.[2] An MTN can solve this problem by confronting the losers with another lobby that may be equally powerful: the set of firms that gain from greater access to foreign markets. Similarly, by requiring reciprocal reductions in trade barriers, the prisoners' dilemma that may in principle confront large countries can be overcome, again improving world welfare (see Chapter 3). Finally, by including many products in the negotiation, losers obtain some automatic compensation through access to cheaper imports.

An MTN is a market in the sense that countries come together to exchange market-access commitments on a reciprocal basis. It is a barter market. In contrast to the markets one finds in city squares, countries do not have access to a medium of exchange: they do not have money with which to buy, and against which to sell, trade policies. Instead they have to exchange apples against oranges: tariff reductions for iron against foreign-market access commitments for cloth. This makes the trade-policy market less efficient than one where money can be used, and is one of the reasons that MTNs can be a tortuous process.

The WTO as a Code of Conduct for Trade Policy

One of the results of the market exchange is a code of conduct. The WTO contains a set of specific legal obligations regulating the trade policies of Member States. These are embodied in the GATT, the GATS, and the agreement on TRIPs, and are intended to help attain the objectives of the founders of the GATT-1947: enhancement of economic growth via non-discrimination and progressive liberalization of trade. The rules and principles of the WTO constrain the freedom of governments to use specific trade-policy instruments. They influence the balance between interest-groups seeking protection and those favouring open markets in Member countries' domestic political marketplace (Tumlir, 1985). The foreign trade policy-making process is generally torn by conflicting objectives of national interest-groups, as well

---

[2] However, in the case of developing countries that do not have a well-developed tax administration, taxing trade flows frequently has a revenue rationale as well (see Rodrik, 1994*a*). More generally, the socio-psychology of protectionism is such that most people tend to be nationalistic in their thinking about economic matters. Trade policy is by definition a nationalistic policy in that it discriminates against foreign producers.

as by external considerations. Industry associations, labour unions, regional authorities, consumer lobbies, and government agencies all interact in determining the policy outcome. The WTO is somewhat analogous to a mast to which governments can tie themselves so as to escape the siren-like calls of various pressure-groups (Roessler, 1985). It is a mechanism through which the political market failure that is inherent in many societies—both industrialized and developing—can be corrected, at least in part, because reneging on liberalization commitments requires the compensation of affected trading partners. This increases both the cost and the visibility of adopting inefficient trade policies to placate domestic interest-groups. However, as will be emphasized throughout this book, much depends on the will of governments to tie themselves to the mast. WTO rules and disciplines—discussed at length in later chapters—embody many holes and loopholes that governments can invoke if they desire to.

The WTO embodies a rule-oriented approach to multilateral co-operation. This contrasts with what can be characterized as a results-oriented approach— agreements on trade flows, market share, or international prices (see Fig. 1.2). The tension between rule-based and outcomes-oriented approaches to international co-operation on trade policy has been a prevailing theme in much of the post-Second World War period. Examples of managed trade include arrangements that involve negotiated agreements on the volume of trade (e.g. barter deals; 'voluntary' agreements to import specific quantities; quotas) and those that attempt to stabilize or set prices (the OPEC cartel being a prominent example). Rule-oriented approaches focus not on outcomes, but on the rules of the game, and involve agreements on the level of trade barriers that are permitted as well as attempts to establish the general conditions of competition facing foreign producers in export markets.

Four basic principles can be identified that are of particular importance in understanding the WTO: (1) non-discrimination; (2) reciprocity; (3) market access; and (4) fair competition. These principles are not always consistent with—or complementary to—each other. There is a tension between non-discrimination and reciprocity on the one hand, and between market access and the notion of fair competition on the other. Of these four principles, non-discrimination is a basic and fundamental formal rule. Reciprocity, in contrast, is a mechanism or tool that is used in MTNs to achieve liberalization and agree on further elaborations of the multilateral code of conduct. Market access and fair competition are best seen as objectives that are pursued through the enforcement and implementation of the non-discrimination principle and other reciprocally negotiated rules of behaviour. Transparency and notification requirements play an important role in this connection.

Result-Oriented Approach

Rule-Oriented Approach

TRADE FLOWS	INTERNATIONAL PRICES	LEVEL OF IMPORT BARRIERS	GENERAL CONDITIONS OF COMPETITION

• Global import commitments (Poland's Protocol of Accession to GATT)
 	
• Long-term commodity contracts (e.g. USSR–Canada Wheat Arrangement)
 	
• Bilateral Barter Agreements
 	
• Voluntary import expansion agreements
 	
• Quotas and voluntary export restrictions
	• Minimum export prices (e.g. International Dairy Arrangement)
	
	• Price provisions of international commodity agreements (e.g. natural rubber and before 1987 sugar and tin)
	
	• OPEC price-setting for crude oil
		• Consolidated tariff rates
		
		• Margins of mark-ups of state trading enterprises
		
		• Ban on quotas
			• Non-discrimination — MFN treatment / National treatment
			
			• Use of trade distorting measures
			  – Tariff binding
			  – Subsidy disciplines
			  – Tariffication
			  – Access to government procurement markets
			  – Use of product standards
			
			• Preferential treatment
			  – Regional integration
			  – Special and differential treatment for developing countries
			
			• Safeguards
			
			• Coping with 'unfair trade' practices
			  – Anti-dumping actions
			  – Measures to countervail subsidies
			  – Protection of intellectual property

FIG 1.2 Trade policy: types of international co-operation

Non-Discrimination

The principle of non-discrimination has two dimensions. The MFN rule requires that at the border, products made in Members' own countries are treated no less favourably than goods originating from any other country. Thus, if the best treatment offered to a trading partner supplying a specific product is a tariff of, say, 5 per cent, then this rate must be applied immediately and unconditionally to the imports of this good originating in all WTO Members. Because the initial set of contracting parties to the GATT was quite small (only twenty-three countries), the bench-mark for MFN is the best treatment offered to any country, including countries that may not be members of the GATT. A similar wording applies under the GATS.

The MFN obligation is complemented by the national treatment rule. This requires that foreign goods—once they have satisfied whatever border measures are applied, including the payment of customs duties and/or other charges—be treated no less favourably in terms of taxes and measures with equivalent effect than domestic goods. That is, goods of foreign origin circulating in the country should be subject to the same taxes, charges, and regulations that apply to identical goods of domestic origin. It is important to note that the obligation is to provide treatment 'no less favorable'. A government is free to discriminate in favour of foreign products (against domestic goods) if it desires subject, of course, to the MFN rule—all foreign products must be given the same treatment. 'No less favorable' does not mean identical treatment, as in many instances it is simply not possible to subject domestic and foreign goods to the same policy. For example, if in practice domestic production is taxed, a government cannot impose the same tax on foreign producers. It is restricted to taxing the foreign products that enter the country. What matters is equivalence.

MFN applies unconditionally, the only major exception being if a subset of Members form a free-trade area or a customs union or grant preferential access to developing countries. These exceptions are discussed in Chapters 9 and 10 below. MFN is one of the pillars of the GATT. Non-discrimination across foreign sources of supply is important for a number of reasons. The first is economic efficiency. Although trade barriers are inefficient instruments, if policy does not discriminate between foreign suppliers, importers and consumers will continue to have an incentive to use the lowest-cost foreign supplier. The second is to provide smaller countries with a guarantee that larger countries will not exploit their market power by raising tariffs against them in periods when times are bad and domestic industries are clamouring for protection, or alternatively, to give specific countries preferential treatment, perhaps for foreign-policy reasons. MFN helps enforce GATT rules by raising the costs to a country of defecting from the trade regime to which it committed itself in an earlier MTN. If it desires to raise trade barriers it must apply the changed regime to all WTO Members, which may then be able to claim compensation.

National treatment also applies unconditionally in GATT (although not in the GATS—see Chapter 5). Its role is to ensure that market-access commitments (trade liberalization) are not offset by countries through the imposition of domestic taxes and similar measures. By requiring that foreign products be treated no less favourably than identical domestic products, it becomes much more difficult for a contracting party to prevent foreign products from competing with domestic ones. The effect is to give foreign suppliers and domestic buyers greater certainty regarding the regulatory environment in which they must operate. This in turn facilitates the organization of production, planning, and so forth. The national treatment principle has often been invoked in dispute-settlement cases brought to the GATT. It is a very wide-ranging rule. The obligation applies whether or not a specific tariff commitment was made, and covers taxes and non-tax policies: all policies must be applied in a non-discriminatory fashion to similar (competing) domestic and foreign products. It is also irrelevant to what extent a policy hurts an exporter; what matters is the discrimination.

Reciprocity

The agreements administered by the WTO are based on a balance of rights and obligations, achieved through the reciprocal exchange of market-access commitments. The principle of reciprocity is a fundamental element of MTNs, i.e. in the process of establishing the code of conduct, and is driven by a desire to limit the scope for free-riding that may arise because of the MFN rule. Thus, trade liberalization occurs on a quid pro quo basis. Although undefined in the WTO, in practice a balanced exchange of concessions is necessary for agreement to be possible (Roessler, 1978). Usually the concessions that are offered would benefit the nations involved even if implemented unilaterally. As noted by Winters (1987*a*), reciprocity in trade negotiations comes in many guises. It may be expressed in quantitative or qualitative terms, and may apply to levels or to changes in protection. While the GATT and the GATS arguably have as underlying goals a broad balance of market-access commitments, MTNs in general and tariff negotiations in particular proceed by agreeing to incremental changes in levels of protection. Convergence in the levels of protection is gradual.

By requiring reciprocity, nations attempt to minimize free-riding. In the case of bilateral negotiations, this is done by a suitable choice of products on which concessions are offered and sought; in the case of multilateral across-the-board negotiations, it is done by a suitable choice of products to be exempted from liberalization. Generally, nations are quite successful in minimizing free-riding. For example, internalization, defined by Finger (1979) as the sum of all US imports originating in countries with whom it exchanged concessions as a percentage of total imports of goods on which concessions were made, was about 90 per cent for the US in the Dillon (1960–1) and Kennedy (1964–7) rounds. Allen (1979), focusing explicitly on bilateral bargains made in the Kennedy round, showed that there was a relationship between the sizes of concessions made on commodity tariffs and the degree of bargaining power a country had on a commodity *vis-à-vis* its major trading partners. Thus, reciprocity is in part a function of the weight a country can bring to bear in a negotiation.

Reciprocity also applies when countries accede to the club. Given that new members obtain all the benefits in terms of market access that have resulted from earlier negotiating rounds, existing members invariably demand that potential entrants pay an admission fee. In practice this implies not only that upon joining the WTO a country's trade regime must conform as much as possible with the rules of the GATT, GATS, and TRIPs, but that the government will be asked to liberalize access to its market as well. Accession therefore involves a negotiation process. The accession commitments of two countries that joined the GATT in 1990 provide an idea of what is demanded of new entrants. Tunisia agreed to bind more than 900 tariffs at levels ranging from 17 to 53 per cent. It also undertook to abolish import licenses and other quantitative restrictions on a wide range of products. Venezuela reduced its maximum tariff from 135 per cent to 50 per cent, pledged to bind its entire tariff schedule at a 50 per cent ceiling, and undertook to lower this further to 40 per cent at a later date. Accession modalities are discussed further in Chapter 2.

Reciprocity is an instrument that allows trades to be made in MTNs. As noted earlier, its theoretical foundation can be found in the political economy literature. The costs of liberalization are generally concentrated in specific industries, which will often be well organized in terms of generating political opposition to a reduction in protection. Benefits, while in the aggregate usually greater than costs, accrue to a much larger group of people, who do not have a great individual incentive to organize themselves politically. In such a setting negotiators need to be able to point to reciprocal, sector-specific export gains to be able to sell the liberalization politically (Tumlir, 1985). By obtaining a reduction in foreign import barriers as a quid pro quo for a reduction in domestic trade restrictions, specific export-oriented domestic interests that will gain from liberalization have an incentive to support it in domestic political markets. A related point is that for a nation to negotiate it is necessary that the gain from doing so be greater than the gain available from unilateral liberalization. By obtaining concessions, these gains are ensured. Box 1.2 explores this issue a bit further.

A major problem associated with the use of reciprocity in the process of trade negotiation is that asymmetry in the size of countries can cause the mechanism to break down. Small nations have little to offer large ones in terms of export potential. A large player such as the EU, Japan, or the USA will not consider bilateral requests by a small economy that offers to substantially liberalize access to its markets without considering the impact of acceding to such requests on its trade relations with other large traders. As discussed in Chapter 3, various methods have been created that attempt to offset this problem. Fundamentally, however, it is a fact of life that small economies (i.e. most developing countries) have little to bring to the negotiating table. This does not mean that participation in reciprocal negotiations is irrelevant to such countries, as signing on to GATT rules will help to lock-in liberalization. Nor does it mean that the value of liberalizing trade for such countries is significantly reduced. What it does imply is that the potential domestic political benefits of reciprocal negotiations are less, and that there must be greater dependence on unilateral efforts to open domestic markets to foreign competition.

Box 1.2 More on the political economy of reciprocity

Oversimplifying for purposes of discussion, in any country interest-groups can be divided into two categories: those with an interest in maintaining domestic trade restrictions and those that are interested in greater access to foreign markets. Assuming that the former groups are powerful enough to prevent a government from pursuing unilateral liberalization, there are then two general options: to provide incentives that (further) induce specific groups to favour liberalization, or to offer compensation to the politically powerful groups that have an interest in maintaining trade restrictions. Under a reciprocity rule the probability of liberalization in the MTN context increases the stronger are the export-oriented groups favouring a reduction in trade barriers.

Hillman and Moser (1995) argue that a useful way to approach reciprocity is to start from the premiss that import-competing industries have 'property rights' to their home markets, a right that has been acquired as a result of past lobbying or political support of governments. In the same way that protection can be explained as the outcome of a political process where governments seek to maximize political support—taking into account the legacy of history, as tariffs are often used for revenue purposes and tend to persist after alternative tax bases are developed—reciprocal liberalization can be explained as the outcome of a political process. In this case the interests of the domestic right-holders (the import-competing industries) are balanced with those of domestic industries seeking equivalent rights in foreign markets. If the latter group offers enough political support, erosion of the former group's rights may prove politically rational. What matters is not economic efficiency, but political support.

Whatever is offered by one country (the demandeur) in an MTN as a quid pro quo for a demand on an issue must be of interest to the government asked to alter its policies. Thus, to be effective the offer must help to meet the objectives of influential foreign lobbies that will then push for the desired change in policy in the latter country. Alternatively, offers might be designed to help the government compensate groups that are likely to lose significantly from a reduction in protection. Options here include a more gradual reduction in the level of protection or acceptance of safeguards.

Although export interests dominate in supporting liberalization in the MTN context, other groups favouring liberalization may also play a role. Examples include consumer or economic development lobbies (the effect of development aid is frequently offset by protection against developing country exports). To mobilize such groups they must be aware of the detrimental impact of existing trade policies on their objectives. The provision of information on the effects of protectionist policies is therefore of great importance. Indeed, the need for such information is quite independent of the MTN process, as in many instances a unilateral change in policy would be welfare-improving. The main point, however, is that what counts is political support. If consumer and other groups favouring a liberal trade policy do not mobilize and have political influence, they will generally be irrelevant. Finally, for reciprocity to work it is important that lobbies favouring open markets do not have other means of getting what they want. Finger (1991) has pointed out that large countries increasingly negotiate increased market access for their exporting firms bilaterally. Such bilateral alternatives weaken the political economy rationale for reciprocity in the multilateral context, as they reduce the incentives for export interests to combat trade restrictions during MTNs.

Market Access

An important goal of the founders of the GATT was the promotion of an open trading system, based on rules fostering competition between suppliers located in different countries rather than on attempts to manage trade flows and determine outcomes. Reciprocal MTNs were foreseen as instruments to enhance market access, while the non-discrimination principle, as embodied in Articles I (MFN) and III (national treatment) of the GATT, was intended to help ensure that market-access commitments were implemented and maintained. Other GATT Articles play a supporting role in either facilitating the contestability of markets, or enforcing market-access commitments. Perhaps the most important of these are Articles II (on Schedules of Concessions) and XI (Elimination of Quantitative Restrictions). The tariff concessions (reductions) agreed to by the GATT contracting parties in an MTN are listed in so-called schedules (lists) of concessions. Such concessions are bound. This means that the country involved cannot raise tariffs above bound levels without negotiating compensation with affected countries. The MFN rule then ensures that such compensation—usually reductions in other tariffs—potentially benefits all WTO Members. Once tariff commitments are bound, other, non-tariff, measures that have the effect of 'nullifying or impairing' the value of the tariff concession may not be used. Hence the importance of GATT Article XI prohibiting quotas (with certain exceptions) and the rules on subsidies (Chapter 4). Quotas are prohibited not only because of transparency or efficiency considerations, but to ensure that tariff concessions are not offset by the imposition of quotas and analogous measures.

If a country perceives that actions taken by another government have the effect of nullifying or impairing a concession (that is, the market-access commitments implied by the tariff bindings and safeguarded by the various rules and disciplines of the GATT), it may bring this to the attention of the government involved and ask that the action be offset. If satisfaction is not obtained, it may invoke the WTO's dispute-settlement procedure. Because the GATT and the WTO are inter-governmental agreements, private parties do not have legal standing before the WTO's dispute-settlement body. The private sector must go through its government. It is also worth noting that in the EU and US domestic legal orders, the GATT is not a self-executing treaty, which means that private parties cannot invoke GATT disciplines in domestic litigation either. Multilateral agreements must be translated into domestic law through implementing legislation. The existence of dispute-settlement procedures gives members an incentive to raise disputes in the WTO, rather than seeking redress through unilateral retaliation. For small countries in particular, recourse to a multilateral body will frequently be their only option, as unilateral actions will not be effective and thus not be credible. Large countries have as great a stake in the functioning of the regime, as in many instances disputes will involve other large trading nations. Moreover, for an export firm what counts is market access, independent of whether it is located in a small or large country, and the WTO helps guarantee that access.

Market access is also facilitated by rules that increase the transparency of trade regimes maintained by Members. Various transparency mechanisms are incorporated into the agreements administered by the WTO. Members must: publish their trade regulations; establish and maintain institutions allowing for the review of administrative decisions affecting trade; respond to requests for information by other Members; and notify subsidy practices to the WTO.

Surveillance of trade policies by WTO Members and the Secretariat also fosters transparency and reduces the scope for countries to circumvent their obligations.

Fair Competition

A final principle embodied in the WTO is 'fair competition'. This should not be confused with the economic conception of fair competition as defined in competition or anti-trust legislation (see Chapter 11). Fair competition in the GATT context is reflected in a number of provisions. Government subsidization of exports is prohibited and/or countervailable by importing countries. Certain types of behaviour pursued by exporting firms (as opposed to governments) are also countervailable. Thus, dumping by exporters—which usually means charging a price in the export market that is less than what is charged in the home market—may be offset by importing country governments through the imposition of an anti-dumping duty if the dumping injures domestic competitors. Governments also have the right to intervene when competition from imports becomes 'excessively' injurious to domestic industries, to safeguard the balance of payments, or to protect public health or national security. The underlying idea is generally that competition should be on the basis of a 'level playing-field', to employ an often used and abused term, and that governments should have the right to step in when competition becomes too vigorous. The objective of fair competition is often in direct conflict with that of market access, as the instrument used by governments to attain fairness is usually a trade barrier. Such barriers are, however, perfectly legal and permitted.

1.3. FUTURE CHALLENGES

The GATT proved very successful as an instrument to induce countries to lower and bind tariffs over time. Its basic philosophy that a rule-oriented approach is superior to a results-based system steadily gained adherents. Whereas many governments in the 1960s and 1970s were engaged in efforts to manage trade—through central planning, barter, or commodity agreements—imposed NTBs and actively pursued international agreements that can be characterized as results-oriented (see Fig. 1.2), this approach proved unsuccessful. Commodity agreements were difficult to enforce, and the prevalence of central planning and state trading was substantially reduced with the dissolution of the CMEA and the USSR.

As discussed in subsequent chapters, many of the issue areas that have given rise to recurring disputes and protectionist policies (agriculture, textiles and clothing, subsidization, protection of intellectual property, and access to service markets) were brought into the system of multilateral rules. Dispute settlement and transparency mechanisms were also bolstered. The system strengthening and expansion should ensure greater adherence to negotiated rules than in the past.

Negotiating the rules (the code of conduct) has become increasingly difficult over time. Recognizing that tariffs were becoming less important as barriers to trade, the agenda of MTNs gradually grew to include mostly non-tariff policies. With the creation of the WTO it is likely that future MTNs will increasingly revolve around non-tariff measures and domestic policies that are deemed to have an impact on trade. The interface between trade policy *per se* and economic policy more generally defined has become increasingly blurred, however. Agreeing on the elimination or reduction of NTMs is more difficult than negotiating downward the levels of tariffs. One reason for this is that it is much less obvious that specific NTMs are detrimental to a country's welfare. For example, attitudes towards environmental quality or product safety differ across countries. In so far as this is reflected in differences in environmental or product standards, it may have a negative impact on trade. Alternatively, a country may seek to offset a market failure with a targeted subsidy programme. Economic theory suggests that under certain conditions subsidies will be the most efficient method of dealing with such problems, even if a side-effect of the subsidy is that it reduces imports. The implication is that negotiations on such issues may be zero-sum games (some countries may lose), in contrast to tariff reductions, which are positive-sum (all countries gain, even though certain groups in each country will lose unless they are compensated). Another problem, again in contrast to tariffs, is that it can be difficult to reduce the trade-restricting impact of NTMs incrementally.

For many NTMs, all that may be feasible is to agree that basic principles of transparency, national treatment, and MFN apply, and to seek to adopt dispute-resolution procedures. However, pressures for the harmonization of policies have been mounting. Although the GATT has traditionally shied away from attempts to agree on common policies, differences in non-trade policies— regarding the environment, labour standards, or anti-trust—are increasingly leading to claims that these result in unfair competition and should be counter-vailed. A key challenge for WTO Members going into the next millennium is to deal with these pressures. This raises fundamental questions regarding the willingness and ability of governments to accept differences in regulatory regimes and market structure. We shall return to these issues in Chapters 11 and 12. The more immediate challenge for the WTO is to implement the many agreements that were reached in the Uruguay round. These are the subject of the Chapters that follow.

Richard Caves and Ronald Jones, *World Trade and Payments: An Introduction* (Boston: Little, Brown, 1985) is one of many good introductory textbooks on international economics. Joan Spero, *The Politics of International Economic Relations* (London: St Martin's Press, 1990) presents a summary of developments in the world economy in the post-Second World War period. A clear and accessible introduction to the legal aspects of the world trading system is presented in John H. Jackson, *The World Trading System: Law and Policy in International Relations* (Cambridge: MIT Press, 1989). Gilbert Winham, 'GATT and the International Trade Regime', *International Journal*, 15 (1990), 786–822, is a leading political scientist's view of the GATT and its role in international relations. Frieder Roessler, 'The Scope, Limits and Function of the GATT Legal System', *The World Economy*, 8 (1985), 287–98 discusses the role of GATT rules as constraints on governments.

For an appraisal and history of negotiations of the Havana Charter and the General Agreement on Tariffs and Trade see William Brown, *The United States and the Restoration of World Trade* (Washington DC: The Brookings Institution, 1950); and William Diebold, *The End of the ITO* (Princeton, NJ: Princeton University Press, 1952). A classic treatise on the Kennedy round is Ernest Preeg, *Traders and Diplomats: An Analysis of the Kennedy Round under the General Agreement on Tariffs and Trade* (Washington DC: Brookings Institution, 1970). A very comprehensive and interesting account and analysis of the Tokyo round is offered by Gilbert Winham, *International Trade and the Tokyo Round Negotiations* (Princeton, NJ: Princeton University Press, 1986). L. Alan Winters, in 'The Road to Uruguay', *Economic Journal*, 100 (1990), 1288–1303 gives a highly recommended, short review of the issues that were dealt with during the Uruguay round and their GATT history. Jeffrey Schott and Johanna Buurman, in *The Uruguay Round: An Assessment* (Washington DC: Institute for International Economics, 1994), offer a summary of the outcome of the negotiations. Will Martin and Alan Winters (eds.), *The Uruguay Round and the Developing Countries* (Washington DC: The World Bank, 1995) contains a series of comprehensive papers analysing the outcome of the Uruguay round, including a number of papers that quantify the gains. *The New World Trading System: Readings* (Paris: OECD, 1994) and Sue Collins and Barry Bosworth (eds.), *The New GATT: Implications for the United States* (Washington DC: Brookings Institution, 1994) contain shorter papers that review the results of the round.

There is a large literature on the political economy of trade policy decisions and institutional design issues. Robert Baldwin, *The Political Economy of U.S. Import Policy* (Cambridge: MIT Press, 1985) and I. M. Destler, *American Trade Politics* (Washington DC: Institute for International Economics, 1992) are important books on US trade policy that take a political economy viewpoint. Arye Hillman, *The Political Economy of Protectionism* (New York: Harwood, 1989) surveys the economic literature. Patrick Low, *Trading Free: The GATT and U.S. Trade Policy* (New York: Twentieth Century Fund, 1993) discusses the changing attitudes of the USA towards the GATT, and the need for—and possibilities of—strengthening the trading system. Robert Keohane, 'Reciprocity in International Relations', *International Organization*, 40 (1986), 1–27 discusses the notion of reciprocity from the perspectives of political science and international organizations; L. Alan Winters, 'Reciprocity', in M. Finger and A. Olechowski (eds.), *The Uruguay Round: A Handbook* (Washington DC: World Bank, 1987) does so from the perspective of an economist; and Frieder Roessler, 'The Rationale for Reciprocity in Trade Negotiations under Floating Currencies', *Kyklos*, 31 (1978), 258–74 from a legal practitioner's perspective.

2

The World Trade Organization

Although the GATT progressively acquired many of the attributes of an international organization, it was increasingly felt in the 1980s that it was not keeping up with the rapid changes in the global economy, and required strengthened dispute-settlement and transparency mechanisms. While this was reflected in the agenda of the Uruguay round, the Ministerial Declaration establishing the round's agenda did not call for the creation of a WTO. Instead, it was agreed that the round would be a 'single undertaking', with all its agreements applying to all GATT contracting parties. In principle, it was not necessary to create an international organization to implement the results of the round, especially in so far as a common dispute-settlement mechanism was agreed to apply to all of the various agreements reached. The suggestion to establish a Multilateral Trade Organization (MTO) by Canada in 1990— supported by the EU—was therefore something of a surprise. An important motivation to establish an MTO was to have a single institutional framework encompassing the modified GATT, its sister bodies on services (GATS) and intellectual property (TRIPs), and all other agreements and arrangements concluded under the auspices of the Uruguay round. The United States initially opposed the idea, but, after further negotiations on the substance of the new organization, agreed to the framework that currently exists, including the name change. Although the US Congress remained suspicious of any limitations to its sovereign powers in trade policy, during the ratification debate it became clear that the establishment of the WTO would not do much to change the *status quo* as far as the infringement of sovereignty was concerned. The GATT-1947 was a binding international treaty, and most of the institutional aspects of the WTO already existed under the GATT.

None the less, the establishment of the WTO was a significant event. Attempts to put the GATT on a more secure organizational footing had been made periodically since the failure of the US Congress to ratify the ITO. During a 1955 meeting to review the GATT, a number of contracting parties proposed to establish an Organization for Trade Co-operation (OTC). This proposal was much less elaborate than the ITO but it also failed to win the approval of the US Congress (Jackson, 1990). The issue of providing an institutional framework for international trade reappeared again in the Economic and Social Council (ECOSOC) of the UN in 1963. A group of experts called for the creation of a new UN agency with universal membership and substantial powers in the sphere of international trade (Kostecki, 1979). The idea was that this body would implement, *inter alia*, recommendations of UNCTAD as well as other relevant policy decisions taken by organs of the UN. The proposal envisaged that the GATT would become the agency's Committee on Tariffs. The proposal did not meet with much interest among the major trading nations. However, the 1964 UN General Assembly resolution establishing UNCTAD provided that it should be concerned with matters relating to the elaboration of a comprehensive trade organization. Nothing concrete came of this—despite lengthy discussions about the need for a New International Economic Order during the 1970s—in large part because of the widely differing philosophies held by industrialized market economies and much of the developing world regarding the appropriate basis for international trade. With the creation of the WTO, an international trade organization exists that is firmly based on GATT principles—reciprocity and non-discrimination.

2.1. THE SCOPE, FUNCTIONS, AND STRUCTURE OF THE WTO

As the principal institution with responsibility for the multilateral trading system, the WTO has the same status as institutions such as the World Bank and the IMF. The WTO has legal personality and has been accorded privileges and immunities similar to those accorded to the specialized UN agencies. It is headed by a Ministerial Conference of all Members, meeting at least once every two years. More frequent participation by trade ministers than occurred in the GATT context is intended to strengthen the political guidance of the WTO and enhance the prominence and credibility of its rules in domestic political arenas. It can be noted, however, that past experience of the GATT with Ministerial meetings suggests that these can easily be an inefficient use of the time of many Ministers from smaller trading nations. This is because in negotiations the controversial issues tend to be solved at the last moment and require agreement between the major players. The latter may take a significant amount of time to strike a deal between themselves, thereby marginalizing the potential for participation by Ministers of smaller countries.

The WTO is charged with providing 'the common institutional framework for the conduct of trade relations among its Members in matters related to the agreements and associated legal instruments included in the Annexes . . .' to the Agreement. There are four such Annexes, which contain the substantive rights and obligations of Members. Annex 1 has three parts: Annex 1A entitled Multilateral Agreements on Trade in Goods, contains the GATT-1994 (the GATT-1947 as amended by a large number of Understandings and supplementary Agreements negotiated in the Uruguay round); Annex 1B, which contains the GATS; and Annex 1C, the Agreement on TRIPs. Annex 2 consists of an Understanding on Rules and Procedures Governing the Settlement of Disputes—the WTO's common dispute-settlement mechanism.

Annex 3 contains the Trade Policy Review Mechanism (TPRM), an instrument through which surveillance of Members' trade policies occurs. Finally, Annex 4—entitled Plurilateral Trade Agreements—consists of Tokyo round codes that were not multilateralized in the Uruguay round, and that therefore bind only signatories. Annexes 1–3 together are called the Multilateral Trade Agreements. All of these instruments are discussed further below and/or in the rest of this book.

The WTO has five functions. It is charged with facilitating the implementation and operation of the Multilateral Trade Agreements; providing a forum for negotiations on already covered or new issues; administering the Understanding on dispute settlement and the TPRM; and, finally, co-operating with the World Bank and the IMF to achieve 'greater coherence in global economic policy-making' (Article III WTO). Between meetings of the Ministerial Conference—responsible for carrying out the functions of the WTO—the organization is run by a General Council at the level of officials. The General Council turns itself, as needed, into a body to adjudicate trade disputes (the Dispute Settlement Body) or to review trade policies of the member countries (the Trade Policy Review Body). Three subsidiary councils operate under the general guidance of the WTO's General Council (see Fig. 2.1): the Council for Trade in Goods; the Council for Trade in Services; and the Council for Trade-Related Aspects of Intellectual Property Rights. Separate Committees exist to deal primarily with the interests of the least developed countries (Trade and Development); surveillance of trade restriction actions taken for balance-of-payment purposes (see Chapters 4 and 10); trade-environment linkages; and the WTO's finances and administration (Secretariat). Additional committees or working parties deal with matters covered by the GATT, GATS, or TRIPs Agreement. There are committees functioning under the auspices of the Council on Trade in Goods dealing with subsidies, anti-dumping and countervailing measures, technical barriers to trade (product standards), import licensing, customs valuation, market access, agriculture, sanitary and phytosanitary measures, trade-related investment measures, rules of origin, and safeguards. Similarly, specific committees address matters relating to the GATS or TRIPs. Committees also exist to administer the Plurilateral Agreements. However, these are not under the guidance of the General Council but operate within the general framework of the WTO and inform the Council of their activities. There were more than thirty councils and standing committees in the WTO in 1995—twice as many as under the old GATT.

The main actors in day-to-day activities are the delegations of Members. The GATT-1947 and the WTO that succeeded it are based on collective input from a large group of constantly changing civil servants who deal with trade issues in each of the Member States. Initiatives for MTNs, monitoring of trade policies, and settlement of disputes are largely the responsibility of WTO Members themselves. The Secretariat provides technical and logistical sup-

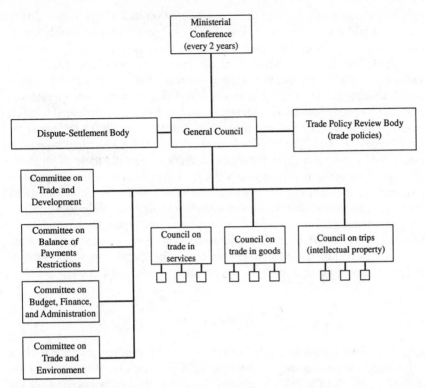

Committees and Working Parties set up to administer the various arrangements that are covered by GATT, GATS, or TRIPS.
Source: WTO.
FIG. 2.1 WTO organizational tree

port, including organizing meetings of governing bodies and preparing background documentation requested by delegations. It also assists the dispute-settlement process, provides legal services when requested to do so, and publishes studies and trade policy reports. The Director-General, the head of the Secretariat, is in some sense the guardian of the collective interest of the Member States. The WTO's rules and procedures allow the Director-General to act as a broker—not a decision-maker—in many situations. A very important figure was the first Director-General of the GATT (or Secretary-General as the post was called in the early days of GATT's existence), Sir Eric Wyndham White, who managed the GATT for over twenty years. The survival and functioning of the GATT and its secretariat in the post-war period was to a large extent the result of his creativity and experience.

The WTO Secretariat is small compared to other international bureaucracies. In March 1995 the total number of professional staff stood at some 450.

For comparison purposes, the OECD has over 3,000 staff, the IMF over 2,000, and the World Bank over 6,000. The WTO's budget is commensurably small. For 1995 it was about US $84m., with staff salaries and related overheads accounting for more than 70 per cent of expenditure. As MTNs give rise to additional work for the secretariat, and because of the increased costs associated with the rental of meeting rooms and dissemination of documentation, since the Kennedy round a supplementary budget has been established for such events. The financial contributions to the budget of the WTO are based on GATT-1947 practice. The WTO's income comes from assessed contributions calculated on the basis of each Member's share in the total trade of all WTO Members, computed as a three-year average of the most recent trade figures (if this share is less than 0.12 per cent, a minimum contribution is assessed). In 1995 the nine largest trading nations contributed approximately two-thirds of total contributions. The EU's contribution is assessed separately for each of its member states, and includes intra-EU trade. Voluntary contributions (grants) are made by industrialized market economies for specific purposes, such as technical assistance or training of the personnel in developing countries.

2.2. DECISION-MAKING

Most decision-making in the WTO follows GATT practice and is based on negotiation and consensus. Consensus is a GATT tradition. While not formally defined in the GATT-1947, it gradually became the *modus operandi* of the institution. Even in cases where GATT rules called for a formal vote—such as on the granting of waivers of GATT obligations to a country—negotiation and consultations would usually be held to arrive at a consensus text before the formal vote was held (Jackson, 1994: 68). Consensus was facilitated by another GATT tradition, which was not to allow progress to be frustrated by one party's obstinacy, unless it happened to be one of the major trading nations. Consensus does not mean unanimity. It signifies that no country physically represented in a meeting of the Council is decisively against a major issue. Those that are not present—or abstain—do not count. Decision-making by consensus is a useful device to ensure that only decisions on which there is no major opposition—and consequently which have a good chance of being implemented—are made. This is important because the WTO has few means of pressing unwilling governments to obey its decisions.

Despite their effective lack of veto power, the consensus practice is of value to smaller countries as it enhances their negotiating leverage—especially if they are able to form a coalition—in the informal consultations and bargaining that precede decision-making. It is in this connection that the quality of a country's delegation can be significant in determining its effective influence. Achieving consensus can be a complex process, in part because it provides a

TABLE 2.1 *Decision-making in the WTO*

Decision-making rule	Type of issue
Unanimity	Amendments relating to general principles such as MFN treatment
Three-quarters majority vote	Interpretation of the provisions of the agreement and waiver of a member's obligations
Two-thirds majority vote	Amendments relating to issues other than general principles such as MFN treatment
Consensus	Where not otherwise specified

context for the establishment of linkages and the exchange of non-veto promises. In order to avoid paralysis, an exchange of votes may be necessary. Bargaining to achieve consensus lies at the heart of both MTNs and the functioning of the system. Consensus reinforces conservative tendencies in the system because a proposal for change can be adopted only if unopposed by a blocking minority.

Recourse to voting is institutionalized under the WTO to deal with issues where a consensus decision cannot be reached. Voting takes place in the WTO only where specified (see Table 2.1). If required, voting is based on the principle of 'one Member–one vote'. This distinguishes the WTO from the IMF and other international economic organizations, where weighted voting is extensively used. Unanimity is required for amendments relating to general principles, such as MFN or national treatment. Interpretation of the provisions of the WTO agreements and decisions on waivers of a Member's obligations require approval by a three-quarters majority vote. A two-thirds majority vote is sufficient for amendments relating to issues other than the general principles mentioned above. Where not otherwise specified and where consensus cannot be reached a simple majority vote is in principle sufficient. As the issues involved will not be central to the functioning of the WTO, this is not likely to lead to conflicts. In all cases, in contrast to the consensus practice, if voting occurs the majority required is relative to all WTO Members; not with respect to those Members that happen to be present in a particular meeting.

Some criteria useful in determining a country's influence in the WTO system are: its share of world trade (which also determines budget contributions); its trade dependence or 'openness' (the ratio of exports and imports to GDP); and the absolute size of its market. A country's trade-policy stance is irrelevant: free-traders do not have any more say in the WTO than countries with highly protectionist regimes. The major players are therefore the EU, Japan, and the USA. The EU is a major player because individual EU Member States do not have sovereignty over trade policy: this has been delegated to the

TABLE 2.2 *Measures of influence, top 20 traders, 1993*

	Share of world merchandise imports, 1993 (%)	Share of exports in GDP, 1992 (%)	GDP 1991 (US $ billion)
USA	15.7	11	5,611
Germany	9.0	24	1,574
Japan	6.3	10	3,346
UK	5.4	24	1,008
France	5.3	23	1,196
Italy	4.1	20	1,150
Hong Kong[a]	3.7	144	81
Canada	3.6	25	584
Netherlands	3.3	54	290
Belgium-Luxembourg[c]	2.9	73	206
China[b]	2.7	20	379
Singapore[a]	2.2	174	10
Korea	2.2	29	284
Spain	2.1	17	528
Taiwan[b]	2.0	43	176
Mexico	1.7	14	287
Switzerland	1.6	35	231
Austria	1.3	41	165
Thailand	1.2	29	110
Malaysia	1.2	78	47
Australia	1.2	18	297
EC-12 (incl. intra-EU trade)	36.0	18	6,189
EC-12 (excl. intra-EU trade)	18.8	9	

[a] A substantial proportion of this trade involves import–export arbitrage activities.
[b] Not a WTO Member as of January 1995.
[c] Data for exports as a share of GDP excludes Luxembourg.

Sources: *The World Bank Atlas* (Washington DC: World Bank, 1993); *Handbook of International Trade and Development Statistics* (Geneva: UNCTAD, 1994); GATT, *International Trade 1994* (Geneva: GATT, 1995).

Commission of the European Communities. For more specific issues in the WTO, the level of influence is also determined by the importance of the matter for the country. For example, Argentina, a relatively small trading nation, is an important meat exporter and has more influence on decisions concerning international trade in bovine meat than on other topics. Issues that arise are often product-specific. What matters then is a country's share of world trade in the product involved. This product-specificity explains much of the bilateral or plurilateral nature of the interactions that take place.

Table 2.2 provides a listing of the major players. While industrialized market economies are clearly the most influential members of the WTO, developing countries are by no means irrelevant. Countries such as Brazil and India have traditionally exerted substantial influence, in part because of their economic size, and in part because they have often acted as spokesmen for other developing countries. Eight of the top twenty countries are developing, although two of these have high incomes (Hong Kong and Singapore), and one is an OECD member (Mexico). Small countries often provide the chairpersons of negotiating groups, and frequently act as honest brokers between larger players or groups of countries.

2.3. TRANSPARENCY: NOTIFICATION AND SURVEILLANCE

Transparency at the multilateral and national levels is essential to reduce domestic pressures for protection and to enforce agreements (GATT, 1985). Efforts to increase transparency and examine Members trade policies take up a large part of the institution's time. The approach is inspired by what Professor Bhagwati has called the 'Dracula principle': problems may disappear once light is thrown on them (Bhagwati, 1988). Transparency provisions of the WTO relate to both the acts of the WTO itself, and the actions of its Members. As far as the WTO itself is concerned, most important WTO documents are made public.[1] WTO decisions, panel findings, and other major documents of the WTO bodies are published in a series entitled *Basic Instruments and Selected Documents* (BISD) edited by the WTO Secretariat in Geneva. The Secretariat also prepares regular newsletters and publishes *ad hoc* studies on particular aspects of the multilateral trading system.

Under GATT-1947 smaller trading nations often perceived a lack of transparency concerning agreements reached between the major players in either MTNs or with respect to the settlement of bilateral disputes or trade issues. While bilateral agreements regarding specific trade issues are not necessarily a matter of concern, they may be detrimental to the interests of third parties who are left to determine the potential effects of the deal on their exporters. More important in terms of generating controversy has been the practice on the part of large traders of coming to an agreement between themselves and then attempting to present the deal as a *fait accompli* in a negotiating group in an MTN or in the Council.

Turning to transparency of Members' policies, the WTO requires that all

---

[1] Exceptions in the past have been unadopted panel reports. However, with the new dispute procedures (see below), adoption of such reports will have to be blocked by all WTO Members — an unlikely event. Another set of documents that have traditionally not been published are the results of tariff renegotiations (see Chapter 7). Moreover, public access to the Secretariat's integrated database of Members' tariff schedules and other trade measures is also restricted.

trade laws and regulations are published. Article X of the GATT, Article III of the GATS, and Article 63 of the TRIPs Agreement all require that all relevant laws, regulations, judicial decisions, and administrative rulings are made public. There are many notification requirements embodied in the Articles of the Multilateral and Plurilateral Agreements, all of which require the existence of appropriate bodies or agencies that have responsibility for satisfying them. A consolidated notification, including all changes in laws, regulations, policy statements, or public notices, must be provided each year by WTO Members to the Secretariat. So-called enquiry points must be created that have the responsibility for answering questions and providing relevant documents regarding health and product standards.

Under the GATS, at least once a year Members must inform the Council for Trade in Services of the introduction of new—or changes to existing—laws, regulations, or administrative guidelines which significantly affect trade in services covered by their specific commitments. By 1997 each Member must establish one or more enquiry points to provide specific information to other Members, upon request, on all relevant measures of general application which pertain to or affect the operation of the GATS. Members must also establish judicial, arbitral, or administrative tribunals or procedures which provide, at the request of an affected service supplier, for prompt, objective, and impartial review of administrative decisions affecting trade in services.

The WTO also has important surveillance activities. The WTO itself periodically reviews the trade-policy and foreign-trade regimes of Members (Box 2.1). Matters of interest to developing countries are reviewed in the Committee on Trade and Development. Multilateral surveillance of trade restrictions for balance-of-payments purposes takes place in the Committee on Balance of Payments Restrictions. The Textiles Surveillance Body reviews bilateral agreements on trade in textiles involving MFA countries and the Textile Committee oversees the phasing out of the Multifibre Arrangement (MFA). Several Committees that oversee the functioning of specific agreements conduct surveillance of the relevant policies of Members at intervals of between every three months and every two years.

2.4. DISPUTE SETTLEMENT AND THE ENFORCEMENT OF RULES

The effective resolution of trade disputes is vital for the smooth functioning of the trading system. The growing number of trade disputes in the 1980s and early 1990s was variously attributed to the intensification of trade conflicts resulting from changing patterns of comparative advantage, in conjunction with the existence of vaguely worded GATT provisions and differences in their interpretation (subsidies, agriculture). Certain disputes were essentially attempts to contest existing provisions with a view to clarifying them. During

Box 2.1. The WTO's Trade-Policy Review Mechanism

The WTO's Trade Policy Review Mechanism (TPRM), established during the Uruguay round, builds upon a 1979 Understanding on Notification, Consultation, Dispute Settlement, and Surveillance negotiated during the Tokyo round, under which contracting parties agreed to conduct a regular and systematic review of developments in the trading system. The objectives of the TPRM are to examine the impact of trade policies and practices of Members on the trading system; and to contribute to improved adherence to WTO rules through greater transparency. The legal compatibility of any particular measure with WTO disciplines is not examined, this being left for Members to ascertain. Country-specific reviews are conducted on a rotational basis. Each WTO Member is requested to submit periodic reports describing its trade policies. The frequency of review is a function of a Member's share of world trade. The four largest players—the EU, the US, Japan, and Canada—are subject to review by the WTO General Council every two years. The next sixteen largest traders are subjected to reviews every four years, and the remaining Members are reviewed every six years. A longer periodicity may be established for least-developed countries.

The WTO's review of trade policies is based on a report prepared by the government concerned and a report by the WTO Secretariat. A weakness of the TPRM is that it involves only limited analysis of global (cross-country) issues in trade policy. An annual Director-General's report called Developments in the Trading System tries to overcome this shortcoming. All reports are published promptly with a view to increasing the awareness of the national trade policies of the country involved. Although the TPRM suffers from important limitations—e.g. reports are not analytical enough to provide an evaluation of the economic effects of various national policies and cannot serve as a basis for dispute settlement (Curzon, 1993; Mavroidis, 1992)—it is an important element in strengthening the multilateral trading system.

MTNs, when a deal is badly needed for political reasons, but substantive agreement cannot be reached, negotiators sometimes opt for a vague arrangement which permits conflicting interpretations (see also Chapter 3). The implicit decision in such instances was that the matter could be addressed further in future dispute-settlement cases, while providing the immediate appearance of the accord that is required for political reasons. Experience has shown that disputes concerning issues where no political consensus could be reached in an MTN have little chance of reaching a satisfactory conclusion through dispute settlement, although further clarification of the issues may be obtained.

A list of major dispute-settlement cases that arose under GATT-1947 between 1984 and 1994 is presented in Annex 3. Although use by developing countries has been increasing (see Chapter 10), the disputes usually involve one of the major trading nations as a party. Dispute-settlement procedures may be invoked whenever a Member believes that an action by another Member has 'nullified or impaired' a concession that was negotiated previously (i.e. a tariff binding) or breaks a WTO rule and 'impairs the attainment' of an objective of the GATT. As under the GATT-1947, complaints may take three forms. The first is a 'violation' complaint, which consists of a claim that one or more WTO disciplines has been violated (e.g. non-discrimination). Second, Members may argue that although no specific WTO rules are violated, a government measure none the less nullifies a previously granted concession. Three conditions must be met in order to bring such a so-called 'non-violation' complaint: first, the measure must be applied by a government; second, it must alter the competitive conditions established by the agreed tariff bindings; and third, the measure must be 'unexpected' in that it could not have been reasonably anticipated at the time the concessions were negotiated. The third possibility is a so-called 'situation' complaint, under which a Member may argue that 'any other situation' not captured by the violation or non-violation options has led to nullification or impairment of a negotiated benefit.

Disputes arising from any WTO agreement are dealt with by the Dispute Settlement Body (DSB), which has the authority to establish panels, adopt panel reports, scrutinize the implementation of recommendations, and authorize retaliatory measures if necessary. The WTO dispute-settlement mechanism covers not only trade in goods, but also trade in services and intellectual property. The same procedures are used for settling disputes across all issues—the WTO has established a unified dispute-settlement mechanism. Although Members are constrained with respect to 'forum shopping' on disputes concerning matters addressed by Agreements based on the Tokyo round codes, these Agreements continue to contain special dispute-settlement provisions. If these special procedures differ from the general WTO provisions, the special procedures apply.

Dispute settlement under the WTO is more timely, automatic, and binding than under the GATT-1947, although to a large extent it codified existing practices. Strengthening was largely due to the elimination of possibilities to block the establishment of a panel or the adoption of panel reports by one of the parties to a dispute—both were possible under GATT-1947—increased opportunities for arbitration, the introduction of time-limits for the various stages of panel proceedings, as well as standard terms of reference for panels and improved surveillance of the implementation of panel reports. Under the WTO, the adoption of panel reports can only be blocked by consensus, a

Box 2.2. Settlement of disputes

Stage I: Consultations and mediation. Members must initially attempt to solve their disputes through bilateral consultations. The good offices, conciliation, or mediation by the WTO Director-General may also be sought, although this is optional.

Stage II: Request for a panel. If parties are not able to secure a solution to their dispute through consultations within 60 days, the Dispute Settlement Body (DSB) may be required to establish a panel. Creation of a panel is automatic. The WTO Secretariat usually suggests the names of three potential panelists to the parties to the dispute. Panelists serve in their individual capacities and may not be subjected to government instructions. They are frequently former representatives to GATT or retired international civil servants knowledgeable in trade matters. The WTO Secretariat provides legal support to the panel and generally prepares the background documentation regarding the facts of the case.

Stage III: The panel at work. The panel usually goes through the following stages: (1) presentation of facts and arguments (Memoranda); (2) meetings with the parties and third countries; (3) rebuttals; (4) additional meetings and submissions, if required; (5) preparation of a report on the facts and the arguments presented; (6) submission of a factual interim report to the parties; (7) conclusions and recommendations are drafted; and (8) the final report is submitted to the parties and the DSB.

Stage IV: Adoption decision. The panel report must in principle be adopted by the DSB within 60 days. A party may appeal if it does not agree with an issue of law or the legal interpretation developed by the panel. A standing Appellate Body, composed of seven persons broadly representative of the WTO's membership, deals with appeals. In principle, appeal proceedings should not exceed 60 days and must be completed within 90 days.

Stage V: Implementation. Prompt compliance with recommendations or rulings is essential for the effective resolution of disputes. If it is impracticable to comply immediately, the offending country is given a 'reasonable period of time' to do so. If it fails to act within this period, it must enter into negotiations to determine a mutually acceptable compensation. If no satisfactory compensation is agreed upon, the complainant may request authorization from the DSB to suspend concessions or obligations against the offending country (i.e. to retaliate). This authorization will usually be granted since a consensus is required to refuse it.

highly improbable event. To allow agreement to be achieved on this major change, WTO Members decided to create a standing Appellate Body. Appeals are restricted to challenges regarding the legal interpretations developed by the panel. If the Appellate Body concurs with the panel report, the Member affected must implement the report's recommendations or pay compensation. If the Member fails to implement a panel report or offer adequate compensation to the Member who won the dispute, retaliatory measures may be taken by the latter after authorization from the DSB. Box 2.2 contains a flow-chart of the WTO's dispute-settlement mechanism that summarizes the various stages involved in settling disputes.

The remedies that tend to be suggested by panels are usually limited to requirements that the Member found to violate a WTO rule and/or nullify or impair a concession take actions to remove the non-conforming measure. Special provisions on remedies in cases of non-violation complaints are included in the WTO's Dispute Settlement Understanding. Article 26 of the Understanding stipulates:

where a measure has been found to nullify or impair benefits under, or impede the attainment of objectives, of the relevant covered agreement without violation thereof, there is no obligation to withdraw the measure. However, in such cases, the panel or the Appellate Body shall recommend that the member concerned make a mutually satisfactory adjustment . . . compensation may be part of a mutually satisfactory adjustment as final settlement of the dispute.

Since there is no obligation to withdraw the non-violating measure, any satisfactory adjustment will concern a different subject-matter; this is a case of cross-compensation.

Compensation or retaliation are the two options available to impose costs on countries that violate a WTO agreement and are unwilling to implement a panel's findings. Obtaining compensation from the transgressor is clearly preferable to retaliation. The latter usually implies shooting oneself in the foot, as the imposition of trade restrictions reduces national welfare. Retaliatory threats will often not be credible, especially if the country is small. A possible way out of this dilemma is for small trading nations affected by a dispute to form alliances and retaliate as a group whenever one of the members is affected. In the multilateral context this could be converted into a rule that violations of non-discrimination result in retaliation by all Members, not just affected Members. This would reduce the costs to the retaliators, while increasing the cost to the transgressor. However, this is not allowed under the WTO. A multiple complaint may be brought by all affected parties; but those not affected cannot participate.

Too much weight should not be given to the threat of retaliation. In practice, 'moral suasion' has been much more effective in inducing trading nations to abide by the agreement. What is needed in general is greater domestic transparency regarding the effects of and changes in government policies (GATT, 1985). Circumvention and abuse of WTO rules are likely to result from successful domestic rent-seeking and thus to be detrimental to the welfare of the country involved. Information regarding the distribution of benefits and costs of actual and proposed policies may be more beneficial than threats of retaliation, both in terms of improving domestic policies and in terms of achieving multilateral agreements. The enforcement issue therefore brings us back to the problem of transparency. While important, in itself transparency is not enough to make politicians, business leaders, bureaucrats, and the public at large rally behind a liberal trade policy stance. Acceptance of multilateral disciplines and liberalization commitments strongly depends on the strategies with which the free-trade message is delivered and promoted among major interest-groups in domestic settings. Appropriate marketing strategies of policy design, communication, and promotion should be in place to mobilize support for trade liberalization and the implementation of the results of MTNs (Finger, 1982).

Summing up, the WTO introduced greater multilateral curbs on unilateral trade action in return for a much stronger multilateral dispute mechanism. Governments have agreed to use multilateral remedies wherever these are available. This considerably narrows the scope for unilateral action by powerful traders. Thus, WTO procedures should reduce the use of controversial national measures such as Section 301 of the US trade law, under which the US Government can take unilateral retaliatory actions against the perceived unfair trading practices of partner countries (see Chapter 6). This is in large part because the WTO's coverage of issues is much wider than that of the GATT-1947—more disputes can therefore be brought to the multilateral forum. However, if an issue is not subject to multilateral rules, the use of unilateral sanctions is not formally constrained by the WTO.

Dispute settlement under the GATT-1947 was considered problematical by many observers, given the opportunities for parties to the dispute to block the process. Will the WTO dispute-settlement mechanism work better? There is a strong presumption that the answer is yes, if only because past experience suggests that GATT dispute mechanisms worked much better than is generally recognized (Jackson, 1989; Hudec, 1993). Of some 120 complaints considered in the GATT under its general dispute-settlement provisions between 1948 and 1990, sixty disputes led to panel reports, the others being settled before a report was produced. Out of the sixty panel reports only four were not adopted. Even in these cases, however, parties settled bilaterally on the basis of the panel's findings (Petersmann, 1994). Hudec (1993) has concluded that overall, over the life of the GATT-1947, the success rate of cases addressed by GATT—that is, disputes settled—was almost 90 per cent.

While dispute-settlement procedures have been substantially improved in comparison to the past, shortcomings can certainly be identified. Many of these are common to any legal system. One is that attempts are generally made to settle trade rows by mutual agreement. At the same time, panels develop GATT case-law. Any political deals that are made on a specific issue will then be embodied in the case-law. This creates scope for inconsistencies. It is important in this connection that formally a panel decision on a matter does not constitute a legally binding precedent that must be followed by future panels. Thus, 'bad' panels can be ignored. However, 'bad' precedents from a purely legal point of view may also be followed in the future. Another weakness is that panels tend to be rather conservative as regards the remedies that are proposed. Usually these are 'cease and desist' orders. Compensation or penalties for actions that violate the rules are not a basic element of the process. A potential problem associated with the tightening of the rules under the WTO is that the institution may come under greater pressure than the GATT-1947, in so far as smaller countries refrained from bringing cases against larger countries that might not adopt reports that found against them. Blocking adoption is no longer possible. If this leads to more cases, one can ask what will happen if large players are unhappy with panel reports that are upheld by the Appellate Body. They may not implement the reports. While this may occur—the outcome then being authorization to retaliate, which petitioning countries will often not want to do—this does not make matters any worse than under GATT-1947.

2.5. AMENDMENTS AND ACCESSION

Article X of the WTO deals with amendments to the Agreement itself or to the Multilateral Trade Agreements. The majority voting criteria that apply in this connection have been discussed earlier. It is noteworthy that a Member is not bound by any amendment that passes a vote if it is opposed to it, and the change is such as to alter the rights and obligations of WTO Members. In such cases, the Ministerial Conference can decide whether to ask a Member that does not accept an amendment to withdraw from the WTO, or to allow it not to be bound by the new rule. As major traders must be part of the WTO for it to retain its value for the rest of the world, it is difficult to conceive of them being asked to withdraw. Large traders cannot therefore be forced to adopt changes they do not like.

GATT-1947 accession procedures have been carried over to the WTO, the main changes being that the deliberations are extended to services and TRIPs as well. The WTO states that 'any State or separate customs territory possessing full autonomy in the conduct of its external commercial relations . . . may accede to the Agreement, on terms to be agreed between it and the WTO' (Article XII). Accession normally follows a number of stages, negotiations usually being the final substantive phase. Summarizing, the procedure involved is as follows: the government communicates its desire to join the WTO by writing a letter to this effect to the Director-General of the WTO Secretariat. In practice, it will usually have requested observer status before this point. The General Council then establishes a working party consisting of interested countries to examine the application.

The government seeking accession must then submit a memorandum describing in great detail its trade regime. On the basis of this memorandum, members of the working party will discuss and clarify the functioning of the trade regime with the applicant, usually through specific questions that are based upon the memorandum, focusing in particular on its consistency with multilateral rules. WTO inconsistent measures will have to be removed, or be subject to negotiated special provisions. The conditions imposed for accession have become more stringent over time. Aspirant Members of the WTO are likely to be requested to bind their whole tariff schedule, and pressure can be expected that such bindings are at, or close to, applied rates. The country seeking accession will usually also have to liberalize access to its markets. Accession tariff negotiations are held between the acceding government and all WTO members that are interested in enhancing their access to the markets of the country seeking membership. Once tariff negotiations have been concluded, the report of the working party is forwarded to the General Council. A draft Decision and Protocol of Accession is attached to the report, as is the negotiated tariff schedule. Accession must be approved by a two-thirds majority of existing Members.

2.6. THE WTO AND OTHER INTERNATIONAL ECONOMIC ORGANIZATIONS

With the two Bretton Woods institutions (the World Bank and the IMF), the WTO can be regarded as one of the three pillars of the international economic order. While each organization has a clear mandate, they are strongly inter-dependent. The World Bank mobilizes resources in support of poverty allevia-tion in—and the sustainable development of—low-income countries. The IMF has the mandate to provide short-term financing to countries that con-front macroeconomic imbalances. The WTO provides a mechanism to induce countries to adopt non-discriminatory trade policies and reduce their barriers to trade, thereby enhancing efficiency and economic growth.

The formal linkages between GATT-1947 and the World Bank and IMF were limited. The only GATT body which worked closely with the IMF was the Balance-of-Payments Committee, which was responsible for conducting consultations on balance-of-payments restrictions that relate to Articles XII, XIII, XIV, XV, and XVIII of the General Agreement (see Chapter 4 and Annex 5). This state of affairs continues to prevail under the WTO. There are none the less numerous links between the WTO and the Bretton Woods institutions, many of which are informal or indirect. Adjustment lending by the Fund and the Bank usually supports trade liberalization, and therefore the goals of the WTO. Linkages may also be more direct. For example, the accession of countries such as Mexico and Morocco to GATT was supported with World Bank lending. Enhancing co-operation between the WTO, the IMF, and the World Bank is one of the goals of the WTO. The objective is to ensure greater consistency between and compatibility of the activities of the three international organizations. The links between trade and financial or macroeconomic policies are important because inappropriate macro policies may give rise to protectionism. Conversely, protectionist trade measures may limit the impact of exchange-rate adjustments introduced to deal with macroeconomic imbalances. The call for greater co-operation between the three agencies may imply that the WTO becomes more of a player in policy co-operation efforts than was the case under the GATT-1947.

There are a number of other international agencies that deal with economic matters in addition to the Fund and the Bank. Examples include the OECD, UN Economic Commissions, ECOSOC, and regional development banks. Most of these have little direct interaction with the WTO. The bodies that have the closest links with the WTO include UNCTAD, the International Organization for Standardization (ISO), the Brussels-based World Customs Organization (WCO) and the World Intellectual Property Organization (WIPO). GATT-1947 and UNCTAD were frequently looked upon as rival organizations, as the two entities have similar areas of interest, but differed greatly in terms of their functions, operations, and underlying ideology. Interestingly, they do co-operate through a joint venture, the International Trade Center (ITC), which provides export promotion and marketing assistance and related training and consulting services to developing countries. The WTO continues to co-operate with UNCTAD in the ITC. The WTO also co-operates with WIPO (through the TRIPs Agreement), the ISO (because of the WTO disciplines on product standards), and the WCO (to develop rules of origin) (see Chapters 4 and 6).

2.7. CONCLUSION

The WTO grew out of the GATT-1947, which successfully developed and oversaw global trading rules in the period after the Second World War. The creation of the WTO can be seen as the fulfilment of the vision of the participants at the Bretton Woods conference in 1944, albeit almost half a century later. Global governance in a rapidly integrating world economy has become increasingly important, as policies can have large and immediate detrimental effects on trade. The stakes involved in trade policies are frequently ill understood except by those who stand to gain from protection. The creation of a firm legal foundation for the institution that manages the multilateral trading system is therefore of great importance. A stronger institution may allow the system of rules and disciplines to be enforced more rigorously than in the past, and should at the very least ensure that the trade policies of Members become more transparent.

Great progress has been made in comparison with GATT-1947 in terms of the surveillance and collection of basic data on trade policy. Much more needs to be done in analysing these data, determining the costs of protection, and publicizing the magnitude and incidence of these costs. It is a truism that to reduce protection and protectionist pressures those negatively affected need to be aware of the costs of such policies. This is not necessarily a task for the WTO Secretariat and the absence of such analysis is not necessarily just cause for criticism. Indeed, a case can be made that it should not be done by the Secretariat. The WTO is a negotiating forum in which governments attempt to reach agreement on specific issues. Each government pursues its self-interest. Even if no overt attempts are made to influence the outcome of analyses undertaken by the Secretariat, WTO Members can be expected to contest the results of analysis that is not to their liking, and Secretariat staff may have a natural tendency towards engaging in self-censorship. Analysis of the data collected by the WTO Secretariat is more suitably done by an independent agency. To safeguard the multilateral trading system, the results of analyses of the costs and incidence of protection and related regulatory policies should be fed into domestic political markets. Discussing these in the WTO Council meetings will have little impact. The clients for the analysis are not governments, but the constituencies in individual countries who are negatively affected by policy (Finger, 1982). A corollary of this is that the institutes that undertake the analysis do not necessarily require public funding. Indeed, such activities should be financed by the parties that have the most to gain: exporters and consumer organizations. It is, however, crucial that the data-collection function of the Secretariat be maintained and enhanced, as this will often require the co-operation of governments, and that access to this data and information must be made available—to all interested parties. The database of tariff bindings and other measures that is maintained by the Secretariat is currently not open to the public.

A very important function of the multilateral trading system is dispute settlement. The dispute-settlement mechanism was changed in the Uruguay round to allow less scope for the parties to a dispute to block the process. With the acceptance of the rule of negative consensus for non-adoption of panel reports, the scope for overt politicization of the process has been reduced. A consequence of this may be that parties to a dispute are induced to politicize the process covertly, by vetoing the selection of specific panelists or by putting pressure on the Secretariat. More generally, under the WTO process panels may have more of an incentive to come to conclusions that are deemed to be as 'balanced' as possible. This has generally been the case as, to a greater or lesser extent, disputes have always been a matter for negotiation. With the elimination of the blocking option, however, the political aspects of the process may become even less transparent. Although the Appelate Body may help to ensure that panels interpret WTO rules appropriately, matters would be facilitated if panelists were selected randomly from a roster of qualified, professional persons, and if parties to a dispute had no veto power over their selection identity. This roster, in turn, might be compiled by an independent competent agency (a management consultancy firm), on the basis of terms of reference developed by WTO Members.

At the time of writing (April 1995) the WTO will have a Director-General, four deputy Director-Generals, as well as two assistant Director-Generals. Given the small size of the secretariat, the organization is quite top heavy. In part this may reflect the fact that there is no Executive Board—formally the WTO receives direction from the Ministerial Meeting, and is managed by the Council, in which in principle each Member has a voice. This is an unwieldy structure. Proposals have been made that the WTO adopt a management structure similar to that of the IMF or the World Bank, where a limited number of Executive Directors represent subsets of the 'shareholders' (Schott and Buurman, 1994). This could help to enhance the authority of the Director-General, and could also help to streamline the organizational chart of the WTO.

2.8. FURTHER READING

For an influential discussion of the design of a successor organization to the GATT-1947, see John H. Jackson, *Restructuring the GATT System* (London: Pinter Publishers, 1990). Jackson discusses the WTO briefly in 'The World Trade Organization, Dispute Settlement and Codes of Conduct', in Sue Collins and Barry Bosworth (eds.), *The New GATT : Implications for the United States* (Washington DC: Brookings Institution, 1994).

A summary of the background and mechanics of the WTO is presented in Philip Evans and James Walsh, *The EIU Guide to the New GATT* (London: The Economist Intelligence Unit, 1994). A history of the Uruguay round negotiations on the WTO is presented in Terence Stewart, *The GATT Uruguay Round: A Negotiating History (1986–1992)* (Deventer: Kluwer, 1994). GATT dispute-settlement procedures and related documents are discussed in Pierre Pescatore, William Davey, and Andreas Lowenfeld, *Handbook of GATT Dispute Settlement* (Irvington-on-Hudson: Transnational Juris Publications, 1993). An exhaustive analysis of GATT dispute settlement can be found in Robert Hudec, *Enforcing International Trade Law: The Evolution of the GATT Legal System* (New York: Butterworth, 1993). An indispensable companion for any analyst of the GATT legal texts is GATT, *Analytical Index* (Geneva: GATT Secretariat, 1994). Official GATT and WTO documents are periodically published by the Secretariat in a series called *Basic Instruments and Selected Documents*.

3

Negotiating Forum

Negotiation is the driving force of the multilateral trading system. Negotiations are used to agree on rules and procedures, to periodically reduce trade barriers, in instances when new countries want to join the club, and to resolve trade conflicts. The WTO is essentially a permanent negotiating forum in which trade issues may be discussed and agreed upon against the background of the provisions of the various agreements already concluded. Negotiations in the WTO context take place in permanent and *ad hoc* bodies, and are often informal. Although it is a multilateral forum, the WTO relies very heavily on bilateral or plurilateral interactions, with whatever agreements that are thus obtained being multilateralized through the MFN requirement.

Much of the discussion in this chapter is of a conceptual nature and centres on the problems that confront negotiators seeking to obtain agreements, the techniques that are used, and the reasons why MTNs tend to have outcomes that do not maximize participants' national welfare. More detailed discussion of the substance of the outcomes of the various MTNs is left to subsequent chapters. Although periodic MTNs such as the Uruguay round clearly attract most of the limelight, the prevalence of negotiations is by no means restricted to MTNs. Indeed, negotiations related to the normal functioning of the WTO are equally important, if less visible. For example, countries acceding to the WTO have to negotiate their 'ticket of admission' (see Chapter 2). This entry payment is a necessary condition for obtaining MFN treatment from existing Members. Negotiations are also conducted to agree on compensation of Members who are negatively affected by the creation of a customs union or a free-trade area (see Chapter 9).

3.1. MULTILATERAL TRADE LIBERALIZATION: CONCEPTUAL ISSUES

As discussed in Chapter 1, the rationale for small economies to engage in reciprocal, multilateral negotiations to liberalize trade (access to markets) rather than doing so unilaterally is political, not economic. It allows governments to offset opposition to liberalization on the part of import-competing industries by creating political support on the part of export interests that obtain greater access to foreign markets. It also allows large countries, that in principle can affect their terms of trade (the prices they get or pay for their exports or imports, respectively) and thus may benefit from trade barriers, to reach higher levels of real income (welfare) through agreeing to mutual disarmament. In the terminology of game theory, large countries are often trapped in an inefficient, non-cooperative equilibrium, while small ones may be held hostage by vested interest-groups.

MTNs can usefully be viewed and analysed with the help of game theory and game-theoretical concepts.[1] The theory of games is the branch of mathematics that analyses situations where actions by decision-makers (players) are interdependent. Outcomes depend on how the game (the interaction) is structured (the rules of the game), the information available to the players, and the way that players form expectations about the actions of other players. There are two basic types of games, co-operative and non-cooperative. The first type assumes that outcomes of games are efficient in the sense that gains from trade are maximized, and what is at issue is the distribution of the possible gains across players. Co-operative games assume that a binding enforcement mechanism exists and that defection by players from the co-operative solution can be observed by other players. Non-cooperative games emerge in settings where there is no central enforcement mechanism and where there is no presumption that outcomes will be Pareto-optimal. A Pareto-optimal situation is one where no party can be made better off without another party being made worse off. The fact that trade policy-makers are driven as much by (internal) political concerns as by economic considerations affects their choice criteria and thus decision outcomes. From an internal political perspective, a Pareto-optimal outcome is one where no party can be made better off without another party knowing that it is being made worse off (Kostecki, 1983). Information is important, therefore, in ensuring that political and economic notions of optimality do not diverge too much.

MTNs held under WTO auspices can be regarded as efforts to set the rules of the international trade game. Countries get together and seek to achieve a consensus as to the type of game they will play in the future. While MTNs are attempts to co-ordinate, the outcome of negotiations will rarely be Pareto-optimal. Perhaps the most appropriate way of looking at MTNs is to regard them as institution-setting exercises. Various situations can be identified that may give rise to the creation of institutions. One very well-known case is the Prisoners' Dilemma, where players choosing individually rational strategies end up in an equilibrium that is not efficient. This situation is discussed in Box 3.1.

While a convenient illustration, it should be noted that the Prisoners' Dilemma is a very special and narrow game, in that there is only a single outcome that makes both players better off, and there are only two players. For practical situations of trade negotiations, there are usually many possible outcomes that make all countries better off and are thus Pareto-superior to the status quo. If players interact over time and are able to communicate and

---

[1] The following paragraphs draw on Hoekman (1993).

Box 3.1. The Prisoners' Dilemma in trade policy

The Prisoners' Dilemma is illustrated in the diagram below. The equilibrium outcome of the game is characterized by both countries imposing trade restrictions (not co-operating), each obtaining a pay-off of zero. It is inferior to the Pareto-optimal free-trade solution, where each party obtains a pay-off of $P - c > 0$, where P is the benefit of obtaining access to the partner country's market, c are the costs of opening up its own market, and $P > c$. These costs consist of political variables, augmented by the possible decline in the terms of trade for certain products.[2] Non-cooperation occurs because it is in each country's interest to impose protection, independent of what the other country does. Whatever policy stance is taken by country B, country A will maximize its pay-off by choosing a protectionist stance, and vice versa for country B. For example, if B chooses free trade, A's pay-off is highest under protection, as $P > P - c$. If B chooses protection, A will again prefer protection, because $-c < 0$. As each country has the same incentive structure, they end up in the non-cooperative, inefficient outcome where each earns a pay-off of zero. If the countries co-operated and both implemented free trade, they would each obtain $P - c > 0$. In instances such as these, where individually rational behaviour by governments is not efficient, the creation of an institution or regime can help solve the dilemma by fostering co-operation.

	Country B	
Country A	Free trade	Protection
Free trade	$P - c, P - c$	$-c, P$
Protection	$P, -c$	$0, 0$

Note: $P > c > 0$.

make credible commitments, the co-operation problem noted above can be regarded as a subset of a more general class of bargaining situations. These are more general because it may be the case that even if countries at any point in time cannot improve upon their joint welfare, there may exist possibilities to

---

[2] This specific formulation of the dilemma is drawn from Garett (1992). Technically, the outcome resulting from non-cooperative behaviour is often assumed to be a Nash equilibrium, that is, each nation acts to maximize its objectives given the actions of all other nations. The Prisoners' Dilemma is an example of such a situation.

achieve outcomes that are superior to these equilibria if countries are willing and able to trade across issues. Conversely, there may exist situations where co-operation is not necessary, and where institutions will not be useful because individually rational strategies lead to a Pareto-optimal outcome. This is the case, for example, in a world where countries cannot affect their terms of trade, markets are perfectly competitive, there are no distortions or rent-seeking interest-groups, and governments believe in *laissez-faire*. In principle no co-operation problem should then exist as the government has no incentive to diverge from free trade. Alternatively—and more realistically—there may exist a dominant country (a hegemon) that enforces co-operation. Conybeare (1987) discusses these and alternative possibilities in greater depth.

In practice, of course, there are rent-seeking groups in each country, governments do not believe in *laissez-faire*, and markets are imperfect. In pursuing national objectives, a country may reduce the welfare of other countries by imposing a negative externality on them. An externality arises when a government does not take into account the impact of its actions on other countries—be they good or bad. The economic literature on externalities has focused on two ways of addressing the problem. One calls for a central authority to impose targeted taxes or subsidies; the other postulates that those affected will attempt to bargain their way to a Pareto-optimal situation. The first approach is not very relevant in an international context, as no supranational entity exists that has the power to levy the required taxes (assuming these can be calculated in the first place). At the heart of the second approach lies the so-called Coase theorem (named after Ronald Coase, a Nobel Prize winner in economics): given the existence of enforceable property rights and in the absence of transaction costs, externalities will be bargained away such that a Pareto-optimal outcome results. That is, the market (i.e. bargaining) will ensure efficiency. In general, for bargaining over rules of behaviour to be possible, it is necessary that players expect to interact with each other over an indefinite time horizon. This creates incentives to co-operate because agreements can be enforced through the threat of retaliation.

The Coase theorem assumes that decision-makers have perfect information regarding the economic setting in which they operate and that they can interact costlessly. This includes information on their own and on other parties' utility functions (preferences). In practice this assumption will often be violated, as will the assumption of zero transaction costs. Thus, usually there can be no certainty that a specific bargaining procedure will lead to an efficient outcome. Bargaining can only solve an externality problem if the external effects are the only cause of market failure, and this is not the case if there is imperfect information. While bargaining will often not be optimal in a technical sense in a world of incomplete information, if institutions exist that allow competitive bidding for property rights, an efficient reallocation of such rights may be achieved (Samuelson, 1985).

In international affairs, reallocation of, or bidding for, property rights may not appear to be very practical at first glance. Nevertheless, property rights do exist, implicitly defined by rules of sovereignty. That is, nation-states that create externalities implicitly have the right to impose them. The existence of rights allows negotiations to take place, while the (mutual) negative externalities created by national trade policies are the inducement for countries to pursue them. Because countries interact continuously, agreements are in principle enforceable as long as defectors can be identified and singled out for retaliation. The WTO puts great emphasis on transparency of procedure and mutual surveillance, which facilitates the identification of violators. Subject to certain conditions, affected countries have the right to retaliate if no or inadequate compensation is offered by the nation violating its WTO obligations (see Chapter 2 above).

To a large extent MTNs comprise barter, that is, trades occur in a setting where there is no generally accepted medium of exchange (money). Barter is possible when there are (enforced) property rights, marginal valuations of goods differ, and potential transactors can meet each other. Any introductory economics textbook will explain that barter is inefficient. Indeed, its inefficiency is one of the historical reasons for the creation of money. However, in international relations there is usually no money and nations are stuck with barter. Three kinds of inefficiencies may arise:

(1) the market (total supply) may not offer any goods a trader is interested in obtaining;
(2) a trader who has something another wants has no interest in what the other has to offer, but is interested in the goods of a third party; and
(3) it may not be possible to equate trader's marginal valuations of goods.

If the first possibility occurs, trade will not be possible and the status quo will be maintained. If the second possibility occurs, trade will only be feasible if a set of potential traders exists such that all members have something that another wants. In this context, economists sometimes speak of barter's need for a double coincidence of wants. Even if this condition is met, trade will only occur if marginal valuations can be (approximately) equated. This is the third potential problem mentioned above. If it cannot be solved, trade may not take place. This problem can occur because goods are indivisible.

All these problems affect MTNs, as these are nothing more (or less) than a marketplace where potential traders meet. To ensure that these traders do not come for nothing (i.e. that there is something to trade), a great deal of care is taken to establish an agenda beforehand. This agenda will have some topics (issues) of interest for all the parties that are willing to trade. Prior to an MTN, national authorities, industries, and bureaucracies will be engaged in a domestic negotiation to determine interests, priorities, and possible trade-offs. It is this work by potential participants that leads eventually to the establishment of the agenda of the MTN. The setting of the agenda of an MTN is a negotiation in itself. Prior to the launching of the Uruguay round it took five years of work in a GATT Senior Officials Group and elsewhere to prepare the agenda that was mostly embodied in the Punta del Este Declaration.

For analytical purposes any trade negotiation can be decomposed into four stages: catalyst, pre-negotiation, negotiation, and post-negotiation.[3] In the catalyst stage there is a visionary. This could be an interest-group or a government. The implied policy vision is the catalyst, defining in broad terms the issues to be negotiated. In the pre-negotiation phase, discussions (negotiations) take place on the agenda of the formal negotiations. The agenda that is established places constraints on the parameters of the formal negotiation that will follow. In the negotiation stage, formal government-to-government bargaining takes place, with interest-group participation. Subject to the implicit parameters established by the agenda, negotiators are lobbied by interest-groups, and their preferences for policy packages change. Ultimately, depending on bargaining strategies, tactics, and time constraints, a formal draft of an agreement emerges. The final stage of an MTN is the post-negotiation, implementation stage, which determines how the agreements are embodied in a country's laws and procedures and enforced by its administration, and judiciary, and legislature. There will frequently be an imperfect correspondence between what was negotiated and what is implemented, making it very important how effective surveillance and dispute-settlement procedures are, and how precisely worded the formal agreement is.

It is often assumed in theoretical treatments of negotiations that countries are unitary actors that seek to maximize national welfare. This is rarely the case. Governments that participate in trade negotiations presumably recognize the potential welfare improvements that can be realized by mutual disarmament, i.e. liberalization. But governments are subject to lobbying by interest-groups that may favour or oppose liberalization (Tumlir, 1985). Even governments that seek to maximize national income must take into account the political realities that constrain what is feasible. Political constraints and incentives offered by interest-groups play a role both in terms of setting the agenda for negotiations and during the negotiations themselves.

The agenda that is established will determine a set of possible policy packages that could emerge as outcomes or solutions to the negotiation. Not all of the possible packages will be feasible. A necessary condition for the adoption of a package by all participants is that it improves upon the status quo ante or upon whatever is expected to be the status quo if negotiations fail (the so-called threat point). In Fig. 3.1, the status quo is represented by point x^{SQ}. If, as is often the case, players have made threats to take actions that will be worse than the status quo for trading partners, the analysis should start from

---

[3] See Leidy and Hoekman (1993). What follows draws extensively on this paper.

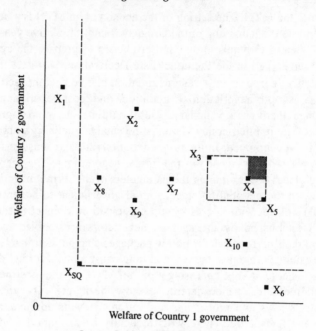

Source: Leidy and Hoekman (1993).
FIG. 3.1 The negotiation space and the set of feasible outcomes

the implied disagreement or threat point. In what follows the status quo point is assumed to incorporate any threats. Assuming for simplicity that there are two parties to the negotiation, and that the vertical and horizontal axes measure their national welfare (abstracting from lobbying for the moment), all possible outcomes that lie to the left or below the dotted lines radiating out from this point are not feasible, as they imply less than the status quo for at least one party. Some policy packages are clearly better for both parties than others. Thus, those packages that form the frontier (x_2 to x_5) dominate all the others for at least one party. The points on the frontier are all Pareto-optimal: if any one of these points is chosen, no other packages exist that make both parties better off. The more possible outcomes there are, the more continuous the frontier will be. In the limit, if what is on the table is perfectly divisible (such as a tariff), the negotiation frontier is a line with an infinite number of Pareto-optimal outcomes. In the more realistic case of a multi-issue negotiation with many non-tariff issues, there will be a large number of feasible policy packages, but moving along the frontier will imply discontinuous jumps from one Pareto-optimal point to another. The location of these various policy packages may change over time, as the result of lobbying pressure, learning, and linkage strategies.

The shape of the frontier is not constant. Lobbying pressure affects the effective preferences that ultimately drive negotiations. In the absence of lobbying activity—i.e. in the absence of political constraints in a certain area—most governments' notional preferences can be assumed to represent the social welfare. Lobbies, however, will generally inform negotiators of the implied political costs of taking certain positions. Once this information is digested and the government has determined the relative political importance of the groups involved, the options available to satisfy their desires, and the costs of these options, the government's effective preferences may well differ from its notional (unlobbied) preferences. As a result the set of feasible policy packages may shrink.

Trades in an MTN can occur both within and across issues. Trade within an issue is exemplified by tariff negotiations. Countries make bids and offers on the level of specific tariffs, or the average tariff level. In principle, if there are enough issues, cross-issue trade may allow agreement if within-issue trade proves insufficient to generate an improvement on the status quo for all concerned. For example, agreement on a definition of subsidies could be made contingent on agreement that stricter rules be imposed on emergency protection against imports. In terms of the negotiating process, linkages play a fundamental role in terms of fostering agreement because they allow side-payments to be made.

In terms of achieving an agreement, issue linkage can potentially play two roles in MTNs (Hoekman, 1993). First, it can be used to achieve reciprocity. That is, it allows a distributional constraint to be met: a balance of benefits and concessions. Linkage is actively used in multilateral trade negotiations to achieve reciprocity. Second, linkage may be used to increase potential gains from trade. In this case linkage is an instrument that allows a more efficient outcome to be attained. As noted earlier, MTNs deal with bargaining problems, that is, the issue is to choose a Pareto-optimal outcome out of a set of many possible such outcomes. Agreement may not occur for procedural reasons, or it may be the case that no better solution exists. Sometimes, this may be the result of not being able to link issues, or of attempting to link the wrong issues. For example, powerful nations may (attempt to) impose linkages on weaker ones. In this case mutual gain is clearly not the objective. Often, such strategies may be counterproductive, especially if attempted by nations that are open to retaliation.

The problem facing negotiators is generally two-fold: when and what to link. The need for linkage depends on whether there are sufficient mutual gains to be achieved by co-operating within a given issue area, and whether these gains are distributed relatively symmetrically. If gains are too small, or are distributed too asymmetrically, cross-issue linkage quickly becomes necessary. The Uruguay round agreements on TRIPs, agriculture, or textiles and clothing would have been considerably different—perhaps non-existent—if no cross-issue linkages had been made. The question of what to link is equivalent to the question of what to trade, and can be answered using the basic microeconomic theory of exchange. The necessary conditions for fruitful issue linkage are that marginal evaluations of different issues differ across nations, and proposed linkages (trades) result in outcomes that make all parties better off than the status quo ante. For linkage to be feasible, parties must agree on the nature of the set of Pareto-optimal outcomes. The less information parties have about the issues, the fuzzier the Pareto-optimal set will be (Tollison and Willett, 1979). The same applies if there is disagreement among the parties regarding the effect of alternative proposals. In general, the choice of issues will be determined on a political level based on various criteria: nations will attempt to offer concessions on those issues they care least about in return for gains on issues they care most about. How much a government cares about an issue is likely to be as much a function of the strength of different domestic interest-groups as of the relative costs and benefits to the nation as a whole. As producers' interests tend to be more concentrated on a specific topic than those of consumers—who are affected by all the issues on the table—the former tend to be much better informed than the latter (Downs, 1954). This is one of the factors skewing the outcome of negotiations.

Issue linkages can be thought of as replacing any two possible policy packages with one that represents a weighted average of the elements of the two. Lobbying efforts might be directed towards achieving linkage for several reasons. As noted earlier, linkage can create a region of mutual advantage where previously none existed, or can expand the set of mutually beneficial agreements. Consider, for example, the set of possible policy packages $\{x_1, \ldots, x_{10}\}$ displayed in Fig. 3.1, and assume that the initial placement of these points corresponds to the unlobbied preferences of negotiators. Assume further that x_4 is now the status quo point. There is no room for agreement without issue linkage. Issue linkage serves to produce a new possible policy package whose value to negotiators, *ceteris paribus*, must fall strictly within the dashed box connecting the linked policy packages. If, for example, proposals x_3 and x_5 were linked, the linked package might fall within the shaded region in Fig. 3.1. If so, the issue linkage makes agreement possible (see Chapter 6 on TRIPs for an example). While such linkage might be pursued directly by unlobbied governments, interest-groups may also pursue issue linkage strategically to move a favoured set of policies to the negotiation frontier. Alternatively they might seek to block consideration of unfavoured policies. Strong supporters of the status quo might even find it efficient to pursue issue linkages in order to empty the effective negotiation set, i.e. to let negotiations break down (Leidy and Hoekman, 1993).

Historically, GATT contracting parties tended to constrain themselves to trade-offs within issue areas, due to their practice of establishing separate negotiating groups for each issue. In practice, attempts to link across issues are generally made at the beginning and at the end of an MTN. In the initial, pre-negotiation phase of an MTN, cross-issue trade-offs occur so as to achieve a balanced negotiating agenda (Winham, 1986). It is only in the final stage of an MTN that positions on issues are completely mapped out and the need for linkage in terms of achieving overall agreement becomes clear. Such trade-offs tend to be made at a high political level under substantial time pressure. The *modus operandi* of the Uruguay round in this connection was the rule that 'nothing is agreed upon until everything is agreed upon'. Linkage in these cases is focused more on achieving a perceived balance of gains and concessions (i.e. reciprocity) than on increasing potential joint gains.

Coalition Formation and the Non-Discrimination Rule

The type of agreement that is likely to emerge from attempts by a group of nations to co-operate will be a function of the number of countries involved, the number of issues, and the extent to which non-participants can be excluded from the benefits of an agreement. Intuitively, the feasibility of achieving agreement among a given group of nations will be in part a function of their identity. This, for example, is likely to influence the choice of agenda and may determine the set of feasible issue linkages. Not only the identity of nations, but also the absolute number of participants may be important. Generally, as the number of participants increases, so will transaction costs. Thus, there will also be a trade-off between the number and types of players and the possibility of achieving comprehensive agreement. The problem then is determining the optimal choice of issues relative to parties in a negotiation. This by no means trivial problem is made even more difficult once the possibilities for coalition formation are taken into account.

The formation of coalitions or clubs of like-minded countries is often regarded as a way to circumvent possible free-rider problems and reduce the transactions costs of MTNs. Limiting the number of parties in a negotiation can be efficient in terms of generating agreement because of reduced negotiation costs. However, this is not necessarily an argument for excluding non-participants from the benefits of an agreement. The primary rationale for exclusion is that it can act as an incentive mechanism to induce participation in the MTN. But the benefits of the WTO have the characteristics of a public good: adding members to the club does not detract from the benefits accruing to existing members. Indeed, the contrary is more likely—implying that efficiency is maximized if all nations are included. Frequently differences of opinion on an issue are extreme enough to prohibit consensus from emerging. If it is difficult for those in favour of a proposal to internalize the benefits of implementing it (to limit free-riding by those that are not in favour), the MFN rule may lead to a breakdown of the discussions. However, if the benefits of agreement between a group of like-minded countries is so large that free-riding by others is not a constraint, the countries involved may agree to form a club. An important example of such 'privileged groups' (Olson, 1965) are the codes that were negotiated between a subset of GATT signatories during the Tokyo round. In most instances signatories to these codes applied them on an MFN basis.

Countries that are like-minded on an issue may also form coalitions so as to maximize their joint bargaining power. Among the various types of coalitions that may arise in the context of an MTN, one can distinguish between agenda-moving, proposal-making, blocking, and negotiating coalitions (Hamilton and Whalley, 1989). The first three of these are the most common in MTNs, as they require only a limited amount of co-ordination between coalition members because there is no need to arrive at a common position. The Cairns group—a coalition of fourteen agricultural exporters (see Chapter 8)—was an example of a proposal-making coalition. Major developing countries frequently acted as an agenda-moving coalition as regards TRIPs, services, and TRIMs in the Uruguay round. In contrast, negotiating coalitions hammer out a common position and thereafter speak with one voice. The major example of such a coalition is the EU. Coalition formation is a relevant strategy for both small and large countries. For the latter the main incentive is likely to be a reduction in transaction costs, and perhaps concern over free-riding in certain instances. For small countries the primary attraction is likely to be the potential increase in negotiating power.

As in the case of issue linkage, coalition formation in MTNs can also be used by lobbies in an attempt to shift the location of policy packages in the preference ordering of their governments (Leidy and Hoekman, 1993). Returning to Fig. 3.1, consider an interest-group in country 2 for whom the policy package x_5 is the worst possible outcome. Assume that country 2 is the EU, country 1 is the US, the lobby is the EU film industry, and x_5 implies far-reaching liberalization that will greatly benefit the US industry. The EU film industry can attempt to remove x_5 from the feasible set in several ways. First, it can lobby for the status quo at home. A small increase in the value of the status quo to its negotiators is sufficient to eliminate x_5 from the effective feasible set. Alternatively, if x_{10} does not contain the offensive provision on film-market liberalization, and is thus ranked higher from the EU film lobby's perspective, it could throw its weight behind domestic and foreign groups supporting package x_{10}. If successful, as reflected in a move of x_{10} to the north-west, it may remove x_5 from consideration. Finally, the industry can also attempt to produce a vertical drop in the valuation of x_5 by its government by directly lobbying against it.

3.2. RECIPROCITY AND THE MECHANICS OF NEGOTIATIONS

A fundamental concept used in GATT negotiations is 'reciprocity'. Very loosely defined, reciprocity is the practice of making an action conditional upon an action by a counterpart. Reciprocity has been a fundamental element in virtually all assaults on barriers to trade, governments generally being unwilling to liberalize unilaterally on an MFN basis. While there have been exceptions to this pattern—e.g. the United Kingdom in the nineteenth century (see Bhagwati and Irwin, 1987) and many Latin American countries in the 1980s—historically mercantilism has reigned. That is, exports were seen as a boon to the economy because they led to an inflow of gold, the hard currency of the times, while imports were bad because they led to an outflow. Even though this makes no economic sense—as was clearly spelled out by the great economists of the eighteenth and early nineteenth centuries (Adam Smith, David Ricardo, and John Stuart Mill)—mercantilism appealed to 'common sense'. Over time the rationales for reciprocity changed somewhat, the primary justification becoming one of preventing free-riding by countries that continued to maintain high trade barriers (i.e. did not reciprocate). Again, the economic foundations for making trade liberalization conditional upon barrier reductions by trading partners is weak, as the cost of holding back to induce others to follow suit may be very high. None the less, reciprocal trade liberalization was even more prevalent in much of the twentieth century than in the nineteenth. For example, the 1934 US initiative for tariff reduction in the 1930s, following the disastrous tariff wars of the early 1930s induced by the passage of the 1930 Smoot–Hawley Act (Conybeare, 1987), explicitly required reciprocal concessions (it was called the Reciprocal Trade Agreements Act).

Article XXVIII bis of the GATT (entitled Tariff Negotiations) states that:

> negotiations on a reciprocal and mutually advantageous basis, directed to the substantial reduction of the general level of tariffs and other charges on imports and exports . . . are of great importance to the expansion of international trade. The CONTRACTING PARTIES may therefore sponsor such negotiations from time to time. Negotiations under this Article may be carried out on a selective product-by-product basis or by the application of such multilateral procedures as may be accepted by the contracting parties concerned. Such negotiations may be directed towards the reduction of duties, the binding of duties at then existing levels, or undertakings that individual duties or average duties of specified categories of products shall not exceed specified levels. The binding against increase of low duties or of a duty-free treatment, shall, in principle, be recognized as a concession equivalent in value to the reduction of high duties.

Three basic principles therefore apply in GATT tariff negotiations: (1) such negotiations are to be on a reciprocal and mutually advantageous basis; (2) concessions are to be bound; and (3) they are to be applied on an MFN basis (through Article I of the GATT). The first two of these principles have tended to apply to developed countries only. Until recently, developing countries have not been required to offer reciprocal concessions or to bind their tariff rates (see Chapters 4 and 10).

Reciprocity in the GATT context has been defined in terms of the 1934

Reciprocal Trade Agreements Act mentioned earlier: it implies the exchange of a reduction in the level of protection in one country in return for an equivalent reduction in the level of protection of another country. Reciprocity criteria or formulae that are used by participants in negotiations may be intra- or inter-issue. An intra-issue criterion provides for the exchange of concessions of an identical nature (e.g. tariff concessions against tariff concessions for a given product or group of products). An inter-issue formula provides for the exchange of concessions of a dissimilar nature (e.g. tariff concessions against removal of quotas). Reciprocity criteria may be product-specific—as in so-called item-by-item negotiations—or more general in nature. Examples of the latter are so-called across-the-board trade barrier reductions, which tend to take the form of a formula: an $x\%$ reduction in average tariffs, or a $y\%$ reduction in the dispersion of tariffs. Both item-by-item and across-the-board approaches can be applied to both tariffs and non-tariff measures, although in the latter case quantification tends to be much more difficult. Formula approaches in the case of non-tariff measures tend to take the form of the adoption of general rules, such as transparency and non-discrimination.

Reciprocity Criteria for Tariffs

GATT members have used a number of criteria to evaluate whether an exchange of tariff concessions is balanced. When considering a reciprocal package or balance of offers, negotiators might be expected to take into account factors such as the effect of a reduction in trade barriers on future trade flows, domestic production, employment, prices, etc. In practice this is often not the case. The methods used to evaluate offers are usually very rough, and have little relationship, if any, with what economic theory would suggest as reasonable yardsticks. The approaches that have been used are best characterized as providing negotiators with a focal point, that is, something tangible enabling parties to set objectives, evaluate the position of others, assess negotiating progress, and identify acceptable compromises. In the case of GATT talks, the focal point is generally nothing more than a measure that takes into account the relative size of different countries (trade volume) and is simple to calculate using data that are readily available. The last point is important: the choice of focal point used in past negotiations has been driven largely by data availability.

There are various examples of focal points that have been used in the past. One method is to focus on 'trade coverage', defined as the reduction in a tariff multiplied by the volume of imports of that product. For example, if imports of a product are US $10 million and the applicable tariff rate is reduced from 50 per cent to 35 per cent, the trade coverage is 0.15 times 10, or $1.5 million. A related method that has been used can be referred to as '50 per cent equivalents'. This also takes into account both the tariff cut on a good and the value of imports of the good before the tariff cut. A 50 per cent equivalent (or one equivalent) signifies that a 50 per cent tariff cut took place with respect to US $1 million worth of imports. A tariff cut of 25 per cent for a product line in which the value of imports is $2 million is also equal to one equivalent. The general formula is:

$$E = (M \times dT)/50$$

where M is the value of imports and dT is the percentage tariff cut. These methods of assessing reciprocal concessions were often used in the earlier MTNs when trade between two negotiating countries was not bilaterally balanced in a specific product.

Another method is the 'average cut'. Generally, weighted averages rather than simple averages are used in this connection. Suppose that country A imports $20 million worth of cotton shirts and $30 million worth of cotton trousers. During trade negotiations it agrees to reduce its tariff on cotton shirts by 5 per cent and its tariff on cotton trousers by 10 per cent. The weighted average cut in import tariffs for cotton imports by country A is then:

$$E = (0.05 \times \$20m. + 0.1 \times \$30m.) / (\$20m. + \$30m.) = 8.$$

The average tariff cut by country A in the cotton sector is thus 8 per cent. Average cuts do not always provide a satisfactory indication of the magnitude of trade liberalization. For example, if a country's tariff is so high as to be prohibitive (no imports come in at all), there will be nothing to weigh the tariff cut by for the product concerned. Use of the formula will then give a biased picture of the extent of tariff cuts. The more restrictive a given import tariff, the less satisfactory is the use of this type of weighted tariff cut average to calculate the value of concessions. Because of such problems, tariff cuts are often also weighted by domestic consumption or production of the products involved, or the global value of trade in the products.

Reciprocity formula may be general (across-the-board) or specific (item-by-item). Negotiations conducted on an item-by-item basis rely on a specific reciprocity formula, i.e. tariff reduction relating to one product line is exchanged for tariff reduction on another product line. Negotiations conducted on an across-the-board basis rely on a general reciprocity formula. Table 3.2 lists some of the major techniques that have been used in the GATT context.

The initial GATT process of negotiations on specific concessions was essentially bilateral. That is, two contracting parties presented each other with lists of requests and offers, and negotiations centred on achieving a bilaterally balanced exchange of concessions. However, this network of bilateral negotiations subsequently acquires a multilateral dimension because: specific tariff concessions once negotiated bilaterally are generalized through the unconditional MFN clause; the bilateral exchange of concessions

TABLE 3.1 *Negotiating techniques for tariff reduction*

Technique	Major Characteristics
Item-by-item approach	Bilateral negotiations based on requests and offers. Principal technique until the Kennedy round; widely used again in the Uruguay round. May consist of only binding a rate without lowering it.
Linear tariff cut	Across-the-board negotiating technique providing for the same rate of reduction for all items; used in the Kennedy round and the Tokyo round. Formula: $T_2 = rT_1$, where T_2 is the reduced tariff, T_1 the original tariff, and r is a coefficient $(0 < r < 1)$, $(1-r)$ being the percentage reduction.
Harmonization formula	An approach aimed at flattening tariff peaks and reducing tariff escalation. In the Tokyo round the so-called 'Swiss formula' was used: $T_2 = RT_1/R + T_1$ where R is a coefficient (16 or 14).
Free trade for a sector or product	Abolition of tariffs for a given sector. This approach was used in the Tokyo round by the signatories of the Agreement on Trade in Civil Aircraft. It was also used in the Uruguay round in the context of so-called zero-for-zero tariff negotiations.

taking place in the MTN context follow procedures laid down multilaterally; and market opening granted by one country is frequently balanced against tariff reductions made by a number of trading partners simultaneously. The rationale underlying the last element is that a generalization of bilaterally negotiated concessions through MFN may create a free-rider problem. Any reduction in trade barriers will also benefit other countries that supply the relevant products, and these countries may not have offered reciprocal concessions. The principle of non-discrimination clashes here with the principle of reciprocity. Under an MFN clause, no conditionality (discrimination) may be introduced once a concession has been granted. However, conditionality (which is the very essence of reciprocity) may be introduced in the negotiating process. Two general techniques have been conceived to deal with the free-rider issue: the principal supplier rule and the practice of balancing concessions in exchange for 'initial negotiating rights'.

Under the principal supplier rule, requests for concessions on a particular product are normally made by, and only by, the principal import suppliers, i.e. the largest suppliers of a product. This limits free-riding, as the concessions granted by an importing country (*A*) to its principal supplier (*B*) of a specific product must be balanced by concessions from that principal supplier (*B*) on products for which *A* is in turn a principal supplier. The principal-supplier mechanism was a long-standing US practice, this being the method used in the negotiation of the network of reciprocal trade agreements starting in the 1930s (Jackson, 1969: 219). The principal-supplier rule effectively reinforces the bilateral character of trade negotiations conducted on a product-by-product basis. Under an unconditional MFN clause governments have few incentives to grant a trade concession to countries that are not its principal suppliers. Granting a concession to a small supplier implies giving away the concession to the principal supplier, since the latter will benefit from it due to the MFN rule. Negotiating a given concession with a small supplier is an ill-conceived negotiating strategy. The principal supplier is the trading nation which benefits the most from a concession and is thus probably prepared to offer more reciprocal trade liberalization than a smaller supplier would be prepared or able to do.

Multilateral product-by-product negotiations based on the principal-supplier rule rely on multilateral balancing. Assume that country A is the principal supplier of good 1 to country B, and that B is the principal supplier of good 2 to A. Negotiations are then feasible. Assume further that B imports $500 million worth of goods from A while A imports only $250 million worth of goods from B. Although an exchange is certainly possible, because trade flows are unbalanced, B may demand that A reduce its tariff by twice as much as B. If A is unwilling to do this, and the reciprocity rule requires equality in cuts as measured by, for example, tariff revenues, negotiations may break down. Involving another country C may allow A and B to circumvent their problem. If country C is the principal supplier of good 3 to A, and exports some $500 million worth of it to A, is the principal supplier of good 4 to country B, with exports being worth around $250 million, and imports from A and B goods worth $250 and $500 million, respectively, for which these countries are principal suppliers, negotiations are balanced. This is, of course, a stylized example. In practice many goods are involved, and precise balancing is impossible to achieve. The main point is that by involving many countries, more trades are possible under the principal-supplier constraint.

While the principal supplier rule reduces the role of smaller supplier countries in multilateral tariff negotiations, it does not eliminate them as players. A factor leading to the involvement of smaller countries is the need for 'end-game' or 'last-minute' balancing. At the end of the bilateral phase of a round, every negotiator knows that his country is not only required to grant the benefits of concessions to other countries but also that it is entitled to the benefits of concessions negotiated between other trading nations. At this stage the negotiators attempt to strike a balance in the global effect of concessions. To achieve that objective they may seek to reshuffle previously made requests and offers. A country which finds out that one of its concessions indirectly benefited another country that refused to make a reciprocal concession to it, always has the possibility to withdraw the original concession. Thus, the granting of concessions to principal suppliers is often made conditional upon obtaining supplementary balancing concessions from a number of other (smaller) suppliers of the product concerned.

The use of the principal-supplier rule with multilateral balancing can be regarded as an explicit attempt by trading nations to form privileged groups in that the share of the costs and benefits of a product-specific liberalization that is internalized by club members (principal suppliers) is sufficiently large so that free-riding by third parties is no longer a source of concern. The use of the principal-supplier rule was in large part a reflection of the fact that the membership of GATT was rather limited in its early days. Contracting parties therefore sought to ensure that non-members were able to free-ride as little as possible, thereby increasing the incentives for them to accede. As GATT membership expanded to include most significant trading nations, the rationale for using the principal-supplier technique diminished, as all parties became involved in the negotiations to reduce barriers to trade.

The practice of supplementary balancing probably resulted in greater trade liberalization than would have taken place under the strict bilateralism which characterized the pre-GATT trading system. The MFN clause prompts requests for concessions from smaller suppliers that would not be presented under a conditional MFN approach, while the fact that the concession-granting country is able to sell its concession to more than one country allows it to obtain greater compensation than under a system of bilateral bargaining. Greater compensation also implies that more can be offered in terms of market opening (Dam, 1970).

Item-by-item negotiations are complex and tedious. They rely on a request-and-offer procedure in a series of bilateral negotiations, the results of which are extended under the GATT to all other member countries through MFN. The item-by-item, principal supplier approach was the main technique used in the first five MTNs (up to the Dillon round). The principal advantage of the item-by-item negotiations is that, being product-specific, they enable negotiators to be very precise, facilitating an evaluation of the trade effects of concessions. This advantage is offset by the fact that item-by-item, principal-supplier negotiations are resource-intensive, facilitate the exemption of industries with political clout, are not very effective in reducing barriers where there are no principal suppliers, and can be micro-managed in a way that allows the MFN obligation to be effectively circumvented.

A good example of how an MFN requirement can be circumvented in the context of an exchange of bilaterally negotiated concessions that are formally subject to MFN comes from a 1904 trade agreement between Germany and Switzerland. Germany committed itself to reducing its tariffs on 'large dapple mountain cattle reared at a spot at least 300 meters above sea level and having at least one month grazing each year at a spot at least 800 meters above sea level' (Curzon, 1965: 60). Although this agreement pre-dates the GATT, it has become the classic illustration of the use of creative tariff-line definition by trade negotiators to avoid MFN. The general approach continued to be used in the GATT context (Finger, 1979).

A general implication of the foregoing is that the number of tariff lines and the trade coverage of item-by-item negotiations is often limited. Moreover, the negotiating process tends to be long and labourious, especially when the number of participants is substantial. Notwithstanding these negative aspects of the item-by-item approach, it was used quite successfully in the early GATT rounds. Over time, however, as the number of participants rose, increasing the complexity of item-by-item negotiations while at the same time reducing their utility (as free-riding became less of an issue), attempts were made to shift towards an across-the-board approach. The Kennedy round thus saw the introduction of a formula approach to tariff reduction. Important in this shift was not only the expansion of GATT membership, but also the fact that the US Congress approved of the approach (having earlier rejected it as infringing on its sovereignty), and EEC concerns about the fact that its average industrial tariffs were lower than those applying in the US and Japan (see Jackson, 1969).

Across-the-board, formula-based negotiations in the GATT have relied on two basic approaches: the linear cutting formula; and a harmonization formula. The linear cutting formula consists in applying the same rate of tariff reduction to all product lines by all participants. It was applied during the Kennedy round, with developed countries agreeing to reduce their tariffs on industrial products by 50 per cent, except for 'sensitive' products. These were put on an exception list, some of which were liberalized on the basis of item-by-item negotiations. As many sensitive items were reduced by a small percentage or totally excluded from the cut, the average tariff reduction in the Kennedy round was only 35 per cent.

The linear approach maximizes the number of tariff lines brought to the bargaining table and leads to the exchange of a greater amount of concessions than negotiations based on a specific reciprocity formula. The formula tends to be particularly beneficial for countries with high import tariffs, since any equal-percentage tariff cut will leave the high-tariff country with higher tariffs in the end than other nations that started from a lower tariff level. Issues such as tariff escalation, high tariffs, and lack of inter- and intra-country uniformity of tariffs may not be satisfactorily addressed under the linear tariff-cutting formula. Negotiators frequently claim that reductions of low tariffs or the total elimination of low tariffs are equivalent to substantial cuts of higher tariffs. Low-tariff nations frequently argue that high-tariff nations should reciprocate with higher percentage cuts. Trading nations maintaining import tariffs characterized by a great disparity of tariff rates frequently favour linear tariff cuts, whereas countries with a uniform or flat tariff structure do not. The latter are usually interested in tariff harmonization, i.e. reducing the import tariffs of all nations to a comparable level. This involves the removal of so-called tariff peaks by trading partners.

Harmonization formulas result in non-linear cuts in tariffs. There are very many options in this respect. One possibility that was discussed in the Tokyo round was to simply cut each tariff by a percentage equal to its initial level. Thus, a 60 per cent tariff would be reduced by 60 per cent, while a 10 per cent tariff would be reduced by 10 per cent. The EEC suggested that this approach be repeated four times, with tariffs over 50 per cent initially not being reduced below 13 per cent. Another proposition made by the United States was to employ the formula $X = 1.5T_1 + 50$, where X is the percentage by which tariffs were to be cut. This formula was to apply to all tariffs below 6.67 per cent, all others being reduced by 60 per cent. This meant that a tariff of 6 per cent would be cut by $1.5 \times 6 + 50$, or 59 per cent, while a 2 per cent tariff would be cut by 53 per cent. This is a clear example of a symbolic harmonization formula, as high tariffs are only subject to a linear cut. From the formulas suggested by the EEC and the USA it is clear that the EEC sought far-reaching harmonization, while the USA did not. Yet another approach, suggested by Switzerland, was to use the formula $T_2 = rT_1/(r + T_1)$. This formula reduced high tariff rates much more than low ones, the ultimate result depending on the value of r that is chosen. In the event the value of r that was chosen by countries ranged between 14 and 16. Thus, a 14 per cent tariff would be reduced by 50 per cent, tariffs below (above) 14 per cent being reduced less (more) than 50 per cent.

A general problem affecting across-the-board formula approaches is that agreement must be obtained on which formula to use and the extent to which exceptions to the use of the rule will be permitted. The larger the scope for exceptions, the less useful it becomes to invest substantial negotiating resources in achieving agreement on the use of a general rule. The shift to a general formula approach used in the Kennedy and Tokyo rounds, while a significant change, did not lead to the demise of item-by-item talks. This was because the formula only applied to products which were not included in the list of exceptions. These exceptions turned out to be rather significant at the end of the day in both negotiations, as the inclusion of a product on this list by one country tended to lead to the reciprocal addition of products to the list by other countries. In the case of products included in the exception list of the Kennedy and Tokyo rounds, item-by-item negotiations took place. In the Uruguay round, negotiators did not use a formula approach, instead reverting to item-by-item (sector-by-sector) negotiations.

Whatever approach is used, item-by-item or general, there are two aspects of the reciprocity concept as practiced in GATT which should be emphasized. First, as noted earlier, reciprocity of market-opening commitments is traditionally measured in terms of incremental rather then absolute trade flows. One dollar of additional market access in one country is exchanged for one dollar of additional market opening in another country. Ernest Preeg, an American negotiator, commenting on the Kennedy round and preceding negotiations, observed that negotiators relying on projected trade impact criteria tended to strike a rough balance between the estimated increases in the value of imports and the forecast rise in the value of exports resulting from the tariff concessions (Preeg, 1970). What is considered *ex ante* advantageous largely depends on the persuasiveness of negotiators. All negotiators will contend that export opportunities gained are greater than import opening conceded, even though logically this cannot be true for all countries at the same time (Curzon and Curzon, 1976). In other words, the bargaining in the GATT forum reflects a balance of perceived advantages at the margin rather than in terms of full equality of market access. Obviously, the complete picture with regard to market-access conditions is never absent from negotiators' perspectives. However, it is the balance of incremental reductions that remains the centre of attention when evaluating reciprocity. Jagdish Bhagwati, using a mathematical analogy, has termed this criterion 'first-difference' reciprocity: what effectively is done is to equate changes in policy (their 'first derivatives'), not absolute levels. Efforts by the USA in the 1980s to move from first difference to full reciprocity criteria created important tensions in the GATT (Bhagwati, 1991; Low, 1993a). This is essentially a move back towards the view of reciprocity held by the USA in the nineteenth century (Bhagwati and Irwin, 1987).

Trade impacts, let alone welfare calculations, are generally not used as measures of reciprocity in the negotiations themselves. Reasons for this include a lack of analytical capacity to undertake the required analysis—especially pre-Kennedy round—and the difficulty of attaining agreement on the many parameters that must enter into the required calculations—e.g. the respective price and substitution elasticities, data on production, trade, and employment, etc. What matters in any event is not so much the precise measure that is used, but the fact that the focus is on incremental changes in market access, not absolute market-access conditions. Tariff concessions mean tariff bindings and not necessarily an increase in market access. A country may liberalize its tariff structure but as long as it does not bind it at a given level, the liberalization is essentially not considered to be a concession in the GATT context. For example, in the Uruguay round many developing countries requested recognition of autonomous liberalization that had been undertaken during the 1980s, but had a hard time, in spite of initial general assurances incorporated in ministerial declarations, of getting this accepted by negotiating partners. Similarly, often the applied tariff rate on a product is less than the bound MFN rate contained in a country's GATT schedule. Again, no credit is obtained from applying lower than bound rates. What matters is the level at which tariff rates are bound. As discussed in Chapter 1, tariff bindings are fundamental in the GATT context, because it is on the basis of claims that bindings have been violated that a Member may initiate dispute-settlement procedures.

Reciprocity Criteria for Non-Tariff Measures

Assessment of the liberalization of NTMs (non-tariff measures) is considerably more complex and more subjective than for tariff concessions. NTMs tend to involve much broader issues than does tariff protection. There are many kinds of NTMs. Some of them are imposed to achieve non-trade objectives and only incidentally restrict imports (e.g. sanitary controls, labelling requirements, standardization etc.) There is also significant difficulty in defining many NTMs. Which measures constitute a barrier to trade and which are legitimate non-protectionist instruments of government regulation? What should be included in an inventory of NTMs?

Reciprocity is relatively easily implemented in the case of tariff negotiations, but becomes much more difficult when the subject of negotiation is broadened to include NTMs, whose effects may be difficult to quantify. The problem is twofold: (1) the 'space' of potential trades is of a much lower dimension than in the case of commodity tariff negotiations; and (2) it is much more difficult to translate the value of issues or proposals into a common denominator (Hoekman, 1993). Because NTM issues are lumpier than tariffs, gains from trade become more difficult to realize, and cross-issue linkages may become more important in achieving agreement. The valuation issue is fundamental. In the context of tariff negotiations, it is usually relatively straightforward to agree on how to value requests and offers. The standard practice has been to focus on the product of the suggested change in the tariff and the existing volume of imports. While of little economic relevance, this procedure does constitute a simple metric and has led to substantial reductions in tariffs over time. Alternative measures that have been used are the variation in tariffs or the magnitude of the cut in the average level of tariffs. A metric for NTM negotiations is much more difficult to establish. As discussed in Chapter 8, in the agricultural setting attempts have been made to agree on methods that convert various types of government intervention into a 'producer subsidy equivalent' or an 'aggregate measure of support'. In the NTM negotiations held during the Tokyo round, the focus was not on principal suppliers and/or change in protection, but on specific measures or rules whose implementation was assumed to increase market access, or on easily quantified variables that were not necessarily related to trade *per se*. For example, in negotiating an agreement on government procurement (see Chapter 4), participants focused on the size of the contracts to be covered and the entities that were to be included (on the basis of past procurement activity). This allowed a balance to be achieved in terms of the percentage of total procurement to be covered by an agreement.

Many of the issues that have appeared on the agendas of recent MTNs are, however, not easily expressed in terms of a simple quantitative metric, so that it is difficult for negotiators to agree on whether they have achieved reciprocity. This is particularly the case when the focus is on agreeing on rules. Often it may not be feasible to make marginal changes in proposed rules without making the rule irrelevant. Instead, it may at times be easier to accept rule x for issue A in return for rule y for issue B, i.e. to engage in issue linkage. In such a context, it becomes very important to have a clear idea of the implications of alternative rules. This requires substantial analysis of the likely effects on both domestic constituents and the multilateral trading system. It is not surprising therefore that the approach taken is often one of adopting 'motherhood' principles such as transparency and perhaps non-discrimination, rather than seeking changes in the substance of regulations.

3.3. A TYPOLOGY OF KEY ASPECTS OF TRADE NEGOTIATIONS

It would seem useful to close this chapter with a summary typology of various aspects of MTNs, drawing upon the discussion in the foregoing sections.

GATT Negotiations are Multi-Issue Barter Exchanges

Barter implies that MTNs involve the exchange of concessions (liberalization commitments). In the process of negotiations participants formulate requests (what they want in terms of liberalization by trading partners) and offers (what they are ready to liberalize themselves). As in any type of market situation, every trader (negotiator) will attempt to get as much as possible in exchange for as little as necessary. Through mutual bargaining negotiators attempt to arrive at a balanced package. The meaning of 'balanced' is likely to differ from case to case, depending on what is being traded. The lack of a fungible medium of exchange requires trade negotiations to have an agenda that allows all the traders to trade something and in so doing improve upon the status quo. Setting the agenda is therefore very important. Actual negotiations are usually preceded by an intensive preparation process in participating countries during which possible issues are identified, preferences are established, issues are ranked, initial positions are formulated, and a proposal is made with respect to the contents of the negotiating agenda. The process that led to the establishment of the negotiating agenda for the Uruguay round took over five years, starting with the ministerial meeting held in 1982, during which the United States sought but failed to obtain agreement to launch a new MTN, and ending with the 1986 Ministerial meeting in Punta del Este, Uruguay, where agreement was finally reached on the agenda of what was to be known as the Uruguay round.

For any given agenda, there are virtually hundreds of economic, legal, and political issues that must be resolved. Each delegation, in evaluating possible final outcomes, must carefully consider and thrash out trade-offs it is ready to accept. The main advantage of dealing with a broad range of issues is that it greatly increases the scope for co-operative behaviour. When it is possible to determine several negotiating issues jointly, the negotiators have an opportunity to considerably enlarge the pie before dividing it among themselves. The larger the range of issues considered, the better the chances are that negotiators will act as co-operative problem-solvers.

The lack of a price mechanism in barter trade situations makes it difficult to reveal true preferences, or, conversely, greatly enhances the scope for employing various tactics intended to increase a country's potential pay-off. Negotiations are frequently in an impasse because negotiators are not willing to make sufficient concessions to reach an agreement. Impasses are also part of the negotiating drama. Tensions, threats of deadlock, and last-minute deals are part of the repertoire of a competent negotiator. When impasses occur, negotiators must attempt to turn to other issues or modify the formulation of issues in search for some alternative terms of possible agreement. Every good negotiating team must maintain a consistent, co-ordinated position in all areas of negotiations, must be able to rank its requests and offers across all issue areas, and must be as well informed as possible about the positions of its negotiating partners. This is difficult, of course. In practice MTNs do not result in Pareto-optimal outcomes because offers are often made on a contingent basis to allow for obtaining further concessions from trading partners. Withdrawal of such contingent offers at the end of the day may lead to the unravelling of a carefully constructed, balanced package, and a move away from Pareto-optimality (Baldwin and Clarke, 1987; Baldwin, 1986).

GATT MTNs are Multi-Stage Games

As discussed earlier, an MTN has a number of stages, starting with a contracting party that acts as a catalyst, initiating the pre-negotiations that lead to the establishment of the agenda, followed by the MTN itself, which is followed in turn by the post-negotiation, implementation stage. The negotiation period, in turn, is in practice usually divided into a number of distinct stages. There is generally a learning period, during which participants signal their preferences on the various issues that are on the agenda, determine the options that exist for forming coalitions of various kinds, and simply engage in a fact-finding exercise with respect to the various solution options that exist. This is then followed by a period in which substantive negotiations take place, with players demanding concessions and responding to the demands of others, thereby mapping out the set of feasible solutions. In this stage, many agreements in principle may be reached, but these are conditional upon the final outcome.

The final stage generally starts close to what is perceived to be the deadline for the conclusion of substantive talks. In practice, this has often been the date the negotiating authority of the US delegation expires.

GATT MTNs are Multi-Party Games

MTNs are games with many players. The complexity of multi-party negotiations greatly exceeds that of those involving only two players. Coalitions may form and each participant must explore what options are available in this connection, and what the implications are of others forming coalitions. Various types of coalitions can be distinguished, ranging from informal and *ad hoc*, session- or issue-specific to formal, multi-issue coalitions. The former tend to be much more prevalent than the latter, as it is generally difficult to agree to negotiate as a bloc. The multi-party nature of MTNs increases the responsibility of negotiators. They are not only engaged in transmitting their country's requests, offers, and negotiating positions, but are also continuously involved in gathering and transmitting information. One of the more important tasks of trade negotiators is to provide feedback on the preferences and interests of negotiating partners, and to feel out to what extent negotiating positions are hard or soft. Such information will help their government in the formulation of instructions for the negotiators, including the pursuit of possible coalition strategies.

MTNs Take Time and are Repeated

In MTNs negotiators bargain together over a substantial period of time, and know that they will meet each other repeatedly. The repeated nature of the interaction fosters co-operation by ensuring that if deals made at one point in time are not implemented (or are reneged upon), not only will recourse to dispute-settlement procedures be feasible, but deals can be renegotiated. History matters in repeated games: actions or positions taken will have an effect on the negotiating stances of trading partners in future interactions. Learning will occur, and participants are given an incentive to invest resources in establishing a reputation and/or coalitions. Reputation is important in terms of generating trust on the part of negotiating partners that agreements will be implemented, and may also help in exploiting the fact that MTNs have deadlines.

As noted earlier, last-minute balancing of concessions is a frequent practice in negotiations where initial bargaining takes place essentially on a bilateral basis. This encourages the squeezing out of concessions through so-called 'salami' tactics. The most important GATT rounds had a defined deadline. This means that the most difficult decisions tend to be made at the last minute. Last-minute decision-making is an element of most negotiations.

Once negotiations have started and have been given publicity, negotiators are under pressure to succeed. The fact that agreements reached on specific issues at intermediate stages of the negotiating process are conditional upon the overall outcome on all the issues further increases the pressure. The pressure resulting from this conditionality may be augmented by tactics of linking problems or issues. Skilful negotiators prepare for the end-game confrontations of an MTN by explicitly seeking to link issues in a way that makes threats possible and credible.

Governments are not Monolithic

Governments participating in MTNs are not monolithic. Participants in MTNs may spend less time negotiating with trading partners than they do internally. There are often large differences in interests within a country on the issues that appear on the agenda—differences among provinces or states, differences between various government departments, as well as differences between consumer, producer, and other associations of interest-groups. One major actor, the EU, is a composite player. It consisted of twelve countries during the Uruguay round, each of which simultaneously internalized the interests of relevant interest-groups on various topics, and agreed with its eleven partners on the common position to be taken in the MTN on these topics.

Both the pre-negotiation stage and the period in which the MTN is held will involve substantial interaction between governments and negotiators, and between governments and domestic industries, consumers, unions, and so forth. The extent to which domestic industries (i.e. producer associations or even particular major companies) influence both the pre-negotiations and the negotiation process that follows varies depending on the country and issue involved. The influence of trade-policy lobbies is particularly important and transparent in the USA, which has institutionalized such interactions through a complex system of general and sector-specific advisory bodies. Because governments are not monolithic, they may at times ask negotiators from other countries to help them in dealing with pressures at home. For example, the US delegation in the Uruguay round made appeals to its negotiating partners to help it to resist protectionist pressures in America. Diversity of internal preferences is therefore another element that leads to the formation of (implicit) coalitions as well as attempts to link issues.

The Set of Feasible Solutions may be Small and can Depend on Threat Strategies

The negotiating process is strongly dependent on whether an agreement on an issue is truly important for the major players. This will depend on whether the status quo on an issue (or the threat point associated with the breakdown of talks) is bad enough. When an agreement is necessary, negotiators may play games, but they know that they finally have to agree. The greater the resources invested (the larger the sunk costs) in an MTN, the lower the probability that they will result in failure. A corollary of this is that if the probability of failure is high, no negotiations will be initiated. A good example is the 1982 ministerial meeting mentioned earlier, where the US sought to launch an MTN including trade in services and intellectual property on the agenda, something that met with broad-based opposition at the time (Low, 1993*a*).

Although care will be taken to only initiate negotiations if there is an agenda that offers the possibility of gains for all concerned, it remains the case that if the status quo on an issue is not all that bad from the viewpoint of one or more major trading nations, agreement may not emerge. In such cases the *demandeurs* on the issue will have to offer enough to substantially improve upon the status quo, something that is not always possible. Alternatively they may try to pursue strategies to affect the value of the status quo. Often, what counts is the threat point—the likely outcome of a failure to reach agreement. This may be much worse than the status quo ante. Indeed, the status quo at any point in time will in part be the result of threat strategies. The USA has made extensive use of threats before and during MTNs. In the 1980s, for example, it began to pursue preferential trade agreements at least partly to pressure GATT members to initiate a comprehensive MTN, and made active use of unilateral trade-policy instruments (Section 301, Super 301, and Special 301) to retaliate (or threaten to do so) against countries pursuing unreasonable (unfair) trade practices in areas that were not subject to GATT discipline (e.g. services, and intellectual property) (see Chapter 6; and Bhagwati and Patrick, 1990).

Negotiators may Seek Symbolic, not Substantive Deals

Sometimes trade negotiations appear more similar to negotiations on the adoption UN resolutions than an attempt to agree to binding, specific commitments. Obviously there are many shades between the two extreme cases of negotiations on words and negotiations on substance. A prominent example of GATT negotiations that led to a symbolic deal was the adoption of Part IV of the GATT on Trade and Development during the Kennedy round, and the so-called Enabling Clause permitting tariff preferences in favour of developing countries in the Tokyo round (Chapter 10). Although these texts are more declarations of intent than firm commitments, they have had an impact on the trading system. The balance of rights and obligations of GATT members frequently extends well beyond legal commitments. Symbolic agreements may become a significant element of that balance. Symbolic deals also have another important function. When an agreement is required for political reasons, but substantive deals are not feasible, a symbolic agreement that incorporates a large zone of ambiguity may still have value for participants.

This is one explanation why certain negotiated agreements are very difficult to understand (e.g. the Agreement on Agriculture—Chapter 8), allow for re-imposition of protection (see Chapter 7), or appear to contain commitments that are 'made of rubber' (e.g. special and differential treatment provisions for developing countries—see Chapter 10).

Equity is more Important than Efficiency

In an investigation of the tariff proposals made during the Tokyo round, Chan (1985) concluded that the proposal finally chosen (the Swiss proposal) is best explained by solution procedures that emphasize fairness considerations. That is, he found that the Swiss proposal distributed the gains from liberalization across players in proportion to the weight (contribution) of each player. Solutions based on efficiency, that is, the maximization of the sum of gains across countries, independent of the distribution, did not work well. A similar result was found by Allen (1979) for the Kennedy round. These findings are quite intuitive as they reflect the reciprocity approach that underlies MTNs. Thus, outcomes can be expected to reward players proportionately.

3.4. FURTHER READING

Useful background reading for international negotiations is provided by Fred Ikle in *How Nations Negotiate* (New York: Harper and Row, 1964). Howard Raiffa, *The Art and Science of Negotiation* (Cambridge: Harvard University Press, 1983) is an excellent discussion of negotiations and bargaining in general. John McMillan, 'A Game-Theoretic View of International Trade Negotiations', in John Whalley (ed.), *Rules, Power and Credibility* (London, Ont.: University of Western Ontario, 1988) explores the applicability of game theory to MTNs. *Game Theory in International Economics* (New York: Harwood, 1986) by the same author applies game-theoretic methods and approaches to international exchange more generally. Jagdish Bhagwati and Hugh Patrick (eds.), *Aggressive Unilateralism: America's 301 Trade Policy and the World Trading System* (Ann Arbor: University of Michigan Press, 1990) contains a set of papers exploring the use of Section 301 by the United States.

Robert Baldwin, 'Toward More Efficient Procedures for Multilateral Trade Negotiations', *Aussenwirtschaft*, 41(1986), 379–94 offers an accessible review of GATT negotiating techniques and problems. The contributions by Baldwin and Winters in M. Finger and A. Olechowski (eds.), *The Uruguay Round: A Handbook for the Multilateral Trade Negotiations* (Washington DC: The World Bank, 1987) provide succinct treatments of GATT negotiating techniques and principles. Gerard Curzon, *Multilateral Commercial Diplomacy*

(London: Michael Joseph, 1965) is a classic reference dealing with the early years of the GATT and its politics and economics.

Robert Tollison and Thomas Willett, 'An Economic Theory of Mutually Advantageous Issue Linkages in International Negotiations', *International Organization*, 33 (1979), 425–49 and James Sebenius, 'Negotiation Arithmetic: Adding and Subtracting Issues and Parties', *International Organization*, 37 (1983), 281–316 discuss the strategy of issue linkage in international negotiations. Mancur Olson, *The Logic of Collective Action: Public Goods and the Theory of Groups* (Cambridge: Harvard University Press, 1965) and Thomas Schelling, *Micromotives and Macrobehaviour* (New York: W. W. Norton, 1978) discuss necessary conditions and incentives for the formation of coalitions or clubs.

PART II

The Multilateral Trade Agreements

The Multilateral Trade Agreements

4

Trade in Goods

Economic theory suggests that trade policy is rarely the most efficient way of achieving a government's objective. Governments pursue trade policies for a variety of reasons, including as a means of raising revenue, to protect specific industries (whether 'infant', 'senile' or other), to shift the terms of trade, to attain certain foreign policy or security goals, or simply to restrict the consumption of specific goods. Whatever the underlying objective, an active trade policy redistributes income between segments of the population by protecting specific industries and the factors of production employed there, usually does so in an inefficient manner, and for that reason tends to be supported by interest-groups that lobby for import restrictions.

The GATT essentially regulates trade policies. It does not address the basic question whether governments should use domestic or trade policies to achieve particular objectives. That is, the issue of efficiency is not addressed directly. The implicit premiss is that inefficiency (i.e. the use of trade policy) must be accepted, and that the best that can be achieved is to discipline the use of different types of trade policies. Thus, while countries are free to use trade policies, they are generally encouraged to use measures that are the least trade-restrictive. GATT rules are mostly consistent with what economic theory would recommend in many circumstances, but only in the sense of moving governments to use second-best rather than third-best instruments. The objective is in some sense to avoid the worst by accepting some bad in government intervention.

Three broad categories of trade-policy instruments can be distinguished: measures that affect quantities, restricting the volume or value of transactions; those that affect prices, involving the imposition of a monetary fee (tax) on foreign suppliers or have an equivalent effect; and those that may indirectly affect quantities and/or prices. Annex 4 provides a list of trade-policy instruments that are often used. Many of the specific policies mentioned are subject to GATT rules, while others are not. Virtually any policy or action by a government may have an effect on trade. As noted in Chapter 2, this is explicitly recognized in the GATT, in that dispute-settlement procedures allow for so-called non-violation complaints to be brought. Any policy— whether or not it is prohibited under GATT—can be contested if it acts to deny a benefit of the Agreement. This chapter summarizes the main GATT disciplines relating to specific instruments of trade control. It must be remembered, however, that the reach of GATT disciplines extends beyond the policy-specific rules that are discussed below. Annex 5 gives a list of the GATT's most important Articles.

4.1. TARIFFS AND PARA-TARIFFS

A tariff is a tax levied on products when passing a customs border. Governments may levy tariffs on imports and exports, but import tariffs are by far the most important in practice. Customs tariffs may be:

(1) *ad valorem* (a percentage of the value of imported products);
(2) specific (a given amount of money per physical unit, e.g., $1.5 per litre of wine);
(3) a combination of the two, e.g. 5 per cent *ad valorem* plus $1 per litre of wine).

The GATT does not favour one type of tariff over another. In practice, most tariffs are *ad valorem*. Each may have advantages in specific situations. *Ad valorem* rates are more transparent, and are indexed: If the value of a product increases (because of inflation for example), then the level of protection and tariff revenue will keep pace with price increases. Specific tariffs have the advantage of not requiring customs authorities to determine the value of imports when entering the country (although they must still classify the product), and are by definition not sensitive to changes in the value of goods. Inflation will erode the protective effect of a specific tariff.

The customs tariff is in principle the only instrument of protection allowed under the GATT. The preference for tariffs is consistent with economic theory, in that tariffs are superior to quantitative trade restrictions. Tariffs are preferable to quotas for many reasons, including the following:

• Tariffs maintain an automatic link between domestic and foreign prices, allowing adjustments in the level of imports or exports to reflect changes in comparative advantage. This link is cut with quotas.

• It is easy to ensure non-discrimination between foreign sources of supply using tariffs; under a quota this is much more difficult. Quota allocation is often the result of arbitrary decisions of officials.

• Tariffs are transparent. Once established, every trader knows the price of market access for specific products. This is not the case under a quota, where the conditions of market access may depend on timing (e.g. under a first-come, first-served allocation scheme), past performance (if quotas are allocated based on historical utilization rates), or even corruption (the need to bribe officials responsible for licensing). Tariffs are also more transparent in that the level of nominal protection under tariff is easily calculated, whereas its estimation is more complex under a quota.

• Tariffs generate customs revenue for the government, whereas under quotas the tariff equivalent may go to the exporters, intermediaries, or governments concerned, depending on how the quotas are allocated. In most cases, governments do not obtain the created rents—the extra revenue per unit sold that is due the price-increasing effect of restricting supply.

• Tariffs are also more efficient because they create more diffuse rents. They benefit the whole industry producing the protected good, reducing the returns to individual firms which lobby for protection. If quotas are an option, traders have an incentive to seek individual quota allocations that are as large as possible for themselves, inducing socially wasteful lobbying.

GATT Rules

There are two basic rules under the GATT with respect to tariffs. First, tariffs must be non-discriminatory (Article I). The main exceptions to the MFN rule are if countries are members of regional integration agreements (Chapter 9), provide tariff preferences in favour of developing countries (Chapter 10), or confront imports from a non-member country. Second, Members are encouraged to bind tariffs. The tariff concessions that are made by Members upon accession or in periodic MTNs are expressed in the form of bound tariff rates that are inscribed in each Member's tariff schedule (Article II GATT). By binding its tariff, a Member undertakes not to impose on a specific product tariffs which are higher then the bound tariff rate. A binding may pertain to: the currently applied rate; a so-called ceiling rate that is higher than the applied rate; or a negotiated rate which is lower than the currently applied rate. The last possibility often arises after an MTN has been completed, with the negotiated rate entering into force at a specified future date. A tariff binding establishes a bench-mark for the conditions of market access that a country commits itself to. Under GATT rules, any measure taken or supported by a government that has the effect of 'nullifying or impairing' the 'concession' implied by its tariff bindings gives cause for complaint by trading partners. There is no need to show an impact on trade. Thus, the binding not only restricts the possibility of raising tariffs, but also limits the possibility of using measures that have an equivalent effect (however, as discussed in Chapter 7, there are various ways around this constraint).

To a very significant extent the content of tariff schedules determines the relevance of GATT rules. GATT is a general agreement—general with respect to products and countries. With respect to tariff commitments, however, the product coverage for each Member is determined by a 'positive list' approach: each Member includes in its schedule the products (tariff lines) on which it is willing to make commitments and the level of the associated bound tariff rate. These schedules form an integral part of the GATT. The comprehensiveness of tariff bindings for Members has traditionally varied considerably. For most

Trade in Goods

industrialized market economies, the share of bound tariffs in the total number of tariff lines has always been very high for manufactured goods and substantial for agricultural products. Moreover, bindings have tended to be at or near applied rates. The coverage of bindings for most developing countries has traditionally been very low or non-existent, and usually pertained to ceiling bindings.

Many GATT-1947 contracting parties joined GATT after becoming independent nations in the 1950s and 1960s. Such former colonies were allowed to accede to GATT without tariff negotiations. Developing countries were also granted 'special and differential' treatment, allowing them not to offer concessions in MTNs. During the Uruguay round an attempt was made to restrain such free-riding by requiring all WTO Members to submit tariff schedules. In contrast to GATT-1947, WTO membership requires a schedule of commitments. While there are no rules concerning the product coverage of the tariff schedules of developing countries, their participation as measured by the scope of tariff bindings increased substantially during the Uruguay round. This largely reflected unilateral liberalization efforts undertaken in the 1980s, and a realization that greater participation in the multilateral trading system was in their interest (see Chapter 10).

Pre- and post-Uruguay-round tariff bindings are presented in Table 4.1. All

TABLE 4.1 *Tariff bindings for industrial products (excluding petroleum) before and after the Uruguay round (number of lines, US $bn. and %)*

Country group or region	Number of lines	Import value	Percentage of tariff lines bound		Percentage of imports under bound rates	
			Pre-	Post-	Pre-	Post-
By major country group						
Developed economies	86,968	737.2	78	99	94	99
Developing economies	157,805	306.2	22	72	14	59
Transition economies	18,962	34.7	73	98	74	96
By selected region						
North America	14,138	325.7	99	100	99	100
Latin America	64,136	40.4	38	100	57	100
Western Europe	57,851	239.9	79	82	98	98
Central Europe	23,565	38.1	63	98	68	97
Asia	82,545	415.4	17	67	36	70

Note: The data cover 26 developing economies accounting for four-fifths of total merchandise imports of all developing country participants in the Uruguay round.

Source: GATT (1994c).

WTO Members have bound all agricultural tariff lines—a major change in comparison with GATT-1947, under which agriculture had largely become exempt from disciplines (Chapter 8). The share of industrial tariff lines bound by developing countries increased from 22 to 72 per cent. Most of these bindings relate to ceilings (i.e. maximum rates), not applied tariffs. Ceiling rates are much less binding than if applied rates were inscribed, but do have some value. Binding places an upper limit on the applied tariff level and is a necessary first step for increased participation in the WTO. It is unclear why developing countries have not bound tariffs at applied rates, especially those that are in the process of moving towards market-determined exchange rates and liberalization of current-account transactions, or have already done so. In some cases it may simply reflect the mercantilism underlying the GATT (i.e. a perception that bindings are negotiating chips), in others it may be that the constituencies in favour of low import barriers are unaware of the potential value of binding rates, complemented by a desire on the part of finance ministries not to give away a revenue-raising tool. More generally, countries with overvalued exchange rates and resulting foreign exchange shortages or rationing often have no wish to be subjected to GATT surveillance in instances where measures are required to safeguard the balance of payments (see Chapter 7).

Other Fees and Charges on Imports

To avoid circumvention of tariff commitments, Members are constrained regarding the use of fees and specific taxes upon imports which are not necessarily called tariffs, but have an equivalent effect. Examples include taxes on foreign-exchange transactions, internal taxes on imports, service fees affecting importers, and special import surcharges. Such 'para-tariffs', as they are sometimes called, are often important in developing countries. Data for a sample of forty-one developing countries in the early 1980s indicated that at least one-third of revenue from import taxation was generated by para-tariffs. Such measures are frequently subject to arbitrary implementation and are non-transparent (Kostecki and Tymowski, 1985). They are often driven by specific interest-groups, who successfully lobbied for earmarked taxes to finance their activities. In contrast to GATT-1947, the GATT-1994 requires that the nature and level of 'other duties or charges' be listed by tariff line in each WTO Member's schedule. All such charges are bound.

There is a loophole as regards the binding of other fees and charges. GATT allows for the imposition of fees or other charges commensurate with the cost of services rendered (Article II: 2c). Article VIII (on fees and formalities related to trade) requires that all service fees must 'be limited in amount to the approximate cost of services rendered and shall not represent an indirect protection to domestic products or a taxation of imports or exports for fiscal purposes' (Article VIII: 1). Examples of such fees include consular transactions, licensing, statistical services, documentation, certification, inspection, quarantine, sanitation, and fumigation. Article VIII applies irrespective of whether a country has bound its tariffs. The term 'services rendered' is somewhat inappropriate, as most customs-related activities are not desired by traders! The possibility of charging cost-based service fees is a potential loophole for countries seeking to raise effective tariffs, in so far as they are able to claim that the fees simply amount to 'cost recovery.' It also offers some scope to interest-groups seeking to circumvent tariff bindings. However, such abuse can be addressed through the dispute-settlement process.

In a 1988 dispute-settlement case brought to GATT concerning the imposition of a uniform *ad valorem* customs user fee by the United States, it was concluded that such fees must be service-specific (GATT, 1994*b*: 251). Thus, imposing an average fee equal to the total cost of customs administration divided by the total value of imports was not acceptable. Although the US altered its customs user fee to conform with these findings, other countries continued to maintain *ad valorem* fees that are presumably inconsistent with the GATT. In part this is because some of the service fees in existence at the time of a country's accession to the GATT were 'grandfathered' and thus immune from scrutiny. Developing countries also appear to have been granted greater leeway than industrialized countries, reflecting the fact that their tariffs were often not bound in any event. Some developing countries have customs user fees of 5 per cent *ad valorem* or higher. It is worth noting that under the WTO, all grandfathered policies that are inconsistent with the Multilateral Agreements must be abolished.

Effective Protection and Tariff Escalation

Goods that are traded internationally are rarely wholly produced in one country. In many cases, inputs or parts of the product are imported. The existence of trade in intermediate products makes a great deal of difference for the economic analysis of tariffs and the measurement of their protective effect. A distinction can be drawn between the nominal rate of protection (NRP) and the effective rate of protection (ERP). The NRP for a product can be measured as the proportional increase in the producer price of a good relative to free trade (i.e. trade undistorted by protection). The ERP differs from the NRP by taking into account the trade barriers that are imposed on the raw materials and intermediate inputs that are used to produce a good. The higher are the tariffs and NTBs imposed on imported inputs, the less 'effective' will be the tariff that applies to goods that are partially produced with these imported inputs. The ERP is a better measure of the extent to which activities are protected than the NRP because it incorporates information on the structure of production (Box 3.1).

Box 4.1. Nominal and effective rate of protection

The nominal rate of protection (NRP) can be defined as

$$NRP = (P-P^*)/P^*,$$

where P^* is the free-trade price and P is the domestic tariff inclusive price of a good ($P=P^*+t$). As the free-trade price of a good cannot be observed in practice, most empirical studies take the world price as a measure of P^*. The effective rate of protection (ERP) can be defined as the proportional increase in value added per unit of a good produced in a country relative to value added under free trade (no protection). The magnitude of the ERP depends not only on the nominal tariff on the final product concerned, but also on the tariffs applied to the inputs used, and the importance of those inputs in value of the final product.

A simple formula for calculating the ERP is:

$$ERP = (V-V^*)/V^*,$$

where V is the domestic value added per unit of the final good including the tariffs on that good and on its inputs, and V^* is valued added under free trade. Value added per unit in turn is defined as the gross value of output minus the cost of inputs used in production, $V = t_f P_f - t_i P_i X$, where t_f and t_i are the tariffs on the final good and inputs, respectively, P_f and P_i are the prices, and X is the amount of input used to produce a unit of the final good. Value added at free-trade prices is the same, except that tariffs in this case do not exist (the value of t is one). For example, suppose one ton of steel is worth $1000 on the world market. To produce it a factory has to buy one ton of iron ore at a world price of $600. Assume for simplicity that nothing more is needed for steel production. Under these circumstances the value added per ton of steel in our factory will be $400. If a 20 per cent nominal tariff rate is imposed on steel imports and no tariff on iron ore, the ERP in those circumstances will be:

$$(1200-600)/400 = 1.5 \text{ or } 50 \text{ per cent.}$$

The ERP in this example is more than double the 20 per cent NRP on steel. If no tariff is imposed on steel but a nominal tariff of 33 per cent is imposed on imports of iron ore, the ERP would be

$$[1000-(600+200)]/400 = 0.5 \text{ or } -50 \text{ per cent.}$$

This example illustrates that an NRP of zero does not necessarily imply that trade is undistorted. As another example, assume that cocoa beans account for 95 per cent of the production cost of cocoa butter. The imposition of a 5 per cent nominal tariff rate on cocoa butter would then imply an effective rate of protection for the cocoa butter industry of 100 per cent.

Although producers care more about the ERP than the NRP, the GATT focuses only on nominal rates of protection (tariffs). There are no obligations with respect to effective rates. This does not mean that the concept of the ERP is not understood by negotiators. On the contrary. The fact that the ERP for most products tends to be higher than the NRP (because governments prefer to protect activities that generate higher added value) explains why tariff negotiations continue to be at the centre-stage of MTNs, even though the absolute level of tariffs has fallen significantly. An average tariff on highly processed goods of only 10 per cent can hide an ERP that is much higher. Interest-groups care about the ERP, not the NRP. While lobbying efforts centre on influencing nominal rates of protection, much of the political manœuvering that occurs in the domestic trade policy arena is driven by the impact of such protection on the ERP. At the multilateral level, in MTNs the focus of attention is often on the dispersion of tariffs. Attempts to reduce dispersion—the difference between the highest and lowest rates—will have the effect of reducing differences in the ERP for specific goods.

Tariff escalation is closely related to the concept of effective protection. One speaks of tariff escalation if duty rates on raw materials and intermediates are lower than rates on processed commodities that embody the relevant inputs. Tariff escalation has traditionally been a problem for developing countries seeking to process commodities before they are exported. The more escalated is the tariff structure maintained in export markets, the greater the difficulty for such countries to generate added value at home, as the low tariffs on raw materials (usually duty-free) provide an incentive not to process commodities before they are exported. A group of products where tariff escalation has often been a source of particular concern are natural-resource-based products, defined in GATT to include non-ferrous metals and minerals, forestry products, and fish and fishery products. As a result of the importance of these products for developing countries a specific negotiating group was established in the Uruguay round to lower tariff barriers and reduce tariff escalation. Tariff escalation declined as a result of the Uruguay round, although much depends on how escalation is defined and on the stage of processing of products. In absolute terms the difference between tariff levels at various stages of processing fell (Table 4.2). At higher levels, escalation increased in proportional terms. An example are average tariffs on natural-resource-based products, where the degree of escalation increased between semi-manufactured and finished products.

The structure of tariffs maintained by WTO Members varies considerably. High tariffs are particularly frequent in developing countries. In the EU, close to one-quarter of post-Uruguay round imports of manufactured goods are duty free, and some 40 per cent are subjected to tariffs below 5 per cent. Tariffs above 25 per cent are imposed on a negligible share of imports. In the United States, duty-free imports account for some 80 per cent of the total; a tariff rate

TABLE 4.2 *Tariff escalation for developing countries' exports before and after the Uruguay round* (US $m. and %)

	Imports	Share of each stage	Tariff	
			Pre-UR (mid 1980s)	Post-UR commitment
All industrial products (excluding petroleum)				
Raw materials	36,692	22	2.1	0.8
Semi-manufactures	36,464	21	5.3	2.8
Finished products	96,535	57	9.1	6.2
Total	169,690	100	6.8	4.3
All tropical industrial products				
Raw materials	5,069	35	0.1	0.0
Semi-manufactures	4,340	30	6.3	3.5
Finished products	4,945	34	6.6	2.6
Total	14,354	100	4.2	1.9
Natural-resource-based products				
Raw materials	14,558	44	3.1	2.0
Semi-manufactures	13,332	40	3.5	2.0
Finished products	5,535	17	7.9	5.9
Total	33,426	100	4.0	2.7

Source: GATT (1994*c*).

of more than 10 per cent is imposed on less than 3 per cent of imports (Table 4.3). High tariffs often exist for items that are no longer produced in a country. They may have been imposed in the past to protect a local industry which disappeared because of technological developments or changes in tastes. Although industries rise and fall, the political economy of the tariff-setting process is such that if domestic industries die, there is no automatic mechanism to abolish the rates. A look at any country's tariff structure usually reveals examples of this. Thus, although the average tariff rate in the US in the late 1980s was below 5 per cent, certain watch parts faced a tariff of 150 per cent (Bovard, 1991: 7).

4.2. QUANTITATIVE RESTRICTIONS AND IMPORT LICENSING

GATT rules on quantitative restrictions (QRs) were written when these types of measures were widespread and constituted a major barrier to trade. Over time, the relative importance of QRs as trade restrictions in OECD countries

TABLE 4.3 *The tariff structure of 44 WTO members, pre- and post-Uruguay round* (US $bn. and %)

Region	MFN import value, excl. oil	Percentage of imports by MFN duty range (*ad valorem* tariffs only)											
		Dute-free[a]		0.1–5%		5.1–10%		10.1–15%		15.1–35%		over 35%	
		Pre	Post	Pre	Post	Pre	Post	Pre	Post	Pre	Post	Pre	Post
North America	325.7	11	39	55	40	22	13	4	2	7	6	0	0
Latin America	40.3	4	2	1	0	6	1	3	3	22	87	65	7
Western Europe	239.7	24	37	28	34	33	18	12	8	3	2	1	1
East Europe	34.7	14	15	27	37	27	35	22	7	10	4	1	0
Africa	18.5	33	19	7	3	7	15	5	16	22	32	26	15
Asia	459.8	40	54	17	9	11	11	5	5	21	15	7	6

[a] Figures refer to tariff lines which were duty-free prior to the Uruguay round, whether bound or not.

Source: GATT (1994c).

has declined substantially. Despite the fact that GATT rules basically prohibit the use of QRs, they have continued to be used by governments to protect domestic import-competing industries. QRs have been particularly prevalent in trade in agricultural products, textiles and clothing, and steel. The economic case against the use of quotas was summarized earlier. Although tariffs and quotas may be equivalent in terms of their impact on trade, a quota cuts the link between domestic and foreign prices, is generally more discriminatory, does not necessarily reflect the changing pattern of comparative advantage, is less transparent, and is more subject to administrative abuse (corruption). For all these reasons interest-groups tend to prefer QRs over tariffs. The primary motivation, however, is generally that QRs are less visible to consumers and that the revenue that otherwise would flow to the government is to a large extent captured by those who manage to obtain the quota rights or licenses.

GATT Disciplines

Articles XI–XIV of the GATT address QRs. Article XI prohibits them in principle, except for agricultural commodities if concurrent measures are taken to restrict domestic production (Chapter 8). The other Articles provide an exception, and allow QRs to be used for balance-of-payments (BOP) reasons (Article XII). If this is done, Article XIII requires that such quotas in principle apply on a non-discriminatory basis, while Article XIV provides an option that Members request that this requirement be waived by the Council. The basic obligation imposed on Members in Article XI: 1 is to refrain from introducing or maintaining QRs. As noted in earlier chapters, QRs are banned not only because of economic considerations, but also to prevent governments from circumventing tariff bindings. Article XIII requires non-discrimination if QRs are used. The economic rationale for this is that a global quota is more efficient than selective QRs. Under a global quota traders (importers) are left free to determine where to source from. The direction of trade (sourcing of imports) will then be responsive to changes in prices, quality, and transportation costs. However, the inclusion of Article XIII is not driven by efficiency considerations. Instead, it simply reaffirms the MFN principle for QRs. The more country-specific the allocation of the quota rights, the greater the danger of discrimination. Country-specific allocation may be used in practice, however, usually based on historical market shares. The GATT rationale is that this reduces all exporters' market-access rights pro-portionally.

Despite the general prohibition on QRs, GATT contracting parties con-tinued to use them. Formal QRs were used especially in the agricultural context (in industrialized countries) and for BOP purposes (in developing countries—see Chapters 7 and 10). A very popular form of QR—used increasingly in the 1970s and 1980s—was the voluntary export restraint

(VER), which was often negotiated under the threat of anti-dumping actions (see Chapter 7). This reflects one of the recurring problems of enforcing the principles of the GATT: there are many formal and informal loopholes that allow for 'forum-hopping' (Finger *et al.*, 1982).

Import Licensing

The GATT recognizes that QRs may be enforced by means of licenses. A separate Agreement on Import Licensing Procedures, which applies to all WTO Members, aims to strengthen general GATT obligations in this domain. The Agreement resembles closely the code on licensing that was negotiated in the Tokyo round. It establishes requirements to enhance transparency of licensing systems, including publication requirements, the right of appeal against decisions, and the length of license validity (see Hoekman, 1995*b*).

4.3. CUSTOMS PROCEDURES

Customs valuation involves classifying and valuing imports for the purpose of levying tariffs and collecting statistics. Customs procedures may become NTBs if officials assign goods to an incorrect classification to which a higher tariff applies or assign goods a value greater than appropriate. An agreement to reduce and bind tariffs would be practically meaningless without a set of rules concerning the valuation and classification of imported goods. Arbitrary customs procedures could then be used to ensure that a government (or its officials) collect as much revenue as desired, independent of the formally negotiated tariff schedule. Import-competing industries might also bribe officials to harass importers. In many countries, customs authorities do not accept importer's invoices as the basis for tariff assessment. To reduce the likelihood that a country's published tariff schedule is not representative of the real nominal tariffs that apply, GATT establishes certain rules and principles regarding customs valuation.

Classification of goods for customs purposes is less troublesome than valuation, as most countries use internationally developed systems. The main coding systems used for classification purposes during the first forty years of the GATT's existence were the Brussels Tariff Nomenclature and the Customs Co-operation Council Nomenclature. More recently, countries switched to the Harmonized Commodity Description and Coding System (HS), which was also developed by the Customs Co-operation Council in Brussels.[1]

---

[1] The Customs Co-operation Council was transformed into the World Customs Organization (WCO) in 1994.

The HS allows for a greater range of products than its predecessors and permits easier classification of new products. As of the early 1990s, most major trading nations were using HS-based systems. While its disaggregation—over 10,000 items are distinguished—facilitates correct classification, ultimately this is still at the discretion of customs.

The provisions on customs valuation contained in the GATT-1947 (Article VII) were not very precise—requiring basically that the valuation basis be the 'actual' value. Before the launch of the Tokyo round (1973), a number of contracting parties, led by the EEC, felt that certain national valuation practices were restricting international trade. A major bone of contention were US methods, in particular the so-called American Selling Price method, which established the value of some imported goods on the basis of the selling price of similar domestically produced goods. Although this violated GATT rules as it was unlikely to reflect the actual value, the USA could employ this method because it had grandfathered the practice when acceding to GATT.[2] In the Tokyo round, a Customs Valuation Code was negotiated which supplemented GATT's valuation provisions. The United States signed the code and abolished the American Selling Price. The Uruguay round extended code rules to all WTO members, and added disciplines on pre-shipment inspection—the practice of requiring the inspection of goods in the country of production before they are shipped—and on rules of origin. The main impact of the Agreement will be on developing countries, as valuation is generally not a policy issue in high-income nations.

The Agreement on Customs Valuation (formally the Agreement on Implementation of Article VII of GATT) aims to establish uniform, transparent, and fair standards for the valuation of imported goods for customs purposes. The main objective of the agreement is to establish a system which outlaws the use of arbitrary or fictitious customs values and which conforms to commercial realities. In principle, valuation should be based on the transaction or invoice value of the goods—the price actually paid or payable for the goods (subject to adjustments concerning freight and several other charges). This method should be applied when:

(1) there are no special restrictions as to the disposal or use of goods;
(2) the buyer and seller are not related;
(3) no proceeds of the subsequent sales accrue to the exporter;
(4) the sale or price is not subject to special conditions that cannot be quantified.

The agreement does not prescribe a uniform system regarding shipping, insurance, and handling charges. A country may opt for a cost, insurance,

---

[2] Grandfathering was possible under GATT-1947 and involved a contracting party exempting a specific policy from the reach of GATT disciplines when acceding to the agreements. This option was eliminated under the GATT-1994.

and freight (c.i.f.), a cost and freight, or a free-on-board (f.o.b.) valuation basis.

If customs authorities have reason to believe that the transaction value is inaccurate, they are required to proceed sequentially through five alternative options:

(1) the value of identical goods;
(2) the value of similar goods;
(3) the so-called deductive method;
(4) the computed value method;
(5) an 'if all else fails' method.[3]

It is only when the customs value cannot be determined under a specific option that the next option in the sequence can be used. However, an importer may request that the computed method be used in preference to the deductive method. In most instances refusal to accept the invoice price will be connected to there being a relationship between buyer and seller. The mere fact of such a relationship is not sufficient grounds for the authorities to reject the invoice price; what matters is that the relationship influences the price. If the value is questioned by customs, the burden of proof is on the importer.

In recognition of fears voiced during the Tokyo round regarding fraudulent invoicing, especially between related parties, a protocol to the code gave developing-country signatories somewhat greater regulatory flexibility in their customs procedures. Technical assistance in implementing code procedures was also made available. Nevertheless, developing-country participation in the code remained limited. Fears of reduced tariff revenue, a wish to maintain discretion in valuing imports, or the administrative burden of implementing code provisions remained concerns. In the Uruguay round, a number of developing countries put forward the view that the need to accept declared values was the main factor prohibiting greater participation in the code. Consequently, they proposed that it be amended to allow more scope for rejecting transaction values.

In the GATT-1994 developing countries that were not party to the code are given the right to delay implementing its provisions until 2000 (an Annex allows developing countries to request extension). Application of the computed-value method may be delayed for an additional three years, and reservations may be entered in respect of any of the provisions of the Agreement if other Members consent. Moreover, developing countries which valued goods on the basis of officially established minimum values can request a reservation

---

[3] The *deductive* value method consists of the unit price at which a significant quantity of imported goods are sold to unrelated persons, subject to deductions for commissions, profit margins, transport, and insurance costs. The computed method consists of summing the cost or value of materials and fabrication or other processing employed in producing the imported goods, and adding an amount for profit and general expenses equal to that applied in sales of similar goods by other producers.

to retain such values on a limited and transitional basis, subject to the terms and conditions required by the other Members. Requests for derogations require approval, and are likely to be conditional. Once fully implemented, the Agreement should be an important tool for strengthening the hand of traders against arbitrary valuation practices, and should reduce the scope for rent-seeking by customs officials and import-competing lobbies.

Pre-shipment Inspection

As the name suggests, pre-shipment inspection (PSI) consists of inspection of goods by specialized firms before they are shipped to the country of importation. Governments of importing countries usually decide to engage the services of PSI firms in order to reduce the scope for exporters and/or importers to engage in either over-invoicing or under-invoicing of imports. Over-invoicing may occur in contexts where there are foreign-exchange controls, this being a classic way to transfer capital outside the country. Under-invoicing is usually driven by attempts at tax evasion: by under-reporting the value of an imported item, traders may seek to reduce their tax obligation (by partially evading applicable tariffs). Government-contracted or mandated PSI should be distinguished from PSI services that are required as part of a contract between buyers and sellers of a product. Most firms that are internationally active in providing inspection services provide pre-shipment certification and inspection of goods because this is required by buyers. Such services focus on the specifications and quality of the goods concerned, not their value. Government-mandated PSI is predominantly concerned with the determination of the quantity and value of goods imported into their territories. PSI became an issue for GATT in the 1980s because exporters objected to some of the methods used by inspection firms (Low, 1995). Governments use PSI in large part because national customs administrations are not able to undertake the required activities. This may reflect a lack of institutional capacity, or problems related to rent-seeking.

Under the WTO Agreement on PSI, countries that use PSI agencies must ensure that such activities are carried out in an objective, transparent, and non-discriminatory manner. Quantity and quality inspections must be performed in accordance with the standards defined by the seller and the buyer in the purchase agreement. If these are not specified, relevant international standards of inspection are to apply. Verification of contract prices must be based on a comparison with the price of identical or similar goods offered for export from the same country of exportation at about the same time. In doing this, PSI entities are to allow for the terms of the sales contract and generally applicable adjusting factors pertaining to the transaction, such as the selling price of locally produced goods, or the export price of other producers; the cost of production or arbitrary prices may not be used for price-verification purposes.

Rules of Origin

A rule of origin is a criterion that is used to determine the nationality of a product or a producer. Rules of origin are necessary when there is a desire to discriminate between sources of supply. The only multilateral convention dealing with rules of origin is the 1974 International Convention on the Simplification and Harmonization of Customs Procedures (known as the Kyoto Convention), negotiated under auspices of—and administered by—the World Customs Organization in Brussels. The Convention provides a list of ten types of products that should be considered to originate in a country because they are wholly produced or obtained there, that is, contain no imported materials. These are largely natural-resource-based products extracted or obtained from the territory of the country concerned. Where two or more countries are involved in the production of a product, the Convention states that the origin of the product is the one in which the last 'substantial transformation' took place, i.e. the country in which significant manufacturing or processing occurred most recently. Significant or substantial in this respect is defined as sufficient to give the product its essential character.

The Kyoto Convention mentions various criteria that can be used to determine if substantial transformation occurred. These include:

(1) a change in tariff heading (CTH);
(2) a list of specific processing operations which do (or do not) imply substantial transformation;
(3) the value of materials embodied in the transformed product;
(4) the value added in the last country or where the good was transformed.

A CTH criterion is equivalent in effect to a value-added criterion, as CTH will require processing—adding value to a product. The difference is that under a CTH the value added may be high or low for a given product. Conversely, a value-added criterion may or may not lead to the same result as a CTH test. A problem with rules of origin is therefore that there can be a wide variance in their economic effects. This may encourage rent-seeking activities, as import-competing lobbies have an incentive to either try to make the rules as restrictive as possible, or to influence the way they are applied. Restrictive rules are a potential problem particularly in the context of preferential trade agreements (Chapter 9). In the application of trade policy more generally, the problem is often vaguely defined criteria. The more discretion officials have in this area, the greater the incentive to lobby. Box 4.2 gives an example.

In contrast to GATT-1947, the WTO includes an agreement on rules of origin. An objective of the GATT-1994 agreement is to foster the harmonization of the rules of origin used by Members. The primary criterion for determining origin is CTH. The Agreement requires a work programme to be undertaken by a Technical Committee, in conjunction with the WCO, with the goal of developing a classification system regarding the changes in tariff

Box 4.2. Origin rules and anti-dumping

One area where the application of rules of origin has become controversial is in the enforcement of anti-dumping (AD) mechanisms. A European case provides a good illustration of how vague rules of origin can be used to achieve the objectives of a specific lobby. In the mid-1980s, the EU imposed a 20 per cent AD duty on twelve Japanese exporters of photocopiers. In 1988, three years after the AD duty was imposed, a so-called anti-circumvention case was brought by the EU industry. It was claimed that the Japanese exporters had circumvented the AD duty by establishing assembly operations inside the EU that imported most of the parts of photocopiers from Japan, adding very little local value. What is relevant here is not the mechanics of AD (see Chapter 7) but the role of origin rules. The aim of AD is to protect a domestic industry that is injured by dumping. But, in a world where companies establish alliances with—and equity stakes in—rival enterprises, establishing which firms constitute the domestic industry is not always easy. In the photocopier AD investigation, Canon (Japan) subsidiaries located in the EU were regarded as foreign firms, while a Xerox (US) affiliate was treated as a European firm. Similarly, in the follow-up anti-circumvention case, the Canon subsidiaries were investigated to determine how much local (EU) value was added in the production process. What is interesting about this case is not only that the composition of the domestic industry was determined rather arbitrarily, but that a number of the firms who petitioned Brussels for protection had value-added performances that were lower than those of the Japanese firms. The reason was simple: these EU firms were basically in the business of importing and distributing photocopiers; they did not produce them. Some even had formal connections with Japanese companies. The AD case was therefore not about dumping or protecting a national industry, but simply part of a strategy used by firms competing for market share. The lack of clearly defined rules of origin introduced one of the elements of discretion that made the strategy attractive to petitioning firms. The Agreement on Rules of Origin will provide a basis for addressing such cases.

Source: Messerlin and Noguchi (1991).

sub-headings based on the Harmonized System that constitute a substantial transformation. In cases where the HS nomenclature does not allow for the expression of substantial transformation, the Technical Committee is to provide guidance regarding the use of supplementary tests such as value-added criteria. After a transitional period—once the harmonization work programme is completed—rules of origin are to be applied equally for all non-preferential commercial policy instruments—tariffs, QRs, AD, and so forth. The Agreement also specifies that rules of origin applied to exports or imports should not be more stringent than the rules applied to determine whether or not a good is domestically produced (as is necessary under AD, countervailing duty (CVD), safeguard, and government procurement procedures). The agreement does not apply to preferential commercial policies such as free-trade agreements and tariff preferences for developing countries.

The economic impact of a rule of origin depends on the specific criterion that is used and on the degree of uniformity with which the rule is applied. Rules of origin have been problematical mostly in the context of preferential trade agreements: exactly the arena where WTO rules do not apply. This was no oversight, and reflects the fact that many countries did not want to see constraints imposed on their policy freedom with regard to regional integration or the mechanics of trade preferences for developing countries (see Chapter 9).

4.4. SUBSIDIES

Subsidies, and appropriate measures to counter their impact on trade, have been an important issue in the GATT system. Subsidization may pertain to import-competing industries or export industries that compete in international markets. To the extent that such subsidization is trade-distorting (i.e. expands or reduces trade above or below the free-trade level) it may threaten to offset market opening commitments negotiated in an MTN. However, in certain circumstances subsidies may be a desirable form of government intervention, whether in the domestic economy or in international trade. Tax-subsidy schemes may in theory be required to bring marginal private costs or benefits into alignment with marginal social costs or benefits. The need for this arises when externalities cause social and private costs or benefits to diverge. Usually this implies that private decision-makers are not given an incentive to take into account the costs or benefits of the actions on others in the economy (for an overview of the theory, see Bhagwati, 1971). Tax-subsidy schemes may be an appropriate means of offsetting externalities or distortions associated with overvalued exchange rates or labour-market rigidities, and may also be used to bring about a redistribution of income. A necessary condition for a more efficient allocation of resources to result from intervention is that the problem has been diagnosed correctly and the policy used targeted appropriately. In practice, governments are prone to fail as often as markets—especially if account is taken of the incentives of interest-groups to lobby for a subsidy or a tax exemption. An advantage that subsidies have from an efficiency or welfare viewpoint is that they are more visible than trade policies—to taxpayers, to the Ministry of Finance, and to foreign traders. They can thus be expected to be subject to greater surveillance.

Governments invariably pursue industrial policies that affect the allocation of productive resources in an economy and/or the distribution of income. These actions may have an impact on the pattern of international trade and investment, and may therefore give rise to frictions and disputes between countries. Industrial policy is difficult to define precisely. For present purposes it can be considered to encompass all actions undertaken by governments that have an effect on the structure of production in an economy. This effect may be intended or not, and can be achieved through a variety of policy instruments. Examples include subsidies to production (output) or inputs (capital or labour), price controls, import restrictions, tax incentives, regulatory regimes, and government procurement policies. All industrial policies can be considered as forms of public assistance or taxation of domestic industries. Theoretically, all possible policies can be expressed in terms of a 'direct subsidy equivalent', which may be greater or less than zero, negative subsidy equivalents implying a burden (tax) instead of a benefit. More generally, the appropriate measure is the effective benefit of government assistance to a firm or to the economy as a whole. It may well be that other policies maintained by the government outweigh any direct support given to a firm or sector. Such general equilibrium measures of effective support are rarely considered by policy-makers. The approach taken in the GATT-1994 context is to focus on subsidies narrowly defined: loosely speaking those policies that directly affect the government budget (the exception to this rule is in agriculture, where use is made of an Aggregate Measure of Support; see Chapter 8). This does not make much economic sense—governments tax and subsidize in so many ways that it is impossible to regulate. In principle it would therefore have been much simpler to maintain a rule of subsidy freedom (Snape, 1987). However, this was not done.

The types of subsidies that may be used by WTO Members to support economic activities include direct payments or grants, tax concessions, soft loans, and government guarantees and equity participation. They may be industry-specific or generally available. Examples of the latter include regional and activity-specific subsidies (such as the promotion of research and development); subsidies that focus on firms of a particular size; and measures aimed at assisting the adjustment of industries, protection of the environment, or the achievement of cultural objectives. Many subsidies may be sector-specific, even though the objective is economy-wide. Examples include subsidies to sectors such as health, education, transportation, and communications. Conversely, subsidies that have an economy-wide rationale may be industry-specific. An example pertains to environmental objectives whose attainment require taxes or subsidies that affect primarily specific sectors such as the chemical or the automotive industry. As of the late 1980s, government subsidies to industry (excluding public services and agriculture) in OECD countries averaged about 2 per cent of the value of industrial output (OECD, 1993). Between two-fifths and three-fifths of subsidies were sector-specific, much of the support going to declining industries such as steel, shipbuilding, and mining. Of the service sectors, available statistics show that rail transport is often highly subsidized, with rates of support varying between 15 and 180 per cent of total value added in this sector.

GATT Rules

GATT disciplines relating to subsidies have a two-fold objective. First, to establish certain rules regarding the use of subsidies, in order to avoid or reduce their adverse effect on Members and to prevent the use of subsidies to 'nullify or impair' concessions made in MTNs. Second, to regulate the use of countervailing measures with which Members may attempt to offset the effects of subsidization of products by other Members. To a significant extent the GATT traditionally allowed a large measure of subsidy freedom, disciplined only by the threat of country-specific countervail. Indeed, subsidy disciplines in the GATT have always gone hand-in-hand with rules regarding contervailing measures, as reflected in the title of the relevant legal instrument: Agreement on Subsidies and Countervailing Measures. Countervail is politically necessary because the substantive disciplines on subsidies were weak. In this respect, the GATT differs substantially from regional integration agreements such as the EU, where much stricter disciplines are imposed on the use of subsidies, and where countervail cannot be used by Member States. Instead, subsidization is subject to EU competition rules. In the GATT context, the objective is to strike a balance between the need to: agree on minimum standards regarding the subsidies that should not be used; and identify what importing countries may do to offset the effects of foreign subsidy programmes. The GATT-1994's rules are such that 'legal' subsidies are 'non-actionable'— they cannot be countervailed. What follows focuses on the rules on subsidies; countervailing measures are discussed in Chapter 7.

Attempts under the auspices of GATT-1947 to deal with the subsidy issue suffered major difficulties. The term 'subsidy' was not defined in the GATT-1947, and agreement on a definition proved elusive. It also proved difficult to determine what are trade-distorting subsidies. These difficulties led to many disputes and panels in the 1970s and 1980s (see Annex 3 for a list of cases in the last ten years). Progress was made on both issues during the Uruguay round, however. Agreement was reached on a definition of the term 'subsidy'. A subsidy is deemed to exist if there is a financial contribution by a government (or public body). This in turn may involve either a direct transfer of funds (e.g. grants, loans, and equity infusion); potential direct transfers of funds or liabilities (e.g. loan guarantees); government revenue that is otherwise due is foregone or not collected (i.e. tax concessions or credits); the provision or purchase of goods or services other than general infrastructure; government funds given to a private body to carry out a function which would normally be vested in the government; any form of income or price support in the sense of Article XVI of the GATT. The definition also requires that a benefit is conferred by the financial contribution. The agreement applies to non-agricultural products; there are separate disciplines for agricultural production and trade (Chapter 8). Members must notify their subsidy programmes to the WTO Secretariat each year, giving information on the type of subsidy; the amounts involved; the policy objective and intended duration; as well as statistics allowing their trade effects to be determined. Any Member may 'cross-notify' alleged subsidies of other countries that the latter have not notified.

Three categories of subsidy are distinguished: non-actionable, prohibited, and actionable. Non-actionable subsidies are legal and may not be countervailed (Chapter 7 discusses countervailing duties). They include all non-specific subsidies: those that do not primarily benefit a firm, industry, or group of industries. Non-specificity requires that allocation criteria are neutral, non-discriminatory, economically based, and do not distinguish between sectors. All export subsidies are deemed specific, whether targeted or not. Certain specific subsidies may be non-actionable. These include R&D subsidies, aid to disadvantaged regions, and subsidies to facilitate the adaptation of plants to new environmental regulations (all subject to conditions). Subsidies contingent, formally or in effect, on exports or on the use of domestic over imported goods are prohibited. An illustrative list of export subsidies is included in the Agreement on Subsidies. Examples are the provision of products or services (including transportation) for use in export production that is more favourable than for domestically consumed goods, and export credits and guarantees or insurance at premium rates which are inadequate to cover the long-term operating costs and losses of the insurer (except if a Member applies the provisions of the OECD agreement on export credits). A necessary condition is that the government, or an institution under its control, provides the subsidy.

Actionable subsidies are subsidies that are permitted but may, if they create adverse effects on a WTO Member, give rise to consultations, invocation of dispute-settlement procedures, or be countervailed. Adverse effects include injury to a domestic industry, nullification or impairment of tariff concessions, or serious prejudice or threat of prejudice to the country's interests. Serious prejudice exists if:

(1) the total *ad valorem* subsidization of a product exceeds 5 per cent;
(2) subsidies cover operating losses of a firm or industry;
(3) debt relief is granted for government-held liabilities.

Serious prejudice may arise if the subsidy reduces the exports of a WTO Member, results in significant price undercutting, or increases the world market share of the subsidizing country in a primary product. If actionable subsidies have an adverse effect on a Member, it may request consultations with the subsidizing Member. Dispute-settlement provisions may be invoked if consultations fail to settle the matter within 60 days.

A number of 'special and differential treatment' provisions for developing and formerly centrally planned countries are included. WTO Members in the process of transformation from a centrally planned to a market economy, may apply prohibited subsidy programmes until 2002. During the same period, subsidy programmes involving debt rescheduling or write-offs are not actionable. Developing-country Members referred to in an annex (least developed and countries with GNP per capita below US $1000) are exempted from the prohibition on export subsidies.[4] 'Graduation' occurs when their GNP per capita exceeds $1000, after which non-conforming subsidies must be eliminated within eight years. Developing country WTO Members that are not listed in the Annex are subjected to a standstill requirement and must phase out their export subsidies over an eight-year period, starting from January 1995. The prohibition on subsidies contingent on the use of domestic goods (local content) does not apply to developing countries for a period of five years (eight years for least developed countries), and further extension may be requested. If granted, annual consultations with the Subsidies Committee must be held to determine the necessity of maintaining the subsidies. Developing countries that have become competitive in a product—defined as having a global market share of 3.25 per cent—must phase out applicable export subsidies over a two-year period.

The traditional difference in rules on subsidies for industrialized and developing countries was narrowed substantially in the Uruguay round, especially as regards export subsidies. But there are still differences. There are possible economic rationales for a more lenient stance for developing countries. Subsidies may be beneficial in stimulating economic development if there are externalities to firms operating in export markets. These may arise through the beneficial effects of learning by doing. Marketing experts have argued that quality upgrading and export marketing of non-traditional products by firms has positive spill-over effects on other potential exporters in a developing country, justifying an export subsidy. Export subsidies may also be used to offset the anti-export bias resulting from an over-valued exchange rate or high rates of protection in cases where first-best policies are not available (devaluation or a market determined exchange-rate and trade liberal-

---

[4] Least-developed countries are those that are designated as such by the United Nations. The following developing countries will graduate when their GNP per capita has reached $1000 per annum (as reported by the World Bank): Bolivia, Cameroon, Congo, Côte d'Ivoire, Dominican Republic, Egypt, Ghana, Guatemala, Guyana, India, Indonesia, Kenya, Morocco, Nicaragua, Nigeria, Pakistan, Philippines, Senegal, Sri Lanka, and Zimbabwe. Market exchange rates are used, not purchasing-power parities.

ization). Export subsidy programmes may also have an important political dimension as they can give credibility to a government's commitment to the maintenance of a policy framework that supports an export-oriented strategy, thus encouraging investment of resources and entrepreneurial energies in the development of foreign markets (Bhagwati, 1988).

In most of these cases subsidies are justified because of distortions created by market failures or other government policies. If the source of the problem is policy-induced, the subsidy is not the appropriate instrument. More often than not subsidy policies are driven by rent-seeking interest-groups, not by a clearly identified market failure. The stricter disciplines that were negotiated in the Uruguay round and are embodied in the WTO are therefore beneficial. Indeed, a case can be made that the disciplines are too weak for developing countries, in that GATT gives developing-country governments little help in identifying the types of subsidies that are harmful to welfare, and little support in opposing domestic interest-groups that are seeking subsidies (Winters, 1994*a*). It is somewhat ironic—although quite typical—that disciplines are weakest for those who can least afford inefficient and thus costly policies.

4.5. STATE TRADING

A government may get involved in international trade not only as a regulator but also as a consumer and as a producer. The GATT pertains to government policies affecting trade, but does so in large part under the assumption that transactions are driven by the decisions of private firms operating in a market environment. Government consumption—the procurement of goods and services—was explicitly excluded from the GATT. In the Tokyo round a code was negotiated on procurement, but only a few countries signed it (see Section 4.8 below). In contrast to government procurement, disciplines were included in the GATT to address state-trading enterprises (STEs) from the start, reflecting a recognition that STEs might not be bound by tariff commitments. However, the relevant provision of the GATT-1947 (Article XVII) gave no clear definition of what constitutes state trading, and a wide range of interpretations of what was meant by 'state trading' was revealed in the notifications that Member countries made to the GATT. The Communist authorities of Czechoslovakia submitted a list of their foreign-trade organizations engaging in export and import transactions. However, in the 1970s Poland and Hungary reported that they did not maintain state-trading enterprises, while Canada reported among its state-trading enterprises certain of its Crown Corporations (e.g. the Canadian Wheat Board), which were considerably more independent of the government than private trading firms in a number of other countries (Kostecki, 1982).

Article XVII covers state-owned enterprises; enterprises granted formally or in effect exclusive or special privileges; marketing boards; enterprises controlled by a Member; and import monopolies. The following working definition of an STE is used in GATT-1994 (in the GATT-1947 the concept was not defined): 'Governmental and non-governmental enterprises, including marketing boards, which have been granted exclusive or special rights or privileges, including statutory or constitutional powers, in the exercise of which they influence through their purchases or sales the level or direction of imports or exports.' STEs may therefore be fully privately owned. What matters is not ownership, but exclusivity. The right of Members to maintain or establish STEs or to offer exclusive privileges is not prejudged by the GATT (Roessler, 1982). The basic obligation imposed is that Members should ensure that STEs not act in a manner inconsistent with the general principle of non-discrimination (MFN). Three qualitatively different legal obligations are imposed by GATT relating to state trading, depending on the type of entity involved (Hoekman and Mavroidis, 1994a). First, as far as import monopolies are concerned, upon the request of trading partners that have a substantial trade in the product concerned, information is to be provided on the import mark-up on the product during a recent representative period, or, if not feasible, the resale price (Article XVII: 4b). Second, in their purchases or sales involving either imports or exports, state-owned enterprises, marketing boards, and enterprises granted exclusive privileges, such firms are to act in a non-discriminatory manner (Article XVII: 1a). Firms granted exclusive privileges are to make purchases or sales solely in accordance with commercial considerations. Third, members must ensure that enterprises in their jurisdiction are not prevented from acting in accordance with the non-discrimination principle (Article XVII: 1c).

In the Uruguay round, negotiators agreed to enhance GATT disciplines on—and surveillance of—STEs. Governments are required to notify all STEs to the GATT for review by a Working Party. The notification requirement does not apply to imports of products for immediate or ultimate consumption by the government or the STE itself (i.e. not for resale or use in the production of goods that are sold). Notifications are to be made for all STEs, independent of whether or not imports or exports have in fact taken place. Any WTO Member which believes that another Member has not adequately met its notification obligation may raise the matter bilaterally. If it is not resolved, a counter-notification may be made, for consideration by the Working Party. The Working Party is to evaluate the adequacy of notifications and to document the kinds of relationships existing between governments and STEs, and the type of activities STEs engage in.

The margins charged by STEs (their mark-ups) may be bound similarly to tariffs (Article II: 4). Once bound, mark-ups may not exceed the resulting tariff equivalent. While tariff commitments have been numerous, commitments regarding STEs have been rare. As far as market economies are concerned, in 1952 Italy undertook not to exceed a 15 per cent mark-up on wheat and rye imported by the Italian government or its agencies. France made a similar commitment regarding wheat imports by the Office National Interprofessionel des Céréales, and undertook a minimum import commitment with respect to lead, tobacco, and cigarettes imported by France's tobacco monopoly from countries other than those of the French Union. Both concessions lapsed with the formation of a common tariff schedule for the EEC.

A frequent companion of state trading is counter-trade: arrangements under which exporters and importers accept reciprocal deliveries in partial or full settlement of the value of their deliveries. Counter-purchase, offsets, advance purchase, buyback, and similar types of barter exchanges are popular forms of contemporary counter-trade (Banks, 1983). There is no reference to counter-trade in the General Agreement with the exception of a passing reference in the Government Procurement Agreement (see below). Counter-trade is a business practice and as such it is not of direct concern to GATT. What is of potential GATT concern are counter-trade regulations adopted by governments, in so far as these imply discrimination or a lack of transparency. The best counter-trade policy is no counter-trade policy. The compatibility of counter-trade regulations with the provisions of the GATT must be examined on a case-by-case basis.

State Trading and Former Centrally Planned Economies

The presumption that WTO Members are market economies has required in the past that centrally planned economies make additional commitments upon accession. Given that tariff concessions by centrally planned economies were meaningless or of limited value, GATT contracting parties negotiated global import commitments with Poland and Romania when these countries sought to accede to the GATT in 1967 and 1971, respectively. These commitments were included in their protocols of accession. The Polish formula provided that, in return for MFN and national treatment, Poland agreed to 'increase the total value of its imports from the territories of contracting parties by not less than 7 percent per annum' and that GATT contracting parties might seek 'agreements on Polish targets for imports from the territories of the contracting parties as a whole in the following year'. The Romanian arrangement stated that Romania firmly intended 'to increase its imports from GATT contracting parties as a whole at a rate not smaller than the growth of total Romanian imports provided for in its Five-Year Plan'. This was equivalent to a promise not to decrease the GATT share of imports in total Romanian imports. However, inflation and a depreciation of the US dollar *vis-à-vis* European currencies made these commitments meaningless in the late 1970s, and too burdensome in the 1980s (Kostecki, 1979).

In the case of Hungary, which acceded in 1973, it was concluded that tariff concessions were meaningful, and no 'voluntary import expansion' was negotiated. In all three cases, however, special safeguard provisions were included in the Protocols of Accession allowing for discriminatory actions to be taken against imports from the acceding country. Recent accession negotiations have revealed that economies that are perceived to be less than fully market-based can no longer accede on terms similar to those granted to the East Europeans in the past. This is not beneficial in any event, as a key benefit of WTO membership is MFN, which was not granted unconditionally to the East Europeans (because of the special safeguard option). All three East European countries are in the process of renegotiating their Protocols. These renegotiations—as well as accession discussions with economies in transition—reveal that WTO Members desire assurances that substantial progress towards privatizing enterprises and establishing a market-based regulatory environment will have been made.

This is an interesting phenomenon and reflects a change in the focus of major trading nations. In moving from the GATT-1947 to the GATT-1994 little was done to strengthen disciplines on STEs beyond improving transparency-related procedures. Formally, STEs are subject only to behavioural rules; there are no prohibitions on their existence or creation. That is, market structure is formally not a matter of concern; what matters is the conduct of STEs. Accession talks with the former centrally planned economies in the mid-1990s illustrated that WTO Members were increasingly concerned with market structure, not just conduct. Countries seeking accession were confronted with many questions regarding not only state-trading, but also the extent of monopolization and progress or intentions with respect to privatization. Underlying these questions was a concern about the contestability of the markets of the countries concerned. As illustrated by disputes between the USA and Japan in the late 1980s and early 1990s (see Chapter 11), perceptions that markets are effectively closed to foreign competition—because e.g. of monopoly or market power in distribution—may give rise to trade conflicts. To some extent accession negotiations in the mid-1990s revealed the increasing interest on the part of a number of WTO Members to ensure the contestability of markets. This is also reflected in suggestions that the WTO consider negotiating disciplines with respect to competition policy matters (see Chapter 11).

4.6. TECHNICAL REGULATIONS AND STANDARDS

Product standards, technical regulations, and certification systems are essential to the functioning of modern economies. Both standards and regulations are technical specifications for a particular product or production process. A standard differs from a regulation in that the former is voluntary, usually being defined by an industry or by a non-governmental standardization body.[5] Technical regulations are mandatory (legally binding), and are usually imposed in order to safeguard public or animal health, or the environment. In most industrialized economies the number of standards far exceeds the number of technical regulations. Certification systems comprise the procedures that must be followed by producers in establishing that their products or production processes conform to the relevant standard or regulation.

In contrast to many other policies discussed in this chapter, product standards are usually under the direct control of firms and industries. Standards, whether for products or aimed at human health and safety, are often welfare-enhancing as well, another difference with many of the other policies that are subject to GATT rules. However, standards may have trade-impeding effects, which is why they are dealt with in the GATT. The tension that arises if welfare-enhancing policies distort trade flows is becoming increasingly important, and extends beyond the case of product standards. Because standards have been dealt with under the GATT for many years already, standards-disciplines are of interest not only in their own right, but also for what they suggest about the feasibility of dealing with related topics (Chapter 11). There are two issues: first, ascertaining whether a standard is indeed welfare-enhancing rather than being the result of rent-seeking by a particular lobby; and second, the determination of the trade impact.

Economic Aspects

For there to be an economic rationale for standards there need to be market imperfections. Possibilities that have been identified in the literature are information asymmetries, uncertainty, market power, and externalities in production and/or consumption. As noted by Kindleberger (1983), many standards have the characteristic of a public good in that use by one person does not reduce other people's consumption possibilities of the good. Indeed, frequently the greater the use made of such standards, the greater the potential gains to users in terms of reduced transaction costs. Examples include standards of measurement and conventions such as driving on one side of the road. In the case of public goods there is a clear-cut argument to be made for harmonization, as a common standard is in the interest of all users. Achieving agreement on a specific standard can be difficult, as different groups may have different preferences. Because of free-rider problems, government intervention may be required to achieve a common standard. But most standards tend to be 'impure' public goods, in that they benefit a specific, identifiable group (usually an industry and its customers). Govern-

---

[5] Examples include the American National Standards Institute (ANSI), the British Standards Institution (BSI), the Deutsches Institut für Normung (DIN), and the Association française de normalisation (AFNOR).

ment intervention is then not necessary. However, there remains a need for interested parties to co-operate, and to the extent that there are costs to developing a standard, there may be an incentive to free-ride. In general, procedures will have to be established that allow a specific standard to be developed and adopted that benefits the major parties concerned.

While adoption of standards may help to achieve technical efficiency, standards may also allow incumbent firms in an industry to increase their market power. Standards are one of the possible instruments through which a firm or a group of firms can raise their rivals' costs. Assuming there are costs involved in meeting the standard, its existence may reduce the contestability of a market because potential entrants find it less attractive to compete or to enter. The greater are the barriers to entry, the greater will be the profit-enhancing effect of the standard, all other things equal. Thus, standardization may well be employed strategically by firms or groups of firms. Whenever the resulting reduction in supply leads to higher profits, it is likely that the standards that are imposed will be too restrictive (in the sense of raising costs too much). To the extent that this occurs, the standard has created rents (excess profits) and the standards-setting activity can be characterized as collusive. The standards that are imposed or proposed are not independent of the conduct of firms or their preferences, and are determined by factors such as the number and relative size of the firms in the industry, their efficiency of production (unit costs), technologies, R&D capability, and the type of good produced. The same applies for regulations. However, in the case of voluntary standards there is no need to lobby governments in order to obtain the rents because the standards are decided upon by industry groups. Government agencies responsible for determining technical regulations can expect to be lobbied by potentially affected parties and may be captured by them.

Because standards can raise unit costs of production and/or transportation, they may inhibit international trade. To the extent that this occurs one speaks of standards forming technical barriers to trade. In general, if standards and regulations differ across countries this will segment markets, even if the same standards are applied by each country to domestic and foreign goods. Prices for similar goods of uniform quality will then not be equal across countries, as the different standards inhibit arbitrage. Research stimulated by the EC-1992 or Single Market programme in the mid-1980s illustrated how significant such standards-induced market segmentation can be. A typical example was building tiles, where voluntary industry standards differ by EC country. Spain was found to be the lowest-cost producer of such tiles, average prices being between 40 and 100 per cent lower than prices charged by producers in other EC countries such as Germany, France, and the Netherlands (Groupe MAC, 1988). Such price differences were maintained as the result of a combination of differing standards and government procurement regulations. In France, for example, non-standard tiles could not be used in public works (about 40 per cent of the market), while private firms are hesitant to use non-standard tiles because insurance companies tend to require that buildings meet industry standards (Groupe MAC, 1988). In Italy pasta purity laws required that pasta be made of durum wheat, a high-quality, high-price type of wheat produced in the south of the country. This increases the cost of pasta in comparison to other EU countries, where pasta tends to consist of a mix of wheat qualities. For numerous other goods and services similar situations exist. These examples illustrate that a lack of uniform or mutually recognized standards and regulations may have a significant negative impact on consumer welfare by restricting trade.

As important are the procedures that are applied to ascertain if a product satisfies mandatory standards. Conformity assessment procedures (testing and certification) may be even more costly to a firm than the fact that standards differ between countries. Much depends in this connection on how products are tested, and if an importing country accepts (recognizes) certification of products by accredited foreign testing bodies, or the test data that have been generated by such bodies. At one extreme, products may be tested individually upon import, a very cumbersome, time-consuming, and costly process. More usual is testing on a random sample basis. Even this can act as a barrier to trade, especially if customs clearance for the whole consignment is dependent upon the sample being approved. Over time, in order to facilitate trade, some countries have agreed to certify specific testing agencies, and allow products tested and certified by such agencies to enter into their territory without additional inspection. Alternatively, they may continue to insist upon certification upon import, but accept foreign test data as long as this meets certain criteria. Rejection of imports by testing bodies, and refusal to accept foreign test data have given rise to many disputes, and was a major factor leading GATT contracting parties to address the topic of standards in the Tokyo round.

GATT Rules

The WTO does not require that Members have product standards. Nor does the WTO develop or write standards. The GATT-1994 Agreement on Technical Barriers to Trade aims to ensure that mandatory technical regulations, voluntary standards, and testing and certification of products do not constitute unnecessary barriers to trade. The Agreement has three major parts: (1) disciplines dealing with the adoption of technical regulations and standards in Member countries; (2) provisions dealing with conformity assessment, testing, and certification; and (3) transparency provisions. The basic rule is that central government bodies do not discriminate and write technical regulations that are no more trade-restrictive than is necessary to meet their legitimate objectives. The latter include national security requirements; the prevention of deceptive practices; and the protection of human health or safety, animal or plant life and health, or the environment. Relevant international standards—if they exist—must be used as a basis for technical regulations, except if this would be inappropriate because of, for example, climatic, geographical, or technological factors. Technical regulations based on product requirements should be worded in terms of performance rather than design or descriptive characteristics. A Code of Good Practice applies regarding the preparation, adoption, and application of standards (as opposed to technical regulations).

Conformity assessment procedures are also subject to MFN. If relevant guides or recommendations issued by international standardizing bodies exist, these are to be used, except if they are inappropriate for national security reasons or are inadequate to safeguard health and safety. In principle, WTO Members are to join and use international systems for conformity assessment. The results of conformity assessment procedures undertaken in exporting countries must be accepted if these are equivalent to domestic ones, once consultations to determine equivalence have been held. Accreditation on the basis of relevant guides or recommendations issued by international standardizing bodies is to be taken into account as an indication of the adequate technical competence of the foreign entity. Members are encouraged to negotiate mutual recognition agreements for conformity assessment procedures, and to apply the MFN and national treatment principles when permitting participation of foreign certification bodies in their conformity assessment procedures.

The third component of standards disciplines is transparency-related, and builds upon the principle of publication of regulations contained in Article X of the GATT. Each Member must establish an 'enquiry point' to answer enquiries and provide documents on:

(1) technical regulations adopted or proposed by bodies which have legal power to enforce them;
(2) standards adopted or proposed by central or local government bodies, or by regional standardizing bodies;
(3) conformity assessment procedures, existing or proposed, applied by bodies which have legal power to enforce technical regulations.

Best efforts are to be made to ensure that enquiry points are also able to answer enquiries regarding standards adopted or proposed by non-governmental standardizing bodies (e.g. industry associations); as well as conformity assessment procedures operated by such bodies. The WTO Secretariat is to establish an information system under which national standards bodies or enquiry points transmit to the ISO Information Centre in Geneva the notifications required under the Code of Good Practice for the preparation, adoption, and application of standards.

Sanitary and Phyto-Sanitary Measures

Sanitary and phyto-sanitary measures (SPMs) are requirements that are imposed by governments to ensure the safety of products for human or animal consumption, or to safeguard the environment. Most governments establish minimum standards that products, plants, or animals must meet in order to be allowed to enter their territory. Usually these norms will apply equally to foreign and domestically produced goods, plants, or animals. However, as is the case with product standards more generally, differences in norms may act to restrict trade. Such differences became increasingly prominent during the 1980s, with many countries alleging that importing countries (more specifically, import-competing industries or lobbies) were using SPMs as NTBs with a view to restricting imports. SPMs can very easily be abused, as they can be defined so strictly as to ensure that no product ever satisfies them. For example, a country with a large sheep industry may prohibit imports of beef to protect its sheep industry by imposing a health-based SPM requiring that beef have a fat content of less than 3 per cent. Alternatively, if it has a beef industry and could consequently be subjected to a claim of violating national treatment, it may require that the drip content of frozen beef be less than 1 per cent—that is, once unfrozen, no more than 1 per cent liquid is allowed in each carcass. This would be a very difficult standard to meet. It could also use an SPM to encourage local processing in cases where it has bound its tariffs. Thus, beef for retail sale might be required to have no more than 3 per cent fat; but beef for further processing could have a fat content of up to 20 per cent. Abuses may also occur in the enforcement of SPMs. Even if a country uses internationally accepted SPMs for a product, governments will still inspect imports to ascertain whether they satisfy health requirements. Such inspections—if not contestable before independent and objective tribunals—may be used as a mechanism to reject imports of politically sensitive goods, even if they meet all health and safety requirements (see Box 4.3).

Box 4.3. International trade and phyto-sanitary restrictions

SPMs may be used to prevent or restrict imports of foodstuffs, plants, or animals. The importance of such regulations can be illustrated by the case of Japanese sanitary rules on the import of apples and the ban on hormonal substances in livestock imported into the EU. Japan formally opened its apple market to foreign competition in 1971. However, in practice market access continued to be restricted in the decades that followed on the grounds that most imports were not sufficiently protected against pests and plant diseases that could harm Japan's pristine orchards. Apple exporters argued that Japan's phyto-sanitary regulations were far more stringent than any other country's, and constituted backdoor protectionism (GATT, 1988). US trade officials cited Japan's apple import regulations as an unfair trade barrier and regularly raised the issue in bilateral discussions, driven by congressional representatives from the state of Washington. After years of tension, Japanese authorities finally gave in to the external pressure, declaring that certain US orchards had taken adequate measures to eliminate viruses and moths. As of January 1995, imports of US apples became possible, and Japanese consumers could be seen munching apples on the streets of Tokyo.

In January 1988 the EU banned the use of hormonal substances for fattening animals intended for slaughter and human consumption. This ban affected US exports of meat to the EU, and caused a dispute between the two partners. The USA argued that the ban had no scientific foundation—since the use of hormones was well within safe margins—and therefore constituted an unjustifiable trade barrier. According to the US Administration, the ban—if fully implemented—would reduce exports by $115 million per year. The dispute was brought before the GATT, with the USA choosing to invoke the procedures of the Agreement on Technical Barriers to Trade (i.e. product standards), this being the only relevant instrument at the time. The EU considered that because the ban was aimed at protecting health and concerned production and processing methods—which were not formally covered by the Agreement at the time—the USA did not have a case. The USA threatened to increase tariffs on certain European goods if the prohibition on the importation and sale of meat treated with hormones was implemented (GATT, 1988; 1989). The EU in turn brought the issue of retaliatory measures by the USA before the GATT Council.

These examples illustrate why an Agreement on SPMs was negotiated during the Uruguay round, and also why the Agreement on Standards was extended to cover processing and production methods. As is invariably the case, the rules of the multilateral trading system expand in a reactive manner: a problem appears, disputes arise, the issue is put on the agenda of an MTN and a compromise emerges. The protectionist nature of food safety and animal and plant health regulations such as those described above will be considerably limited under the WTO's expanded disciplines on SPMs.

An Agreement on the Application of Sanitary and Phyto-Sanitary Measures was negotiated as part of the Uruguay round Agreement on Agriculture. It applies to all SPMs that may affect international trade. An SPM is defined as any measure applied to protect human, animal, or plant health from risks arising from the establishment or spread of pests and diseases; from additives or contaminants in foodstuffs; or to prevent other damage from the establishment or spread of pests. SPMs include all relevant regulations and procedures, including product criteria; processes and production methods; testing, inspection, certification, and approval procedures; quarantine treatments; provisions on relevant statistical procedures and risk-assessment methods; and packaging and labelling requirements directly related to food safety. As in the case of product standards, there is no requirement that Members adopt SPMs. The Agreement simply establishes disciplines if Members implement SPMs.

SPMs may not unjustifiably discriminate between WTO Members, be more trade-restrictive than required to achieve their objectives, or constitute a disguised restriction on international trade. They should be based on international standards, guidelines, or recommendations, if these exist, unless it can be proven with scientific evidence that an alternative is preferable. The Agreement requires that SPMs be based on scientific principles, including an assessment of the risks to human, animal, or plant life or health, taking into account risk-assessment techniques developed by relevant international organizations. In the assessment of risks, available scientific evidence must be considered, as well as relevant processes and production methods, inspection, sampling and testing methods, and the prevalence of specific diseases or pests and environmental conditions. SPMs may not be maintained without sufficient scientific evidence. In choosing an SPM, economic factors must be considered as well, including the potential damage in terms of loss of production and cost of control in the event of the spread of a pest or disease and the relative cost-effectiveness of alternative approaches to limiting risks. WTO Members must accept the SPMs of other Members as equivalent—even if they differ from their own—if the exporting country can demonstrate that its SPMs achieve the desired level of protection. Negotiations to achieve bilateral or multilateral agreements on recognition of the equivalence of specified SPMs is encouraged. Conformity assessment procedures and fees are to be based on MFN and national treatment, procedures and criteria should be published, confidentiality should be respected, and an appeals procedure established.

The Committee on Sanitary and Phyto-Sanitary Measures may grant developing countries specified, time-limited exceptions in whole or in part from meeting the requirements of the Agreement. Least-developed-country Members may delay application of the provisions of the Agreement until mid-2000. Other developing countries have until mid-1997, subject to certain conditions. The Committee is to develop a procedure to monitor the process of international harmonization and to establish a list of international standards or guidelines relating to SPMs that have a major impact on trade. As under the Standards Agreement, an enquiry point must exist to provide answers to SPM-related queries from trading partners and to provide relevant documents. Whenever the content of a proposed regulation is not substantially the same as the content of an international standard, guideline, or recommendation, and if the regulation may have a significant effect on the trade of other Members, the WTO

Secretariat must be notified of the products covered by the regulation together with a brief indication of the objective and rationale of the proposed regulation.

In the case of both the Agreements on Standards and on SPMs, WTO disciplines are valuable because they establish mechanisms to contest arbitrary decisions by customs, health, or agricultural authorities to reject goods on the basis of not meeting standards. No attempt is made to agree to the substantive content of standards, or to define minimum standards. Instead, reference is simply made to the relevant international bodies that address standards-related matters, and countries are encouraged to adopt internationally developed—and therefore consensus-based—standards. Countries remain free to define their own technical regulations for products, but must notify diverging national standards and justify their use. Especially in the case of SPMs—where such justification requires scientific evidence—much may depend on how such evidence is evaluated by panels should disputes be brought before the WTO. Publication and notification requirements foster transparency, and help ensure that traders know the regulatory situation that prevails in Members States. A weakness of the Standards Agreement is that language on voluntary product standards developed by industry associations is largely of a best endeavours nature. But this reflects the fact that the WTO disciplines government actions—not the private sector. All in all, the WTO's standards disciplines are a valuable, if often neglected, component of the multilateral trading system.

4.7. TRADE-RELATED INVESTMENT MEASURES

Trade-related investment measures (TRIMs) are policies used by governments with a view to forcing foreign investors to attain certain performance standards. The most prevalent are local content requirements—a condition that a minimum proportion of inputs used or value added by an investor must be of domestic origin—and export performance requirements. In most realistic circumstances such measures are inefficient. This is because they either act like a tariff on intermediate goods (this is the case for a local content requirement, where manufacturers are forced to use higher-cost local inputs)—or as a QR (this is the case with a so-called trade-balancing requirement, which acts to restrict imports to a certain quantity). Note that a local content requirement, while equivalent to a tariff, is inferior to one because the government does not collect any tariff revenue. In a distorted environment, a TRIM can be welfare-enhancing, but invariably there will be more efficient policies that could be used. For example, if a country with a large market has high import tariffs, this may induce foreign firms to invest there for local production (so-called tariff wall-jumping). A government may then impose a TRIM on such investment to obtain some of the excess profits (rents) that accrue to the foreign firm from the protected environment. In general, however, welfare would be better served if the government were to liberalize its import regime. None the less, many developing countries maintain various TRIMs as part of their arsenal of trade policies. Disciplining the use of such measures is likely to be welfare-enhancing, and to increase the incentive for governments to liberalize. Trade and investment are increasingly interdependent, complementing each other. Companies must increasingly engage in joint ventures in the countries from which they source their products. The development of an integrated framework addressing policies affecting both trade and investment in both goods and services is likely to be one of the issues the WTO will confront in the next decade. The TRIMs agreement is a first modest step in that direction.

TRIMs were initially one of the more controversial topics on the agenda of the Uruguay round negotiations. Many developing countries were of the view that attempting to agree to broad-ranging multilateral disciplines on policies affecting investment went far beyond the scope of the GATT, and that the GATT was not necessarily the appropriate forum for such an agreement (or attempt). Certain OECD countries, and the United States in particular, were of the view that policies distorting investment flows could have a significant impact on trade flows, and should be subject to multilateral disciplines. At the start of the Uruguay round, the USA sought disciplines on a long list of measures, including local content, export performance, trade balancing, minimum or maximum domestic sales, technology transfer and licensing, remittances, ownership limitations, and investment incentives (see Annex 4).

The TRIMs agreement that emerged is, not surprisingly, a compromise. It explicitly affirms that GATT disciplines (Articles III and XI, on national treatment and the prohibition of QRs) apply to investment policies in so far as this directly affects trade flows. Although this was a point of view that was long held and defended by most OECD countries, it had been resisted by developing countries. Thus, TRIMs that violate the GATT's national treatment rule or its prohibition on the use of QRs are banned. Technically this implies that the TRIMs agreement is subordinate to the GATT—it does not go beyond GATT disciplines. An illustrative list of measures that are considered to violate GATT rules is included in the agreement. Of these, performance requirements (such as local content and trade-balancing policies) are the most important. The agreement prohibits both mandatory measures and those 'with which compliance is necessary to obtain an advantage' (e.g. a tax concession or subsidy). All TRIMs that are inconsistent with the GATT must be notified to the WTO Secretariat, and Members must eliminate such measures within two, five, or seven years (for industrialized, developing, and least developed countries, respectively).

The TRIMs agreement is somewhat ironic, since WTO Members were given grace periods to phase out measures that were already violating the GATT.

However, as noted earlier, many developing countries were of the view that the GATT did not apply. Agreement on the scope of the GATT was the main outcome of negotiations. Moreover, the agreement is to be reviewed within five years of the establishment of the WTO, at which time the need for more general disciplines on investment, competition policy, and the scope for expanding the illustrative list of prohibited TRIMs is to be determined. Perhaps the most serious shortcoming of the TRIMs Agreement is that it does not address export performance requirements (Low and Subramanian, 1995). This is somewhat inconsistent with the GATT's prohibition on the use of export subsidies, as the two instruments are very similar in effect.

4.8. GOVERNMENT PROCUREMENT

The WTO has a few agreements relating to trade in goods that apply only to signatories. These agreements—of which that on government procurement is the most important—are formally known as 'plurilateral' trade agreements. The other agreements concern civil aviation, dairy products, and bovine meat (Chapter 8). The Agreement on Government Procurement was originally negotiated during the Tokyo round. It requires national treatment and non-discrimination for purchases by government entities, and establishes rather detailed rules to enhance the transparency of tendering procedures. The trade-off for introducing competition in procurement—a large market in any country—was that its disciplines apply only to governments that sign it, and then only for the entities that are listed in the Annexes (schedules) of each country. The revised agreement negotiated during the Uruguay round enters into force in January 1996.

Government procurement and sourcing policies often include preferences given to domestic over foreign firms in bidding on public-procurement contracts. Examples of policies pursued by governments include outright prohibitions of foreign sourcing (e.g. US civil servants must fly with US airlines); formal criteria for foreign sourcing to be permitted (e.g. minimum cost or price differentials; offset or local content requirements); and informal procedures favouring procurement from domestic firms. An example of the latter are selective or single tendering procedures under which no competitive bidding for a contract is initiated, the government instead directly approaching a specific (usually domestic) firm for a bid. Such discriminatory practices can be very important in terms of restricting access to markets. The market for government procurement is quite substantial. In the USA, for example, total procurement by government entities was over $1 trillion in 1991, or almost 20 per cent of GDP.

The Government Procurement Agreement (GPA) in principle prohibits preferences for domestic firms by imposing GATT's national treatment and non-discrimination principles. These apply to both trade (cross-border supply) and tenders by foreign firms that are locally established. The GPA thus goes beyond the GATT, which does not deal with establishment-related transactions. There are three types of entities that are in principle covered by the GPA: central government entities (e.g. ministries); sub-central government entities (e.g. those of a Province); and a catch-all of 'all other entities' that are required to follow the GPA's rules (in practice public utilities). The last two categories were added as a result of the Uruguay round. The extent to which bodies belonging to each of these three groups are covered, depends on the schedules that are negotiated between the signatories. The GPA applies to all contracts above SDR 130,000 (calls for tender) by listed central government entities. Higher thresholds apply to procurement by sub-central entities (usually around SDR 200,000) and utilities (around SDR 400,000). The GPA's scope was enhanced in the Uruguay round not only by the expansion of the entities covered, but also by the inclusion of services and construction contracts. Procurement of the latter product categories is again covered only for listed entities, and then only for those services that are explicitly listed in annexes to the GPA for each signatory. In general, only construction contracts above SDR 5 million are subject to the GPA. To give an indication of the orders of magnitude involved in the extension of the GPA's coverage to sub-central entities and services, the offers made by the USA and the EU covered some $100 billion of purchases (Schott and Buurman, 1994: 74).

The GPA contains detailed rules regarding the tendering procedures that are to be followed by covered entities. It reduces the scope for so-called single or limited tendering, where a firm is directly approached and invited to bid (or simply awarded the contract outright). Tendering is to be competitive, either being open to all firms, or open to all pre-qualified firms. If qualification is a pre-condition, the GPA establishes detailed rules regarding the procedures and modalities for allowing foreign firms to qualify and ensuring that this process does not work to shut out foreign competition. There are also detailed requirements concerning technical specifications used in invitations to bid; publication requirements; time-limits; and the content of tender documentation to be provided to potential suppliers. It also requires signatories to establish mechanisms allowing awards to be contested by bidders before domestic courts or similar bodies, and to compensate them should it be found that a decision violates GPA rules and procedures. Although in principle no discrimination is allowed in favour of domestic firms by covered entities, the GPA allows developing countries to negotiate 'mutually acceptable exclusions from the rules on national treatment with respect to certain entities, products, or services that are included in their lists of entities.' Such negotiations may also be initiated *ex post*, after signing the agreement (Article V: 5). Some scope therefore exists for maintaining discriminatory policies.

Many countries have concluded that the GPA is too far-reaching in its implications. Membership of the GPA is quite limited, with only eleven signatories (counting the EU as one). Indeed, not all OECD countries have signed it. A major challenge facing WTO Members in the coming years is to bring procurement of both goods and services into the WTO, i.e. to multilateralize the GPA. Public-procurement markets are too big to be left beyond the reach of the multilateral trading system, and strong pressures can be expected by export interests in the more open countries to improve their access to such markets. The history of GATT attempts to deal with this issue suggests that progress will require creativity on the part of negotiators. One option that might be explored in this connection is to allow developing countries to grant price preferences to local bidders (Hoekman and Mavroidis, 1995).

4.9. CONCLUSION

Despite the complexities of the details of the GATT, it is basically a simple agreement. The key disciplines are non-discrimination, tariff binding, and the prohibition on QRs. The pressure for protection that emerged in domestic political markets in the 1970s and 1980s led to circumvention of all three principles. Circumvention was often not blatant—VERs were called 'grey-area' measures for good reason. The incentive for interest-groups—especially import-competing industries—to lobby for protection and government support cannot be regulated away.

But the GATT in its dual role of market and code of conduct proved able to deal relatively well with recurring pressures for protection. Great achievements in this regard were the agreements negotiated in the Uruguay round to reintegrate agriculture and textiles and clothing into the GATT, and the Agreement of Safeguards that prohibited the use of VERs (see Chapter 7). Although always under attack, support for multilateral rules and disciplines has generally been strong enough to allow their gradual expansion over time. With the establishment of the WTO the institution was much strengthened, creating both a stronger mast to which governments could tie themselves, and a firmer foundation for settling trade disputes co-operatively in Geneva.

The tariff bindings and GATT's non-discrimination rules establish a benchmark for the conditions of competition facing foreign products on any Member's markets. Over time, attempts—often successful—have been made to extend the set of disciplines to non-tariff measures, thus expanding the scope to bring complaints that market access concessions were violated. The contestability of markets can be affected by many policies: export subsidies, procurement practices, standards, customs procedures, and so forth. Many of these have been addressed in the GATT. The rules often make economic sense in so far as they encourage transparency and push governments to use more rather than less efficient instruments, although their reach is often affected by language allowing for exceptions or exemptions. Indeed, the main problem relates to the loopholes contained in the GATT that allow for the legal imposition of protectionist measures, rather than circumvention of GATT obligations. The most important of these is probably anti-dumping (see Chapter 7).

Co-operation in the GATT has always been based on what has been called shallow integration—agreements not to do certain things (use QRs; raise tariffs above bound levels; discriminate against foreign products). Over time, contracting parties increasingly came to be confronted with the trade-distorting effects of non-tariff policies. Efforts to agree on reducing the trade-restricting effect of such policies proved much more difficult than negotiating downward the average level of tariffs. As it is difficult to exchange concessions on NTMs incrementally, disciplines were largely limited to the application of basic principles, such as non-discrimination and transparency. A basic question confronting WTO Members is how much further the pursuit of shallow integration can take countries. A premiss underlying the GATT has always been that regulatory regimes are taken as given: to use the language of business economics, what mattered were the conditions of competition, not market structure. Thus, state involvement in the economy was tolerated (state-owned enterprises, state trading), but subject to the non-discrimination rule. As tariffs have fallen to very low levels, and many NTBs have been subjected to multilateral disciplines, attention is turning increasingly to differences in the structures of the economies of WTO Members, and in particular to the contestability of markets. This has been reflected in accession talks involving former centrally planned economies (Section 4.5), but also in the interest of many countries to negotiate rules pertaining to the service sector and intellectual property regimes. It is also a major factor underlying efforts to expand the WTO further to include competition and investment policies (Chapter 11).

The question of whether and how to deal with differences in the structure of economies—how much regulatory competition is acceptable—can be expected to be a central element in much of the future work of the WTO, especially given the prospective accession of China and Russia. But the issue goes much beyond integrating these two large economies into the system. As the WTO struggles with the problem of regulating domestic policies that have an impact on trade, a number of fundamental issues will have to be confronted. One relates to the extent to which governments are willing to accept a loss in sovereignty by agreeing to harmonize regulations or accept to apply the principle of mutual recognition. Another is that the WTO binds central governments, while economic policies are increasingly being decentralized. This has been a problem in areas such as standards and government procurement, and pertains to many types of regulatory policies. Although WTO Members will be confronting such difficult issues in the years to come, the traditional GATT approach of shallow integration still has a lot of potential life to it. Certain policies have so far been left untouched. As mentioned, the government procurement agreement has virtually no developing-country signatories, and a challenge for the future will be to multilateralize this agreement. Another policy area where the GATT imposes no disciplines is with respect to export taxes. Governments remain free to impose such taxes, despite the fact that export taxes can be equivalent to import duties. As discussed further in Chapter 11, if WTO Members decide to initiate discussions on competition policies, disciplining this area can also be expected to be put on the agenda.

4.10. FURTHER READING

There is no economics textbook that looks at the economics of all of the policies addressed by the GATT. W. Max Corden, *Trade Policy and Welfare* (Oxford: Oxford University Press, 1974) remains a classic. A more recent modern study that has a good treatment of the concept of effective protection and also discusses the GATT is Neil Vousden, *The Economics of Trade Protection* (Cambridge: Cambridge University Press, 1990). Alan Deardorff and Robert Stern, *Methods of Measurement of Nontariff Barriers* (Geneva: UNCTAD, 1985) is an excellent discussion of the economic impact of different NTBs. John Jackson, *The World Trading System: Law and Policy of International Economic Relations* (Cambridge: MIT Press, 1989) is a recommended complementary source of reading on the GATT. The contributions in J. M. Finger and A. Olechowski (eds.), *The Uruguay Round: A Handbook* (Washington DC: World Bank, 1987) are a good source of information on GATT rules, practices, and history.

For a comprehensive discussion and analysis of government-mandated PSI (used by some thirty countries, mostly in Africa), and customs valuation more generally, see Patrick Low, *Preshipment Inspection Services*, Discussion Paper no. 278 (Washington: World Bank, 1995). Rules of origin systems are discussed further in Edwin Vermulst, Paul Waer, and Jacques Bourgeois (eds.), *Rules of Origin in International Trade: A Comparative Study* (Ann Arbor: University of Michigan Press, 1994). Subsidy issues are explored in greater detail by Richard Snape, in 'International Regulation of Subsidies', *World Economy*, 14 (1991), 139–64. Michel Kostecki, in *State Trading in International Markets* (London: Macmillan, 1982), explores the role of state trading in global trade as of the early 1980s. Counter-trade and the GATT are discussed in Frieder Roessler, 'Counter-trade and the GATT Legal System', *Journal of World Trade Law*, 19 (1985), 604–14. Bernard Hoekman and Petros Mavroidis, in 'The WTO's Government Procurement Agreement: Expanding Disciplines, Declining Membership', Discussion Paper no. 1112 (London: CEPR, 1995) analyse the GPA.

5

Trade in Services

Modern economies are service economies. Services—construction, transport, distribution, finance, education, and so forth—account for over 60 per cent of GDP in OECD countries. The service industry in these countries has become increasingly diverse and specialized in recent decades. An efficient service sector is a pre-condition for economic development. Without an adequate telecommunications and transport infrastructure, without a good educational system, and without the availability of high-quality business services a country will find it difficult to foster private-sector investment and economic growth. Trade and foreign direct investment will often play a crucial role in developing the service sector. One of the results of the Uruguay round was the creation of a General Agreement on Trade in Services (GATS). By establishing rules and disciplines on policies affecting access to service markets, the GATS greatly extended the coverage of the multilateral trading system. This chapter starts with a brief overview of global trade flows in services. This is followed by a summary of the main elements of the GATS and a discussion of some of the political economy forces that help explain the structure and content of the Agreement. The chapter concludes with brief evaluation of the GATS.

5.1. TRADE FLOWS AND CONCEPTUAL ISSUES

The introduction of services on the MTN agenda reflects their increasing importance in domestic economies and international trade. In the late 1970s, the United States began to perceive that it had a comparative advantage in services, and sought to link further liberalization of goods trade to progress in liberalizing trade in services. Driven by innovations in information technology, increasing specialization and product differentiation, as well as government policies such as deregulation and liberalization in the 1980s, trade in services has grown faster than trade in merchandise throughout the last decade. As shown in Table 5.1, in 1993 global services trade stood at some US $930 billion. This was equal to 22.2 per cent of global trade (goods plus services), as compared to 18.8 per cent in 1980. Both industrialized and developing countries have seen the relative importance of trade in services increase, although services account for a larger share of the total trade of OECD countries. In 1993 OECD countries accounted for 81 per cent of global exports of commercial services, up from 79 per cent in 1982.

128

Trade in Services

TABLE 5.1 *Global trade flows, 1980 and 1993* (US $bn. and %)

	1980	1993	Average annual change
Total trade in services	358	934	8.3
OECDᵃ	283 (79)	752 (81)	8.6
Rest of worldᵃ	75 (21)	182 (19)	6.8
Services as share of goods and services	17.0	22.2	2.2
OECD	18.8	23.1	1.6
Rest of world	12.7	19.1	3.5

Note: Data pertain only to countries reporting to the IMF.
ᵃ Percentage shares in parentheses.
Source: World Bank (1995).

Trade in services differs from trade in goods. Services are often intangible and cannot be stored. Proximity between providers and demanders is then usually required for exchange to be feasible (Bhagwati, 1984; Sampson and Snape, 1985). Certain transactions may occur across borders (i.e via telecommunications media, without there being a need for provider or demander to move), but others will require that provider and consumer are in the same place at the same time. This can be achieved through the physical movement of consumers to the location of service providers (e.g. tourism), or via temporary entry of service providers into the territory of a consumer (e.g. consulting). In a statistical sense all three of these modes of supply are considered to be trade and are registered as such in the balance of payments. They all involve exchanges between the resident of one country and the resident of another.

In the GATS context, trade is defined to also include sales by foreign firms that have established a commercial presence in a country. Many services are not tradable, in that cross-border, long-distance exchange or temporary physical movement of provider or consumer does not suffice for an exchange to be feasible. Producers of such services can contest foreign markets only through establishing a long-term physical presence there, that is, by engaging in foreign direct investment (FDI). FDI in services accounts for a large share of the total stock of inward FDI in most host countries. As of the early 1990s, some 50 per cent of the global stock of FDI was in services activities, and the share of annual flows to many countries was even higher (roughly 60 per cent). The relative importance of trade in services (as registered in the balance of payments of a country) as opposed to sales of services by affiliates is not known. This is because the latter are not registered in the balance of payments. Once established, foreign firms are considered to become residents of the host country. Conventional wisdom holds that FDI is likely to be the dominant mode of supply for many services. US data, (the USA is one of the few

TABLE 5.2 *Shares of global service exports, 1980 and 1992*

Country group	Travel		Transport		All Other	
	1980	1992	1980	1992	1980	1992
Share in global trade						
OECD members	75.0	79.1	79.8	80.5	81.4	85.2
Rest of the world	25.0	20.9	20.2	19.5	18.6	14.8
Relative specialization						
OECD members	1.01	0.96	1.10	1.02	1.13	1.06
Developing countries	0.93	1.12	0.65	0.82	0.65	0.74
Small LDCs (1 million people or less)	2.19	3.45	1.19	1.85	0.39	1.11

Note: Relative specialization if defined as the ratio of exports of a product category to a country's total exports of goods and services, divided by the same ratio for the world: RCA = $[X_{ij}/Y_j]/[X_{rw}/Y_w]$, where X_{ij} are exports of product i by country j, Y_j are total exports of goods and services by country j, and w stands for the 'world': the sum of all countries. The value of this index may range from zero to a very large number. If the index is greater than one this implies that the country is relatively specialized in the product concerned.
Source: Hoekman (1995*a*).

countries to collect data on sales of services by affiliates of US parent companies), suggest that trade and sales are of roughly the same importance.[1] Not too much can be inferred from this, however, as both trade and sales via FDI will in part reflect the barriers to the various modes of supply that are imposed by partner countries. Quantitative measures of these barriers do not exist.

Available data on trade in services are very weak compared to those on merchandise. Only a limited number of industrialized countries collect and report statistics on trade in services at a relatively disaggregated level (e.g. ten categories or more). Most non-OECD countries only report data on trade in 'commercial services' broken down into 'transport' (largely freight and passenger transport by sea and air), 'travel' (expenditures by non-residents—mostly tourists—while staying in a foreign country), and 'other services'. The last category includes items such as brokerage, insurance, communications, leasing and rental of equipment, technical and professional services, income generated by the temporary movement of labour, as well as property income (royalties). Table 5.2 provides an overview of the relative importance of these three main categories of trade for major country groups. Although in aggregate value terms global trade in services is dominated by OECD countries, many developing countries are—or could become—

[1] In 1987 foreign sales by US majority-owned affiliates were 15 per cent smaller than service exports; by 1992 they had grown to be 20 per cent larger (World Bank, 1995).

relatively specialized in exporting services. Table 5.2 shows that small developing countries in particular (defined as those with less than one million people) are highly specialized in exports of services. Moreover, their relative specialization have increased significantly during the last decade. These countries have higher than average export intensities for all three services categories, but are clearly most highly specialized in travel, that is, tourism. The relative importance of travel receipts was about twice the world average in 1980, rising to over three times in 1992.

Cross-country data on the magnitude of barriers to trade in services do not exist. Because services are generally intangible and often cannot be stored, barriers to trade do not take the form of import tariffs. Instead, trade barriers take the form of prohibitions, QRs, and government regulation. QRs may limit the quantity and/or value of imports of specific products for a given time-period; or restrict the number and/or market share of foreign service providers. Such discriminatory QRs are often complemented by measures that apply to both foreign and domestic service providers. These may consist of limitations on the number of firms allowed to contest a market, or on the nature of their operations. Frequently, this involves either a monopoly (e.g. telecommunications) or an oligopolistic market structure (e.g. insurance). Considerations relating to consumer protection, prudential supervision, and regulatory oversight often induce governments to require establishment by foreign providers or to reserve activities for government-owned or controlled or regulated entities.

The non-existence of tariffs as a restraint to trade greatly complicates the life of negotiators seeking to agree to incrementally reduce barriers to services trade. As discussed in Chapter 3, negotiators require a focal point—some tangible variable enabling parties to set objectives and assess negotiating progress. In past merchandise trade negotiations, the focus of negotiators centred on the value of bilateral trade flows and the associated tariffs. Lack of data on trade and the complexities associated with identifying and quantifying barriers to trade in services focused the attention of negotiators on rules. Thus, a substantial amount of time and resources was devoted to determining whether and how GATT-like concepts such as national treatment and MFN could be applied to service sectors. Rather than focusing on the identification, quantification, and reduction of barriers, subjective notions of sectoral reciprocity became the norm in services negotiations. This contrasts with the first-difference approach to reciprocity used in GATT tariff negotiations.

5.2. A SYNOPSIS OF GATS DISCIPLINES

The GATS consists of four main elements:

(1) a set of general concepts, principles, and rules that apply to all measures affecting trade in services;

(2) specific commitments that apply to service sectors and sub-sectors that are listed in a Member's schedule;

(3) an understanding that periodic negotiations will be undertaken to liberalize trade in services progressively; and

(4) a set of attachments and annexes that take into account sectoral specificities and Ministerial Decisions that relate to the implementation of the Agreement.

The GATS applies to measures imposed by Members that affect the consumption of services originating in other Member States (Article I). The Agreement applies to all of the four modes of supply that are possible in exchanging services:

(1) cross-border supply (not requiring the physical movement of supplier or consumer);

(2) provision involving movement of the consumer to the country of the supplier;

(3) services sold in the territory of a Member by foreign entities that have established a commercial presence; and

(4) provision of services requiring the temporary movement of natural persons.

'Trade in services' in the GATS context therefore covers both trade in the balance-of-payments sense and local sales by foreign affiliates. The Agreement does not apply to services supplied in the exercise of governmental functions.

The Basic Rules: MFN, National Treatment, and Market Access

The core principle of the GATS is non-discrimination, as reflected in MFN and national treatment rules. The reach of these principles is less all-encompassing than under the GATT. Although MFN is a general obligation, the GATS contains an Annex allowing countries to invoke exemptions to MFN. The coverage of MFN for each GATS Member is therefore determined by a so-called negative list—it applies to all services except those listed in the Annex by each Member. The sectoral coverage of national treatment is determined by a positive list—it only applies to sectors listed in a Member's schedule of commitments, and then only in so far as existing measures are not exempted.

MFN exemptions may only be made once: upon the entry into force of the agreement (however, GATS allows for the formation of economic integration agreements between a subset of Members—see Chapter 9). Once a Member, further exemptions can only be sought by requesting a waiver from the Ministerial Conference of the WTO (which must be approved by three-quarters of the Members). MFN exemptions are in principle to last no longer than ten years and are subject to negotiation in future MTNs, the first of which must take place within five years of the entry into force of the agreement. The need for an annex on MFN exceptions arose from concerns on the part of some industries that MFN allowed competitors located in countries with relatively restrictive policies to benefit from their sheltered markets while enjoying a free-ride in less restrictive export markets. This concern was expressed vividly in GATS discussions on financial services and telecommunications, prompting industry representatives in relatively open countries to lobby for MFN exemptions as a way to force sectoral reciprocity.

In the closing days of the Uruguay round it became clear that a number of participants were ready to invoke the Annex on MFN exceptions for financial services, basic telecommunications, maritime transport, and/or audio-visual services. Rather than allow a situation to develop where countries would withdraw already tabled commitments in these areas and/or exempt them from the MFN obligation, a compromise solution was reached under which negotiations in these sectors were to continue after the establishment of the WTO. Negotiations on financial services, basic telecommunications, and maritime transport were restarted in the spring of 1994, with those on financial services to be concluded by July 1995, the others by mid-1996. If negotiations are not successful, Members are free to invoke an MFN exemption for the sector concerned.

Over sixty GATS Members had submitted MFN exemptions by mid-1994, with three sectors in particular being affected: audio-visual services, financial services, and transportation (road, air, and maritime). Exemptions in the audio-visual area tend to be justified on the basis of cultural objectives, allowing for preferential co-production and/or distribution arrangements with a limited number of countries. Exemptions for financial services are usually motivated by reciprocity concerns: countries seeking the flexibility to retaliate against Members that do not offer reciprocal access to financial service markets. The goal of many Members in this connection was to maintain some leverage *vis-à-vis* the USA. Exemptions in the transport area by developing countries were often motivated by the UNCTAD Liner Code—under which they may reserve up to 40 per cent of liner shipping routes for their flag vessels.

National treatment is a so-called specific commitment that applies only to the services inscribed in a Member's schedule, subject to whatever qualifications or conditions are listed. It is defined as treatment no less favourable than that accorded to like domestic services and service providers. Such treatment may or may not be identical to that applying to domestic firms, in recognition of the fact that identical treatment may actually worsen the conditions of competition for foreign-based firms (e.g. a requirement for insurance firms that reserves be held locally). In addition to national treatment, the GATS introduces another specific commitment: a market-access obligation. Six types of market-access restrictions are in principle prohibited. These consist of limitations on:

(1) the number of service suppliers allowed,
(2) the value of transactions or assets,
(3) the total quantity of service output,
(4) the number of natural persons that may be employed,
(5) the type of legal entity through which a service supplier is permitted to supply a service (e.g. branches vs. subsidiaries for banking), and
(6) participation of foreign capital in terms of a maximum percentage limit of foreign shareholding or the absolute value of foreign investment.

While in principle prohibited, if a Member wants to maintain one or more of these six measures, it may do so as long as it lists them in its schedule.

The introduction of a market-access commitment reflects the fact that the contestability of service markets is frequently restricted by measures that apply to both foreign and domestic entities. The market-access article explicitly covers a number of such measures that were felt to be of particular importance. To a degree it is the equivalent of GATT Article XI, which prohibits the use of QRs. Note, however, that the market-access obligation overlaps with the national-treatment requirement, as prohibited measures may be discriminatory as well as non-discriminatory (e.g. limitations on foreign equity participation violates market access and is discriminatory). This overlap creates potential for confusion and disputes.

Other GATS obligations address issues such as transparency, recognition of licenses and certification of service suppliers, policies regarding payments and transfers for services, domestic regulation, and the behaviour of public monopolies. Article III (Transparency) requires all Members to establish enquiry points to provide specific information concerning any laws, regulations, and administrative practices respecting services covered by the Agreement. Article VI (Domestic Regulation) requires that Members establish disciplines to ensure that qualification requirements, technical standards, and licensing procedures are based on objective and transparent criteria, are no more burdensome than is necessary to ensure the quality of the services concerned, and do not constitute a restriction on supply in themselves (thereby possibly circumventing a specific commitment). Article XI requires Members to refrain from applying restrictions on international transfers and payments for current transactions relating to their specific commitments—it does not apply generally. Article VII (Recognition) promotes the establishment of procedures for (mutual) recognition of licenses, education, and/or experience granted by a particular Member. It is noteworthy in requiring Members to 'afford adequate opportunity' for other Members to negotiate their accession to an existing bilateral or plurilateral recognition agreement. Monopoly or oligopoly supply of services is allowed under the GATS, but governments are required to ensure that such firms do not abuse their market power to 'nullify' any specific commitments relating to activities that fall outside the scope of their exclusive rights.

Many of the GATS' disciplines apply only to the extent that specific commitments are made. This is a serious shortcoming, and is a consequence of the positive list approach taken for scheduling commitments. The MFN, national-treatment, and market-access obligations of the GATS do not extend to government procurement of services. This greatly reduces the coverage of the GATS, as procurement typically represents a significant share of total demand for many services—e.g. professional services, consulting engineering, and construction. Negotiations on this issue are to be initiated by the end of 1997. Nor does the GATS impose general disciplines on subsidy practices, only subjecting subsidies to the Agreement's general obligations (i.e. transparency, MFN, and dispute settlement). Negotiations are also called for on this topic, the time-frame to be determined by a future work programme. Article IX recognizes that business practices of service suppliers that have not been granted monopoly or exclusive rights may restrain competition and thus trade in services, but no obligations are imposed regarding the scope and enforcement of competition policy rules.

There are a number of articles of a safeguard nature, including Article X (Emergency Safeguard Measures), Article XII (Restrictions to Safeguard the Balance of Payments), and Article XIV (Exceptions). Article X allowing for possible industry-specific safeguard actions is largely a shell, and the Agreement again calls for negotiations on this topic before the end of 1997. The balance-of-payments provision only applies to those services for which specific commitments have been undertaken. It requires that such measures be non-discriminatory, temporary, and phased out progressively as the invoking Member's balance-of-payments situation improves. As in the GATT context, no recognition is expressed that import restrictions are second-best instruments to deal with balance-of-payments difficulties. Article XIV on exceptions is similar to what is found in the GATT, providing Members with the legal cover to take measures to safeguard public morals, order, health, security, consumer protection, and privacy. The WTO's Dispute Settlement Body is responsible for disputes under GATS. It is noteworthy in this regard that retaliation from goods to services and vice versa is possible if this is necessary (so-called cross-retaliation).

Specific Commitments

As described previously, specific commitments on national treatment and market access apply only to service sectors listed by Members, subject to sector-specific qualifications, conditions, and limitations that may continue to be maintained. As commitments are scheduled by mode of supply as well as by sector, these exceptions may apply either across all modes of supply or for a specific mode. Members also make horizontal commitments that apply to

TABLE 5.3 *Format and example of a schedule of specific commitments*

Commitments	Mode of supply	Conditions and limitations on market access	Conditions and qualifications on national treatment
Horizontal commitments (i.e. across all sectors)	Cross-border supply	e.g. 'none'	e.g. 'none' other than tax measures that result in differences in treatment with respect to R&D services.
	Consumption abroad	e.g. 'none'	e.g. 'unbound' for subsidies, tax incentives, and tax credits.
	Commercial presence (FDI)	e.g. 'maximum foreign equity stake is 49 per cent'	e.g. 'unbound' for subsidies. Under Law *x*, approval is required for equity stakes over 25 per cent; new investment that exceeds *y* million.
	Temporary entry of natural persons	e.g. 'unbound' except for the following: intra-corporate transferees of executives and senior managers; specialist personnel for up to one year; specialist personnel subject to economic needs test for stays longer than one year; service sellers (sales people) for up to three months.	e.g. 'unbound' except for categories of natural persons referred to in the market-access column
Specific commitment: e.g. architectural services	Cross-border supply	e.g. 'Commercial presence required'	e.g. 'unbound'
	Consumption abroad	e.g. 'None'	e.g. 'None'
	Commercial presence (FDI)	e.g. '25 per cent of senior management should be nationals'	e.g. 'Unbound'
	Temporary entry of natural persons	e.g. 'Unbound, except as indicated in Horizontal Commitments'	e.g. 'Unbound, except as indicated in Horizontal Commitments'

Source: Hoekman (1995*a*).

modes of supply, rather than sectors. Table 5.3 illustrates the complicated format of schedules of commitments. A consequence of the decisions to distinguish between general and specific obligations, to schedule specific commitments by mode of supply, and to allow for MFN exemptions is that very much depends on the content of the schedules. In comparison to the GATT, general rules and principles are less important (binding).

The sectoral commitments of GATS Members, while of a qualitative nature, can be quantified to determine the extent to which measures have been bound, and the share of sectors where such binding relates to free trade. Virtually all commitments made in the Uruguay round are of a standstill nature, i.e. a promise not to become more restrictive than was the case at the time of negotiation for listed sectors. As liberalization did not occur, sectoral coverage indicators provide useful information on the extent to which Members were willing to bind the status quo. Sectoral coverage ratios are also an indicator of the openness of countries if attention is limited to those sectors that GATS Members subject to market-access and national-treatment obligations without any qualifications.

Table 5.4 reports sectoral coverage indicators for national treatment and market-access commitments for three groups of countries: (1) high-income countries (HICs)—OECD members, Hong Kong, Korea, and Singapore; (2) all other countries; and (3) a group of 'large' developing countries—Argen-

TABLE 5.4 *Sectoral coverage of specific commitments* (%)

	High-income countries	All other countries	Large developing nations
Market access			
Average count (sectors or modes listed as a share of total)	53.3	15.1	29.6
Average coverage (sectors or modes listed as a share of total, weighted by restrictiveness and binding scale factors)	40.6	9.4	17.1
No restrictions as a share of total	30.5	6.7	10.9
National treatment			
Average count (sectors or modes listed as a share of total)	53.3	15.1	29.6
Average coverage (sectors or modes listed as a share of total, weighted by restrictiveness and binding scale factors)	42.4	10.2	18.8
No restrictions as a share of total	35.3	8.5	14.6

Source: Hoekman (1995a)

tina, Brazil, Chile, China, Colombia, India, Indonesia, Israel, Malaysia, Pakistan, Philippines, Poland, South Africa, Thailand, and Venezuela.[2] Three indicators are reported. First, the share of sectors where a commitment was made. Second, the weighted average coverage of the commitments, adjusted for whether there are qualifications (see Hoekman, 1995a for details of the calculations). Third, the share of sectors where commitments include no exceptions or qualifications on national treatment or market access. The higher the number, the more liberal the country. These ratios are conceptually similar to NTB frequency and coverage indices (see Deardoff and Stern, 1985).

HIC members made commitments of some kind for 53.3 per cent of all services, as compared to 15.1 per cent for developing countries. Commitments made by large developing countries, arbitrarily defined as those with GDP of US $40 billion or more, were substantially higher than the developing country average, accounting for 29.6 per cent of the total possible. This largely reflects the fact that many developing countries made very limited commitments. Indeed, over one-quarter of developing countries scheduled less than 3 per cent of their service sector. The weighted average coverage of market-access commitments—adjusting for whether exemptions are listed and policies are bound—for the HIC group is 40.6 per cent; that for developing countries 9.4 per cent; and that for large developing countries 17.1 per cent. Table 5.4 also reports the importance of 'no restriction' commitments relative to the maximum possible. Such commitments by HIC members account for 30.5 per cent of the total. For developing countries as a whole the figure is 6.7 per cent; for the large developing country group the number is 10.9 per cent. Identical ratios were calculated for national-treatment commitments, which are very similar. The numbers vividly illustrate how far away GATS members are from attaining free trade in services, and the magnitude of the task that remains.

Most of the potential gains for developing countries associated with GATS membership will result from liberalizing access to their own markets. There is substantial evidence that many of the constraints that reduce the economic efficiency of service industries are home grown, in that governments have not always pursued the appropriate policies (UNCTAD and World Bank, 1994). Thus, policy measures should focus on augmenting domestic productive capacity, increasing quality, establishing a reputation for reliable supply, etc. Services are often intermediate inputs into the production of goods, so that the availability of higher quality and/or lower cost services will increase the output of goods and make them more competitive on world markets. The level of specific commitments suggests that governments did not grasp the opportunity to fully bind the status quo, let alone to liberalize access to service markets.

---

[2] Mexico is included in the high-income countries, reflecting its membership in the OECD.

This raises the question why so little was achieved in the Uruguay round, and whether substantial liberalization will occur in the future.

5.3. THE POLITICAL ECONOMY OF THE GATS

Why did this rather convoluted and non-transparent structure emerge? A synopsis of initial negotiating stances is a good point of departure to address this question. Before and during the 1986 ministerial meeting establishing the agenda of the Uruguay round, many developing countries defended the view that there should not be an MTN addressing services. This position was defended by the so-called G-10, which included many of the large and more influential developing countries (e.g. Argentina, Brazil, Egypt, and India) (Bhagwati, 1987). While these countries could not block the inclusion of services, they managed to put services on a separate track in an attempt to prevent cross-issue linkages between traditional GATT issues and services. In the course of initial negotiations many developing countries argued that the lack of data on services trade justified excluding service transactions involving establishment by foreign providers from any agreement. In this they were supported by UNCTAD, which proposed that trade in services be defined to occur only when the majority of value added is produced by non-residents (UNCTAD, 1985). This definition excluded virtually all transactions through FDI, as foreign factors of production that relocate are generally considered to become residents of the host country for statistical purposes. Great emphasis was put on the need for governments to be able to impose conditions on inward FDI and support domestic industries. A consequence of this was that a generally applicable national-treatment obligation was considered to be unacceptable.

The EU's initial negotiating position was that trade should be defined so as to include all types of transactions necessary in a sector in order to achieve 'effective' market access. A 'regulations committee' was proposed that would determine the 'appropriateness' of regulations, criteria to determine this to be negotiated. Inappropriate measures were to be subject to liberalization over time, the goal being to achieve 'comparable' market access on a sector-by-sector basis for all participating countries. Any framework agreement was to involve only limited obligations of a generally binding nature. In particular, national treatment was to be only an objective. The implication of this was that any binding commitments were to apply on a sector-specific level. The United States' initial proposal was the most liberal: MFN was to apply to all signatories and national treatment was to be a binding, general obligation. Trade was to be defined broadly, including FDI (commercial presence). All measures limiting market access for foreign service providers were to be put on the table.

Thus, both the EU and major developing countries expressed an early preference for an agreement with soft obligations—the EU arguing that national treatment should only apply to specific sectors, major developing countries opposing even that. Only the USA and a number of small open economies—both OECD members and newly industrialized countries like Singapore—were in favour of a hard agreement along GATT lines from the start, with generally binding obligations and universal sectoral coverage. At the end of the day the original EU and developing-country preference for a soft framework agreement prevailed. In return for acceptance that trade in services be defined to include the four possible 'modes of supply', and agreement that certain non-discriminatory measures restricting market access were in principle negotiable, national treatment became a specific commitment, and it was agreed that scheduling of specific commitments would be on a sector-by-sector and mode-of-supply basis. The softness of the general disciplines may also have been a factor underlying the pressure for MFN exemptions. The case for such exemptions would have been much weaker if national treatment or market access had been general obligations. The positive list approach to determining the sectoral coverage of specific commitments emerged in large part because many developing countries apparently felt they did not have the administrative resources required to determine all the measures that currently applied to each sector and to decide which they would want to exempt. As many of these countries did not appear to have the intention of making very substantial commitments to liberalize access to their service markets in any event, they much preferred a positive-list approach.

What does the structure of the GATS imply as regards the likelihood of future liberalization? Negotiations in the services area were (and will be) sectoral, largely driven by the concerns and interests of major industries and firms in Member States. As in the GATT context, a necessary condition for co-operation on trade in services is that a balance of 'concessions' be attained. Services are traded less than tangible goods, as is reflected in ratios of trade to output of marketed services. In OECD countries, for example, the ratio of exports to output is on average over six times less for services than for goods. In many instances, potentially tradable services are simply not traded at all, i.e. barriers—whether natural or man-made—are prohibitive. As a result, the number and political weight of import-competing sectors may greatly exceed that of export-oriented service sectors interested in obtaining access to foreign markets.

The existence of multiple modes of supply may imply that standard predictions of lobbying interests will change. In the short run, it is generally assumed that sector-specific factors of production employed in inefficient protected industries will oppose the liberalization of market access. In the services context this may not be the case. For example, to the extent that establishment is the most efficient mode of contesting a market, sector-specific labour interests may not be opposed to liberalization, in so far as they expect that net employment in the sector will not change much upon liberalization due to the establishment of foreign-owned firms. This in turn will depend on the type of technology (production methods) that are used by new foreign entrants.

While the introduction of establishment as a possible mode may result in less opposition to liberalization, this is not necessary, of course. Labour interests in general may oppose the liberalization of the longer-term movement of foreign service providers. Reduced opposition to liberalization may also be offset by the interests of regulatory agencies. Many service activities are highly regulated. The regulatory agencies involved may then have a vested interest in defending their turf, complicating the necessary inter-agency co-ordination and co-operation (Feketekuty, 1988). Again, however, much may depend here on whether establishment is allowed or not. If not, regulators may have greater objections to liberalization, as it is more difficult for them to control industries that are located in foreign jurisdictions. Indeed, regulators may prefer that establishment is required as a mode, as this ensures that they will maintain their control of the activity involved.

There are therefore reasons to suspect that if governments are willing to liberalize, they are likely to have a preference for liberalizing the commercial presence mode of supply. This may help to offset the political economy problem that the relatively small size of potential exporters of services poses in terms of reducing the potency of reciprocity as a motor of liberalization. Whatever the relevance of the foregoing speculations, fewer commitments on the cross-border movement of services and service providers (i.e. labour) were offered by developing countries. Commitments tended to be least restrictive on the establishment mode of supply. No doubt this reflects a perception that establishment is the best in terms of generating domestically produced added value. However, FDI may not be the optimal mode of supply for a particular service, so that the policy preference for FDI may be second-best. Such piecemeal liberalization may then be welfare-reducing.

The structural weaknesses of the GATS may hamper the realization of the goal of progressive liberalization. The design of the country schedules makes commitments less than transparent. The GATS generates no information on sectors, sub-sectors, and activities in which no commitments are scheduled— most often the sensitive ones where restrictions and discriminatory practices abound. This is a serious shortcoming given that the impediments to trade in services are mostly regulatory in nature. It makes future progress more difficult, as negotiators will have limited information—indeed, to a large extent they are dependent on export interests for information. The GATS à la carte approach to liberalization may also allow countries to schedule commitments whilst maintaining significant degrees of regulatory discretion. For example, commitments relating to commercial presence may be subject to the right to maintain or impose authorization and/or screening procedures. The

Trade in Services 141

criteria that underpin such procedures may not be adequately specified in the schedule.

5.4. CONCLUSION

With the negotiation of the GATS, policies affecting access to service markets are firmly on the multilateral trade-policy agenda. Only time will tell how effective the GATS will prove in terms of liberalizing world trade in services. As it stands, the impact of the GATS is limited. Much depends on how important its architectural shortcomings turn out to be. The key issues here are whether the GATS will stimulate significant liberalization in the future, and whether it will prove helpful to governments that seek to liberalize trade in services and enhance the efficiency of their service industries. Participation in a multilateral agreement imposing certain disciplines and constraints on national policy formation may help a government in pursuing or implementing desired changes in domestic policies. Membership in the GATS may both increase the credibility of initial reform and help governments resist demands from politically influential interest-groups for altering policies in the future. The GATS imposes costs on backsliding, reflected in Article XXI on Modification of Schedules. This provision allows parties to withdraw concessions subject to negotiation with—and compensation of—affected parties. In the event that bilateral negotiations result in inadequate offers of compensation for affected parties, the GATS foresees arbitration. If the Member State withdrawing a concession does not comply with the suggestions of the arbitration panel retaliation may be authorized. The existence of Article XXI will help governments to oppose attempts by domestic industries and other interest-groups desiring to restrict market access at some point after liberalization has occurred.

But, this is all conditional upon significant liberalization taking place. Will membership of the GATS help governments pursue liberalization efforts? The standard rationale for the pursuit of multilateral (reciprocal) liberalization efforts is that increased access to foreign markets is likely to be of interest to domestic export-oriented industries, and that these are then given an incentive to oppose lobbying by import-competing industries against the opening of domestic markets. This political dynamic is arguably less strong in the GATS context because developing countries tend to have less of an interest in service exports (or, more accurately, many of the services where they are likely to have or develop a comparative advantage require movement of labour, and this is a mode of supply that has mostly been kept off the table).

What does the GATS do to help a government liberalize in the face of opposition by powerful domestic lobbies? The non-generality of national treatment is an important negative factor in this connection, as is the sector-specificity of market-access commitments. A government cannot tell its lobbies that because of the GATS it must automatically abide by the national-treatment principle for all sectors and offer foreign firms access to service markets. Instead, it must explicitly list each and every sector to ensure that national-treatment and market-access obligations will apply. This clearly makes matters much more difficult for governments that need an external justification for resisting protectionist pressures. Another weakness of the GATS in this regard is Article XIX, which allows for 'appropriate flexibility for individual developing countries for opening fewer sectors, liberalizing fewer types of transactions, progressively extending market access in line with their development situation and, when making access to their markets available to foreign service suppliers, attaching to it conditions aimed at achieving the objectives' of increasing the participation of developing countries in world trade. This is a guideline for the conduct of future MTNs, not an obligation. But it does give developing countries substantial scope to limit the sectoral coverage of their offers.

More generally, GATS imposes few limitations on national policy, leaving a Member pretty much free to do as it likes in the policy domain, subject to the constraint that no discrimination across alternative sources of supply occurs. It allows parties to implement policies that are detrimental to—or inconsistent with—economic efficiency. A good example is the article specifying the conditions under which measures to safeguard the balance-of-payments may be taken, such measures being inefficient. It can also be noted that the GATS does not require a participating country to alter the regulatory structure of certain service sectors, or to pursue an active anti-trust or competition policy. Liberalization of trade and investment may need to be augmented by regulatory change (frequently deregulation) and an effective competition policy in order to increase the efficiency of service sectors such as finance, transportation, and telecommunications. If liberalization is simply equated with increased market access for (certain) foreign suppliers, this may have little effect in markets that are characterized by a lack of competition. The main result will then simply be to redistribute rents across firms.

While it is important to recognize the weaknesses of the GATS, it must also be recognized that much can be done within its confines if governments prove willing to substantially liberalize international transactions in services. The GATS is just the first step in what will hopefully prove to be a fruitful path leading to substantial liberalization of international transactions in services. The Agreement is likely to be changed over time, especially as experience reveals which of its shortcomings are serious, and which not.

5.5. FURTHER READING

Geza Feketekuty, in *International Trade in Services: An Overview and Blueprint for Negotiations* (Cambridge, Mass.: Ballinger, 1988), offers an excellent and comprehensive discussion of issues relating to services trade; why services were put on the agenda; and what the US goals were in the Uruguay round. See Julian Arkell, 'Lobbying for Market Access for Professional Services', in Michel Kostecki (ed.), *Marketing Strategies for Services* (Oxford: Pergamon Press, 1994) for an insider's account of lobbying and marketing strategies employed by service sectors in the GATS negotiations and in other fora to enhance their access to foreign markets. Various GATS-related topics are discussed in depth in Patrick Messerlin and Karl Sauvant, *The Uruguay Round: Services in the World Economy* (Washington: World Bank, 1990), which also includes a number of country-specific viewpoints. UNCTAD and World Bank, *Liberalizing International Transactions in Services: A Handbook* (Geneva: United Nations, 1994) provides an integrated treatment of the policy issues that arise in liberalizing services, focusing on all four modes of supply. Bernard Hoekman, in 'Tentative First Steps: An Assessment of the Uruguay Round Agreement on Services', in Will Martin and Alan Winters (eds.), *The Uruguay Round and the Developing Economies* (Washington: The World Bank, 1995), offers a detailed analysis of the GATS, the commitments made by Members, and a discussion of the weaknesses of the agreement.

6

Intellectual Property

Multilateral co-operation in the field of intellectual property (IP) dates back more than a century. Although the issue has always been of some relevance to the multilateral trading system—largely in terms of trade in counterfeit goods—it was not until the creation of the WTO that multilateral rules and enforcement mechanisms for a broad range of trade-related IP issues were accepted by trading nations. This chapter provides an overview of the economic rationales for protection of IP and explains why the issue increasingly became related to trade. Some of the major conflicts of interest that shaped the Agreement on Trade-Related Intellectual Property Rights (TRIPs) are summarized, as are the basic elements of the substantive disciplines that are imposed. The TRIPs Agreement is unique in the WTO context in that it imposes obligations upon governments to pursue specific, similar policies. This is in stark contrast with the GATS and the GATT, which consist of agreements not to use specific policies. The TRIPs Agreement is the first example of successful harmonization of policies under GATT auspices.

6.1. INTELLECTUAL PROPERTY PROTECTION AND INTERNATIONAL TRADE

IP can be defined as information with a commercial value. Intellectual property rights (IPRs) have been defined as a mix of ideas, inventions, and creative expression on which there is a public willingness to bestow the status of property (Sherwood, 1990). IPRs comprise industrial property as well as copyrights and so-called neighbouring (related) rights. Industrial property principally concerns protection of inventions through patents and trade marks. The subject-matter of copyright is usually described as 'literary and artistic works'. (For definitions of the various concepts see also the References at the end of this chapter.) Although the rationale for government protection of intellectual property rights (IPRs) depends considerably on the characteristics of the knowledge that is involved, protection of patents, copyrights, and neighbouring rights, industrial secrets and industrial designs have some broad similarities. They differ substantially from trade marks and appellations of origin, which are protected essentially to allow product differentiation and improve consumers' information. The following discussion of the rationale for IP protection focuses on patents, copyrights, and neighbouring rights, and industrial design which falls within the broad category of intellectual property. Trade marks—while clearly intellectual property in the sense of being intangible, are not really knowledge goods. Marks of origin are not 'intellectual' but will be regarded as IPRs in this chapter as they are covered by the TRIPs Agreement. However, the importance of appellations of origin in trade—and as potential protectionist devices—should not be overlooked (see Box 6.1).

Box 6.1. What is 'Noix de Coquille Saint-Jacques'?

National regulations concerning the description or geographical origin of a product may be used as a protectionist device. While appellations of origin are intended to 'protect' a product—in a sense being a guarantee of quality and helping to reassure a consumer about what is being bought, they can be protectionist if used to place identical foreign goods at a disadvantage. This often is attempted by producers of goods that confront import competition. A case in point was a 1993 French regulation concerning the description of scallops, which reserved the use of the expression 'noix de coquille St Jacques'—under which scallops are sold in France, to French production. Canadian harvested scallops were forbidden to be labelled as noix de coquille St Jacques. This negatively affected Canadian exports of scallops to France. Exports of this product stood at some $10 million before the regulation entered into force, equivalent to almost 11 per cent of French imports of scallops. This policy clearly significantly weakened the competitive position of the Canadian scallops on the French market, and could only reduce the level of Canadian exports. After consultations between Canada and the EU, the French legislation was amended to eliminate the discrimination against Canadian producers. Canada is a large trader, and has significant negotiating leverage. In such situations developing countries have much less ability to use negotiations to offset protectionist attempts by import-competing industries.

Source: *GATT Activities*, 1993.

Knowledge often has the characteristics of a public good. That is, its stock does not diminish with its consumption: the marginal cost of disseminating knowledge is often zero. Consequently, from a static efficiency perspective the optimal allocation of resources requires that such goods have a zero price. However, this does not take into consideration that inventions have to be produced and that inventive acts, and especially the development of techno-logical innovations, can require considerable investments and thus costs. With a zero price for knowledge, investors have no pecuniary incentive to invest in research and development (R&D) activities. A zero price is therefore socially sub-optimal in a dynamic sense, since it discourages future innovations and technological progress. Empirical evidence suggests that protection by patent is needed not so much to promote inventions (many of which would occur anyway) but to provide an incentive to engage in costly R&D activities which turn inventions (pure knowledge) into innovations (products or production processes that can be used in industry). The degree of protection afforded to innovations has an impact on inventors' profits and therefore on the amount of money invested in R&D activities.

Patents or copyrights grant an inventor or author a temporary monopoly over the use of the invention or the reproduction of a work, and prevent competitors from sharing or using their knowledge without payment. This enables the owners to recoup their investments and secure their economic interests, thus creating an incentive for the production of knowledge. IP protection also contributes to more rapid public disclosure of inventions. It is often suggested that in the absence of such protection certain types of industrial inventions and the associated technical information would be kept secret much longer. Governments are generally concerned with establishing an optimal balance between the need for monopoly and the benefits of free access to knowledge. In formulating their IPR policies they must reconcile static efficiency considerations (which imply that knowledge should be free) with the longer-term objectives of encouraging innovation and technological progress. There is no unique answer to this conundrum. Whether a given policy of IP protection is optimal or not depends on the objectives and circumstances of countries and the economic sectors involved. Conflicts of interest between countries can easily occur.

IPRs became a trade issue for a number of reasons. International trade in goods embodying IP has increased substantially in recent decades. A number of industrialized market economies, concerned with the erosion of the competitiveness of their industries, increasingly felt that inadequate protection of IP in technology-importing countries reduced their competitive advantage in the high-technology area. Although trade in counterfeit goods had been around for a long time, as technologies for duplication became more advanced and the reproduction of IP easier and cheaper, trade in goods embodying stolen IP became an increasingly contentious issue. Examples of counterfeit include imitations of premium goods such as fake Cartier watches, Lego toys, Sony Walkmen, or Vuitton handbags, as well as copies of compact discs, software, and video films. Resulting disputes were frequently addressed through bilateral channels, with trade sanctions used as the stick with which to induce acquiescence. The United States played a particularly prominent role in using unilateral threats of sanctions to deal with perceived IP infringements. The two main instruments used were Section 337 of the 1930 US Tariff Act, and

Section 301 of the 1974 Trade Act, as amended by the 1988 Omnibus Trade and Competitiveness Act (see Box 6.2).

Box 6.2. Sections 301 and 337 of US trade law

Section 301 of the US Trade Act of 1974 gives the President authority to retaliate against foreign-trade practices which discourage US exports. What these practices could be were not spelled out in the legislation. It was left to the discretion of the President whether to retaliate. A Section 301 action is initiated by private parties in the USA, and will usually result in pressure on the foreign government to adopt different policies. In cases where this is not possible or is deemed to be insufficient, 301 cases may involve attempts to negotiate 'voluntary import expansion' agreements. If negotiations fail, the USA may retaliate by restricting access to its market.

The Omnibus Trade and Competitiveness Act of 1988 introduced changes to 301, rendering it much more threatening to foreign traders. Because Congress felt that the President had not been vigorous enough in pursuing the unfair trading practices of other nations, the 1988 Act required formal investigations of private complaints, and created a new procedure—the so-called 'Super' 301—that required the Administration—the US Trade Representative (USTR)—to create an inventory of 'unfair' practices in foreign countries; select priority targets from that list; set deadlines for removal of the offending measures; and restrict the exports of these countries if the practices concerned were not eliminated. Super 301—which dealt with identification of and action on trade liberalization priorities more generally, was complemented by a new 'Special' 301 provision that pertained to the identification of countries whose protection of intellectual property was inadequate. It is Special 301 that is relevant to this chapter.

Section 337 of the US Tariff Act of 1930 allows for investigations to be initiated to determine whether foreign producers of goods that are imported into the USA are supported by unfair trade practices and are injuring an efficiently operating US industry; act to prevent the establishment of such an industry; or are anti-competitive (restrain trade). What these practices are is not defined precisely, but many of the cases brought under Section 337 have involved claims of infringement of US-held IPRs. The Omnibus Trade and Competitiveness Act of 1988 eliminated the injury test from Section 337 if the unfair practices concerned violation of IPRs.

US law targets imports, since grievances can be brought only when goods whose production infringes upon the IPRs of Americans are brought to the USA. The law applies US standards of IP protection. The EU has similar instruments, Regulation 2641/84 on illicit commercial practices being the main example. In part, recourse to unilateral instruments reflected the fact that the International Court of Justice, the main dispute-settlement forum in this area, requires agreement between the interested parties to submit the case to it. More generally, some of the countries targeted under instruments such as Special 301 were not members of the relevant international conventions in this field, so that recourse to international dispute settlement was not available. Of course, that does not necessarily justify the unilateral threat-based approach employed by the USA (see Bhagwati and Patrick, 1990).

The use of US trade-law provisions was challenged under GATT dispute-settlement provisions on a number of occasions. In a case concerning certain automotive springs assemblies brought to the GATT by Canada in 1981, the dispute-settlement panel found in favour of the United States, concluding that the US law could be justified as falling under Article XX: d (General Exceptions—see Chapter 7). The panel's findings were endorsed by the Council on the understanding that this did not foreclose future examinations of the use of Section 337 to deal with patent infringement cases. A subsequent panel considered an EEC complaint concerning a Section 337 action against exports of aramid fibres by Akzo, a large Dutch multinational. This panel concluded that Section 337 was inconsistent with Article III: 4 (national treatment), as it discriminated against imported products alleged to infringe US patents. Another IP-related case was initiated by Brazil, after a decision by the USA—following a Section 301 investigation—to increase tariffs on a range of Brazilian products in retaliation against a perceived lack of adequate patent protection for pharmaceuticals and fine chemicals in Brazil. After negotiations, Brazil promised to review its IPR regime and the matter was settled bilaterally. (See Hudec, 1993, for more on these cases.)

Business communities in OECD countries maintained that infringements of IPRs constituted a straightforward matter of piracy and theft, and called for multilateral rules and enforcement of IPRs. Many developing countries initially opposed this strongly, arguing that protection of IP was a policy matter, that non-protection of IP on their part had a negligible impact on producers in OECD countries, and that the adoption of OECD levels of IP protection would be quite detrimental to the welfare of their populations and the development process. For example, patent protection was held to be potentially detrimental to food security by raising the costs of inputs (seeds, fertilizers) or the health of poor populations (which would have to pay more for patent-protected pharmaceutical products). However, interest-groups in developing countries also existed that favoured stronger IP protection. Examples were domestic IP-creating or IP-using industries and sectoral interests where transfer of technology generally requires inward FDI, which in turn is generally conditional on the existence of strong IP protection. Developing countries' acceptance of the TRIPs deal in the Uruguay round stemmed from a mix of fear that without it they would be increasingly vulnerable to unilateral arm-twisting by the USA and the EU, and a growing perception that IP laws also had benefits in terms of allowing participation in knowledge-creating activities, providing consumers with access to new products, and giving industries better opportunities of obtaining cutting-edge technologies.

6.2. INTERNATIONAL CONVENTIONS AND GATT HISTORY

Several international conventions exist which lay down standards for the protection of intellectual property. These include the Paris Convention (on patents and trademarks), the Berne Convention (on copyright), the Rome Convention (on neighbouring rights), and the Treaty on Intellectual Property in Respect of Integrated Circuits (see Table 6.1). These and other conventions are administered by the World Intellectual Property Organization (WIPO), a Geneva-based UN body. Both the Paris and Berne Conventions date from the nineteenth century, but have been periodically updated and expanded. The need for international co-operation on IPRs arose as early as the nineteenth century because IPRs are country-specific, created by national legislation. As creators of IP must file for an IPR in each jurisdiction where they want protection, they have an incentive to seek that governments adopt similar procedures and standards. Little harmonization occurred, however, and most international conventions did not go much beyond an agreement to apply the national treatment principle.

Most net exporters of IP or IP-intensive goods were not fully satisfied with the existing conventions and sought to fill certain gaps through the TRIPs Agreement. For example, the Paris Convention does not stipulate the minimum duration of patents or define what should be patentable. No international agreements existed on proprietary business information (trade secrets). Better protection of computer software and sound recordings was needed in the view of the industries concerned. Many countries considered that existing agreements dealt inadequately with counterfeiting and that national laws on trade marks were often too weak or poorly enforced. Finally, it was perceived that an effective multilateral dispute-settlement mechanism was needed to deal with IP-related issues. As noted earlier, existing conventions did not contain binding, effective procedures in this regard. A major attraction of the GATT (WTO) was that trade remedies (sanctions) could be made available to enforce the substantive content of the Agreement.

GATT-1947 provisions and work related to IP was limited. Among the GATT provisions referring specifically to IPRs are those on marks of origin

TABLE 6.1 *Major international conventions on intellectual property*

Agreement	Description	Administered by:
Paris Convention* (1883; 129 signatories; revised in 1967)	Protection of patents, trade marks and service marks, trade names, utility models, industrial designs, indications of sources or appellations of origin and the 'repression of unfair competition'. Allows for compulsory licensing.	WIPO
Berne Convention* (1886; 111 signatories; revised in 1971)	Basic copyright treaty based on principles of non-discrimination and national treatment (like Paris Convention).	WIPO
Madrid Agreement (1891; 31 signatories)	Allows imported goods bearing a false origin indication to be seized on importation.	WIPO
Universal Copyright Convention (1952; 57 signatories)	Copyright treaty accommodating US statutory requirements and based on principles of non-discrimination and national treatment.	UNESCO
Lisbon Agreement (1958; 17 signatories)	Protection of appellation of origin.	WIPO
Rome Convention* (1961; 47 signatories)	Protection of neighbouring rights (performers, producers of phonograms, broadcasting organizations).	ILO, UNESCO, and WIPO
Geneva Convention (1971; 52 signatories)	Protection of producers of phonograms against the making of duplicates in another country.	WIPO, ILO, and UNESCO
IPIC Treaty* (1989; 8 signatories)	Treaty on Intellectual Property in Respect of Integrated Circuits.	WIPO

Note: Agreements marked with a * are explicitly referred to in the TRIPs Agreement. The IPIC Treaty had not yet entered into force as of March 1995.

(Article IX)—which require that these not be used so as to restrict trade—and Articles XII:3 and XVIII:10 which state that a condition for using QRs for BOP purposes is that these do not violate IP legislation. A general exceptions provision of the GATT (Article XX:*d*) states that measures necessary to protect IP are not subject to GATT as long as they are non-discriminatory. However, GATT rules such as national treatment (Article III), MFN (Article I), transparency (Article X), and nullification and impairment (Article XXIII) can apply to actions taken in connection with the enforcement of IPRs. As discussed below, a number of IP-related disputes were brought to the GATT. More generally, the relevance of GATT provisions for IPRs was limited, in so far as no substantive disciplines existed with respect to IP protection by contracting parties, and GATT rules (e.g. national treatment) relate to products, whereas those of the IP conventions concern persons. IP-related matters raised in the GATT mainly concerned trade in counterfeit goods. They also arose under the Multifibre Arrangement (trade-mark and design infringement), the Agreement on Trade in Civil Aircraft (counterfeit civil aircraft parts), the Agreement on Technical Barriers to Trade (access to and misuse of certification marks), and the Customs Valuation Agreement (appraisal of the value of IPRs in connection with goods being imported), and marks of origin (prevention of unwarranted impediments and distortions to international trade arising from marking requirements).

The two closest links between IPRs and GATT arose in discussions on counterfeit goods and in a number of dispute-settlement cases. Informal negotiations on trade in counterfeit goods were held during the Tokyo round, and led to the tabling of a draft code on the subject by the United States. However, no agreement on this issue proved possible (Winham, 1986). The issue was first put formally on the GATT agenda in November 1982, when Ministers asked the Council to determine whether it would be appropriate to take joint action in the GATT framework on trade in counterfeit goods and, if so, what this action should be. In 1985 a Group of Experts established to advise the Council concluded that trade in counterfeit goods was a growing problem that needed multilateral action, but could not agree on whether the GATT was the right forum for this. This question was resolved at the Ministerial meeting at Punta del Este that launched the Uruguay round, with the agreement to put TRIPs on the agenda.

6.3. THE URUGUAY ROUND NEGOTIATIONS

TRIPs was one of the more difficult issues on the Uruguay round agenda, both politically and technically. The issue was new to GATT and involved a North–South confrontation. Industrial countries, led by the United States, sought an ambitious and comprehensive agreement on standards for protection of IP of all kinds. They argued that negotiations should consider a wide range of IP issues and that enforcement through the WTO's dispute-settlement system as well as through domestic laws and customs procedures was a must. These demands were of great concern to many developing countries. Led by the same countries that opposed comprehensive discussions on services—India, Brazil, Egypt, Argentina, and Yugoslavia—they sought to draw a firm distinction between work on trade in counterfeit goods and that on TRIPs more broadly defined. They were willing to co-operate on the former, but opposed the latter.

The first order of priority for poor countries was to ensure that unilateral measures to protect IP did not cause barriers to legitimate trade. There was a general concern that greater protection of IPRs would strengthen the monopoly power of multinational companies, and detrimentally affect poor populations by raising the price of medicines and food. Given that the duration of patent protection—if granted at all—was generally shorter than in developed countries, this was a valid concern.

The first two years of negotiations were dominated by disagreements over the mandate of the negotiating group. Areas of disagreement included standards of protection, the use of unilateral sanctions, the reach of competition policy, and the need for—and length of—transitional periods. One of the most difficult questions was how far new rules could go to protect intellectual property. Was it acceptable for GATT contracting parties to draft substantive standards on intellectual property and embody them in an international agreement? Some developing countries, led by India, argued that GATT or its successor organization was not the right place for setting and enforcing IP standards. They felt that this was a task for WIPO—which already administered numerous multilateral conventions—and for individual governments themselves. As far as unilateral sanctions were concerned, developing countries wanted industrialized nations to renounce the option of unilateral trade sanctions. They called for a credible commitment to multilateral dispute-settlement procedures. This aspect of the negotiations was further complicated by the initial US refusal to change its legislation (Section 337), which a GATT panel had found to be discriminatory in nature. The USA linked modifying its laws to conform with the panels recommendations to 'satisfactory' progress in the TRIPs discussions. In the event, the USA did agree to comply with the panel's findings, although implementation was problematical (Hudec, 1993). In contrast to the rest of the agenda, the TRIPs negotiations were not about freeing trade, but about more protection. As IPRs create market power, developing countries sought assurances that action could be taken against the abuse of monopoly rights by IPR holders. Adoption of stricter IP protection takes time. Moreover, given the complete absence of such rights in many countries, enforcement of IPRs would entail adjustment costs. Developing countries therefore insisted on a long transitional period during which changes in domestic legislation could be implemented.

The foregoing summary illustrates that the TRIPs talks neatly divided developed countries—the major net exporters of IP—from many developing countries—all net importers. But gains from trade were clearly available, as each group had things to offer that the other wanted. Developing countries wanted to control the USA; maintain sufficient discretion to safeguard national interests; and minimize the adjustment costs of strengthening IP protection. OECD countries sought stronger standards, multilaterally agreed, with multilateral enforcement. Incentive structures also differed over the course of the

Uruguay round. It is important in this connection that developing countries were not really a cohesive bloc on the TRIPs issue. Some of the poorer nations that had tightened their domestic protection of IPRs unilaterally so as to attract FDI and technology or as a response to the threat of US action, feared to be undercut by competitors in other developing countries (Mansfield, 1994). Potential cross-issue trade-offs further enlarged the scope for a successful conclusion. In exchange for progress on TRIPs, poor nations and transition economies could seek more open markets for their agricultural products and better market access for their textile exports. They also increasingly felt that stricter IP protection was in their interest, if only because it was a necessary component of a more general move towards a market economy.

6.4. WTO RULES

The TRIPs Agreement is an integral part of the WTO. It is a far-reaching, complex Agreement—with seven major parts and 73 Articles—that covers copyrights and related rights (rights of performers, broadcasters, and phonogram producers), layout-designs of integrated circuits, geographical origin indications, trade marks, industrial designs, and patents. The Agreement:

(1) establishes minimum substantive standards of protection of the above rights;
(2) prescribes procedures and remedies which should be available in Member States to enforce rights;
(3) makes the general dispute-settlement mechanism of WTO available to address TRIPs-related conflicts; and
(4) extends basic GATT principles such as transparency, national treatment, and MFN to IPRs.

However, some exceptions are allowed on non-discrimination, in recognition of the fact that a number of international conventions permit such discrimination in specific circumstances.

Minimum Standards of Protection

The Agreement is built upon the main international conventions negotiated under the World Intellectual Property Organization (WIPO). With respect to copyrights, Members are required to comply with the substantive provisions of the Berne Convention for the protection of literary and artistic works, except as concerns protection of moral rights. Computer software is to be protected as a literary work under the Berne Convention. The conditions under which databases should be protected by copyright are clearly specified. A very significant addition to international rules on copyrights are the provisions on rental rights, giving authors of computer programs and producers of sound recordings the right to authorize or prohibit the commercial rental of their works to the public. A similar exclusive right is also applicable to films. Performers are to be given protection from unauthorized recording and broadcast of live performances (bootlegging). The protection for producers of sound recordings and performers is to be for at least fifty years, while broadcasting stations are granted a twenty-year period during which use of their programmes requires their authorization.

The Agreement defines the types of marks eligible for protection as a trade mark or service mark. It also specifies the minimum rights that Members must grant to mark owners. Marks that have become well-known in a particular market enjoy additional protection. For example, owners of foreign marks may not be forced to use their marks in conjunction with local marks. Governments must provide means to prevent the use of any geographical indications that mislead consumers as to the origin of goods and are required to discourage any use which would constitute unfair competition. Trade marks containing a geographical indication which misleads the public as to the true origin of the product are to be refused or invalidated. Geographical indications for wines and spirits are given more effective protection. A multilateral system of registration and notification of geographical indications for wines is to be negotiated in the future. The protection of industrial designs is considerably improved. Such designs are to be protected for a minimum period of ten years. Owners of such designs may prevent the importation, sale, or production of products bearing a design which is a copy of the protected one.

WTO members are required to comply with the substantive provisions of the Paris Convention (1967) on patents. At least twenty-year patent protection is to be provided for almost all inventions, including both processes and products. The twenty-year lower limit implies harmonization towards the standards maintained by industrialized countries (e.g. Indian patent length for pharmaceutical production processes was only seven years as of the late 1980s, whereas no patents were provided at all for pharmaceutical products). The permitted exclusions from patentability comprise plants and animals (other than micro-organisms) as well as essentially biotechnological processes. Plant varieties, however, have to be given protection. This can be done either by patents or by a *sui generis* (special or more specific) system, which may be akin to those defined in applicable international conventions.[1] Inventions may also be excluded from patentability for reasons of morality, public order, or because of therapeutic, diagnostic, or surgical usefulness.

There are detailed rules concerning compulsory licensing and government

---

[1] The main international convention in this area is the Union for the Protection of Plant Varieties (UPOV), which deals with breeders' rights. The TRIPs Agreement does not require membership of the UPOV (Braga, 1995).

use of patents without the owner's authorization. As a general rule rights conferred in respect of patents for processes must extend to the products directly obtained by the process. The Treaty on Intellectual Property in Respect of Integrated Circuits (1989) provides the basis for the protection of layout designs of integrated circuits. The TRIPs Agreement goes beyond this Treaty by requiring a minimum protection period of ten years and extension of rights to articles incorporating infringing layout designs. Trade secrets and know-how of commercial value are protected against acts contrary to honest commercial practices such as breach of confidence. Test data on agricultural or pharmaceutical chemicals submitted to the authorities in order to obtain marketing approval must also be protected against unfair commercial use.

WTO members are obliged to provide procedures and remedies under their domestic law for effective enforcement of IPRs by right-holders (both foreign and national). Such procedures should be fair and equitable, should entail reasonable time-limits, and not be unnecessarily complicated or costly. Requirements on the civil and administrative procedures and remedies include provisions on evidence of proof, injunctions, damages, and other remedies. In cases when delay is likely to result in irreparable harm to the right-holder, prompt and effective provisional measures must be available. The Agreement also deals with measures to be taken at the border by customs authorities against pirated or counterfeit goods.

All Members have one year following the date of entry into force of the WTO to implement the provisions of the TRIPs agreement. Developing countries are entitled to a delay of an additional four years for all provisions of the Agreement with the exception of national treatment and MFN. If countries in the process of transition to a market economy are facing special problems in the preparation and implementation of intellectual property laws, they may also request the right to benefit from the four-year period. Least-developed countries have ten years to conform with the Agreement, and may request extensions of this period. To the extent that a developing country must extend product patent protection to areas of technology that currently cannot be protected in its territory (e.g. pharmaceuticals or agricultural chemicals), it may delay the application of the provisions on product patents to these areas for an additional period of five years, bringing the total to ten.

While it has been claimed that these transition periods are long (especially by the pharmaceutical industry in the USA), it should be kept in mind that transition periods for the abolition of the MFA and agricultural liberalization by OECD countries are also long. Implementation of the TRIPs Agreement will involve adjustment costs for developing countries. While these costs are not incurred gradually (as is the case with incremental implementation of liberalization commitments on e.g. textiles and clothing), the transition period reduces the aggregate cost. Similarly, while there may remain some holes in the TRIPs agreement as far as OECD industry is concerned, these are less large than those allowing, for example, for the imposition of contingent protection against developing-country exports. A case can be made that as far as the structural adjustment associated with the Uruguay round is concerned, developing countries committed themselves to doing as much, if not more, on the new IP issue as OECD countries did with regard to an old issue such as protection of their textiles and clothing industries (see Chapter 8).

6.5. CONCLUSION

The GATT and the GATS are similar in that an attempt was made to agree to general rules and principles relating to trade policies, and to obtain country-specific liberalization commitments. No harmonization of policies was pursued. This is in marked contrast to the TRIPs agreement, which establishes minimum standards of intellectual property protection that must be achieved by all members of the WTO. The TRIPs agreement is noteworthy in the multilateral trade context in that it obliges governments to take positive action to protect intellectual property rights. GATT and GATS do not require governments to pursue specific policies; they merely impose disciplines on (constrain) signatories regarding the types of policies they may pursue. The question of whether seeking harmonization of policies and regulatory regimes that indirectly affect trade is a desirable approach in the multilateral context has attracted increasing attention recently (see Bhagwati, 1994*a*; and Chapter 11). Abstracting from the important normative issues, the TRIPs agreement, as well as the agreement relating to sanitary and phyto-sanitary measures (Chapter 4), illustrates that multilateral agreement on minimum standards is possible. The approach taken in the TRIPs Agreement is somewhat analogous to a Directive in the EU context: the Agreement specifies certain objectives (minimum standards), but leaves it to signatories to determine how these requirements will be implemented (Article 1: 'Members shall be free to determine the appropriate method of implementing the provisions of this Agreement within their own legal system and practice').

The final outcome of negotiations suggests that US pharmaceutical, entertainment, and informatics industries, which were largely responsible for getting TRIPs on the agenda, obtained much, if not most, of what was desired when the negotiations were launched. US industries sought multilaterally agreed minimum standards of IP protection in GATT member countries, an obligation to enforce such standards, and the creation of an effective multilateral dispute-settlement process. Much was achieved in terms of negotiating an agreement with substantive obligations and few loopholes. It is fair to say that developing countries agreed to substantially more than even an optimist might have hoped for in 1986 when the round began.

There are no definitive empirical estimates of the impact of the TRIPs agreement on developing countries (see Maskus and Eby-Konan, 1994). Much depends in this connection on the dynamic effects of the agreement. The static impact is unambiguously negative for those countries that do not provide patent protection, but even here the magnitude is unknown. Market structure and conduct is very important. However, as noted by one economist, 'all evidence and arguments . . . point to the conclusion that, to a first-order approximation, TRIPs is a redistributive issue: irrespective of assumptions made with respect to market structure or dynamic response, the impact effect of enhanced IPR protection . . . will be a transfer of wealth from [developing country] consumers and firms to foreign, mostly industrial-country firms' (Rodrik, 1994*b*: 449). Countries perceiving a loss from protecting IP will obtain off-setting gains from greater access to export markets for their goods.

At some level, it seems clear that a trade-off was made between TRIPs and the rest of the agenda (the MFA, a services agreement that accorded well with the preferences of many developing countries, and a stronger dispute-settlement mechanism), although it is not possible to identify specific (formal) linkages. Thus, e.g., reversals on the MFA-front may give rise to non-implementation on the IP-front. The regime shift that occurred among many developing countries in the 1980s in their attitudes towards inward FDI also played a role in inducing their acceptance of the Agreement. Attracting FDI in certain higher-tech sectors requires enforcement of IPRs. Other variables were no doubt the threat of unilateral action on the part of the United States (but also the EU), the acceptance by OECD countries of long transition periods for developing countries, and a recognition that without a deal on TRIPs, ratification of the Uruguay round package in the US Congress was unlikely given the political weight of the US industries supporting strong IPR disciplines.

6.6. FURTHER READING

An overview of various forms of intellectual property and a brief discussion of international conventions on IPRs is included in: WIPO, *General Information* (Geneva: World Intellectual Property Organization, 1988). A comprehensive review of the interaction between protection of intellectual property rights and trade is presented in a special issue of the *Vanderbilt Journal of Transnational Law*, 22/4 (1989). The linkages between protection of IP and development are explored in Wolfgang Siebeck (ed.), *Strengthening Protection of Intellectual Property in Developing Countries* (Washington DC: The World Bank, 1990) and Robert Sherwood, *Intellectual Property and Economic Development* (Boulder, Colo.: Westview Press, 1990).

For an account of the US multifaceted programme in the 1970s to improve the international protection of IPRs and efforts to address the issue in the GATT, see William Walker, 'Private Initiative to Thwart the Trade in Counterfeit Goods', *The World Economy* (March 1981). The role of the United States in bringing the issue of IPRs onto the agenda of the Uruguay round is described in A. Jane Bradley, 'Intellectual Property Rights, Investment, and Trade in Services in the Uruguay Round: Laying the Foundations', *Stanford Journal of International Law* (Spring 1987), 57–98. A brief negotiating history of trade-related aspects of IP in GATT and the Uruguay round is presented in Michel Kostecki, 'Sharing Intellectual Property Between the Rich and the Poor', *European Intellectual Property Review*, 13 (1991), 271–4. Carlos Primo Braga, in 'Trade Related Intellectual Property Issues: The Uruguay Round Agreement and its Economic Implications', in Will Martin and Alan Winters (eds.), *The Uruguay Round and the Developing Countries* (Washington DC: The World Bank, 1995), provides a comprehensive summary of the TRIPs negotiations, an analysis of the outcome, and the likely economic impact of the Agreement.

PART III
Holes and Loopholes

7

Safeguards

Virtually all existing international trade agreements or arrangements contain safeguard provisions. The WTO is no exception. Broadly defined, the term 'safeguard protection' refers to a provision in a trade agreement permitting governments under specified circumstances to withdraw—or cease to apply— their normal obligations under the agreement in order to protect (safeguard) certain overriding interests. Safeguard provisions are often critical to the existence and operation of trade-liberalizing agreements, as they function as both insurance mechanisms and safety-valves. They provide governments with the means to renege on specific liberalization commitments—subject to certain conditions—should the need for this arise (safety-valve). Without them governments may refrain from signing an agreement that reduces protection substantially (insurance motive). This chapter focuses largely on the safeguards embodied in the GATT. Those of the GATS are either very similar or still in an embryonic stage.

The GATT's safeguard provisions can be separated into two categories. The first are those that can be used in the event of the occurrence of a pre-defined set of circumstances which legitimize temporary increases in import barriers. The second constitute permanent exceptions to the general obligations of the GATT. The first category can be further divided into those dealing with so-called 'unfair' trading practices (such as exports benefiting from actionable subsidies or dumped exports) and those which can be applied without having to demonstrate 'unfairness'. In this chapter, the term 'safeguards' covers all of the possibilities noted above. Safeguard provisions in the GATT that allow for the temporary suspension of obligations include:

Anti-dumping (AD): measures to deal with dumping—pricing of exports below what is charged in the home market—that materially injures a domestic industry (Article VI);

Countervailing duties (CVDs): measures to offset the effect of subsidization that causes or threatens material injury to a domestic industry (Article VI);

Balance of payments (BOP): restrictions on imports to safeguard a country's external financial position (Articles XII and XVIII:*b*);

Infant industries: governmental assistance for economic development, allowing import restrictions to protect infant industries (Articles XVIII:*a* and XVIII:*c*);

Emergency protection: temporary protection in cases where imports of a product cause or threaten serious injury to domestic producers of directly competitive products (Article XIX); and

General waivers: allowing Members to ask for permission not to be bound by an obligation (Article XXV). In contrast to the other mechanisms, this requires formal approval by the GATT Council.

Provisions of the GATT allowing for permanent exceptions from the general obligations of the Agreement include:

General Exceptions: measures to safeguard public morals, health, laws, and natural resources, subject to the requirement that such measures are non-discriminatory and are not a disguised restriction on trade (Article XX);

National security: allowing intervention on national security grounds (Article XXI); and

Tariff renegotiation: allowing for the withdrawal of certain tariff concessions (i.e. tariff reductions that were bound) if compensation is offered to affected Members (Article XXVIII).

Summarizing, there are at least eight GATT safeguard provisions, with the following objectives: (1) facilitating adjustment of an industry (Art. XIX); (2) establishment of an industry (Art. XVIII:*a* and *c*); (3) combating 'unfair' trade (Art. VI); (4) allowing for a permanent change of mind, through renegotiating of tariff concessions (Art. XXVIII); (5) seeking a derogation (waiver) from specific GATT rules with the agreement of a majority of members (Art. XXV); (6) dealing with macroeconomic (balance-of-payments) problems (Articles XII and XVIII:*b*); (7) achieving health, safety, and related objectives (Art. XX); and (8) maintaining national security (Art. XXI). The first five allow for the protection of a specific industry; the last three have an economy-wide rationale. All the industry-specific instruments are (imperfect) substitutes for each other, as to a large extent they all address the same issue: protection of domestic firms from foreign competitive pressures. Indeed, in practice the BOP provision is also often used to protect specific industries by developing countries. All these measures are GATT-legal.

It is noteworthy that the GATS does not have provisions allowing for AD actions, CVDs, or infant-industry protection. Moreover, its analogue to GATT Article XIX remains to be drafted. This suggests that some learning may have occurred from GATT experience. Although the GATS does not embody a provision allowing for the request of a waiver from some of its disciplines, Article IX of the WTO allows for waivers to be granted for any of the multilateral agreements under the WTO (see Chapter 2). The GATS does contain provisions allowing for actions to safeguard the balance of payments, for general exceptions, and for renegotiation of commitments. These provisions are similar to those of the GATT, except the one on modification of schedules. This differs from GATT by calling for mandatory arbitration if no agreement can be reached on compensation.

The goal of the drafters of the GATT-1947 was that Article XIX would be the main escape clause used to grant temporary protection to industries finding it too difficult to adjust to increased import competition following trade liberalization. AD and countervailing options were included in large part at the behest of the USA, which had such statutes on the books, although they were rarely used. Over time, industrialized countries increasingly shifted away from invoking Article XIX, using AD and CVD procedures to obtain relief from import competition, often in conjunction with—or as an alternative to— the negotiation of VER agreements. The preference for unfair trade remedies became ever more clear during the 1970s and 1980s. Between 1980 and 1986, the EU took 213 AD actions, as compared with only ten Article XIX actions. In the same period, the USA imposed five Article XIX measures, as compared with some 195 AD actions (Finger and Olechowski, 1987: 147, 265). The dominance of AD and VERs in OECD countries reflects the fact that the conditions that need to be satisfied to obtain Article XIX protection have been stringent. Until this was changed in the Uruguay round, Article XIX actions had to be non-discriminatory and affected exporters had the right to claim compensation (or failing adequate compensation, could seek authoriza- tion by the GATT Council to retaliate). Governments often preferred to use other instruments, either because they sought to exempt certain countries, or because they wished to avoid the need for compensation.

Developing countries have frequently invoked Article XVIII:*b* of the GATT to justify 'temporary' protection, generally because of a desire to use QRs. If developing countries desired to impose tariffs for BOP reasons, they usually would not have to invoke Article XVIII, because most had either not bound their tariffs or had bound them at high ceiling rates. In such cases countries are free to impose higher tariffs without being confronted with a compensation requirement (see also Chapters 1 and 3). Over time the use of Article XVIII: b by developing countries has declined, in part due to efforts by the IMF and the World Bank to induce a shift towards more effective and efficient instruments to deal with BOP problems. Table 7.1 provides a brief summary of the frequency with which various safeguard instruments have been invoked.

Safeguard actions, being trade restrictions, distribute income from consu- mers to import-competing (and/or foreign exporting) industries. In general, the mere existence of safeguard instruments may reduce competition between foreign exporters and domestic import-competing firms. Scope may also exist for the capture and abuse of such procedures by import-competing interests, further enhancing such threat effects. Consequently, the gains from the liberal- ization negotiated under an MTN or implemented unilaterally are reduced, and perhaps even eliminated, for certain sectors or for the economy as a whole. In so far as the cause of an import-competing industry's problems lie in a shift in comparative advantage, it needs to adjust to changed circumstances. Protection is generally an inappropriate policy in this regard. Whatever the political

TABLE 7.1 *Frequency of use of safeguard provisions*

Instrument	Frequency of use
Periodic— three-year— renegotiations (at the initiative of the country wanting to increase a bound rate), Arts. XXVIII: 1 and XXVIII: 5.	January 1955–March 1994: 206 renegotiations
Special Circumstances Renegotiations (requires GATT authorization), Art. XXVIII: 4.	64 renegotiations since 1948.
Withdrawal of a concession to provide infant-industry protection, Art. XVIII: *a*.	9 withdrawals, through March 1994.
Waivers, Art. XXV.	Through March 1994: 113 waivers granted, 44 still in force.
Release from bindings to pursue infant-industry protection, Art. XVIII: *c*;	9 countries granted release in 47 years.
Restrictions for BOP purposes by developing countries, Art. XVIII: *b*.	Used by 24 countries at least once during 1974–86; over 3,400 product categories restricted.
Emergency actions to protect an industry, Art. XIX.	1950 through 1984: 124 actions (3.6 a year) 1985 through 1994: 26 actions (3.25 a year)
Countervailing duties, Art. VI.	July 1985–June 1992: 187 investigations (27 a year), of which 106 by the USA, 38 by Australia.
Anti-dumping duties, Art. VI	July 1985–June 1992: 1148 investigations (164 a year), of which 300 by the USA, 282 by Australia, 242 by EU, 124 by Canada, 84 by Mexico.

Source: Finger (1995).

rationale for safeguard instruments, their mere existence may reduce competitive pressure on domestic import-competing firms (by raising prices, reducing incentives to innovate, etc.). They are also all inefficient, in the sense that the costs to consumers are almost invariably larger than the benefits that accrue to the protected industry. In addition, industries can be expected to exploit substitution possibilities across instruments if these exist, making it more difficult for governments to control trade policy.

The various safeguards allowed under the GATT—and AD in particular—are an important hole in the trading system. They can seriously undermine the liberalizing dynamic of the WTO, and limit the usefulness of the WTO to governments that seek 'protection' from protectionist lobbies. Any international agreement must allow for Members to diverge from the relevant disciplines if events require this. The GATT is no exception. A major problem, however, is that there are too many loopholes that permit a Member to reimpose protection. Some progress was made in strengthening the rules in the Uruguay round. Much more remains to be done.

7.1. RENEGOTIATION OF CONCESSIONS

The GATT allows governments to renegotiate tariff concessions and schedules (Article XXVIII). Renegotiation concerns the compensation that must be offered as a quid pro quo for raising a bound rate. Modification of schedules takes three basic forms:

(1) 'open season' renegotiations, which may be conducted every three years following a binding;
(2) 'special circumstances renegotiations', which may take place when approved by GATT members; and
(3) 'reserved right renegotiations', which may occur at any time during the three-year period following a binding if a notification is made by interested governments to that end (Dam, 1970).

Developing countries may follow a simplified procedure to modify or withdraw concessions. In negotiating the compensation required, account is taken of the interests of the country with which the concession was originally negotiated (which has so-called 'initial negotiating rights'—INRs), the interest of the country having a 'principal supplying' interest, as well as that of countries having a 'substantial interest'. Principal or substantial supplying interest requires a major or a sizeable share, respectively, in the market concerned, determined on the basis of import statistics for the last three years for which information is available.[1]

Countries having a substantial interest in the concession concerned (the negotiated tariff binding) have consultation rights only, whereas countries that have INRs or are principal suppliers have negotiation rights. In disputed cases it is up to the Council to determine whether a given country is a principal supplier or whether it has a substantial interest in the concession withdrawn. No such cases arose under GATT-1947, however. The main objective of the principal-supplier rule is to provide for the participation in the negotiations, in addition to the country with the INRs, of countries with a larger share in the trade affected by the concession than the country with INRs might have. This allows a balance to be maintained between the old, previously negotiated situation and new trade patterns that emerge over time. Exceptionally, when the concession to be withdrawn affects trade which constitutes a major part of

---

[1] Principal supplying interest is determined with reference to the share in the export market; substantial supplying interest is determined in relation to a country's total volume of exports.

the total exports of a given country, the country may also enjoy principal-supplier status (Article XXVIII: 1). If no agreement is reached on compensation, affected countries may withdraw 'equivalent concessions'. The WTO Understanding on the Interpretation of Article XXVIII enhanced the opportunities of affected exporters to participate in tariff renegotiations. The GATT Member for which the relative importance of exports of the product on which a tariff is increased is the highest (defined as exports of the product to the market concerned as a proportion of the country's total exports) will be considered to have a principal supplying interest if it does not already have so (or an INR) under pre-existing GATT-1947 procedures.

The mechanisms for—and disciplines on—modification of tariff schedules have seen steady use. Before the completion of the Uruguay round, on average renegotiation of concessions occurred every year with respect to some 100 items, as compared to some 80,000 tariff lines bound. During the 1955–95 period over thirty GATT contracting parties utilized the renegotiation option more than 200 times. In comparison with AD, CVD, and BOP actions, tariff renegotiations have been of relatively minor significance. In any event, in contrast to the former, renegotiations imply that affected parties are compensated for increases in tariffs.

7.2. WAIVERS

Tariff renegotiations are limited in nature: by definition they only pertain to instances in which a country wants to raise tariffs above bound levels. Article XXV: 5 of the GATT allows a Member to ask to be excused from one or more other obligations of the GATT. As noted before, Article IX of the WTO allows waivers to be requested for any obligation imposed under a Multilateral Trade Agreement. The conditions under which waivers are granted are negotiated. Table 7.1 shows that over 100 waivers were granted in the first forty-five years of GATT history, of which forty-four were in effect in 1994. From a systemic perspective, the waiver option allows for Members to obtain an exemption from a specific rule in situations where they might otherwise have been forced to withdraw from the Agreement because of political imperatives at home. Waivers can be good or bad from an economic perspective. For example, a number of waivers were granted to countries under GATT-1947, allowing them to impose surcharges on imports for BOP purposes. Although this is an inferior instrument to deal with a BOP problem, at least it is better than the instrument called for by the relevant GATT Article—i.e. QRs. The option of asking for a waiver in such situations was welfare-improving.

By far the most famous waiver was one requested by the United States in 1955. As noted in Chapter 4, QRs are allowed under Article XI of the GATT for agricultural commodities as long as concurrent measures are taken to restrict domestic production or to remove a temporary domestic surplus. Although it was the USA that drafted this rule when negotiating the GATT, it proved too stringent for Congress. The latter did not wish to be bound by any international agreement and forced the Administration to ask for a waiver of this obligation in 1955. The waiver was necessary as existing US programmes supported domestic industries such as sugar and dairy without incorporating any incentives to reduce output. The root of the problem was Section 22 of the Agricultural Adjustment Act, which states that the Secretary of Agriculture must advise the President if he believes any agricultural commodity is being imported so as to interfere with Department of Agriculture price-support programmes. Depending on the finding of an investigation into the matter, he may impose fees or QRs. Because Section 22 violated GATT rules, US Administrations were reluctant to apply it. However, Congress had no such inhibitions, and amended Section 22 in 1951 to require the President to carry out its provisions regardless of international agreements, i.e. the GATT (Evans, 1972: 72).

Under the WTO, disciplines on waivers were tightened (Article IX WTO). Any waiver in effect at the entry into force of the WTO was agreed to expire by January 1997, unless extended by the WTO Ministerial Conference by a three-quarters majority. This compares with the two-thirds requirement under GATT-1947. Waivers under the WTO must have an expiry date— which was not required under GATT-1947—and must be reviewed annually to ascertain if the 'exceptional circumstances' requiring a waiver continue to exist. These changes substantially strengthened the disciplines over the use of this loophole.

7.3. ARTICLE XIX: GATT'S GENERAL INDUSTRY-SPECIFIC SAFEGUARD

Article XIX is GATT's general escape clause. It permits governments to impose 'emergency protection' in order to protect producers that are seriously injured by imports. The main rationale for the general safeguard clause is to allow some 'flexibility' with respect to tariff commitments, thereby promoting trade-liberalization efforts. Article XIX is a safety-valve. Designing a safeguard mechanism in such a way that a balance is achieved between making it difficult to open the safety-valve and avoiding an explosion of the boiler is not easy. The drafters of the GATT chose to be rather strict in this regard. Necessary conditions for the invocation of Article XIX under GATT-1947 were: (1) the existence of increased imports; which (2) resulted from unforeseen developments; (3) were the consequence of trade liberalization negotiated in an MTN; and (4) caused or threatened serious injury to domestic producers. Safeguard measures had to be imposed on a non-discriminatory basis. The interests of affected exporting countries were protected by a requirement that they be compensated. If no agreement was reached in consultations on compensation, an exporting country could be authorized to retaliate (or suspend equivalent concessions or other obligations) against the safeguard-taking country. The compensation requirement made Article XIX a substitute for Article XXVIII, the main difference being that the latter allows for a permanent change. However, although in principle Article XIX actions were temporary, no formal time-limits were imposed. As a result some actions taken by contracting parties lasted for many years (Sampson, 1987).

Only 150 official safeguard actions were taken by GATT contracting parties up to 1994. Of these, twenty involved payment or offer of compensation—mostly in earlier cases—while retaliation occurred in thirteen instances (GATT, 1994*b*). Article XIX was therefore used relatively infrequently: alternative instruments—Article XXVIII renegotiations, AD, and VERs—were preferred by industries and governments. Reasons for this included the requirement that safeguard actions be non-discriminatory (that they affect all exporters), a preference for QRs (which are much more difficult to implement in a non-discriminatory manner than a tariff), the need to offer compensation, and the fact that in some jurisdictions (such as the USA) granting of emergency protection is subject to the discretion of the President, who is required to take into account the impact of a positive action on the economy. The relatively stringent conditions for obtaining Article XIX cover for protection reflected the fact that such protection violates earlier tariff commitments. This is not the case under AD. As dumping is defined to be 'unfair', actions are legitimized as long as it is shown that dumping occurred and that it materially injured domestic industries.

In addition to AD—discussed below—VERs became a favourite 'safe-guard' instrument in the 1970s and 1980s (Kostecki, 1987). Although illegal under the GATT if governments negotiated or enforced them, (GATT, 1994*b*: 434), VERs did not lead to any formal dispute-settlement cases. Third-country exporters, including the 'principal suppliers' with which original tariff concessions on the goods involved had been negotiated, often did not have an incentive to oppose VERs restricting competitors. Affected exporters tended to accept VERs because they were better than the alternative—often an AD duty—as they allowed them to capture part of the rent that was created. Instead of being confronted with a tariff, the revenue of which is captured by the levying government, a VER involves voluntary cut-backs by exporters in their supplies to a market. This reduction in supply will raise prices—assuming that other exporters do not take up the slack. Exporters may therefore get more per unit sold than they would under an equivalent tariff. There is a very large literature on VERs that will not be discussed here (see Section 7.10 on Further Reading). The key point to remember about VERs is that they imply some direct compensation of affected exporters and selectively target exporters. Thus, they partially meet GATT-1947's compensation requirement, while allowing for the circumvention of its non-discrimination requirement. It should also be recalled that provisions such as Articles XIX or XXVIII are only relevant if tariffs have been bound. If this is not the case, countries may employ other types of safeguard policies. A good example is the EU's agricultural policy, under which variable levies are imposed on imports so as to insulate domestic farmers from the vagaries of international markets. For GATT's rules to bite fully, tariffs must be bound. As discussed in Chapter 8, one result of the Uruguay round was that all agricultural tariffs are to be bound.

By the time of the Uruguay round, the major objective of 'target' countries was to constrain the use of AD and VERs and assert the dominance of Article XIX in safeguard cases—those where the problem relates to the need to facilitate adjustment by slowing the growth of imports: the majority of all cases. The problem was how to achieve this goal. Two options were available: either to tighten the disciplines on the use of AD, or to reduce the disincentives to use Article XIX. Both approaches were pursued. In the event the first avenue did not prove very fruitful, and attention centred instead on making Article XIX more palatable to 'invoking' countries or lobbies.

The Uruguay Round Agreement

A major achievement of the Uruguay round Agreement on Safeguards is a prohibition of VERs and similar measures on the export or the import side (such as export moderation, export-price or import-price monitoring systems, export or import surveillance, compulsory import cartels, and discretionary export or import licensing schemes). Any such measure in effect as of January 1995 must be brought into conformity with the substantive requirements of the agreement on safeguards or phased out before mid-1999. However, one specific measure may be maintained by each Member until the end of 1999 as long as this is mutually agreed between the Members directly concerned and notified to the Committee on Safeguards.

Safeguard measures may only be taken if an investigation demonstrates that imports have increased so much as to have caused or to threaten serious injury to an import-competing domestic industry. Investigations must include reasonable public notice to all interested parties and public hearings or other mechanisms through which traders and other affected parties can present their views as to whether a safeguard measure would be in the public interest. Investigating authorities must publish a report setting forth their findings and reasoning. Serious injury is defined as a significant overall impairment in the situation of a domestic industry. In determining injury, the domestic industry is defined as those firms whose collective output constitutes a major share of total domestic production of the good concerned. In the investigation to determine whether increased imports have caused serious injury, all relevant quantifiable factors must be considered, including the magnitude of the increase in imports, their change in market share, and changes in the level of sales, production, productivity, capacity utilization, profits, and employment of the industry. A causal link must be established between increased imports and serious injury or threat thereof. When factors other than increased imports are causing injury to the domestic industry at the same time, such injury may not be attributed to increased imports.

Protection should be limited to what is necessary to prevent or remedy serious injury. If a QR is used, it may not reduce imports below the average level of the last three representative years, unless clear justification is given that a different level is necessary to prevent or remedy serious injury. While in principle safeguard actions must be non-discriminatory, quota rights may be allocated on a selective basis if the Committee on Safeguards accepts that imports from certain Members have increased 'disproportionately' in comparison with the total increase in imports, and the measures imposed are 'equitable' to all suppliers of the product. Such measures may be maintained for four years at the most. QRs may also be administered by exporters if this is mutually agreed. Thus, although VERs are prohibited, something analogous may be used if implemented as part of a GATT-conforming procedure. Safeguard actions that are based on absolute increases in imports and are consistent with the provisions of the Agreement do not require compensation of affected exporting countries for the first three years. All actions are subject to a sunset clause—of maximum duration of eight years—and are to be degressive. In principle, safeguards should not last more than four years. If extended, a necessary condition is that the industry is adjusting. If individual market shares of developing countries are less than 3 per cent of total imports, and the aggregate share of such countries is less than 9 per cent of total imports, they are exempt from safeguard actions.

On balance, the Agreement on Safeguards constitutes a significant improvement over the status quo ante. As has been the GATT practice in other areas— AD is the prime example, see below—existing practices have to some extent been brought inside the tent, but their use is now subject to multilateral surveillance and rules. Thus, VER-type measures are allowed by the WTO under certain conditions—in contrast to GATT-1947. While this implies a move away from economically preferred policies in an abstract sense, this is an inappropriate bench-mark. The right counterfactual to use for comparison purposes is continued circumvention of GATT-1947 disciplines, which had become increasingly irrelevant. The ban on VERs is a major achievement. Much will depend, however, on its implementation, which in turn will be a function of the willingness of WTO Members to cross-notify VERs and initiate dispute-settlement procedures. Past experience suggests that governments may not have a great incentive to do so. A beneficial step in this connection would be to make VERs unenforceable in domestic law, opening up participating firms to potential anti-trust liability (see Chapter 11). Another key issue is whether the compromises that were made in the safeguards area will prove sufficient to induce a reduction in the use of AD. Given that the injury test is in practice the major barrier for industries seeking protection, and the criteria under Article XIX remain more strict than under AD, doubts can be expressed in this regard.

7.4. ANTI-DUMPING ACTIONS

Loosely defined, dumping occurs when products are sold by a firm in an export market for less than what is charged in its home market for the same product. Dumping is also said to occur if the export price of a product is below the costs of production. GATT rules allow action to be taken against dumped imports if dumping causes or threatens material injury to a domestic import-competing industry. As is the case with other safeguards, AD is an option. GATT disciplines apply only if the option is invoked. Some 2,000 AD investigations have been initiated since the late 1970s, of which over 1,000 occurred in the 1985–1992 period alone (Table 7.2).

The main users of anti-dumping procedures have traditionally been Australia, Canada, the EU, and the USA. More recently, other countries have also become users. As about half of all investigations affect industrialized country exporters, relative to their share in world trade, AD affects developing countries more than proportionately. AD became increasingly controversial during the 1980s as its use expanded. Fifteen AD actions taken by contracting parties were challenged in the GATT between 1989 and 1994, of which five led to the creation of a panel. In all cases the panel found against the country that had taken the AD action, and in a number of instances it recommended that AD duties be removed (Petersmann, 1994). As a result, dispute settlement itself became a major issue in the Uruguay round, with users seeking to circumscribe the power of panels to conclude that specific AD actions violated GATT requirements.

A Brief Summary of GATT Disciplines

The basic GATT provision dealing with AD is Article VI. Starting in the Kennedy round, reflecting increasing use of AD, attempts began to be made to further define multilateral disciplines in this area. An AD Code negotiated in the Kennedy round was opposed by the US Congress, and in practice was only applied in so far as its provisions were consistent with existing US legislation. In the Tokyo round, the AD Code was renegotiated. This Code—which only bound signatories—became the basis of the Uruguay round Agreement on AD that is embodied in the WTO (formally entitled the Agreement on Implementation of Article VI).

Safeguards

TABLE 7.2 *Anti-dumping investigations initiated, 1985–1992*

A	B Total number of cases		C Industrialized countries		D Eastern Europe (including FSU)		E Latin America developing countries		F African and Middle East developing countries		G Asian developing countries	
Initiating Country	No.	(%)	No.	(%)	No.	(%)	No.	(%)	No.	(%)	No.	(%)
Australia	278	(27)	144	(52)	15	(5)	22	(8)	10	(4)	87	(31)
Austria	4	(0)	0	(0)	4	(100)	0	(0)	0	(0)	0	(0)
Brazil	14	(1)	3	(21)	3	(21)	3	(21)	0	(0)	5	(36)
Canada	128	(12)	73	(57)	13	(10)	10	(8)	1	(1)	31	(24)
European Union	159	(15)	42	(26)	46	(29)	14	(9)	6	(4)	51	(32)
Finland	13	(1)	2	(15)	11	(85)	0	(0)	0	(0)	0	(0)
India	5	(0)	1	(20)	0	(0)	3	(60)	0	(0)	0	(0)
Japan	3	(0)	0	(0)	1	(33)	0	(0)	1	(33)	1	(20)
Korea	9	(1)	8	(89)	0	(0)	0	(0)	1	(33)	1	(33)
Mexico	63	(6)	37	(59)	0	(0)	10	(16)	0	(0)	16	(11)
New Zealand	31	(3)	7	(23)	0	(0)	0	(0)	0	(0)	24	(25)
Poland	24	(2)	24	(100)	0	(0)	0	(0)	0	(0)	0	(77)
Sweden	11	(1)	2	(18)	9	(82)	0	(0)	0	(0)	0	(0)
United States	298	(29)	131	(44)	30	(10)	45	(15)	12	(4)	80	(27)
Total	1040	(100)	474	(46)	132	(13)	107	(10)	30	(3)	297	(29)
All countries												
Developing countries	91	(9)	49	(54)	3	(3)	16	(18)	0	(0)	23	(25)
Industrialized countries	949	(91)	425	(45)	129	(14)	91	(10)	30	(3)	274	(29)

Notes: The total number of cases initiated (column *B*) by each country is the sum of the number of cases of all the exporting groups (i.e. columns *C* to *G*).
Percentages in column *B* are shares in the total number of cases for the initiating countries (i.e. 1040).
Percentages in columns *C* to *G* are percentages of the total for the initiating country (given column *B*).
Source: Finger (1994: 110).

Dumping is defined in GATT as offering a product for sale in export markets at a price below 'normal value'. 'Normal value' is defined as the price charged by a firm in its home market, in the 'ordinary course of trade'. Trade is considered not to be ordinary if over an extended period of time (normally one year) a substantial quantity of goods is sold at less than average total costs (i.e. the sum of fixed and variable costs of production plus selling, and general and administrative costs). If sales on its domestic market are too small to allow price comparisons, the highest comparable price charged in third markets or the exporting firm's estimated costs of production plus a 'reasonable' amount for profits, administrative, selling, and any other expenses is to be used to determine normal value (so-called constructed value). In cases where there is no export price or where it appears to the investigating authorities that the export price is unreliable because of a relationship between the parties to a transaction, the export price may also be 'constructed'. This should be based on the price at which the imported products are first resold to an independent buyer, or if they are not resold to an independent buyer, 'on such reasonable basis as the authorities may determine'. The comparison of the export price and the normal value must be made at the same level of trade (normally ex-factory level) and as close as possible to the same time, allowing for differences in factors such as the conditions and terms of sale, the quantities involved, physical characteristics, and differences in relevant costs. In an investigation, exporters must be allowed at least sixty days to adjust their export prices to reflect sustained movements in exchange rates during the period of investigation.

Actions against dumping may only be taken if it can be shown that it has caused or threatens material injury of domestic import-competing firms. Injury determinations must be based on positive evidence and must involve an objective examination of the volume of the dumped imports, their effect on prices in the domestic market, and the impact on domestic producers of like products. A significant increase in dumped imports, either in absolute terms or relative to production or consumption in the importing country, is a necessary condition for finding injury. Significant price undercutting of domestic producers, a significant depressing effect on prices, or the level of the dumping margin are other indicators that may be used. The term 'significant' is not defined. While differences in views as to what is significant might be dealt with through the dispute-settlement process, this possibility is constrained as panels are constrained in their ability to overrule substantive decisions taken by domestic investigating authorities (see below).

An illustrative list of injury indicators is given in the Agreement, including actual and potential decline in sales, profits, output, market share, productivity, return on investments, or utilization of capacity; factors affecting domestic prices; the magnitude of the margin of dumping; actual and potential negative effects on cash flow, inventories, employment, wages, growth, ability to raise capital, or investments. This list is not exhaustive, and no single factor or combination of factors can give decisive guidance. Dumped imports must be found to cause injury because of dumping. The necessary causality must be established on the basis of 'all relevant evidence before the authorities'. Any other factors that are known and that are injuring the domestic industry at the same time must be taken into account, and may not be attributed to the dumped imports. A number of factors that may be relevant in this respect are mentioned, including the volume and prices of imports not sold at dumping prices, contraction in demand or changes in the patterns of consumption, trade restrictive practices of—and competition between—the foreign and domestic producers, developments in technology, and the export performance and productivity of the domestic industry.

The Agreement on Antidumping is very 'legalistic': the wording is technical and complex, and many of its Articles are only decipherable for lawyers specialized in this particular area of trade law. The wording of the Agreement reflects numerous compromises reached in the Tokyo and Uruguay rounds. It is a combination of elements of the domestic laws and practices of major WTO Members and periodic attempts by target countries to limit the protectionist biases that are inherent in the use of AD in most jurisdictions. These biases have proved impossible to eradicate. The reason for this is simple: AD is fundamentally flawed from an economic perspective and cannot be fixed by tinkering with the methodological arcana of investigations. For all practical purposes, there is nothing wrong with dumping, as it is a normal business practice. The problem is anti-dumping. As argued by Finger (1993*a*), the only way to deal with AD is through efforts by negatively affected parties to alter domestic implementing legislation to allow their interests to be represented in AD cases.

What's Wrong With Dumping?

Dumping is not prohibited by the GATT. All GATT does is to establish certain rules that apply to governments that seek to offset dumping. Why dumping occurs is not considered relevant under GATT rules. From a normative, economic, perspective this is important, however. What's wrong with dumping? A typology of business motivations for dumping is presented in Table 7.3.

Sporadic dumping may occur without any deliberate intention if the exporting company has to decide on how much to produce before demand conditions or exchange rates are known. Sporadic dumping may also arise from a lack of experience in pricing a new product or may reflect unconscious pricing by a firm from an economy where domestic price systems are distorted. The trading environment facing a firm is usually uncertain, so dumping will often be beyond the control of a firm. For example, unexpected changes in exchange rates may lead a firm to dump even if it had no intention of doing so. Market

TABLE 7.3 *Motivations for dumping*

Type of dumping	Company's objectives
Sporadic	No deliberate intention to engage in dumping
Price discrimination	Profit maximization
Cyclical	To cover at least variable costs or to ensure job security during periods of slack demand
Defensive	To minimize losses resulting from excess capacity which is maintained to deter entry by competitors
Scale	To attain economies of scale or full capacity
Market-creating	To establish a company as a market leader in a newly invented product
Head-on	To attack a market leader in an export market
Predatory	To establish monopoly in a foreign market

Source: Kostecki (1991).

structure and firm strategy may then become irrelevant as a determinant of dumping, and dumping can arise in any context. However, in most cases dumping reflects a deliberate business strategy followed by exporting companies and constitutes a conscious, premeditated pricing practice aimed at the accomplishment of specific business objectives.

The best known motivation is simple price discrimination between markets. The wording of GATT rules specifically targets this rationale. A firm having some control over prices and operating in two separate markets may find it advantageous to discriminate in its price formation in favour of foreign consumers in order to maximize profits. Price discrimination across markets will occur whenever demand for a product is more elastic in export markets than at home (that is, for any change in price, foreign consumers change their demand more than domestic customers). Dumping in the sense of spatial price discrimination requires that there are barriers to the re-importation of the dumped product into the exporter's home market. Otherwise, price differentials across markets would tend to be eliminated through arbitrage, allowing for transport and transactions costs. This suggests that the problem with dumping—if any—is the barriers (tariffs, etc.) that prevent such arbitrage.

As noted above, selling below average total cost can also constitute dumping, and it is not strictly necessary that prices charged in the export market be below those charged at home. Issues of trade policy and differing price elasticities then become irrelevant.[2] The cost-dumping case is important in

---

[2] The price elasticity of demand for a product is defined as the ratio of the percentage change in the quantity demanded to the percentage change in the price. For example, if prices increase by 5% and the corresponding quantity decreases by more than 5%, demand is price elastic. See e.g. McClosky (1982).

practice, because many exporters produce exclusively or predominately for export, or sell only specific products for export. Often it may be in a firm's interest to sell below variable or even marginal costs (the cost of producing an extra unit of output) for a while. By doing so the firm will make a loss in so far as its fixed costs are not recovered. Accepting losses in the short run may be a requirement to establish (or increase) market share, and/or to enable the firm to move down its learning curve, thus increasing expected long-run profits.

A company may practice cyclical dumping to stabilize its production over the business cycle. Dumping arises as the firm reduces prices to cover only average variable costs during periods of slack demand. This can be perfectly rational, if the firm expects better times in the future and perceives the costs of laying off workers and reducing capacity to be higher than continuing production without covering all costs. Indeed, differences in labour markets and employment practices of firms across countries are one factor explaining why firms from some countries are more prone to engage in cyclical dumping than others (Ethier, 1982). If it is very costly for a firm to lay off workers— because of high legislated redundancy payments for example—it will continue to produce more than a firm which confronts a very flexible and less regulated labour market.

Certain forms of dumping have a pronounced strategic dimension. Exporting at prices below production cost may help deter entry by potential competitors into a firm's home market. This can be called defensive dumping (Davies and McGuinness, 1982). A firm may also price exports below production cost on a longer-term basis if such a strategy permits it to realize economies of scale (i.e. if unit costs decline as output expands), or to attain full capacity utilization. Losses incurred in the export market must then be offset by profits realized in other markets. Alternatively, a firm may need to move down its learning curve as fast as possible. As output increases, production workers tend to become more efficient and unit costs of production fall. Dumping in these cases is part of a strategy to attain an optimal scale of production.

A related rationale for dumping arises in cases of newly developed high-technology products (such as video recorders in the 1970s and early 1980s). Here a firm may attempt to discourage domestic firms from engaging in the development of a competing product by establishing a large market share. Products where there is proprietary technology may foster dumping in the early stages of the product cycle. Such products often involve the need to encourage consumers to choose a specific standard. To return to the video case, in the 1970s there were two main competing standards or formats: VHS and Betamax. Both needed to attract enough adherents to form a large enough customer base to recoup investment in R&D. When firms are trying to establish market share quickly, dumping may be part of an effective competitive strategy. A firm may also choose to export at prices which do not cover even marginal cost when, instead of maximizing profit, it prefers to maximize sales subject to a profit constraint. Such head-on dumping may be used as part of a frontal attack on a price leader in a given export market. Head-on dumping was extensively practised by Japanese exporters of semi-conductors and electronic products in the US and European markets in the 1980s (Kotler *et al.*, 1987).

With the exception of sporadic dumping most forms of dumping have a clear strategic dimension. Dumping is part of a pricing strategy of business firms that is driven by market structures, business cycles, or the characteristics of the products that are produced. Of these deliberate strategies, only one is potentially detrimental to the welfare of the country importing the dumped product: predation. Predation was the original rationale for US AD legislation in the first decades of this century. The fear was that a foreign firm (or cartel) could deliberately price products low enough to drive existing domestic firms out of business and establish a monopoly. Once established, the monopolist could more than recoup its losses by exploiting its market power. Note that the monopolist (cartel) must not only eliminate domestic competition, it must also be able to prohibit entry by new competitors. For this to be possible it must either have a global monopoly or it must convince the host government to impose or tolerate entry restrictions. It is not clear why a government would do this. Not surprisingly, in practice, post-Second World War cases of successful predatory dumping remain undocumented.

Proponents of AD often have a narrower definition of predation than the economic one described above. Their concern, implicitly if not explicitly, relates to the continued existence of national firms that produce a good. The fact that competition from other, outside sources will in most realistic circumstances prevent the formation of a monopoly is considered irrelevant. What matters is the maintenance of a domestic industry. But AD will not help in achieving this objective. What is needed is adjustment of the industry, something that AD is unlikely to encourage. Import-competing firms usually object to underselling, but not to price discrimination or selling below cost. This has been emphasized by de Jong (1968), who noted that 'popular opinion refers to dumping when foreign producers are able to undersell the domestic supplier in his own market.' As described by de Jong, this notion was translated as 'social' dumping in early discussions concerning AD legislation. While this term was not clearly defined, it was apparent that it referred to underselling by foreign firms in the domestic market, made possible by lower labour costs abroad (i.e. comparative advantage). In practice, it is underselling that importing-competing firms consider unfair, which reflects their inability or unwillingness to meet the price set by a foreign competitor.

What's Wrong With Anti-dumping?

The foregoing calls into question the economic justification for AD law. AD is simply a packaging of protectionism to make it look like something different.

By calling dumping unfair, the presumption is that AD is fair and thus a good thing. It levels the playing-field, and what can be wrong with fair play? Unfortunately, AD is not about fair play. Its goal is to tilt the playing-field. There has been a concerted attack on AD by economists during the last decade. AD is a major loophole in the GATT, used strategically by firms.

Defenders of AD have marshalled a number of arguments in favour of AD that go beyond the standard first line of defence: AD is GATT legal; end of discussion. For example, advocates of AD policies have argued that AD is a justifiable attempt by importing-country governments to offset the market-access restrictions existing in an exporting firm's home country that underlie the ability of such firms to dump. Such restrictions may consist of import barriers preventing arbitrage, but may also reflect the non-existence or non-enforcement of competition law by the exporting country. The US has claimed that lax Japanese anti-trust enforcement permits Japanese firms to collude, raise prices, and use part of the resulting rents to cross-subsidize (dump) products sold on foreign markets.

Garten (1994: 11–13) offers a representative policy-maker's defence of AD that emphasizes entry barriers in the exporter's home market. Four major conditions are argued to be most likely to give rise to dumping: closed home markets of exporters, anti-competitive practices in the exporting coun-try market which permit export sales below cost, government subsidization, and non-market conditions (mainly referring to state-trading enterprises in economies in transition to a market system). Garten goes on to defend the active application of AD laws to address these conditions. Arguing against those who suggest that if lack of competition is the problem, competition laws should be applied,

The Administration supports increased global standards in the area of competition law and believes that, with success in this effort, the need to invoke the AD law will be reduced. Competition laws can and do work effectively alongside the AD law, but are not a substitute for it. The need for vigorous enforcement of the U.S. AD law will continue for the foreseeable future. (Garten, 1994: 20)

Whatever the merits of this argument—the issue of the relationship between competition and trade policy is discussed further in Chapter 11—AD is an inferior instrument to address foreign market closure as it does not deal with the source of the problem, i.e. the government policies which artificially segment markets, or allow this to occur. An AD duty may put pressure on affected firms to lobby their government to eliminate such policies—or to abolish private business practices that restrict entry—but does so in a very indirect manner. Once investigations are initiated, any changes in policies or practices cannot have an impact on the finding. In many cases there will not be significant barriers to entry, so there is not much to be done by exporters to improve access to their home markets. Indeed, under current procedures no account is taken of whether price discrimination or selling below cost is the result of market-access restrictions.

A key problem with AD is the discretion that often is granted to investigating authorities—or, alternatively, the guidelines under which such authorities are forced to operate by law—to follow procedures that can make the instrument blatantly protectionist. In practice methodologies used to determine whether dumping has occurred and the size of the dumping margin may be such as to ensure that high positive margins are found in almost any circumstance. A practice often used in this connection is to calculate dumping margins by using methodologies that raise the normal value and lower the average export price, thereby increasing the dumping margin. Normal values can be biased upward by not including sales in the home market that are made at prices that are considered to be below cost, and by excluding sales in the export market that are above the calculated normal value. The latter procedure has been justified on the basis that 'sales at a high price should not be allowed to conceal dumped sales' (Hindley, 1994: 97). In cases where the normal value is constructed by authorities on the basis of costs, the dumping margins can be inflated in various ways. One way this may be done is through the inclusion of high profit and overhead margins in the calculation of the normal value, but not allowing for this in the calculation of the costs of sales for export. The use of such biased procedures will often guarantee that a positive dumping margin is found.

Another problem is that injury criteria may be manipulable by firms. This is potentially of greater importance, as the injury test tends to be the main factor constraining the access of import-competing industries to protection (Finger and Murray, 1990). Indicators of injury include trends in market share, employment, profits, capacity, capacity utilization, import penetration, and price underselling (i.e. the exporters' supply price being less than that of the import-competing industry). Many of these will not be closely linked to trends in imports, but will depend on business-cycle influences. While all of these indicators may to some extent be correlated with 'injury', many can be manipulated by firms, thus creating an incentive for indirect rent-seeking by either feigning that criteria have been met, or by deliberately taking actions that will induce injury as defined in the law (Leidy, 1994a). This enhances the threat effect of AD, and may foster the cascading of protection. Protection follows automatically if the criteria are found to be satisfied by the administering authority. Potentially countervailing forces—such as users and consumers—remain outside the administrative process and are effectively neutralized by the law. By invoking instruments of contingent protection, an upstream industry that produces an input may have the power to significantly injure a downstream industry that uses the input. This increases the probability that downstream firms will seek and gain protection in turn. Indeed, by initiating and winning an AD action, upstream suppliers may be able to manipulate the health of downstream firms to the advantage of both (Hoekman and Leidy, 1992*a*). As a result, instances of contingent protection may cascade along the chain of production.[3]

This vertical linkage across instances of contingent protection illustrates just one way in which AD procedures may foster *de facto* cartelization along the production stream. AD and similar laws may also facilitate tacit or explicit collusion by enforcing existing cartels and substantially reducing price competition in affected markets (Messerlin, 1989; 1990*a*). Others have argued that a credible threat of invocation of unfair-trade laws provides a means for industries to engage in implicit collusion that could not otherwise be maintained (e.g. Leidy, 1994*a*). AD and similar procedures are initiated by private parties (firms or industry associations). These interested parties are active in pursuing the adoption of more restrictive rules, and employing credible threats of invocation of procedures to negotiate VERs. The expansion of the scope and use of unfair-trade laws has been characterized as reflecting the *de facto* privatization of trade policy (Messerlin, 1990*b*).

The Uruguay Round Agreement

The WTO Anti-Dumping Agreement somewhat constrains the protectionist bias of investigating methodologies used in the 1980s. A sunset clause has been added: AD duties are to be terminated within five years of imposition, unless a review determines that both dumping and injury caused by dumped imports continues to persist or that removal of the measure would be likely to lead to the recurrence of dumping or injury. *De minimis* rules were agreed to. Duties may not be imposed if dumping margins are less than 2 per cent, or if the level of injury is negligible, or the market share of a firm is less than 3 per cent and cumulatively less than 7 per cent for exporters each supplying less than 3 per cent. Discretion with respect to methodologies used to determine dumping and injury margins was reduced. In effect, practices such as the statistically biased averaging methodologies described earlier were authorized, but subjected to certain constraints. This made AD somewhat less protectionist. However, many of the practices that have been identified as leading to significant protectionist biases remain untouched.

For example, although the Agreement calls for an 'average-to-average' comparison of home and export prices in the determination of dumping, authorities may compare a normal value that has been calculated on a

[3] Research by Feinberg and Kaplan (1993) provides evidence of cascading. In a statistical analysis of all anti-dumping and countervailing duty cases during the period 1980–6 brought by US producers and users of metals, they found that user industries tended to file for protection after upstream industries, and that the share of all cases accounted for by downstream industries increased significantly over time. An analysis of cases involving producers and users of chemicals led to the same finding.

weighted average basis with the prices of individual transactions (i.e. not take into consideration export sales above normal value), if they 'find a pattern of export prices which differ substantially among different purchasers, regions, or time periods and if an explanation is provided why such differences cannot be taken into account appropriately by the use of a weighted average to weighted average or transaction-to-transaction comparison' (Article 2.4.2). As the first condition will usually be met, much depends on the extent to which explanations are demanded. As no objective criteria have been established—simply an 'explanation'—this does not appear to be much of a constraint. Moreover, home-market or third-country prices may be discarded if they are below constructed costs, if this methodology is used. However, given that in the United States, for example, investigating authorities consistently refused to use average-to-average comparisons, the explicit requirement under the WTO to do so—even though subject to loopholes— was an improvement (Palmeter, 1995).

Procedural biases and methodological abuses are very difficult, if not impossible to regulate away given the definition of dumping. Little was done to compensate for the fact that AD authorities retain substantial discretion in applying regulations and defining criteria, and do not require any investigation into the market-access conditions prevailing in the exporter's home market, or the threat to the competitive conditions existing in the importer's market. For example, the new requirement that AD duties be terminated within five years would appear to be a major improvement from the viewpoint of economic welfare. In practice this may not be a binding constraint, however, as it is conditional upon the findings of a review investigation into whether both dumping and injury caused by dumped imports continue (or threaten) to persist. Another example pertains to the definition of an 'interested party' in AD cases. This provides users and final consumers of the import with a voice during the investigations, but restricts them to providing evidence that is relevant to the determination of dumping, or injury to domestic firms that compete with the imported product. The fact that a duty may injure their proper business is not a factor that can be brought forward. Nor does the Agreement require any consideration of the economy-wide impact of AD duties, their impact on existing users of imports, or the state of competition in the domestic market.

The AD Agreement also embodies language on dispute settlement. Although the WTO's general mechanism applies, Article 17.6 of the Agreement greatly restricts the ability of panels to focus on the substance or merits of a case, as they are required to accept any 'reasonable' interpretation of the Agreement's substantive rules. In cases where the Agreement can be interpreted in more than one way, a decision by AD authorities must be accepted if it is based upon one of the permissible interpretations. New information that was not available or used by investigating authorities cannot be used by a panel to overturn an

AD action (Hindley, 1994; Finger, 1995). In many cases panels will be limited to determining whether the procedural requirements of the Agreement were violated. As noted by Palmeter (1995), a major goal of US user industries in the Uruguay round was to limit the ability of GATT panels to overturn domestic AD decisions. The standard of review embodied in the Agreement reflects the power of the industries supporting AD. This lobby was strong enough to make this specific issue a deal-breaker for the United States, and it obtained most of what it sought. The lobby also targeted the modalities of dispute-settlement panels relating to AD, apparently pushing for greater involvement of GATT Secretariat staff responsible for providing support services to the AD Committee rather than the GATT's Legal Division (Petersmann, 1994: 1204, 1224; Palmeter, 1995).

Little happened in the Uruguay round negotiations because the talks were essentially conducted between the users of anti-dumping measures on the one hand, and the countries that pursued export-oriented development strategies on the other. This meant that the negotiations differed substantially from those in the Tokyo and the Kennedy rounds, where the negotiating process mainly involved user countries. The user–exporter dichotomy made it difficult to come up with a balanced package deal in the Uruguay round. Exporting country governments had little to offer in the negotiations as dumping cannot (and should not) be prohibited. Exporters such as Japan, Hong Kong, Korea, and Singapore considered that their trade was detrimentally affected by AD measures, and made many proposals to discipline the use of methodologies that were biased towards finding high dumping and/or injury margins. In this they had some success, in that practices that were tolerated but not explicitly subject to GATT disciplines were 'disciplined': they became subject to multi-lateral rules (regulation) specifying the conditions under which they could be used.

A number of contentious practices could not be resolved in this manner. A good example pertains to so-called anti-circumvention measures, which Japan and Korea sought to subject to multilateral rules. Exporting firms may try to circumvent AD actions by establishing assembly plants either in the importing country (where the final product has become subject to AD duties) or in third countries. Anti-circumvention became an important issue in AD enforcement as of the late 1980s. In June 1987 the EU adopted legislation allowing measures to be imposed to prevent circumvention of anti-dumping measures on finished products. Such measures could be applied to products assembled or produced in the EU, using imported materials or parts. In the year following the adoption of this Regulation, the EU initiated investigations on electronic typewriters, electronic scales, excavators, and photocopiers. All of these products were assembled or produced by Japanese-related companies in the EU.

Japan challenged the anti-circumvention measures before the GATT, arguing that the existence of dumping and injury related to imported components was not investigated; the provision contained GATT-inconsistent local-content requirements as it stipulated that duties could be imposed if the value of components originating in the country subject to the initial AD duty exceeded the value of all other parts by a specified margin; and that the duties were only imposed on manufacturers associated with foreign companies that were already subject to AD duties. Domestic producers were not affected even if they used the same imported components (discrimination). Australia, Hong Kong, and Singapore made detailed submissions critical of the EU circumvention regulation. The EU argued that the anti-circumvention provision was adopted after experience had shown that the initiation of AD action was frequently followed by the establishment of an assembly operation in the EU to circumvent AD duties. The USA supported the EU's objective of combating circumvention of AD duties, it having similar concerns and mechanisms.

The GATT panel that considered the case concluded that the anti-circumvention duties on the finished products, being levied on products manufactured within the EU, were not customs duties but internal taxes. Because these were levied on a discriminatory basis, they were contrary to GATT's national treatment principle. The EU was requested to bring the application of its anti-circumvention mechanism into conformity with GATT obligations. Although Japan won this battle, as adopted panel reports become part of the GATT case-law, it did not win the war. No agreement emerged on anti-circumvention in the Uruguay round, as negotiators could not agree on a specific text. The matter was referred to the Committee on Anti-dumping Practices. It remains to be seen what the implications of this will be.

Summing up, dumping is rarely an anti-competitive practice. Predatory pricing is possible, but will not be profitable as long as governments ensure that markets remain contestable. At the same time, AD creates a large number of distortions. The threat of AD induces rent-seeking behaviour on the part of import-competing firms, and leads exporting firms to alter production, allocation, and production-location decisions in ways that can easily reduce welfare at home and abroad. These threat effects are important, as they can imply substantial uncertainty regarding the conditions of market access facing exporters, and the costs of goods for importers. Similar effects can arise under Article XIX-type, emergency protection procedures, but these will generally be less distorting as they are more transparent, less arbitrary, and less prone to capture. AD mechanisms are simply an option allowed under the WTO's rules; they are not required. The best option for governments that are concerned with both equity and efficiency is not to pass AD legislation, or to abolish it if it exists. The problem is that powerful vested interests support AD. As revealed in the Uruguay round, these interest-groups did not confront much domestic opposition. A policy implication is that there is a great need for greater domestic transparency in this area.

7.5. MEASURES TO COUNTERVAIL SUBSIDIZED IMPORTS

Countervailing duty (CVD) or anti-subsidy procedures, similar to AD, are allowed under Article VI of the GATT. The objective is again to ensure fair competition. As noted in Chapter 4, while the GATT prohibits export subsidies on manufactures and limits the use of export subsidies on primary products, it allows for other types of subsidies. However, unless a subsidy is in the so-called 'green box' (i.e. permitted and not countervailable), GATT members that consider that their industries are materially injured by imports benefiting from subsidies may impose countervailing measures. A necessary condition is that an investigation determines that imports have been subsidized and have caused material injury to domestic industry. The procedures to be followed in subsidy-injury investigations are described in great detail in the Agreement on Subsidies and Countervailing Measures, which in turn is largely based on the Tokyo round Subsidies Code. As in the case of AD disciplines, the injury test is the key element underlying the agreements's implicit objective of reconciling presumably legitimate national government subsidy policies with the interests of nations affected by those policies.

The United States has been by far the largest user of CVD mechanisms, initiating over 100 investigations since 1985 (Table 7.1, above). While a substantial number of these CVD cases were not brought to a conclusion, this may be attributed in large part to the introduction of trade-restricting bilateral agreements, as in the case of many steel products. Other countries, including major traders such as the EU and Japan have made little use of the CVD mechanism. In part this is because other policies for safeguarding producers' interests are available and are easier to implement, and in part because many countries apparently fear that initiation of CVD investigations could lead to retaliatory investigations. As the USA does not devote many resources to explicit subsidization of manufacturing, its government has never felt constrained in its use of CVDs.

Rationales for Countervailing Duties

There are two possible rationales for countervailing foreign subsidy policies via import restrictions. The first is to offset the injurious effect of such policies on domestic industries. The second is to induce the foreign government either to change its policy or to refrain from subsidizing. The first rationale has little economic merit, as the imposition of import barriers (countervailing duties) simply further distorts the behaviour of consumers and producers, and reduces the welfare of the country concerned. If the goal is to offset the effect of the foreign intervention, superior instruments exist. It is also important to note that an explicit subsidy granted to a foreign firm will generally only be one aspect of the industrial policy that is applied by a foreign government. Such governments will also pursue direct and indirect tax policies, engage in investments in infrastructure, etc. Given the difficulty of determining the real (general equilibrium) effect of any kind of foreign industrial policy, it will always be very difficult, if not impossible, to determine the appropriate counter action. Imposition of a countervailing measure may benefit the domestic industry, but is equivalent to a tax on the rest of the economy.

The argument that restricting imports of products that have benefited from unfair government assistance can be justified as a means of inhibiting the use of such measures has greater economic merit (Deardorff and Stern, 1987). Indeed, it may be the case that even though a CVD will not be the appropriate instrument and will be welfare-reducing, the threat of CVDs is required to induce governments to refrain from engaging in certain types of behaviour. The relevance of this argument depends on whether a number of conditions are met. For example, the cost to the foreign country of a CVD must be greater than the benefit resulting from the subsidy policy. This may not be the case, especially if the policy has an economic rationale or is driven by non-economic considerations.

For there to be an economic rationale for the various policies affecting a country's industrial structure it is necessary that the policies offset market imperfections. In the absence of market failure, subsidy policies can only reduce the economic welfare of a country, due to the deadweight losses caused by distorting the behaviour of producers and consumers. Among the most frequently invoked reasons for market failure are the existence of externalities and informational asymmetries. The latter may be an important source of capital-market imperfections leading, for example, to interest rates that exceed the socially optimal level or to inefficient rationing. However, in practice, with the exception of measures aimed at achieving environmental objectives, subsidy policies affecting the output of sectors are rarely intended to offset a market imperfection. Instead, they are often used to offset a government failure—e.g., macroeconomic distortions created by overvalued exchange rates.

Whatever the case may be, CVDs are superior to AD in that at least the instrument is better targeted at the source of the perceived externality: government intervention. In contrast to the case of dumping by firms, in the subsidy context it is at least possible to build a case for 'unfair competition'. Countervailing subsidies will rarely make economic sense, however, unless the subsidy is expected to be temporary. In the case of agricultural subsidization by OECD countries, for example, the policy is best regarded as structural, in that affected producers are well advised to adjust to the situation. Governments can provide such producers with income support if they desire, but the imposition of CVDs is equivalent to throwing good money after bad. After all, the subsidy is equivalent to a transfer from a foreign government to the consumers of the importing country. If a tariff is imposed on these imports, the economy will be worse off than if nothing is done. Moreover, the same types of capture and manipulation problems that affect AD also arise in the CVD setting (see Leidy, 1994*b*).

WTO Disciplines

The GATT history on CVDs revolves around the use made by the United States of this instrument, it being the primary user. The fact that CVDs were allowed under Article VI reflects the fact that the USA had a CVD instrument. Despite this, when the USA acceded to GATT, it grandfathered its existing legislation. The negotiation of a Code on Subsidies and Countervailing Measures in the Tokyo round was driven by a desire by targeted countries to see the USA adopt an injury test (which was not required under its law). This attempt was somewhat successful, in that the USA signed an agreement that required an injury test. However, in practice, this was made conditional upon bilateral commitments with respect to subsidy policies. US CVD policies therefore continued to be a source of controversy.

In the Uruguay round the issue of subsidies and CVDs was substantially clarified. GATT-1994 makes a distinction between different types of subsidies, depending on their trade impact and their objective (Chapter 4). Subsidies that have an economy-wide impact (education, general infrastructure, basic R&D) or have a non-economic rationale (regional disparities, income support) are permitted and are not subject to the threat of CVDs. Subsidies that are not in this 'green box' may be countervailed. In the case of both prohibited and actionable subsidies, WTO members may initiate CVD investigations or invoke dispute-settlement procedures. Both routes may be pursued simultaneously. However, only one remedy may be applied. Necessary conditions for CVDs are that the existence of a subsidy is demonstrated, a domestic industry producing similar (like) products is shown to be materially injured, and a causal link is established between the subsidization and injury. Injury requires that the volume of subsidized imports has increased; that this has had an impact on price levels or is reflected in price undercutting of domestic firms; and that this in turn has had a detrimental effect on the domestic industry. At least 25 per cent of the firms in the domestic industry must support the launching of a countervailing duty investigation.

Detailed requirements and deadlines are established regarding the different phases of investigations, including the collection of evidence, the rights of interested parties, the calculation of the extent to which a subsidy benefits the recipient, the determination of injury, possible remedies, and access to judicial review of the decision that is made. After five years a countervailing duty is to be eliminated, except if a review determines that the abolition of protection would be likely to lead to the continuation or recurrence of injury. When confronted with countervailing duty investigations, developing countries benefit from *de minimis* thresholds. If the subsidy is less than 2 per cent of the per-unit value of products exported, developing countries are exempt from countervail (for least-developed countries the threshold is 3 per cent). An exemption also applies if the import market share of a developing country is less than 4 per cent, and the aggregate share of all developing countries with shares less than 4 per cent is below 9 per cent of total imports.

7.6. TRADE RESTRICTIONS FOR BALANCE-OF-PAYMENTS PURPOSES

GATT permits the imposition of trade restrictions to safeguard a country's external financial position (Articles XII and XVIII:*b*). The inclusion of such provisions reflects the fact that when the GATT was created, a system of fixed exchange rates existed (Bretton Woods). Given the presumption of fixed exchange rates, this removed an instrument through which governments could seek to deal with BOP disequilibria. If a country running a deficit could not devalue, or not do so easily, and if prices on labour markets were relatively inflexible as well, there could be a case for allowing the imposition of temporary import restrictions. Indeed, the imposition of an across-the-board tariff in conjunction with a subsidy to exports is under certain conditions exactly equivalent to a nominal devaluation of the currency (Vousden, 1990).

In practice, the BOP provisions of the GATT were widely used by both industrialized and developing countries. The former used Article XII as cover, the latter Article XVIII:*b*. Use of QRs for BOP purposes by developed, mostly European, countries occurred mostly in the 1950s during the post-war reconstruction when many currencies were not convertible. In contrast, use of Article XVIII:*b* by developing countries has been fairly constant (Table 7.1, above). Most developing countries had no need to use Article XIX safeguard actions to protect their industries if needed, as their tariffs were generally not bound or were bound at high levels. They did need GATT cover to use QRs, however, and this was the role of Article XVIII—it permits, indeed encourages, the use of QRs for BOP purposes. This is an idiosyncrasy of the GATT-1947, and contradicts the general preference for price-based instruments such as tariffs. In general, an import surcharge would be less distortionary than QRs.

The challenge to negotiators in the Uruguay round was to close the BOP loophole, which in practice was simply an avenue to legally impose QRs, albeit subject to GATT surveillance. Closing the loophole should have been facilitated by the move away from the fixed exchange-rate system—which had already occurred in the 1970s. The move towards flexible (more easily adjustable) exchange rates reduces the rationale for resorting to trade restrictions to safeguard a country's external financial position. Exchange-rate adjustment provides an automatic and effective mechanism for adjustment of current account imbalances if complemented by supporting measures (fiscal and monetary discipline). Experience clearly demonstrates that QRs are not the right instrument to deal with BOP problems. The IMF and World Bank routinely obtain agreements with borrowing governments not to introduce import restrictions for BOP purposes in their adjustment lending to developing countries (Finch and Michalopoulos, 1988). The IMF and the OECD have also attempted to contain the use of BOP measures through political declarations of intent (Roessler, 1980).

Most developing countries responded to this line of argument by emphasizing that their foreign-exchange shortages did not stem so much from their own policies as from the protectionist policies of their trading partners. Although this was a disingenuous argument at best, given that the maintenance of overvalued exchange rates was usually the primary cause of foreign-exchange shortages and rationing, it was against this background that the issue of BOP escape clauses was considered in the Tokyo round. A 1979 Declaration on Trade Measures Taken for Balance-of-Payments Purposes reinforced scrutiny over the trade and adjustment policies of industrial countries, but asserted that developing countries should be allowed greater latitude in safeguarding their foreign-exchange reserves. During the 1980s, industrialized countries argued increasingly that the clause rendered the participation of developing countries in GATT to a large extent meaningless. This damaged both the trading system (because it undermined adherence to the principles on which the system rests) and the imposing developing country which has no effective means within the GATT context to counter powerful protectionist interests at home (see Chapter 1 on the domestic policy function of GATT). The measures imposed tended to be permanent, whereas BOP difficulties are mainly of a cyclical nature. The trade restrictions were also often imposed on selected products, rather than being applied across the board as would be necessary for BOP purposes.

WTO Disciplines

In the Uruguay round, new language on Article XVIII was agreed that reduced the scope to use QRs, and strengthened the surveillance of BOP actions. GATT-1947 contracting parties committed themselves to publicly announce time-schedules for the removal of restrictive import measures taken for BOP purposes. They also agreed to give preference to those measures which have the least disruptive effect on trade. Such measures include import surcharges, import deposit requirements, or other equivalent trade measures with an impact on the price of imported goods. The use of new QRs for BOP purposes requires a justification that such price-based measures are not able to arrest a sharp deterioration in the external payments position. Only one type of restrictive import measure taken for BOP reasons may be applied on a product. The emphasis on the use of price-based measures is a significant improvement over the GATT-1947.

In principle, surcharges or similar measures must be applied on an across-the-board basis. However, exemptions may be made for certain essential products, necessary to meet basic consumption needs or which help improve the BOP situation, such as capital goods or inputs needed for production. A WTO Member applying new restrictions or raising the general level of its existing restrictions must consult with the BOP Committee within four months of the adoption of such measures. Each year a Member taking BOP actions is to provide the WTO Secretariat with a consolidated notification, including all changes in laws, regulations, and policy statements, and complete information at the tariff-line level on the type of measures applied, the criteria used for their administration, product coverage, and trade flows affected. Countries applying BOP measures must engage in periodic consultations for which a report is prepared that includes:

(1) an overview of the BOP situation and prospects and the domestic policy measures taken to restore equilibrium;
(2) a full description of the restrictions applied and steps taken to reduce incidental protective effects;
(3) measures taken since the last consultation to liberalize import restrictions;
(4) a plan for the elimination and progressive relaxation of remaining restrictions.

The Secretariat also prepares a report, using data obtained from the IMF, regarding the macroeconomic situation in the country concerned. The IMF is represented at Committee meetings.

There is therefore in principle rather close surveillance of BOP actions. Very much depends, however, on the willingness of the BOP Committee to insist that measures are no longer or are not justified. Past experience suggests that not too much should be expected from this Committee (see Eglin, 1987). In practice the main source of discipline comes from the international capital markets, from the international financial institutions, and from bilateral pressure by WTO Members on one another to stop invoking Article XVIII as a cover for trade restrictions. A number of countries disinvoked Article XVIII during the Uruguay round following such pressure. Multilateral surveillance exercised by the BOP Committee played a role in this, but in conjunction with the GATT dispute-settlement system. For example, Korea's use of Article XVIII: *b* was challenged in the 1980s by beef exporters, who alleged that Korea no longer had a BOP problem and that restrictions on beef could therefore not be justified by this Article, as claimed by Korea. The panel that dealt with this case found in favour of the petitioners and recommended that Korea be required to eliminate its import restrictions on beef. A total of ten developing countries disinvoked Article XVIII during the 1980s and early 1990s, largely following the adoption of more appropriate macroeconomic policies and unilateral liberalization efforts.

7.7. INFANT-INDUSTRY PROTECTION

Article XVIII:*a* allows for the removal of tariff concessions if necessary to establish an industry in a developing country. It does not differ much in substance from Article XXVIII (renegotiation of tariffs), as compensation negotiations must be initiated. Article XVIII:*c* permits the use of QRs or other non-tariff measures by developing countries for infant-industry purposes. This provision requires the approval of WTO Members, and compensation may also be requested. The infant-industry exceptions were widened considerably in 1979 to allow for measures intended to develop, modify, or extend production structures more generally, in accordance with a country's economic development priorities. It has rarely been invoked as a cover for the use of import quotas, probably due to the fact that the BOP loophole embodied in Article XVIII:*b* was preferred. In comparison to the latter, surveillance and approval procedures under the infant-industry provision are more strict, and the possibility of retaliation is more likely (Chapter 10).

In most circumstances the economic rationale for the invocation of Article XVIII:*c* is very weak, as a QR in itself will do very little to stimulate the establishment of a competitive industry. Any justification for a government to help in the establishment of an industry must be based on market failure. Even if it is assumed, heroically, that a government can correctly identify the market failure, a QR will never be appropriate in targeting the source of the distortion. Usually a subsidy of some type will be a less inefficient instrument to promote an industry. From an economic viewpoint, the drafters of the GATT were therefore justified in placing relatively stringent conditions on the use of infant-industry protection. But, as has been the case with other GATT disciplines as well, the result of this was to induce a shift towards invoking substitute GATT-cover: the BOP route.

7.8. GENERAL EXCEPTIONS

Both the GATT and the GATS contain Articles entitled General Exceptions, which allow Members to take measures that may violate a rule or discipline if necessary to: protect public morals and health or safety of human, plant or animal life; to prevent imports of goods produced with prison labour; to conserve natural exhaustible resources (as long as applied to domestic production or consumption as well); or to secure compliance with laws or regulations that are not inconsistent with GATT or GATS provisions. A necessary condition for the invocation of the exceptions provision is that measures are not applied in a manner which would constitute arbitrary or unjustifiable discrimination between countries, or a disguised restriction on international trade. Members are also exempt from the multilateral rules and disciplines in so far as measures are required to safeguard national security interests.

The general-exceptions Articles are broadly and rather vaguely worded (Jackson, 1969). There are no compensation or approval requirements. There is also no notification requirement. This implies that the only source of discipline is the dispute-settlement mechanism. Many panel cases have involved an investigation whether the provisions of Article XX are applicable in specific instances. This is because it happens relatively frequently that if a Member feels that another is taking a measure that violates GATT rules and initiates dispute-settlement procedures, the latter attempts to justify the policy on the basis of Article XX. In many such cases it is the task of the panel to decide if the measure in question is necessary to achieve the government's purported objective. For example, in the case of a Thai policy prohibiting imports of cigarettes, the panel found that this violated Article XI (prohibition on QRs). An argument by the Thai government that the ban was necessary to control smoking was rejected, because other instruments were available to restrict smoking (so the QR was not necessary). Moreover, because domestic cigarette production was not treated equivalently to foreign products, the ban not only violated national treatment, but was inconsistent with achieving the government's stated goal (so the ban was again not necessary).

7.9. CONCLUSION

Political realities, especially in countries that are in the process of moving from highly distorted trade regimes to a more liberal policy stance, often dictate that there be a mechanism allowing for the temporary reimposition of protection in instances where competition from imports proves to be too fierce to allow the restructuring process to be socially sustainable. Indeed, a safeguard mechanism is likely to be a pre-condition for far-reaching liberalization to be politically feasible. Governments desire loopholes that allow legal backsliding (Finger, 1995) for a variety of reasons. One that has not been discussed so far is a sympathy motive. Societies tend to have sympathy for groups severely affected by large, exogenous shocks. They support granting assistance to such groups because they too may be affected some day. This insurance motive is complemented by what has been called the conservative social welfare function: governments tend to oppose large absolute reductions in the real incomes of any significant portion of society (Corden, 1974; Deardoff, 1987).

GATT does little in terms of providing guidance to policy-makers wishing to rationalize or create an economically sound system to deal with 'market disruption caused by imports'. This is not only an important question in systemic terms, but of direct relevance to many (developing) nations that are (or may be) contemplating the creation of such a system in the context of ongoing or planned trade-liberalization programmes. In many cases the first stop is at the GATT; the second is to take existing legislation in developed market economies as a model. This is unfortunate, as most instruments that are used in OECD countries tend to be very costly. While improvements in industrialized nations are usually hindered by the difficulty of revoking a law once it has been enacted, many (developing) countries are still in the position of starting *de novo*. They should thus in principle be able to implement a rational system of emergency protection (Hoekman and Leidy, 1990).

Allowing for the possibility of emergency protection sends a signal to firms that the government cannot or will not commit itself to a given level of intervention or support. This can negatively influence the performance of particular firms—who may build this insurance into their management decisions. This can in turn give rise to so-called time-inconsistency problems. If a government is pursuing a liberalization programme, but firms do not adjust because they expect to be able to obtain further protection in the future, it may not be optimal (politically) for the government not to grant such protection (or alternatively, to remove the temporary, emergency protection). The design of the mechanism and the rules or criteria that apply are therefore important. External obligations—such as those applying under the WTO—can help in reducing possible time-inconsistency problems, but cannot eliminate them.

An efficient system of emergency protection should have two basic elements. First, there need to be hard requirements (rules) to obtain protection that are not subject to discretion on the part of investigating agencies or the political authorities. Second, criteria and indicators must be such that the scope for firms to manipulate them is minimized. While the rules will have to be GATT-consistent, GATT disciplines are so widely worded that interest-groups can easily push for language which is favourable to them, but detrimental to the economy as a whole. The rationale for safeguard protection is to give an industry time to adjust to vigorous import competition. The rules embodied in the GATT Agreement on Safeguards reflects a large number of compromises that are less than optimal from a national point of view. Safeguard protection should be applied on a non-discriminatory basis, be subject to time-limits, be phased out gradually over this time-period, and offer some compensation for affected exporters (Hoekman and Leidy, 1990). As safeguards should be intended to give an industry a breathing space in which to adjust or restructure to the new, more competitive environment, they should be non-renewable (in contrast to the GATT, which allows for another four-year extension). A decision to award protection should be taken by the President or Prime Minister, after a consideration of the impact this would have on the economy as a whole. The specific criteria (necessary conditions) need to be well defined in the law. Clearly import growth must be such as to greatly increase foreign market share, and injury criteria should be such as to ensure that the domestic industry as a whole is making substantial losses. Import penetration is relatively insusceptible to strategic behaviour and directly tied to the presumed source of difficulty. Threat of injury should not be a criterion at all. Instead, procedures should be such that action—if deemed necessary—can be taken rapidly. Very importantly, a national-interest criterion should be incorporated, where this is defined in such a way that it requires a published cost–benefit analysis by an independent agency of the economy-wide effects of imposing protection.

Designing 'Unfair-Trade' Laws[4]

Nothing in the GATT requires Members to implement AD laws. The best practice here is clear: do not exercise this GATT option. If unavoidable, there is nothing that prevents the adoption of AD laws that are designed to minimize the protectionist biases that can easily arise under a GATT-consistent AD mechanism. If AD is maintained, the basic objective should not simply be to focus on the existence of injury to competitors (i.e. to the domestic industry producing the like product), but to establish that dumping is injurious to competition (i.e. to the economy of the importing country as a whole). AD duties should be imposed only if a cost–benefit analysis determines that the advantages created by the imposition of duties for the economy as a whole outweigh the disadvantages. The rules should include a clearly defined public-interest clause. Public-interest clauses generally require that before duties are imposed, investigating authorities examine the impact this would have on the users of the alleged dumped import and the final consumers of goods that embody the imports concerned. For a public-interest clause to be effective, it is important that it allows potentially negatively affected parties to defend their interests by giving them the opportunity to present their arguments to investigators, and that they have the legal standing to do so. Governments interested in reducing the anti-competitive effects of AD can also introduce much higher *de minimis* standards than those required under the GATT Agreement. A necessary condition for the imposition of duties should be that an exporter has a significant market share. Concepts developed and employed in the anti-trust area can be useful. For example, a foreign firm or cartel could be required

---

[4] What follows draws on Hoekman and Mavroidis (1994*b*).

to have at least 40 per cent of the domestic market before an investigation can be launched.

Trade policy is usually inefficient in that it tends to create more distortions than it solves. Indeed, Deardorff and Stern (1987) have likened trade policy to doing acupuncture with a two-pronged fork; even if one of the prongs finds the right spot, the other prong can only do harm. This applies to protection in response to market disruption as well. Protection is also a very costly form of intervention, both in a static sense (as demonstrated by studies of costs per job saved), and in a dynamic sense (due to the distortions that reduce economic growth). In practical terms, however, given a socio-political need to address market disturbance, temporary contingent protection may be the best response in situations where import penetration has increased substantially. The issue, then, is to design and implement procedures that are effective, equitable, and that minimize distortions. The start of this process should be to have only one mechanism, and one consistent with GATT Article XIX. A problem with the GATT is that it allows for numerous types of safeguards—AD, CVD, Article XIX, BOP actions—many of which make no economic sense. Countries in the process of developing or reforming their trade laws are well advised not to implement all the options allowed under the GATT to impose trade barriers, as it will make it much more difficult to control the trade-policy formation process (Hoekman, 1995b). Those countries already caught in the morass need to enhance domestic transparency regarding the economic costs of contingent protection and their distribution across groups in society. Greater information is a crucial necessary condition for changing the status quo.

7.10. FURTHER READING

The issues of safeguard protection for import-competing industries have been analysed extensively in the economic literature. Robert Baldwin, in 'Assessing the Fair Trade and Safeguards Laws in Terms of Modern Trade and Political Economy Analysis', *World Economy*, 15 (1992), 185–202; and Michael Leidy, 'Trade Policy and Indirect Rent Seeking: A Synthesis of Recent Work', *Economics and Politics*, 6 (1994), 97–118 provide further discussions of the (political economy) issues and summarize some of the recent literature. Gary Sampson, 'Safeguards', in J. M. Finger and A. Olechowski (eds.), *The Uruguay Round: A Handbook* (Washington DC: World Bank, 1987) is an excellent review of the history of Article XIX in the GATT. Alan Deardorff, 'Safeguards Policy and the Conservative Social Welfare Function', in Henryk Kierzkowski (ed.), *Protection and Competition in International Trade* (Oxford: Basil Blackwell, 1987), and Bernard Hoekman and Michael Leidy, 'Policy Responses to Shifting Comparative Advantage: Designing a System of Emergency Protection', *Kyklos*, 43 (1990), 25–51 discuss why governments need safeguard instruments, and explore the possible design of an efficient mechanism. Brian Hindley, 'GATT Safeguards and Voluntary Export Restraints: What are the Interests of the Developing Countries?', *World Bank Economic Review*, 1 (1987), 689–705 discusses the incentive effects of VERs.

Richard Eglin, 'Surveillance of Balance-of-Payments Measures in the GATT', *World Economy*, 10 (1987):1–26 reviews the GATT experience with Article XVIII actions and Committee reviews. Michael Finger (ed.), *Antidumping: How it Works and Who Gets Hurt* (Ann Arbor: University of Michigan Press, 1993) is an excellent set of papers identifying why AD makes no economic sense. Patrick Messerlin, 'Antidumping Regulations or Procartel Law? The EC Chemical Cases', *World Economy*, 13 (1990), 465–92 illustrates on the basis of a particular case how an industry can capture AD procedures to enhance its market power. The contributions by Finger, Hindley, and Winters in *The New World Trading System* (Paris: OECD, 1994) are good summaries of what was agreed on contingent protection in the Uruguay round. Michael Finger, 'Legalized Backsliding: Safeguard Provisions in the GATT', in Will Martin and Alan Winters (eds.), *The Uruguay Round and the Developing Economies* (Washington DC: World Bank, forthcoming) is a comprehensive discussion of the various loopholes in the GATT that allow for backsliding.

8

Sector-Specific Arrangements

This chapter focuses on trade in agricultural products and in textiles and clothing, which were gradually removed from the reach of GATT-1947 disciplines starting in the 1950s. After many abortive attempts to reintegrate these sectors into the GATT, success was achieved in negotiating agreements in the Uruguay round that re-establish multilateral disciplines for both sectors. Once fully implemented, the WTO will embody few sector-specific arrangements. The three exceptions are so-called plurilateral agreements on civil aircraft, bovine meat, and dairy products. These only bind signatories (see Annex 2), and do not add much to general GATT disciplines.

8.1. AGRICULTURAL PRODUCTS[1]

Agricultural products (food) accounted for 12 per cent of world trade in 1993; textiles and clothing accounted for 7 per cent. Together, these sections therefore represented nearly one-fifth of global trade (GATT, 1995).

Agriculture provides a good example of a sector where the potential economic gains from liberalization greatly outweighed the costs, but negatively affected producer groups (farm lobbies) were able to exert significant (political) pressure in favour of maintaining—indeed, expanding—government support. Past MTNs, recurring bilateral trade disputes, and the discussions in the Uruguay round context illustrate that agriculture is 'special'. A major problem facing countries seeking to reduce government intervention was to offer sufficiently attractive carrots to the countries asked to liberalize. A lesson of over thirty years of GATT discussions on agriculture is that in the absence of domestic interest-groups favouring liberalization, MTNs are unlikely to make much progress. Agriculture is an area where reciprocity broke down as a driving force for liberalization, because major players—the EU, Japan—pursued protectionist policies for reasons that could not be offset by internal groups that would benefit from greater access to foreign markets. Potential export interests were not agricultural—these not being competitive and/or compensated by export subsidies—but industrial. Numerous attempts by the United States to link the two areas failed, however, in large part because the cost of not engaging in mutual reductions in trade barriers on industrial products outweighed the potential benefits of getting something on agriculture.

[1] This section draws in part on Hoekman and Crémoux (1993).

Historically, agricultural trade policy has been driven by short-run phenomena. Food crises led to export controls, while gluts led to import measures. In terms of relatively recent history, protectionist measures in agriculture of a permanent nature became increasingly prevalent at the end of the nineteenth century. One cause of this was the steady expansion of American production, which lowered world prices. While some nations reacted to the resulting change in incentives by adjusting, e.g. the Dutch became more specialized in livestock as the price of feed grains fell, others reacted by protecting existing producers and subsidizing exports (e.g. France, Germany, and Austria-Hungary). During the interwar period, agricultural protection and domestic market regulation increased further. After World War II, farmers and agricultural ministries were basically able to exempt agriculture from GATT disciplines and recurrent MTNs. With the creation of the EEC in 1957 and the Common Agricultural Policy (CAP), agricultural intervention in Europe became an institutional fixture.

The CAP is the pre-eminent example of how farmers became insulated from competition from foreign farmers. The CAP provides for an 'intervention' or support price at which the Community guarantees to purchase the agricultural output from farmers, and a 'threshold price' (that is higher than the internal support price) below which no imports are allowed. In order to isolate the EU market from international competition a 'variable levy' equal to the margin between the threshold price and the lowest representative offer price on world markets is imposed on imports. Moreover, an 'export restitution' amounting to the difference between the average world price and the internal EU price is granted to European exporters. The programme is extremely costly. Domestic support to agricultural producers averaged more than $92 billion per year in the EU during 1986–90. However, the EU is not alone. Domestic support in Japan and the USA over the same period averaged $35 and $24 billion, respectively. In Japan, rice was produced at a cost four times that of competitive producers elsewhere. The same applied to Swiss meat and butter. Budgetary support in the USA, the EU, and Japan accounted for some 15 per cent of government spending; a figure comparable to what was spent on education.

Relative to other sectors of the economy, as of the early 1990s agriculture in many industrialized countries was regulated, subsidized, and centrally planned to an exceptional degree. Market forces were restrained by production quotas, state purchasing and distribution, subsidies, and administered pricing. These often worked at cross purposes: in the EU, support programmes were so effective in stimulating output that they had to be complemented by production quotas and incentives to take land out of production (so-called set-asides). Matters were not much better in many developing countries. Marketing boards—monopoly buyers and distributors of food—were often established that set prices for farm products. Farm gate prices were frequently kept low— below world market levels—in a deliberate attempt to lower the cost of subsidizing the prices of basic foodstuffs for the urban population, or in an attempt to tax tradable commodities and generate revenue for the government. The result was often a drop in agricultural output; migration to the cities; and rising imports of food. This pattern was complemented by the effect of food aid from OECD countries—which further reduced the incentive to adopt a more economically rational agricultural policy.

As a consequence of agricultural intervention, countries without comparative advantage in agriculture not only became major producers but net exporters. Production support policies had to be complemented by export subsidies to allow surpluses to be sold. These in turn led to numerous trade conflicts. As farm surpluses were dumped at subsidized prices in international markets, agricultural trade increasingly became managed trade. During the 1986–90 period, OECD economies annually subsidized exports averaging 48.2 million tons of wheat, 19.5 million tons of coarse grains, 1.8 million tons of sugar, 1.2 million tons of beef, and 1.2 million tons of cheese and butter. Average annual export subsidies in the EU during 1986–90 were more than $13 billion, with most of the money allocated to exports of bovine meat, wheat and coarse grains, and butter and other milk products (GATT, 1994c). The loss of developing-country export revenue resulting from agricultural protectionism in the USA, the EU, and Japan was significant. For sugar and beef alone, it was estimated to be the equivalent of about half of total international development aid (World Bank, 1986).

Why do governments intervene in agriculture? Rationales that are often offered include: (1) to stabilize and increase farm incomes; (2) to guarantee food security; (3) to improve the BOP; (4) to support the development of other sectors of the economy; and (5) to increase agricultural output (Fitchett, 1987). The reasons for agricultural intervention are in large part non-economic and/or driven by special-interest politics. The political influence of the agricultural sector is substantial in many countries. Agriculture is mostly food, and food is often very political. President Nyerere of Tanzania used to say that if he needed shoes, and South Africa under the apartheid system was the only place where he could get shoes, he would not go to South Africa, but if he needed corn and the only place where he could get corn was apartheid South Africa, he would go there. Food shortages can lead to riots, revolutions, and wars. In many developing countries this has led to policies that tax agriculture and subsidize the food consumption of the population living in the cities. In industrialized countries exactly the opposite pattern can be observed: the urban population is taxed to support farm production and thus incomes. In both cases, governments are motivated to regulate, promote, distribute, store, and trade in agricultural products using subsidies, trade barriers, state trading, and government purchases (Winters, 1987b). Box 8.1 discusses this issue further.

Box 8.1. Why do poor countries tax, and rich countries subsidize agriculture?

It is an empirical regularity that average rates of protection for industries tend to decline across countries as capital–labour ratios increase. Thus, industrialized countries with large capital stocks—both physical plant and equipment and human capital—relative to labour are more open to trade than countries with large stocks of labour relative to capital (i.e. developing countries) (Rodrik, 1994a). However, rich countries tend to be much more protectionist towards agriculture (supporting production by granting financial subsidies and closing off domestic markets against import competition). In contrast, poor countries tend to promote imports, either explicitly through import subsidies, or implicitly by taxing domestic production. Kym Anderson (1993a) argues that this can be explained as follows. In a poor country, food accounts for a large share of total household consumption, whereas in rich countries food accounts for only a small share of expenditure. Moreover, agriculture is the main source of employment in a poor country, while it typically accounts for less than 5 per cent of the labour force in a rich one. In poor countries agriculture is also much less capital-intensive than in rich ones. These stylized facts can do much to explain the different policy stances that are observed. If agriculture is protected in a poor nation, the resulting increases in food prices have a large impact on the demand for labour (given the size of the sector) and thus on economy-wide wages (because labour is mobile). The wage rise will be offset to a greater or lesser extent by the rise in food prices, food being so important in consumption. At the same time the wage increase puts upward pressure on the price of non-tradables (services). The increase in wages has a large negative impact on industry as it lowers profits. As the gains per farmer of protection are low, and the loss per industrialist is high, the latter will be induced to invest resources to oppose agricultural support policies. Supporting agricultural production in a poor country may therefore not make political sense. The converse applies to rich nations, where agricultural support has much less of an impact on wages—the sector being small—on the prices of non-tradables, and industrial profits.

A simulation model that incorporates the basic differences between poor and rich countries reveals that a 10 per cent rise in the relative price of manufactures (that is, a tax on agriculture) will reduce farmers incomes by only 2 per cent, while raising those of industrialists by 45 per cent. In contrast, a 10 per cent tax on industry in a rich country (that is, a policy of supporting agriculture) raises incomes of farmers by over 20 per cent, while reducing those of industrialists by only 3 per cent.

These differences in costs and benefits for different groups in society—in conjunction with the differences in sizes of the various groups—does much to explain why farmers in rich countries are willing to invest substantial resources to obtain and maintain protection, and why industrialists in developing countries are able to obtain support at the expense of farmers.

From GATT-1947 to GATT-1994

GATT-1947 rules applying to agricultural trade were weaker than those that applied to manufactured goods. The reason for this is that many nations regarded agriculture as a sector of economic activity that should be accorded special status. This attitude manifested itself during the post-war negotiations on the ITO in US insistence that the ITO not affect its agricultural policies. Although the ITO was never ratified, GATT rules on agriculture were in part written to fit existing US agricultural policies. Disciplines for agriculture differed in two major respects from those on trade in manufactures: neither QRs nor export subsidies were forbidden. QRs were allowed under GATT Article XI for agricultural commodities as long as concurrent measures were taken to restrict domestic production or to remove a temporary domestic surplus. Quotas could also be used to deal with shortages of food or other essential exportables.

Although export subsidies on primary products were permitted, there was not complete subsidy freedom. A constraint was that such subsidies not lead to 'a more than an equitable share' of world trade for the subsidizing country. What this meant in practice was not clear, however. This condition was used as the basis of a number of disputes brought to the GATT but was too vague to give guidance to panels. Further flexibility in the use of QRs and other non-tariff barriers in the agricultural sector was introduced under special waivers (e.g. for the USA—see Chapter 7); in protocols of accession (e.g. Switzerland); through limited tariff bindings on agricultural imports—opening the way for the use of variable levies under the CAP; by maintaining 'residual' grandfathered restrictions on imports of agricultural goods; and a proliferation of various grey area measures such as VERs, orderly marketing arrangements (OMAs), and 'bilateral quotas' on trade in agricultural products.

Increasing intervention in agriculture had serious implications for MTNs. By accepting—implicitly or explicitly—the notion that agriculture is unique, it proved to be virtually impossible to make cross-sectoral linkages or trade-offs in MTNs. As noted by Josling (1977: 11) the establishment of separate negotiating groups for agriculture in recurring MTNs, staffed 'by civil servants experienced in the defence of domestic farm-support policies . . . [was] a way of avoiding a trade-off between agriculture and industry'. This constraint on the scope for general liberalization was made even more binding by the commodity-specific approach that was usually taken in MTN talks on agriculture. Throughout the 1960s and 1970s, agricultural discussions between the two major players—the EU and the USA—were based on two totally different world-views. The EU basically sought to manage world trade in a way that facilitated the functioning of the CAP, while the USA—supported by countries such as Australia, Canada, and New Zealand—wanted to achieve significant liberalization.

Very little progress was made on agriculture in the Kennedy and Tokyo rounds. In both MTNs, the basic premiss of the EU was that the principles of the CAP were non-negotiable, and that the focus of discussions should be on stabilizing world agricultural markets. Thus, the Community proposed that international commodity agreements be negotiated for products such as cereals, rice, sugar, and dairy. The United States, in contrast, emphasized the need to expand agricultural trade and to end the special status of agriculture in the GATT. It felt that restrictions on agricultural trade should be covered by agreements reached in other MTN fora where NTBs, tariffs, and safeguards were being discussed. In the Tokyo round these incompatible positions deadlocked the negotiations for a long time as the USA refused to allow progress to be made on issues such as subsidies and standards without seeing some progress made on the agricultural front. This deadlock was broken only after the new Carter Administration took over in 1977 and Robert Strauss was appointed as Special Trade Representative. President Carter put greater weight on the successful conclusion of the round than his predecessor and was willing to give in on the issue. Subsequent bilateral bid–offer negotiations resulted in the reduction of certain tariffs and an increase in various quotas, but did nothing to achieve general US objectives. Two sectoral agreements were negotiated: the Agreement on Bovine Meat and the International Dairy Arrangement. Neither was far-reaching. The agreement on meat was ostensibly aimed at increasing trade and the stability of the world market. It implied no binding obligations, however, and in practice has had little effect, if any. The dairy agreement was more substantive in that it set out minimum prices for certain major dairy products. However, these prices proved to be unenforceable in practice. A number of disputes occurred regarding circumvention of the minimum prices by certain signatories (especially the EU), which led the United States to withdraw from the agreement in February 1985. Both arrangements remain in force as Plurilateral Agreements under the WTO.

As of the early 1980s, a constituency gradually emerged in the EU that favoured a reduction in agricultural support. Agricultural subsidies were a significant burden for heavily strained government treasuries, and became increasingly difficult to defend as the ideological balance swung towards greater reliance on competition and deregulation. Two successive oil shocks financed by inflationary policies had led to large fiscal deficits, compounding the pressure on government finances. A decision by the USA to engage in a 'subsidy war' with the EU in the 1980s—partly driven by a decline in international food prices, which raised opposition to EU export subsidization—also helped to increase the financial pressure. Agricultural lobbies remained very strong, however, making multilaterally based reform potentially more attractive than unilateral actions. Better to share the pain than to go it alone. At the same time, agricultural disputes became more intense, and further enhanced the incentive for dealing with agriculture in the GATT context. As discussed previously, MTNs have an important socio-psychological dimension: governments may find it useful to be able to tell their farmers that they are not alone in having a hard time.

Thus, the Ministerial meeting that launched the Uruguay round proved able to put agriculture on the table in a comprehensive manner for the first time. The negotiating mandate broke new ground first, in that there was an explicit reference to liberalization, with all policies affecting agricultural trade to be discussed, including domestic and export subsidies; and second, that the special status of agriculture was not mentioned explicitly. This contrasts with the Kennedy and Tokyo round Ministerial Declarations, which emphasized the status of agriculture as a special (unique) sector and were oriented towards the negotiation of commodity-specific agreements. As the negotiations commenced, it rapidly became clear that discussions would continue to be dominated by what was known in GATT-jargon as 'transatlantic ping-pong' between the two largest agricultural traders—the EU and the USA—which together accounted for about 40 per cent of international trade in food. Any agreement required a deal that these two partners could live with. But they were by no means the only players. Other significant actors included the EFTA countries and Japan (with highly protectionist systems and basically in the EU camp) and a group of traditional agricultural exporters that sought significant liberalization. This coalition of fourteen countries was called the Cairns Group and was an ally of the USA. It included Argentina, Australia, Brazil, Canada, Chile, Colombia, Fiji, Hungary, Indonesia, Malaysia, New Zealand, the Philippines, Thailand, and Uruguay.

The Cairns Group's objective was to gradually attain free trade in agricultural commodities, to eliminate production distortions, and to bind undertakings to this effect. The United States sought the complete liberalization of trade in agriculture. It was particularly concerned about export subsidies, and sought their rapid and unconditional elimination. It also insisted on the need to introduce a clear-cut separation between income support for agricultural producers and the level of farm production. Income support could be accepted only if decoupled from production. The EU initially proposed that negotiations should first concentrate on 'emergency measures' for certain sectors, including cereals, sugar, and dairy products. This could be followed by the liberalization of trade and a reduction of support policies, it being understood that the goal was not free trade, but achieving stability and equilibrium in world agricultural markets. It proposed to follow a bid–offer process for specific products along the lines of previous MTNs. The Community emphasized that liberalization of trade first required the removal of the structural disequilibria on world markets. It also maintained that its existing zero (or low) tariff bindings on oil-seeds led to severe distortions in the EU market and sought to negotiate a rebalancing of its agricultural protection to make it more uniform. This desire for rebalancing became one of the more contentious issues of the negotiations.[2] Japan's general support for allowing market forces to determine production and trade was qualified by an insistence that certain social and other considerations could require government intervention. Japan supported the idea of a freeze on export subsidy expenditures as a short-run step, to be followed by a gradual phasing-out, but suggested that domestic subsidies be permitted to maintain a minimum (unspecified) level of self-sufficiency for national security reasons.

The wide disparity in positions led to heated exchanges and some acrimony. Bridging the gap between the EU and the US/Cairns positions proved extremely difficult, not only because of fundamental, substantive differences, but also because of the negotiating strategies that were pursued. Although clearly unacceptable to the EU, for the first two years the USA maintained its demand for a total reduction in trade-distorting support policies within ten years. The resulting stand-off led to the breakdown of the Midterm Review of the round held in Montreal in December 1988. After a four-month period of informal consultations it was agreed that the long-run objective in the agricultural area was to be 'substantive progressive reduction' in agricultural support. This compromise allowed negotiations to continue. In the final phase of the MTN, discussions remained very contentious, with serious differences of opinion emerging within the EU as well as between the EU and other GATT members. At the December 1990 Ministerial meeting that was supposed to conclude the round, no agreement could be achieved on agriculture, leading to a breakdown of talks on all the issues on the agenda. In effect, the EU refused to accept the compromise text that was proposed by the Chairman of the negotiating group—which would have averaged a cut of about 25 per cent in protection levels—as going too far in disciplining export subsidies and the use of specific policies. The proposal would have had significant implications for the CAP—the reform of which was under active discussion at the time. The EU needed to settle its internal debates on agriculture first—in particular to placate the French, who opposed any significant move towards

---

[2] In early MTNs a number of European countries bound tariffs on cotton, soybeans (oil, meal, and seeds), vegetables, and canned fruit at low or zero levels. When these countries joined the EEC, their obligations were assumed by the community. Once the CAP had led to a significant rise in the price of grains, European producers began to import large quantities of products with low tariff bindings, especially soybeans and related products. This was a major source of irritation for the EC Commission, which unsuccessfully attempted to close this 'gap in the CAP' in subsequent years.

meeting US/Cairns Group demands. Conversely, the Cairns Group stood firm in opposing any significant weakening of the Chairman's proposed text.

An agreement between the EU and the USA was eventually reached—after much brinkmanship—with the so-called Blair House Accord in November 1992. By that time internal CAP reform proposals had been developed by the EC Commission, allowing a deal to be struck. The EU obtained agreement that its compensation payment policies—under which farmers were paid to take land out of production—would not be included in the definition of the Aggregate Measure of Support (AMS)—that the AMS would not be product-specific, and that the extent of liberalization be reduced to a cut of about one-sixth over six years, or less than 3 per cent per year (Anderson, 1993b). While French farmers in particular continued to oppose the deal, the EU Commission contained this by arguing that the internally agreed reform of the CAP—driven by budgetary considerations and helped along by the multilateral discussions—was consistent with the Accord.

WTO Rules

The Agreement on Agriculture has four main parts, dealing with market access, domestic support, and export competition. On market access it was agreed that NTBs be converted into tariffs at the entry into force of the WTO, and that industrial countries reduce their average tariffs by 36 per cent over six years compared to a 1986–8 base-period average. All agricultural tariffs—both pre-existing and new—are bound. Reflecting the general non-prohibition on state trading (Chapter 4), marketing boards and similar monopolies are only subject to the general prohibition on the use of QRs. Because of so-called 'dirty' tariffication by many countries—i.e. the setting of tariffs above the tariff-equivalent of existing restrictions (see Chapter 4)—the extent of liberalization is less than 36 per cent. WTO members also have considerable scope to concentrate tariff reductions in commodity groups with relatively little effect on trade (Josling, 1994). The immediate impact of the tariff reductions was therefore modest, with benefits being more pronounced for processed and higher value, non-traditional products. However, at the level of the tariff line, tariffs per commodity must fall by at least 15 per cent. So as to ensure some market opening, the market-access package also requires that by 2000 at least 5 per cent of the market for commodities subject to tariffication be satisfied by imports.[3] Special safeguard mechanisms are available to protect

---

[3] Countries seeking to delay tariffication were permitted to do so for six years (ten for developing countries) if imports were below 3 per cent of domestic consumption in the 1986–8 base-period, no export subsidies were granted, and measures to restrict output are implemented. In such cases the minimum market-access requirement is higher, increasing from 4 per cent in 1995 to 8 per cent in 2000.

domestic producers if imports exceed specific trigger quantities or are priced below trigger price levels.

Domestic production support to agriculture as measured by an Aggregate Measure of Support (AMS) is to decline by the year 2000 by 20 per cent (relative to a 1986–8 base-period). WTO members are required to enter their base-period AMS in their schedules, as well as the Final Bound Commitment Level for the AMS. All these levels are bound. The AMS includes expenditures on domestic subsidies as well as market price-support policies such as administered prices, and therefore captures both border and non-border policies. In principle it covers all support policies that affect trade. This distinguishes it from concepts such as the producer subsidy equivalent (PSE) which has been used by the OECD to estimate the total amount of support given to agriculture. The AMS is aggregated over commodities and programmes. Given the goal of reducing the trade-distorting effects of agricultural policies, the AMS excludes instruments that in principle have minimal effects on production and trade. These include programmes that support agriculture generally and do not involve direct transfers to farmers, income transfers that are decoupled from production, policies that contribute less than 5 per cent of the value of production, and direct payments under production-limiting programmes if these are based on fixed areas and yields and are made on 85 per cent or less of base-period production. EU compensation payments and US deficiency payments—both of which affect production—were also excluded. In contrast to the tariff reduction obligations, which apply at the tariff line, the AMS reduction requirement pertains to the sector as a whole, not on a commodity basis.[4]

Export subsidies are to be reduced by 36 per cent in value terms and the volume of subsidized exports is to decline by 21 per cent from a 1986–90 base-period average. Reductions are to be made on a commodity-by-commodity basis. The volume decline requirement diverges from the general GATT principle that negotiated disciplines should not focus on results but on incentives, the rules of the game. There is a prohibition on the use of export subsidies, except for those agricultural commodities which are subject to reduction commitments. Export subsidy levels are bound, as are tarriffs and the AMS.

Developing countries only need to reduce tariffs, support, and export subsidies by two-thirds of the levels mentioned earlier, and have ten years to implement this. They are also exempt from the tariffication requirement for

---

[4] There is a similarity between the AMS and the *'montant de soutien'* concept which was introduced by the EU during Kennedy round (see Evans, 1972). The *montant de soutien* was defined as the difference between the world price of a product and the price received by a domestic producer. In other words, it was the nominal rate of protection taking into account all instruments affecting producer prices. However, in the Kennedy round the intention was that support measures would be calculated per commodity.

those products that are primary staples in a traditional diet, as long as imports are at least 4 per cent of consumption by 2005. Only production support that exceeds 10 per cent is subject to reduction. Input subsidies for low-income farmers are permitted, as are generally available investment subsidies and export subsidies related to export marketing and internal distribution or transport. It is unclear what the tariff reductions imply in terms of the effective liberalization of agricultural markets by developing countries, as they were not committed to use a particular base year for tariffication. In effect, developing countries have the freedom to impose tariffs at whatever level they choose to. While this basically eliminates any reduction in protection, tariffication in itself is a great achievement. The tariffs that are imposed are frequently, but not always, specific. As they are bound, over time price increases will reduce their effectiveness, independent of future trade negotiations.

While the results of the Uruguay round fell far short of US and Cairns group objectives, agreement was reached to re-insert agriculture into the multilateral trading system. The Agreement is general and systemic in nature, rather than commodity-specific, reflecting the fact that intra-sectoral trade-offs were made (in contrast to earlier MTNs). Agriculture remains 'special', but has at least been put on a progressive liberalization track. The goal is not free trade but to reduce trade distortions. Tariffication may initially increase the level of protection for some countries, but improves transparency and provides an explicit basis for future liberalization. If fully implemented, the Agreement should achieve this. And pressure to continue liberalizing the sector will persist, not least because the shift towards decoupled income support will have budgetary implications that can be expected to be more closely scrutinized by finance ministries. Notwithstanding these positive considerations, it must also be recognized that—as is often the case in MTNs—the ultimate deal is less liberalizing than it appears. This was a necessary condition for agreement by the EU. A binding constraint for the EU was that an MTN deal not oblige it to go beyond what had been agreed internally on CAP reform.

8.2. TEXTILES AND CLOTHING

Textiles and clothing was the second major sector that came to be effectively exempted from GATT-1947 disciplines. Being labour-intensive and relatively low-technology activities, developing countries began to acquire comparative advantage in basic textile and clothing products in the early 1960s. As domestic industries in high-income nations came under pressure from cheap imports, they successfully lobbied for trade restrictions. Bilateral trade restrictions gradually expanded in terms of product and country coverage. By the early 1990s a global web of QRs existed. Protectionism was driven by a desire to maintain employment of unskilled or semi-skilled workers. These industries were often regionally concentrated, and as of the 1960s still accounted for a substantial share of total manufacturing employment in many OECD countries. Rather than allow market forces to lead to a reallocation of productive resources, a choice was made to accede to pressure to limit imports. Despite the protection, total employment in the sector declined steadily. The income of low-skilled workers was also negatively affected by the policy. The price-raising effect of protection on lower-quality garments impacts especially hard on lower-income groups. Estimates for Canada revealed that in relative terms the burden of protection is four times higher for low-income consumers than for higher-income groups (UNCTAD, 1994).

How to deal with cheap labour imports from the developing world has been a recurring issue in OECD countries since the 1950s. It was on the occasion of Japan's accession to GATT in 1955, at which time it was still a developing economy and an exporter of textiles and clothing, that the concept of 'market disruption' was first extensively discussed in the GATT. In the late 1950s QRs began to be used. The restrictions imposed on developing-country garment exports were contrary to Articles I and XI of the GATT. Given the objective, the appropriate instrument would have been an action consistent with Article XIX. However, as discussed in Chapter 7, there was a strong preference to avoid GATT disciplines. To legalize the use of QRs industrialized nations sought a multilaterally negotiated derogation from the GATT rules.

The first step towards the creation of managed trade was the Short-Term Arrangement on Cotton Textiles, introduced during the Dillon round (1961). This rapidly evolved into a Long-Term Arrangement (1962), which in turn led to four successive Multifibre Arrangements (1974–94) (Table 8.1). The discriminatory character of the MFA was progressively intensified and country and product coverage were considerably extended. Not only cotton fabrics, but wool, man-made fibres, all vegetable fibres, and silk blends have been covered since 1986. The first MFA was concluded in 1973. By 1994, MFA-IV had forty-five signatories, including thirty-one developing and Central and Eastern European countries (CEECs) that exported textiles and clothing.[5] Exports covered by the MFA were subject to bilaterally agreed QRs or unilaterally imposed restraints. As textiles and clothing accounted for about 45 per cent of total OECD imports from developing countries the MFA was a cornerstone of

---

[5] As of the early 1990s, the MFA covered eight importers. Among these, Austria, Canada, the EU, Finland, Norway, and the United States applied restrictions, while Japan and Switzerland did not. The following exporting trading nations were signatories of the MFA-IV in 1994; Argentina, Bangladesh, Brazil, China, Colombia, Costa Rica, Czech Republic, Dominican Republic, Egypt, El Salvador, Fiji, Guatemala, Honduras, Hong Kong, Hungary, India, Indonesia, Jamaica, Kenya, Macau, Malaysia, Mexico, Oman, Pakistan, Panama, Peru, Philippines, Poland, Republic of Korea, Romania, Singapore, Slovakia, Slovenia, Sri Lanka, Thailand, Turkey, and Uruguay.

TABLE 8.1 *A chronology of managed trade in textiles and clothing*

Date	Action
1955	Japan introduces 'voluntary' exports restraints on cotton textiles to the USA. Restraints are continued in 1956, at the request of the USA.
1959–60	UK introduces 'voluntary' restrictions on export of cotton textiles from Hong Kong, India, and Pakistan.
1961	The US textile and clothing industry makes its support for the 1962 Trade Act conditional on interim restrictions to deal with 'market disruption' caused by surges of imports from low-cost countries. The Short Term Arrangement on Cotton Textiles is negotiated in July 1961.
1962	The Long Term Arrangement Regarding International Trade in Cotton Textiles (LTA) imposes a 5 per cent growth limit on imports of cotton products and places an important portion of the North–South trade in textiles under a managed trade regime.
1967	The LTA is extended for the next three years.
1970	The LTA is extended for another three years.
1973	To gain the support of the textile industry for the 1974 Trade Act (granting negotiating authority to participate in the Tokyo round), the US Administration persuades major developing-country garment exporters to accept a Multifibre Arrangement (MFA). The Arrangement was more liberal as regards allowed import growth than the LTA.
1974	The MFA limits the growth of textile and clothing imports to 6 per cent per annum. A Textiles Surveillance Body supervises the implementation of the MFA under the auspices of the GATT Textiles Committee, which is composed of the parties to the arrangement.
1977	An extension is agreed for a five-year period (MFA-II), including a provision for 'jointly agreed reasonable departures' from MFA rules under special circumstances.
1982	MFA-III is negotiated, extending the arrangement for five more years. The 'reasonable departure' clause is dropped.
1985	Developing countries covered by the MFA establish an International Textile and Clothing Bureau to promote the elimination of the arrangement and the return of trade in textiles and clothing to the GATT.
1986	The MFA is extended until 1991 (MFA-IV).
1991	The MFA is extended again until 1994.

the institutional framework for North–South trade. The MFA's restrictive effect on trade was substantial. Without it, it was estimated that trade would have been some 25 per cent higher for clothing and 10 per cent higher for textiles (Yang, 1994).

As in the case of agriculture, it was only in the Uruguay round that textiles and clothing could be put on the agenda of an MTN. The reasons were not the same, however. In agriculture, important factors were the financial burden of agricultural support programmes and the trade tensions that these programmes had caused. In textiles and clothing there was no pressure from finance ministries, and while consumer organizations in high-income countries undoubtedly did not much like the cost-increasing effect of the MFA, their voice was barely heard. What happened was that an implicit link was established between the demands by the USA and the EU to address new issues, such as services and TRIPs, and the desire of developing countries to see an improvement in the market-access conditions for their manufactured exports, in particular clothing.

This is not to say that negotiations were easy. Not surprisingly, they were quite difficult. Major areas of disagreement concerned the application of strengthened GATT rules, the modalities for phasing out the MFA, the duration of the transitional period and its product coverage, and the need for transitional safeguards. However, these areas were all addressed without the type of brinkmanship that characterized the agricultural negotiations. The WTO stipulates that the MFA will be phased out, and trade in textiles and clothing will be integrated into GATT rules and liberalized over a ten-year period (1995–2004). Integration means that GATT rules prohibiting QRs will enter into effect. Products covered by the Agreement on Textiles and Clothing will be integrated into GATT in three stages. In 1995 at least 16 per cent of HS categories under MFA restrictions in 1990 are to be integrated. In 1998 (stage two) another 17 per cent of tariff lines are to be integrated, followed by a further 18 per cent in 2002 (stage three). By the end of 2004 the remaining 49 per cent are to be integrated. Integration is therefore heavily backloaded, putting most of the difficult liberalization off to the future.

While this naturally raises the possibility that at the end of the day importing countries will not deliver, the Agreement requires that quotas grow substantially over the ten-year transition period. This will ensure that import-competing industries are gradually subjected to more competition, and should therefore facilitate the removal of QRs on schedule. Quotas are to grow by 16 per cent in stage 1, 25 per cent in stage 2, and 27 per cent in stage 3. Thus, a 6 per cent permitted growth rate in 1994 will become 7 per cent per year during 1995–7; 8.7 per cent during 1998–2001; and 11 per cent per year during 2002–4. Markets for textiles and clothing will also be liberalized through reductions in average tariffs. The trade-weighted tariff average for developed countries is to fall to 12.1 per cent, as compared to 15.5 per cent prior to the Uruguay round.

The demise of the MFA will be a major achievement. In part the agreement to integrate this sector into the GATT reflects the change in the negotiating position of developing countries. They insisted that progress in this area was a quid pro quo for the agreements on TRIPs and services. Full realization of free trade was not achieved, of course, and should not be expected in the near future. Tariffs will remain significantly higher than average for most countries, and domestic producers in OECD countries can be expected to use AD actions increasingly in the future. Indeed, the abolition of the MFA—in conjunction with the prohibition on VERs—will put much more pressure on AD. Disciplining this instrument of contingent protection is likely to be one of the main issues confronting developing countries in the post-MFA period.

8.3. THE CIVIL AIRCRAFT AGREEMENT

The Agreement on Trade in Civil Aircraft is something of an anomaly in the WTO in that it is a sector-specific agreement that binds only signatories. We mention it here for completeness. It aims at the reduction of both tariffs and NTBs affecting world trade in civil aircraft, and was the only specific sector agreement covering manufactures that was successfully negotiated in the Tokyo round. It eliminates import duties on trade in civil aircraft and the bulk of aircraft parts for signatories. The Agreement also reinforces disciplines on non-tariff barriers to trade in aircraft. Signatories to the agreement account for all leading civil aircraft exporters except the Russian Federation. The agreement is supervised by the Committee on Civil Aircraft. Its continued existence is to some extent a legacy from the past, as the Agreement's creation was due in part to the lack of progress that was made in the Tokyo round on subsidies. As the WTO Agreement on Subsidies applies to civil aircraft—as do all other GATT disciplines—the rationale for a sectoral agreement declined. It is not redundant, however, as the Agreement covers a high-technology sector. As such, it provides signatories with a forum in which to discuss issues that are of more general relevance to high-tech industries and high-tech competition.

8.4. CONCLUSION

If GATT was perceived to lack teeth, it was in part due to the *de facto* exclusion of trade in agriculture and textiles and clothing from the reach of its disciplines. The agreements reached in the Uruguay round therefore constituted a significant step forward in the process of reasserting the relevance of GATT's general principles of multilateralism, non-discrimination, and open markets. Without these agreements the WTO would have been much less credible as an organization.

What does the sectoral experience suggest about the political economy of multilateral liberalization and negotiations? The agriculture case illustrates that if a lobby is strong and is supported by other groups for non-economic reasons multilateral co-operation can break down. Standard reciprocity does not work in the sense that intra-sectoral trade-offs are not feasible. Only if domestic industrial lobbies had existed that had a great interest in obtaining access to foreign markets could the mechanism have worked. But such lobbies could be satisfied through negotiations that were limited to manufactures. The gains from trade within industrial trade policies were more than large enough. No linkage was required with agriculture, and US attempts to impose such linkages failed because they were not credible. The cost of the total breakdown of an MTN merely because of lack of agreement on agriculture was simply too great. Progress was made in the late 1980s because new interest-groups appeared that sought to control agricultural support programmes: finance ministries; the Maastricht Treaty with its targets for government deficits and public debt in the run-up to the establishment of a single European currency; the prospect of future enlargement of the EU to include many CEECs; and the emergence of environmental lobbies who opposed the intensive and polluting farming encouraged by existing production-support policies.

As noted earlier, a different story applies in textiles and clothing. Here there were also powerful lobbies that had been successful in obtaining protection for decades. But there were no direct budgetary implications that put pressure on abolishing such protection. While very regressive in income distribution terms, the protection of textiles and clothing was not subject to strong opposition from consumer or welfare groups. The explanation for the agreement to integrate textiles and clothing into the GATT in this case is more in line with standard GATT reciprocal negotiating dynamics. Developing countries insisted on liberalization as a quid pro quo for agreeing to sign on to other agreements. Indeed, to some extent the progress that was achieved can be explained by the fact that developing countries participated fully in the negotiations and that the lower-quality garments industry had declined substantially in size as compared to the 1970s, reducing its political clout. However, it must be recognized that liberalization will occur only over a ten-year period, and that the import-competing industries are very well aware of the existence of AD, and can be expected to invoke this or the special safeguard mechanisms allowed for under the Agreement if the competition gets too hot. Indeed, one of the reasons that it proved so difficult to agree to discipline AD significantly was strong opposition by textile and clothing lobbies.

8.5. FURTHER READING

T. Warley, in 'Western Trade in Agricultural Products', in *International Economic Relations in the Western World 1959–1971* (London: Royal Institute of International Affairs, 1976), provides a historical overview of agricultural policies and the trade of OECD countries.

L. Alan Winters, in 'The Political Economy of the Agricultural Policy of

Industrialized Countries', *European Review of Agricultural Economics*, 14 (1987), 285–304 discusses the question of why farmers have been able to obtain high levels of protection. The same author, in 'The So-Called "Non-Economic" Objectives of Agricultural Support', *OECD Economic Studies*, 13 (1989), 238–66, critically addresses the rationales that have been offered for such policies. Tim Josling, 'Agriculture and Natural Resources', in *The New GATT: Implications for the United States* (Washington DC: Brookings Institution, 1994) gives a summary evaluation of the Uruguay round Agreement on Agriculture. Richard Higgott and Andrew Cooper, 'Middle Power Leadership and Coalition Building: Australia, the Cairns Group and the Uruguay Round', *International Organization*, 49 (1990), 589–632 discuss the formation and operation of the Cairns group.

Carl Hamilton (ed.), *Textiles Trade and the Developing Countries: Eliminating the MultiFibre Arrangement in the 1990s* (Washington DC: The World Bank, 1990) contains a set of papers that analyse and describe the workings of the MFA. Irene Trela and John Whalley's contribution to that volume provides quantitative estimates of the impact of the MFA. Craig Giesse and Martin Lewin give a detailed review of the history of the MFA in 'The Multifiber Arrangement: Temporary Protection Run Amuck', *Law and Policy in International Business*, 19 (1987), 51–170. Another good source is Vinod Aggarwal, *Liberal Protectionism: The International Politics of Organized Textile Trade* (Berkeley: University of California Press, 1985).

9
Regional Integration

Although a fundamental principle of the WTO is non-discrimination in the application of trade policy by member countries, both the GATT and the GATS make explicit allowance for preferential trade agreements among a subset of Members. To avoid abuse of this possibility, both GATT and GATS impose conditions that must be met for an agreement to be permissible and provide for an examination of regional schemes by WTO Members. This Chapter discusses the rationale for regional integration, the rules of the GATT and the GATS, and the challenges that regionalism poses for the multilateral trading system.

9.1. MOTIVATIONS FOR REGIONAL ECONOMIC INTEGRATION

Regional integration agreements (RIAs) may take several forms, depending on the degree of integration. In a free-trade area (FTA), trade restrictions among member countries are removed, but each country retains its own tariff structure against outsiders. A customs-union is a free-trade area with common external trade policies. A common market is a customs union that also allows for the free movement of factors of production. An economic union is a common market that includes some degree of harmonization of the national economic policies of member states, while a monetary union is a common market or economic union that has adopted a common currency. In practice, RIAs are often a combination of these ideal types, with harmonization in the case of economic and/or monetary union occurring in policy areas that are chosen on the basis of political factors.

Between 1948 and 1994, over 100 preferential trading agreements were notified by contracting parties (GATT, 1994b). Many of these notifications occurred in GATT's later years, starting in the 1970s. Between 1989 and 1994 alone, some forty agreements were notified to the GATT Secretariat. Most of these involved the European countries: many were FTAs negotiated between the EU or the European Free Trade Agreement (EFTA) and many CEECs. Major non-European agreements that have been notified recently include the North American Free Trade Agreement (NAFTA)—Canada, Mexico, and the USA—and MERCOSUR (the Southern Cone Common Market)—Argentina, Brazil, Paraguay, and Uruguay. Virtually all OECD countries are now a member of one or more RIAs—Australia and New Zealand have a long-standing preferential trade relationship, dating back to the 1960s.

Why go regional? Before going on to focus on economic aspects, it should be recognized that RIAs are often driven by considerations of foreign policy and national security. Indeed, these may predominate, any economic costs being regarded as the price to pay to achieve the non-economic objectives. Taking this as given, there are a number of possibilities with regard to economic motives. The first is that a subset of like-minded countries may be able to go much further in liberalizing trade flows than the larger set of WTO Members. The second is that RIAs are a way for countries to enhance their market power and/or circumvent the GATT's non-discrimination requirement. Of course, the first possibility does not exclude the second, and this is why GATT and GATS have rules on regional integration. In principle it is considered to be beneficial for the world—after all, if far-reaching enough, an RIA has the effects of fully integrating two or more economies, in effect making them one country—but only if the RIA does integrate the economies involved and does not in the process increase barriers to trade with non-members. Another economic motivation for the pursuit of RIAs is as a mechanism to lock in liberalization or regulatory reform. A final rationale that should be mentioned is to seek membership of an RIA in order to guarantee access to markets.

As discussed in Chapter 1, at any point in time the political market of a country will determine an equilibrium level of market-access restrictions. Assuming for purposes of discussion that unilateral liberalization is not an option, interest-groups will have a choice between pursuing regional or multi-lateral trade agreements. What determines interest-group preferences regarding these two options? An RIA by definition involves substantially fewer countries than an MTN; indeed, some RIAs involve only two countries. This should make them easier to negotiate. The set of possible policy packages that could make all parties better off may well be larger under an RIA, including issues that could not even appear on the negotiating agenda of an MTN. Issue linkage or side-payments may be more feasible, facilitating agreement. RIAs may also involve formal mechanisms to transfer income from one region to another; in the MTN-context this is rarely possible. The more similar countries are in their endowments and income levels, the likelier it is that intra-industry trade will be significant. This may facilitate liberalization (see Box 9.1).

Globally oriented exporting firms may be indifferent between the status quo and an RIA as long as external trade barriers are not raised, and may actively support it if they perceive that the negotiating power of the RIA enhances the probability of obtaining greater access to third markets. Regional liberalization may also be considered to be less uncertain. The closer are countries' regulatory regimes, the smaller may be concerns regarding the free-riding of competitors in potential partner countries. Thus, a preferential agreement to

---

Box 9.1. Intra-industry trade and pressures for protection

The magnitude of intra-industry trade is often regarded as an indicator of the extent to which significant adjustment pressures are likely to arise as a result of liberalization. Adjustment costs are likely to be lower if intra-industry trade is high, because jobs lost due to customers shifting to more efficient foreign suppliers may to a large extent be offset by the job-enhancing expansion in foreign demand for similar goods produced domestically. The political opposition to liberalizing and expanding intra-industry trade tends to be much more muted than in instances where trade flows are predominantly of the inter-industry type. In the latter case industries that are less competitive than those abroad will generally be forced to contract substantially. This is not to say that intra-industry trade will not lead to adjustment and thus pressure for protection. Specialized and relatively immobile factors of production injured by import competition can be expected to seek protection. But the injury in this case is more at the firm than at the industry level. Other firms in the industry will expand. This makes it more difficult to maintain protection, as there will be conflicting interests within industries. The relevance of this for regional integration is that intra-industry trade is high among countries with similar endowments and per capita income levels—those that have traditionally tended to form RIAs. Aggregate adjustment costs associated with an RIA may then be much lower than under an MTN, as such countries' trade consists importantly of intermediate and differentiated products. Levels of intra-industry trade between the members of the most successful RIAs—the EU, EFTA, and the more recent North American FTAs—are high, both for trade in goods and trade in services (Globerman, 1992; Edwards and Savastano, 1989; Greenaway, 1987; Primo-Braga *et al.*, 1994).

---

liberalize trade may allow greater internalization of the benefits. The implied reduction in uncertainty with respect to the outcome of liberalization—the distribution of gains and losses—may facilitate its negotiation. The smaller the required changes in regulatory regimes and the greater the confidence that regulations will be enforced in all jurisdictions, the more certain are the conditions of competition *ex post*.

RIAs may also allow more credible commitments to be made, in so far as monitoring implementation of the agreement is facilitated. The limited number, similarity, and proximity of member countries may imply that industries are better informed regarding actions by rivals or foreign governments that violate the agreement. Some RIAs have supranational enforcement mechanisms, the EU being the primary example. This will reduce uncertainty regarding implementation and enforcement. Finally, RIAs can be good instruments through which to experiment with issues that have not yet been addressed in the multilateral forum and/or to exert pressure on trading partners. Thus, if an MTN on a set of issues cannot be agreed upon, the subset of countries seeking agreement on the issues involved may pursue an RIA in part with a view to inducing other countries to agree to their position. The United States decided to negotiate FTAs with trading partners in the 1980s in part because of dissatisfaction with the refusal of GATT partners to initiate an MTN in 1982 (Schott, 1989).

Much attention has been devoted to the question of whether RIAs are detrimental to non-members, both in the short run (impact effects) and in the longer run (taking induced growth effects into account). The impact of regional integration on both member and non-member countries will depend on the type of agreement concerned (i.e. FTA, customs union, or common market) and on the degree to which intra-regional trade is liberalized. The more extensive internal liberalization is, the greater the resulting increase in competition within internal markets. While this is welfare-enhancing for member countries—and presumably the object of economic integration—it may also be associated with greater adjustment pressures for inefficient industries located in member countries. The latter may attempt to shift some of the adjustment burden onto third countries by seeking increases in external barriers. Account therefore needs to be taken of the magnitude of implicit discrimination (due to the preferential nature of liberalization) and possible additional explicit discrimination against third countries in the form of greater barriers to imports *ex post*. Regional integration *per se* can also be detrimental to non-members by inducing a shift away from trading with them. To use economic jargon, the formation of a trading bloc can give rise to trade diversion (a shift from an efficient outside supplier, to a higher cost regional one, induced by the elimination of tariffs on intra-regional trade).

Some observers—e.g., Hirschman (1981), and Tumlir (1983)—argue that regionalism must involve greater intra-regional trade for political reasons, even though such trade may involve member countries importing from each other higher-cost products than those available from non-member countries. Trade diversion may be necessary for political reasons. But although member countries may decide that any economic costs are outweighed by the (non-economic) benefits more broadly defined, the rest of the world does not experience such benefits, and is simply confronted with the costs. Third countries may also be harmed through so-called investment diversion. This involves enterprises deciding to invest inside RIAs and produce locally, rather than produce in the least-cost location and ship products to the RIA. Box 9.2 presents the case of Mercedes-Benz, which illustrates how multinationals take into account the incentives created by RIAs in formulating their globalization strategies.

Box 9.2. Mercedes-Benz, regional integration, and globalization

The impact of trade liberalization on international business is strongly felt in corporate quarters. Multinationals continuously face very complex decision problems regarding what and where to produce. Purely economic considerations are tempered by socio-political ones: whatever the economics, it often makes sense to become a local in terms of enhancing one's influence with host country governments (both central and local) by building a support base (through employment creation, etc.). A representative example of a large firm that is increasingly driven to think global and act local is Mercedes-Benz's commercial vehicle division. More than 40 per cent of 1994 turnover originated in plants outside Europe. NAFTA and MERCOSUR (see above) have helped to determine where the firm has established production facilities in the Americas. It owns Freightliner, a US producer of trucks, and operates a plant in Mexico that produced 12,000 trucks and buses in 1994. It has reacted to the negotiation of the MERCOSUR deal by restructuring its Latin American operations, and deciding to begin construction of vans in Argentina in 1996.

Firm production strategies are, of course, by no means driven by regional integration alone. The main trend is towards globalization: sourcing from whatever location is the best in terms of price, quality, and reliability. Mercedes is a global firm and will remain one. For example, an Indonesian subsidiary that has been selected to begin pilot manufacturing of a new truck (the MB700) will source engines from Spain, power-steering from Japan, axles and drive-trains from India, and other parts from Thailand, Taiwan, and Turkey. The whole operation will be co-ordinated from a regional logistics centre in Singapore. While globalization will continue, regional integration can affect investment decisions at the margin: rather than expand its Mexican operations, new investment might go to a MERCOSUR country. Or, rather than ship trucks from Indonesia to Argentina, the RIA may induce investment there. The specific policies of the RIA will be important in this connection.

Source: *Financial Times*, 15 October 1994.

9.2. GATT ARTICLE XXIV: CUSTOMS UNIONS AND FREE-TRADE AREAS

Article XXIV of the GATT allows FTAs and customs unions to exist as long as:

(1) trade barriers after integration do not rise on average (Article XXIV: 5)
(2) agreements eliminate all tariffs and other trade restrictions on 'substantially all' intra-regional exchanges of goods within a 'reasonable' length of time; and
(3) they are notified to the GATT which may decide to establish a Working Party to determine if these conditions are satisfied.

The rationale for the first condition is obvious. Clearly, if restrictions on imports from non-member economies are no higher than before, the extent of possible reductions in imports from non-members is limited. A practical problem faced by the drafters of Article XXIV was that the formation of a customs union involves changes in the external tariffs of member countries as they adopt a common external tariff. The rule that applies to customs unions is that duties and other barriers to imports from outside the union may not be 'on the whole' higher or more restrictive than those preceding the establishment of the customs union (Article XXIV: 5a). The interpretation of this phrase became a source of much disagreement among GATT contracting parties. The rule for FTAs was unambiguous, however. Duties applied by each individual country are not to be raised (Article XXIV: 5b).

The second condition is somewhat counter-intuitive in that maximum preferential liberalization in itself is likely to be more detrimental to non-members than partial liberalization. Requiring it, however, ensures that countries are limited in their ability to violate the MFN obligation selectively. As noted by Finger (1993b), the rationale behind the second condition is a public choice one: it is an attempt to ensure that participants in regional liberalization efforts 'go all the way'. There is a high probability that due to the political dynamics of trade negotiations, negotiators able to pursue partial preferences will tend to cut tariffs on items previously imported from non-member countries. It is precisely for such items that the risk of trade diversion is greatest. What really matters as far as the welfare of non-members is concerned is the impact on trade flows (see below) and this is not recognized in Article XXIV. Even if the two requirements are met, and even if net aggregate imports do not contract, imports of particular products by the region may decline *ex post*, harming producers in the rest of the world. No compensation can be claimed *ex post* under GATT rules if the RIA has been approved and/or *ex ante* compensation was granted. In any event, satisfaction of the GATT tests does not give a green light to an RIA—in principle what matters are the conclusions of the Working Party and the Council.

The GATT's experience in testing FTAs and customs unions against Article

XXIV has not been very encouraging. Various aspects of the rules and their application, including approval by the CONTRACTING PARTIES of regional arrangements before they could be said to have entered into force, have proved unsatisfactory. After the examination of the Treaty of Rome establishing the EEC in 1957, almost no examination of agreements notified under Article XXIV led to a unanimous conclusion or specific endorsement that all the legal GATT requirements had been met. As noted by the Chairman of the Working Party on the 1989 Canada–United States Free Trade Agreement, commenting on the inability to reach a consensus, 'Over fifty previous working parties on individual customs unions or free trade areas have been unable to reach unanimous conclusions on the compatibility of these agreements with the GATT—on the other hand, no such agreement has been explicitly disapproved' (*GATT Focus*, November–December 1991). As of the late 1980s, only four working parties had agreed that a regional agreement satisfied the requirements of Article XXIV (Schott, 1989) three of which pre-dated the EEC. It is not much of an exaggeration to say that GATT rules were largely a dead letter, although the consultations that occurred allowed interested non-members to exert some influence.

The reasons underlying this impotence are largely political. A conscious political decision was made by contracting parties in the late 1950s not to closely scrutinize the formation of the EEC, as it was made clear by the original six EEC member states that a GATT finding that the EEC violated Article XXIV could well result in their withdrawal from GATT (Snape, 1993). To paraphrase Finger (1993*b*), at the end of the day the GATT 'blinked'. Given that the EEC probably did not meet all the requirements of Article XXIV, this created a precedent that was often followed subsequently. A result has been that most RIAs notified to GATT embody many holes and loopholes. Indeed, even serious attempts at regional liberalization—and until recently there were not very many of these—did not go much further than the GATT (Hoekman and Leidy, 1993). Although regional agreements have been tolerated for political reasons, the criteria and language of Article XXIV are also ambiguous. Legitimate differences of opinion may exist as to what constitutes 'substantially all' trade, how to determine whether the external trade policy of a customs union does not become more restrictive 'on average', or what is a 'reasonable length of time' for the transition towards the full implementation of an FTA or customs union. Some of these issues were addressed in the Uruguay round.

The GATT-1994 Understanding on the Interpretation of Article XXIV reaffirms that RIAs should facilitate trade between members and should not raise barriers to the trade of non-members. In their formation or enlargement, the parties to RIAs should 'to the greatest possible extent avoid creating adverse effects on the trade of other Members' (GATT, 1994*a*: 31). It was recognized that the effectiveness of the role of the Council for Trade in

Goods—see Chapter 2—in reviewing agreements notified under Article XXIV needed to be enhanced. This was to be pursued in part by clarifying the criteria and procedures for the assessment of new or enlarged agreements, and by improving the transparency of all agreements notified to GATT under Article XXIV. Under the WTO, the evaluation of the general incidence of the duties and other regulations of commerce applicable before and after the formation of a customs union is to be based upon 'an overall assessment of weighted average tariff rates and of customs duties collected'. The assessment must be based on import statistics for a previous representative period (to be supplied by the customs union) on a tariff-line basis, broken down by WTO member country of origin. The WTO Secretariat is to compute the weighted average tariff rates and customs duties collected. The duties and charges to be taken into consideration are to be the applied, not the bound rates. If quantification of the incidence of trade policies is difficult, the impact of individual regulations may be analysed on a case-by-case basis.

Article XXIV: 6 requires GATT members seeking to increase bound tariff rates upon joining a customs union to enter into negotiations—under Article XXVIII (Modification of Schedules, see Chapter 7)—on compensatory adjustment. In doing this, reductions in duties on the same tariff line made by other members of the customs union must be taken into account. If such reductions are insufficient compensation, the Understanding requires the customs union to offer to reduce duties on other tariff lines, or to otherwise provide compensation. Where agreement on compensatory adjustment cannot be reached within a reasonable period from the initiation of negotiations, the customs union is free to modify or withdraw the concessions and affected Members are free to withdraw substantially equivalent concessions (i.e. to retaliate).

The Understanding also established a ten-year maximum for the transition period for implementation of an agreement, although allowance is made for 'exceptional circumstances' (to be explained to the Council for Trade in Goods). Working parties are to make appropriate recommendations concerning interim agreements—those with a transitional period—as regards the proposed time-period and the measures required to complete the formation of the customs union or FTA. If an interim agreement does not include a plan and schedule, the Working Party must recommend one. Parties to an agreement may not implement it if they are not prepared to modify it in accordance with the recommendations. Implementation of the recommendations is subject to subsequent review.

Developing countries may, if they wish, invoke provisions of the GATT allowing them to establish FTAs that do not meet the conditions of Article XXIV. The 1979 Decision on Differential and More Favorable Treatment of Developing Countries (the so-called Enabling Clause) allows for regional arrangements between developing countries to apply lower tariffs to each other's trade than are applied to imports originating in non-members. If governments so desire, agreements that do not meet the requirements of Article XXIV—e.g. they pertain to a limited set of products, or entail reductions in tariffs rather than elimination—can be and have been justified under the Enabling Clause (see Chapter 10). A relevant recent example was the Mercosur (a customs union), which was notified to GATT under the Enabling Clause, not under Article XXIV. In this case, however, the United States argued that Mercosur should be notified under Article XXIV, and the matter was given to the Committee on Trade and Development to review. This is a good example of the interface between the code of conduct aspect of the WTO and its role as a forum for negotiations.

9.3. GATS ARTICLE V: ECONOMIC INTEGRATION

The GATS is similar to the GATT in allowing for RIAs subject to conditions and surveillance. The relevant provision, Article V of the GATS, is entitled Economic Integration, not Free Trade Areas and Customs Unions (as in Article XXIV of the GATT), reflecting the fact that the GATS covers more than cross-border trade in services. It also covers three other modes of supply:

(1) provision implying movement of the consumer to the location of the supplier;
(2) services sold in the territory of a member country by entities originating in other Members through a commercial presence; and
(3) provision of services requiring the temporary movement of service suppliers who are nationals of a Member (see Chapter 5).

Analogous to Article XXIV of the GATT, Article V of the GATS imposes three conditions on economic integration agreements between signatories of the GATS. First, such agreements must have 'substantial sectoral coverage'. An interpretive note states that this should be understood in terms of the number of sectors, volume of trade affected, and modes of supply. Economic integration agreements may not provide for the a priori exclusion of any mode of supply. Second, regional agreements are to provide for the absence or elimination of substantially all discrimination (defined as measures violating national treatment) between or among the parties to the agreement in sectors subject to multilateral commitments—i.e. those where specific commitments were made (see Chapter 5). This is to consist of the elimination of existing discriminatory measures and/or the prohibition of new discriminatory measures, and must be achieved at the entry into force of the agreement or on the basis of a 'reasonable' time-frame. Third, such agreements are not to result in higher trade and investment barriers against third countries.

The 'substantial sectoral coverage' requirement is weaker than the 'substantially all trade' criterion of Article XXIV. The same conclusion applies regarding the criteria on the magnitude of liberalization required. Article XXIV of the GATT requires that 'duties and other restrictive regulations of commerce' be eliminated on substantially all intra-area trade. Under the GATS, a mere standstill agreement may be deemed sufficient. The GATS requirement is not elimination of existing discriminatory measures and prohibition on new measures, but elimination of existing discriminatory measures and/*or* a prohibition on new measures. As under the GATT, economic integration agreements are not to raise the overall level of barriers to trade in services originating in other GATS Members. However, a difference is that the GATS requires that barriers not be higher in the relevant sectors or sub-sectors — those where specific commitments were made. This sector-specificity means that a Member cannot argue — in contrast to GATT — that the average level or 'general incidence' of protection has not changed, regardless of what might occur at the level of individual products (sub-sectors).

In both the GATT and GATS, compensation of non-members is only foreseen for increases in explicit discrimination (i.e. the raising of external barriers), not for rises in implicit discrimination. The latter is a central — and inherent — feature of RIAs and is 'tolerated' by Members so long as the necessary conditions noted above are met. Members of the GATS engaged in economic integration efforts intending to withdraw or modify specific market access and/or national treatment commitments (i.e. to raise external barriers) must follow the procedures set out in GATS Article XXI (Modification of Schedules). Members intending to alter previously negotiated specific commitments must notify the Council of the GATS of their intentions, and engage in negotiations with affected parties regarding compensation (which must be applied on an MFN basis). In contrast to GATT, the GATS allows affected Members to request binding arbitration if no agreement on compensation emerges. If arbitration recommendations are not implemented by the Members(s) modifying a specific commitment, affected Members that participated in the arbitration may 'retaliate' without needing authorization by the GATS Council. In this respect the GATS also goes beyond GATT, which only provides for countries concerned to refer disagreements regarding compensation to the Council for Trade in Goods, who may in turn 'submit their views'.

Both the GATT and GATS contain provisions relating to transparency and surveillance matters. Countries intending to form, join, or modify a preferential agreement must notify them, make available relevant information requested by WTO Members, and may be subjected to the scrutiny of a working party to determine the consistency of the agreement with multilateral rules. In both the GATT and GATS, consequent to a working party's report on the consistency of an agreement, 'recommendations' may be made by the Council 'as they deem appropriate'. The GATT differs from the GATS, however, in that Article XXIV contains stronger language than Article V on the 'conditionality' attached to the time-frame for implementation. As noted earlier, Article XXIV requires that if a working party finds that the plan or schedule for an interim agreement is not likely to result in a GATT-consistent customs union or FTA, its members 'shall not maintain or put into force . . . [an] agreement if they are not prepared to modify it in accordance with . . . the recommendations.' No such provision exists in Article V, perhaps reflecting the difficulty of past working parties to come to agreement.

Article XXIV of GATT and Article V of GATS both contain loopholes allowing for the formation of agreements that do not fully comply with multilateral disciplines. For example, Article V: 2 of the GATS allows for consideration to be given to the relationship between a particular regional agreement and the wider process of economic integration among member countries. Article V: 3 gives developing countries involved in an RIA flexibility regarding the realization of the internal liberalization requirements and allows them to give more favourable treatment to firms that originate in parties to the agreement. That is, it allows for discrimination against firms originating in non-members, even if the latter are established within the area. These 'special and differential treatment' type of provisions are unlikely to be very effective in achieving their presumed objective: attracting inward foreign direct investment. More importantly, they weaken the scope of multilateral disciplines, giving governments (or interest-groups) an opportunity to pursue agreements that are not beneficial to the trading system.

9.4. TRADING BLOCS AND THE MULTILATERAL TRADING SYSTEM

Economists argue that a necessary condition for preferential liberalization to be deemed multilaterally acceptable is that the volume of imports by member countries from the rest of the world should not decline on a product-by-product basis after the implementation of the agreement (Kemp and Wan, 1976; McMillan, 1993). Import volumes are a function of the extent of trade diversion, the trade-policy stance taken *vis-à-vis* the rest of the world, and the impact of regional liberalization on the growth of member economies. The latter will in turn depend on how comprehensive the regional agreement is with respect to sectoral coverage and the elimination of intra-regional barriers to contesting markets. The trade volume test will capture these various kinds of effects, but only after the fact. While in principle it could be used as the basis for *ex post* compensation claims by countries that turned out to be negatively affected by the formation or enlargement of an RIA, neither GATT nor the GATS allows for such claims, nor is a trade-effects test required.

The empirical literature suggests that the trade-volume test has been met in the past. Although the intensity of intra-regional trade has increased this century, the propensity of regions to trade with the rest of the world, expressed as a percentage of their GDP, has also expanded (Anderson and

Norheim, 1993). Global integration—as measured by trade flows and capital flows—does not appear to have been affected negatively by regional integration efforts. However, this cannot be said with certainty, as no one knows what would have happened without RIAs. Whatever past history may suggest regarding the effect of RIAs on non-members, there clearly are causes for concern about the proliferation of RIAs observed in the last ten years. What matters is not just the economic impact of a particular agreement, but the systemic effects of RIAs. For example, the threat of contingent protection, especially AD, has become an important incentive for third countries to seek to join RIAs as opposed to the pursuit of MTNs (Hindley and Messerlin, 1993). Whether RIAs tend to be consistent with multilateral liberalization depends on the incentives that are created inside RIAs with respect to their external trade-policy stance, and the reactions of non-members.

Member Countries' Trade Policies

There are various means by which RIAs may constrain national interest-groups and thus foster a more liberal external trade policy (De Melo *et al.*, 1993). A first can be called the 'preference-dilution effect': because regional integration implies a larger political community, each of the politically important interest-groups in member countries will have less influence on the design of common policies. The second is the 'preference-asymmetry effect': because preferences on specific issues are likely to differ across member countries, the resulting need for compromises may enhance efficiency. The creation of RIAs may disrupt the formation of rent-seeking interest-groups, as these have to reorganize at the regional level, establishing an institutional structure that allows them to agree on a common position. But, RIAs may also facilitate the adoption of less liberal policies. Consumer interests may be harder to defend in an RIA than at the national level, whereas producer interests are more likely to be strengthened than weakened (Tumlir, 1983). Each national producer group may face less opposition when seeking price-increasing policies, and may indeed find support from other producer groups in other countries that pursue their own interests. The need for striking compromises may then result in a less liberal regulatory regime. Moreover, it may be in the interest of national politicians to let a regional organization satisfy national pressure-groups as this is less transparent for domestic voters and can be justified as being necessary to maintain the agreement (Vaubel, 1986).

Much will generally depend on the type of regional integration agreement that is involved. Two basic types can be distinguished: an FTA, as opposed to a customs union or common market. Both types imply non-discrimination between the members of the agreement: any benefit granted to member country *B* by member country *A* is also available to member country *C*. The major difference between an FTA and a customs union or common market is that the latter have a common external trade policy. Whatever the extent of internal liberalization of trade and competition, implementation of a common external trade policy can give rise to an upward bias in the level of external protection over time, especially if import-competing industries pursue instruments of contingent protection such as anti-dumping actions. The scope for expansion in the use and coverage of AD actions in a customs union is amply illustrated by the experience of the EU (Hindley and Messerlin, 1993). Thus, there may be no net increase in external trade barriers at the formation of a customs union, but there can easily be an upward trend if contingent protection is maintained as an option. In contrast, FTAs have a different dynamic, as members in some sense compete in their external trade policies. Box 9.3 discusses the political economy of FTAs versus customs unions further.

Box 9.3. Pressures for protection: FTAs and customs unions

Under a customs union or common market the potential returns to protection-seeking will be higher than under an FTA or under multilateral arrangements: the expected pay-off for a unit of lobbying effort increases because the size of the protected market is bigger. Moreover, liberal-minded governments that join a customs union may find it impossible to prevent domestic industries from seeking protection or to block the imposition of protection. For example, it may be the case that certain countries did not use (or make available) contingent protection before joining a customs union. However, once a member country, any domestic firm has access to the central trade-policy authority and will be able to petition for an AD investigation, and cannot be prevented from doing so by the home country government. Indeed, the welfare gains to liberal countries from joining a GATT-consistent customs union that employs contingent protection are reduced, as consumers are faced with higher expected levels of protection—without knowing *ex ante* which industries will be affected (Hoekman and Leidy, 1993).

More generally, once a common external trade policy applies, decision-making structures may be biased towards more rather than less protection or intervention. This is illustrated by the EU. As discussed at greater length in Winters (1994*b*), EU trade policy-making is characterized by the restaurant-bill problem. If a group goes to a restaurant and shares the cost of the bill, each has an incentive to order more expensive dishes than they would if they ate on their own, as to some extent the others are expected to pick up part of the cost. The same is true in the EU. The costs of protection are borne by all EU consumers, and are roughly proportional to each country's GDP. Benefits accruing to producers are proportional to the share of each country in the EU's production of the good concerned. This establishes an incentive for each government to pursue protection for those products where their share of total EU production exceeds their country's share of EU GDP. Thus, the Netherlands may not like the EU-wide protection for cars sought by France and Italy, but may accept it if other policies are adopted for products in which it is relatively specialized (such as agriculture). Indeed, to the extent that larger countries are able to get the Commission to propose protectionist policies in specific areas, all EU Member States have an incentive to ensure that some of their producers also obtain protection. Matters are compounded by the desire of the EC Commission to safeguard its prerogatives in the realm of trade policy. Thus, if a Member unilaterally takes an action to restrict imports, such restrictions may be extended to the EU as a whole in an attempt to keep control of policy.

The external trade-policy bias towards protection that may arise under a customs union will be weaker in an FTA. Because there is no common external trade policy, member countries compete in their external trade policies. Industries cannot lobby for area-wide protection. While import-competing firms in member countries may have an incentive to obtain such protection, each industry will have to approach its own government. The required co-ordination and co-operation may be more difficult to sustain than in a customs union, where the centralization of trade policy requires firms to present a common front. In any particular instance, some member country governments will award protection, whereas others will not. If industries in member countries are all competing against third suppliers, protection by one member may benefit industries in other Member States. Such free-riding can result in less protection than in the absence of the FTA (Deardorff, 1992). This benefit may, however, be offset by other aspects of FTAs. An example is the need for rules of origin, which may allow industries to limit the extent of intra-area liberalization and can be detrimental to non-members (see Box 9.4, below).

Both customs unions and members of an FTA may negotiate FTAs with non-member countries. To the extent that the countries involved do not have FTAs with each other, a hub-and-spoke system may emerge (Wonnacott, 1991). A hub-and-spoke system essentially consists of a set of bilateral trade agreements. Because there is discrimination between the members of such a system, less liberalization is likely to result than under an FTA. Moreover, it may be more difficult to reduce the magnitude and scope of the sectoral exclusions and loopholes over time. Because a hub-and-spoke system involves separate agreements between the hub country and the spoke countries, there is more scope to exclude sensitive sectors from the coverage of each bilateral agreement (Snape *et al.*, 1993). Each spoke is likely to have comparative advantage in a somewhat different set of such sectors. In an FTA the scope for exceptions will generally be less because members will have different preferences concerning the extent to which the coverage of the agreement is incomplete. Similarly, the scope under a hub-and-spoke system for maintaining policies that imply an effective reduction in the scope of liberalization of internal trade will also be greater. If each country maintains the contingent protection option (AD, safeguards) *vis-à-vis* member countries, powerful import-competing industries in the hub country will have an interest in including wide-ranging safeguard clauses and relatively stringent rules of origin—as is the case in the Association Agreements negotiated between the EU and various CEECs in 1992 (Winters, 1995). By allowing bilateral deals regarding sectoral coverage and the obligations imposed by the agreement, vested interests may be created that can prove more difficult to dislodge in future attempts to achieve further liberalization than if the agreement had been applied on a non-discriminatory basis. As summarized by Bhagwati (1993) such groups may argue that the region 'is our market', and that 'our markets are large enough'.

Rules of origin will play an important role in hub-and-spoke arrangements, as they are crucial to ensure that trade flows are not diverted through the hub country or customs union from one spoke to another. Rules of origin are a corollary of all free-trade agreements, and constitute a major disadvantage of FTAs as compared with customs unions.

Box 9.4. Rules of origin in free-trade agreements

The extent of liberalization under an FTA depends on its rules of origin. Upon the formation of an FTA, non-member countries may not only be confronted with trade diversion due to the preferential nature of the abolition of barriers to trade, but also because of an effective increase in protection even if no changes are made to external tariffs. Assume that an intermediate product enters a country free of duty and that this country accedes to an FTA. Industries using this input that export to RIA members may then have an incentive to shift to higher-cost regional producers of intermediates in order to satisfy the rules of origin for their product. In effect, the rule of origin is then equivalent to a prohibitive tariff for the original third-country suppliers of components. An additional important factor is whether the rule is cumulative. Suppose a product is imported that has been processed in at least two countries, both of which have preferential status. An origin system is cumulative if the importing country only requires that 'sufficient' processing of the product has occurred in any of the countries to which the preferential agreement applies. That is, it allows the exporting country of the final product to add (cumulate) the value added in other beneficiary countries to that added by itself. If the value-added criterion is 40 per cent, and 30 per cent was added in country 1 and 20 per cent in country 2, the product would meet the criterion under a cumulative origin system. Under a non-cumulative system of origin 40 per cent would have to be added in each country. Non-cumulative rules of origin are much more restrictive than those that allow cumulation.

The more restrictive the rules of origin, the more they will hinder the liberalization goal from being attained. In an empirical analysis of trade between the EU and individual EFTA countries—each of which is in principle allowed duty-free access to the EU—Herin (1986) found that the costs associated with satisfying the rules of origin imposed by the EU were high enough to induce 25 per cent of EFTA exports to enter the EU by paying the relevant MFN tariff. More important for the trading system is the possibility of trade diversion (Krueger, 1992). Article XXIV: 5*b* of the GATT requires that duties and 'other regulations of commerce' applied by members of a free-trade area are no more restrictive than those applying prior to the formation of the area. The question of whether rules of origin are one of the 'other regulations of commerce' referred to in Article XXIV: 5*b* has not been settled. Nor are preferential rules of origin embodied in a regional trade agreement addressed by the WTO agreement on rules of origin (see Chapter 4), even though they are clearly of concern to third countries. As argued by the USA in connection with the 1972 FTAs between the EEC and EFTA states, the rules of origin would 'result in trade diversion by raising barriers to third countries' exports of intermediate manufactured products and raw materials. This resulted from unnecessarily high requirements for value originating within the area. In certain cases . . . the rules disqualifies goods with value originating within the area as high as 96 per cent. The rules of origin limited non-origin components to just 5 per cent of the value of a finished product of the same tariff heading [for] nearly one-fifth of all industrial tariff headings. In many other cases a 20 per cent rule applied' (GATT, *Basic Instruments and Selected Documents*, 1974: 152–3).

Non-Members

The systemic impact of RIAs depends not only on their internal political dynamics, but also on what non-members do in response to them. The most obvious trade-policy reaction of third countries is to induce the RIA to reduce its barriers to external trade, perhaps in part in order to obtain compensation for any increases in tariffs. Thus, the first part of the Dillon round (1960–1; see Chapter 1), was devoted to renegotiating a balance of concessions subsequent to the implementation of the EEC's common external tariff (Patterson, 1966). In practice, regional integration (in particular by the EU) has been a recurrent reason for third parties to engage in MTNs under GATT auspices. The second component of the Dillon round was to reduce the level of the common external tariff of the EEC, thereby limiting potential trade-diversion effects.

The same type of objectives played a role in the Kennedy and Tokyo rounds. At the time of the Kennedy round the margins of preference for EEC members had increased substantially, as most of the internal elimination of tariffs had been achieved. 'The record leaves no doubt that a compelling factor in the decision of Congress to pass legislation authorizing a 50 per cent linear cut in tariffs [in the Kennedy round—see Chapter 3] . . . was the belief that the Common Market posed a potentially serious threat to the growth, and perhaps even maintenance of American exports.' (Patterson, 1966: 176). Thus, 'the task of the Kennedy Round . . . was to attempt to mitigate [the] disruptive trade effects of European economic integration' (Preeg, 1970: 29). In this, third countries were somewhat successful, as the Kennedy round reportedly prevented one-third to one-half of the trade diversion that might have occurred from European integration (Preeg, 1970: 220). The first enlargement of the EEC in 1973—to include Denmark, Ireland, and the United Kingdom—was one factor behind the launching of the Tokyo round, as was the impact of the CAP. A major objective of the United States was to improve its market access for agricultural products and to curb the EU's use of export subsidies. Links between regional integration and the Uruguay round included the adoption of the Single European Act (the EC-1992 programme), the implementation of the Canada–USA FTA, the negotiations on the NAFTA, and the continuing distortions of world agricultural trade induced by the EU's CAP. The foregoing does not imply that RIAs are good because they give countries an incentive to pursue concurrent MTN-based liberalization. Without the EEC, much more progress might have been made towards multilateral liberalization (Winters, 1994*b*).

Another trade-policy option for third countries is to seek to join existing RIAs. The primary example here is again the EU, which expanded from six to currently fifteen member states, with a number of additional accessions likely in the coming years. In North America, Mexico was induced to seek accession to Canada–US FTA, the result being a renegotiated trilateral FTA, the NAFTA. Other Latin American countries have also expressed their interest in joining NAFTA, Chile being the first candidate. To some extent accession is motivated by market-access insurance motives, as well as non-economic objectives. The goal is not so much to obtain duty-free access to the regional market, as average MFN tariffs are relatively low for most products, and many potential members tend to be treated preferentially in any event. More important is the elimination of the threat of contingent protection and a desire to enhance the credibility of recent unilateral liberalization and structural reform efforts.

An alternative to accession—which frequently will either not be on offer by member states or will be considered by third countries to involve too great a loss in sovereignty—is to seek alternative forms of association with an RIA. Frequently this will take the form of a preferential trade arrangement with the members of an RIA. Examples of this strategy abound, especially in the European context. The EU has negotiated some two dozen preferential trade agreements with third countries (Xafa *et al.*, 1992). Recent examples are the FTAs between the EU and the CEECs, many of which are expected to accede to the EU at some point. The EU also has many co-operation and association agreements with Mediterranean countries. These agreements illustrate the hub-and-spoke nature of European integration. A major difference with accession is that they offer less insurance in terms of market-access guarantees. Instruments of contingent protection generally remain applicable.

The creation of an RIA may also create incentives for third countries to pursue economic integration in turn. This defensive rationale appears to have been important in practice and continues to be so. Regional integration efforts in Africa and Latin America were driven in part by a wish to strengthen their bargaining position *vis-à-vis* major trading partners, reflecting a belief that this would allow them to 'better defend themselves against discriminatory effects of other regional groups' (Patterson, 1966: 147). The EFTA is an important case in point. It was established in 1960 in reaction to the formation of the EEC, its membership consisting of European countries that did not want to join the EEC because of concerns relating to its supranational aspects and the likely level of the common external tariff (most EFTA countries tended to be relatively liberal). The EFTA reaction to the formation of the EEC was not unique. Japan informally proposed a Pacific Free Trade Area with the USA, Canada, Australia, and New Zealand in the mid-1960s for the same reason (De Melo and Panagariya, 1993). More recently, Pacific nations agreed to pursue regional free trade under the auspices of the Asian-Pacific Economic Cooperation (APEC) agreement.

Harmonization is another possible trade-policy response for third countries. In general, the larger the region and/or the more important it is as a trading partner, the greater the incentive for a country to adopt the regulatory standards of the RIA. Third countries will have an interest in adopting identical product standards, and perhaps even similar competition and environmental rules. There will often be a link here—implicit or explicit—between harmonization of regulatory regimes and the threat of contingent protection. One factor driving harmonization is to reduce the possibility of being confronted with allegations of social or environmental dumping. As RIAs are increasingly instruments for such harmonization—or for the adoption of mutual recognition procedures—the potential cause for concern on the part of non-members is again obvious.

9.5. CONCLUSION

Participation in a regional integration agreement is an option allowed under the WTO. Although subject to conditions contained in Articles XXIV of the GATT and V of the GATS, WTO disciplines are relatively weak. An example is the absence of any disciplines with respect to preferential rules of origin in the WTO (Box 9.4). Another is the lack of a requirement that RIAs be open to new members that are willing to satisfy their obligations (Bhagwati, 1993). Multilateral surveillance is limited—the WTO Secretariat has no mandate to monitor the trade effects of RIAs. WTO-consistency is not sufficient to ensure that RIAs are a complement to the multilateral trading system. As mentioned previously, developing countries may be able to opt out of GATT's disciplines on RIAs altogether by invoking the Enabling Clause, and negotiate preferential tariff-reduction agreements for a limited number of products. Such agreements can greatly distort trade flows, generating substantial welfare-reducing trade diversion. More generally, much depends on the various holes and loopholes that are embodied in an RIA.

Notwithstanding these caveats, RIAs may embody many good practices and some go far beyond the WTO in terms of liberalizing markets. Thus, in the EU there are no tariffs, no safeguard mechanisms, and full binding of policies. To a large extent the current bench-mark for good practice in trade policy is the set of policies and rules that apply to the movement of goods, services, labour, and capital inside the EU. However, this is certainly not the case as regards EU external trade policies that apply to non-member countries. The challenge then is to pursue multilaterally what the serious RIAs are implementing internally. This has been the trend. Indeed, it appears that developments in RIAs are frequently reflected in analogous developments on the multilateral front. Differences between the RIAs and the GATT/WTO at any point in time have been limited in part because efforts to negotiate RIAs have stimulated concurrent—and largely successful—efforts to achieve further multilateral trade liberalization (Hoekman and Leidy, 1993).

RIAs represent both a challenge and an opportunity for the multilateral trading system. The opportunity is to use them as experimental laboratories for co-operation on issues that have not (yet) been addressed multilaterally. Examples of such issues are discussed in Chapter 11. The challenge is to control them. Multilateral control under WTO auspices will depend importantly on the willingness of affected WTO Members to invoke compensation and dispute-settlement mechanisms, and on ensuring that RIAs are open and

232   *Regional Integration*

transparent. Transparency—through multilateral surveillance—is important, as enforcement of WTO rules requires that violations are identified. The slower non-Member countries are to recognize the impact of policies that discriminate against them, the greater the incentive may be for an RIA to use them. As in the case of AD, the key is not more multilateral disciplines, but greater internal scrutiny of regional trade policy to ensure that the interests of all groups in society are considered. Transparency is again crucial in this connection, as without information interest-groups will be represented asymmetrically in the political market. Ideally, an institution with a statutory mandate to act as a watchdog should be established, with the mandate to scrutinize, analyse, and publish reports on the aggregate impact and distributional effects of the policies that are maintained by the RIA. This cannot be mandated through a multilateral institution, although multilateral surveillance can be helpful as an objective source of information and analysis. Ultimately, domestic transparency requires domestic political will.

9.6. FURTHER READING

The economics of regional integration and its relationship to the GATT is discussed in depth by the contributors to two conference volumes: Kym Anderson and Richard Blackhurst (eds.), *Regional Integration and the Global Trading System* (London: Harvester-Wheatsheaf, 1993) and Jaime de Melo and Arvind Panagariya (eds.), *New Dimensions in Regional Integration* (Cambridge: Cambridge University Press, 1993). For an excellent historical discussion of the issue of regionalism and preferential liberalization in the GATT context, see Gardner Patterson, *Discrimination in International Trade: The Policy Issues, 1945–1965* (Princeton: Princeton University Press, 1966). Augusto de la Torre and Margaret Kelly, *Regional Trade Arrangements*, Occasional Paper no. 93 (Washington DC: IMF, 1992) is a more recent review of RIAs. Alan Winters, 'The EC and World Protectionism: Dimensions of the Political Economy', Discussion Paper no. 897 (London: Centre for Economic Policy Research, 1994) is an insightful and thought-provoking analysis of the political economy of trade-policy formation in the EU. Bernard Hoekman and Pierre Sauvé, in *Liberalizing International Trade in Services*, Discussion Paper no. 243 (Washington DC: World Bank, 1994) explore the relationship between regional and multilateral liberalization of trade in services.

PART IV
Future Challenges and Opportunities

10

Developing Countries and the WTO

For a long time, the GATT was basically a club that was primarily of relevance to OECD countries. Developing countries did not participate fully. With the creation of the WTO this changed, significantly expanding the global significance of the organization. Fuller participation on the part of developing countries constitutes both a challenge for the WTO and an opportunity. This chapter briefly reviews the history of developing countries' involvement in GATT.

10.1. SPECIAL AND DIFFERENTIAL TREATMENT

The terms of developing countries' participation in the multilateral trading system has oscillated over time. Three stages can be identified:

(1) small-scale membership of low-income countries in GATT based on a formal parity of obligations, although from the very start developing countries maintained that they should be granted special treatment (1947–64);

(2) substantial broadening of developing-country membership based on the concept of 'more favorable and differential' treatment (1964–86); and

(3) deepening integration of developing countries into the GATT-WTO system, with a return to reciprocal responsibilities (1986–   ).

Table 10.1 provides a short list of important events.

Although the initial premiss underlying GATT-1947 was essentially parity of obligations between rich and poor trading nations (Hudec, 1987), the concept of giving preferential treatment to developing countries existed from the start. It gained prominence in the mid-1950s, when a large number of colonies approached independence. Two types of preferential treatment can be distinguished. The first consisted of a request for preferential access to rich-country markets through tariff preferences. Such preferences were already in effect, largely reflecting economic relationships built up by France and the UK with their colonies. A second form of preferential treatment consisted of exemptions from GATT rules and mechanisms. Preferences were justified in various ways. One argument was so-called export pessimism. The fear was that if developing countries relied upon exports for growth their supply of commodities would exceed what could be absorbed by the world. The resulting predicted decline in the terms of trade was considered to justify trade restric-

TABLE 10.1 *GATT and developing countries*

Date	Event
1947	Ten what would now be called low-income countries accede to the GATT on essentially the same terms as developed countries. An infant-industry protection clause (Article XVIII) is the main development-specific provision in GATT. Only one BOP Article existed: Article XII.
1954–5	Article XVIII is modified to include XVIII:*b* allowing for QRs to be used for BOP purposes whenever foreign-exchange reserves are below what is considered necessary for economic development. This vague test constitutes much weaker discipline than Article XII. It has been invoked extensively (see Chapter 7).
1964	Establishment of UNCTAD. A committee for Trade and Development is created in the GATT to address development-related concerns; the Internation Trade Center (ITC) is charged with assisting developing countries to promote exports.
1965	A new Part IV on Trade and Development is added to the GATT, which defined the notion of non-reciprocity for developing countries. However, Part IV contains no legally binding obligations.
1968	The USA accepts the Generalized System of Preferences (GSP)—as called for by UNCTAD—under which industrialized countries were to grant tariff preferences to developing countries on a non-reciprocal basis. Such preferences were voluntary, not mandatory, and granted unilaterally. The ITC becomes a joint venture with UNCTAD.
1971	A GATT waiver is granted authorizing tariff preferences under the GSP. Another waiver is adopted for the Protocol on Trade Negotiations among Developing Countries (Geneva Protocol).
1973–9	More than 70 developing countries participate in the Tokyo round. The Enabling Clause is adopted which introduces the concept of 'special and differential treatment' (S&D) *inter alia* making the 1971 waivers permanent and including language on graduation. Most developing countries abstain from signing the various Tokyo round codes.
1986	Developing countries approve launching of the Uruguay round with a ministerial declaration that contains many references to S&D.
1994	All developing-country GATT contracting parties join the WTO, adopting the results of the Uruguay round as a Single Undertaking.

tions by developing countries—in effect, they had to impose an optimal tariff to improve their terms of trade (Prebisch, 1952; Bhagwati, 1988). Given their reliance on exports of commodities, export pessimism was complemented by the view—persuasively argued by Prebisch (1952)—that developing countries needed protection to achieve industrialization and economic development, and that a new world trade order was required to break the 'vicious circle of underdevelopment'. Developing countries, it was argued, suffered from foreign-exchange shortages requiring protectionist policies to protect their balance of payments. International trade was also seen by some as an instrument of exploitation and self-sufficiency as beneficial. More generally, it was argued that development strategies required freedom to pursue import-substitution policies.

The institutional expression of this line of thinking was embodied in the creation of UNCTAD in 1964, and the formation of a political bloc of developing countries in the UN called the 'Group of 77'. One year later, in 1965, developing-country demands for special status in the multilateral trading system led to the adoption of a new Part IV of the GATT. Part IV defined non-reciprocity for developing countries. To a large extent the inclusion of Part IV can be seen as a reaction of the GATT contracting parties to the creation of UNCTAD. As of that moment, special and differential treatment (S&D) for developing countries reigned supreme for the next 20 years. Developing countries were not expected to grant tariff concessions and bind tariffs, instead being granted the 'privilege' of free-riding through the operation of the MFN principle.[1] However, these privileges were not formally embodied in the GATT, as the provisions of Part IV were of a best endeavours nature.

Developing nations successfully invoked the principle of non-reciprocity as cover for not engaging in reciprocal reductions of trade barriers. For example, the 1973 ministerial meeting that established the agenda of the Tokyo round stated that the MTN should secure additional benefits for developing countries in order to achieve a substantial increase in their foreign-exchange earnings, diversification of their exports, and an acceleration of the rate of growth of their trade. It confirmed that the developed countries should not expect reciprocal concessions from developing economies. The inconsistency between these goals and the policy of allowing developing countries to maintain protection and GATT-inconsistent trade regimes was not openly remarked upon. During the negotiations, developed countries repeatedly voiced their dissatisfaction with the reluctance of developing countries to accept GATT disciplines. This found its expression in the negotiation of codes on various issues in which membership was voluntary—see Chapter 4—avoiding the veto that was likely by developing countries if an attempt was made to amend the GATT to include new obligations.

The Tokyo round also resulted in a Framework Agreement, which included the so-called 'Enabling Clause'. Officially called Differential and More Favorable Treatment, Reciprocity and Fuller Participation of Developing Countries,

---

[1] It should be noted that much depended here on how a country acceded to the GATT. Most developing countries joined GATT under Article XXVI, under which former colonies could undertake to accept the obligations initially negotiated by the metropolitan government. As the latter generally had not established separate tariff schedules for colonies, newly independent states were able to accede without a tariff schedule. Countries that were not ex-colonies were generally required to negotiate accession under Article XXXIII, and establish a tariff schedule (bind tariffs).

it provided for departures from MFN or other GATT rules. The Enabling Clause created a permanent legal basis for the operation of the general system of preferences (GSP) established under UNCTAD auspices. It codified principles, practices, and procedures regarding the use of trade measures for BOP purposes (Articles XII and XVIII), giving developing countries 'flexibility' in applying trade measures to meet their 'essential development needs'. The quid pro quo for this codification was the inclusion of a graduation principle. This was also vague, however, and was more in the nature of a statement of principle.

The idea that the most successful developing trading nations should begin to move back towards a parity of obligations and benefits first appeared in the late 1970s. The basic objective of OECD countries was to progressively integrate into the GATT system developing countries with large markets or substantial trade levels and growth. This strategy was not so much inspired by growing evidence that economic development required liberal trade and pro-market policies, but because a number of countries had managed to grow sufficiently to have become attractive markets. The fact that many such countries often had large positive trade balances with industrialized countries provided the latter with an additional incentive to try to impose graduation criteria. A problem in this regard was the definition of developing countries. This has always been a highly arbitrary and political concept. No agreement has ever been reached in the GATT context on how to define developing countries. Indeed, the issue was carefully avoided. For example, when Portugal and Israel claimed developing-country status in the GATT Balance-of-Payments Committee so as to be able to invoke Article XVIII:*b*, the committee avoided pronouncing on the matter. It is left to countries to self-declare their status, and individual WTO Members can decide whether to treat a particular trading partner as a developing country. An exception concerns the group of least-developed countries, where the UN definition tends to be used. Graduation is in practice left to bilateral interaction and has been restricted to obvious candidates. The disinvocation of Article XVIII restrictions by Korea (discussed in Chapter 7) is a representative example.

Although the rationale for S&D from a developing-country perspective was largely based on prevalent theories that import substitution was the path to development, it should also be noted that GATT's reciprocity dynamic is less effective in a developing than in an industrialized economy. A necessary condition for reciprocity to work is that decision-makers confront lobbies that favour or need better access to foreign markets. One problem in this connection was noted in Chapter 1—developing countries often do not have enough to offer large traders in the reciprocity game. Another problem was that potential gainers from such greater access—export industries—often did not exist or were small. Moreover, those that might have favoured domestic liberalization as a quid pro quo for better access to foreign markets often benefited from preferential (GSP or related) treatment, reducing their incentive to go head-to-head with domestic import-competing firms. Frequently, export industries were also granted exemptions from tariffs on their imported inputs, further reducing incentives to oppose protection. Problems were generally compounded by economic mismanagement that led to high unemployment, inflation, and support for uncompetitive industries. Policy-makers in developing countries were also highly sceptical of the benefits of full participation in the GATT. While the key problem was not GATT and its reliance on reciprocity, but the pursuit of inappropriate economic policies, GATT did little to help convince governments to adopt more liberal trade policies. Only if a country managed through its own efforts to adopt better policies, grow, run a trade surplus, and become a potentially attractive export market were pressures exerted to bring the country into the fold. Global foreign policy considerations also played a role in the acceptance of S&D. Some developed countries believed that an insistence on reciprocal obligations might help to push poor countries to join the Soviet bloc (Kostecki, 1979). A concerted decision by major Third World states not to participate in the GATT would have been contrary to Western interests.

The Value of S&D

The corollary of S&D—free-riding—was not that beneficial to developing countries (Hindley, 1987). It meant that MTNs were essentially conducted among developed trading nations, who concentrated on their own trade interests. As discussed in Chapter 3, the principal-supplier rule used in MTNs was also used to ensure that free-riding was minimized (Finger, 1974; 1979). Issues of major importance to developing countries, such as agriculture or textiles and clothing, were either excluded from GATT or granted protectionist treatment on an *ad hoc* basis. Indeed, as noted in earlier chapters, the fact that developing countries were out of the game is one explanation for the continued existence of highly protectionist policies on textiles and clothing in OECD countries. Once governments started to pursue liberalization unilaterally, such protection mobilized export lobbies in developing countries to push for their governments to start playing the GATT game. Moreover, as industrialized country trade barriers were reduced over time, the value of tariff preferences was eroded, further reducing the benefits of non-reciprocity. The value of preferences was also diluted because of the uncertainty regarding their applicability over time. Preferences were granted unilaterally, and could be removed unilaterally. The rules determining eligibility to benefit from preference schemes were also at the discretion of granting countries. This not only contributed to the uncertainty dimension, but also eroded the value of the preference margin by imposing costs on developing countries (see Box 10.1).

Box 10.1. Unilateral preferences are uncertain

To benefit from preferential access, a country must be able to document that exported products do indeed originate in their countries. The rules of origin used in the context of GSP schemes are therefore important. Some examples from the United States illustrate how rules of origin have been used to restrict competition from goods benefiting from GSP treatment. In 1983 the USA adopted the Caribbean Basin Initiative, which granted Caribbean countries duty-free access to the USA for many products. To determine whether a product was eligible for preferential treatment, a value-added criterion of 35 per cent was required. That is, at least 35 per cent of the value of the good imported into the USA must have been generated in the Caribbean. The preference scheme induced foreign investment in the Caribbean. Among such investors were companies that established operations in Costa Rica and Jamaica to convert surplus European wine into ethanol, which was then exported to the USA. This production process met the 35 per cent value-added test. Two years later, with production and exports doing well, the exporters were hit by a rule change: a US Congressman introduced an amendment to a tax bill raising the value-added requirement for ethanol to 70 per cent—an impossible requirement to meet for the Caribbean producers. Interestingly, the US industry that had lobbied for this rule change was not threatened by imports—which never exceeded 3 per cent of US consumption (Bovard, 1991: 22).

10.2. DEVELOPING COUNTRIES AND THE WTO

The developing-country stance towards trade policy and the GATT changed in the early 1980s, under the influence of the debt crisis, the demonstration effect of the benefits of the neutral external policy stance taken by the dynamic economies of South-East Asia, advice from the World Bank and the IMF, and research efforts by the academic community. As national trade policies became more liberal and the interest in obtaining better access to industrialized country markets expanded, the willingness to engage in reciprocal bargaining in the GATT forum increased.

In the Uruguay round, a major shift occurred in both the strategy and the tactics of developing countries. They participated actively in the MTN, and were willing to engage in a reciprocal exchange of concessions. In contrast to the Tokyo round, the Uruguay round was agreed to be a single undertaking: all agreements were to apply to all members, and all were to have schedules of concessions and commitments. Developing countries were strongly involved in shaping the WTO agreements. They had significant impact on issues such as GATS, textiles and clothing, agriculture, tropical products, TRIMs, and dispute settlement. This influence was already manifested at the 1986 ministerial meeting in Punta del Este, where a group of smaller developing and developed economies (the Swiss–Colombian coalition) played a mediating role between the USA, the EU, and large developing countries such as Brazil and India. This marked a sea change: developing countries could no longer be regarded as a bloc. Instead, they pursued their self-interest in a much more open way than in the past. The Cairns Group—as discussed in Chapter 8— was a prominent example.

The creation of the WTO does not mean that S&D is dead. Ending S&D was not on the Uruguay round agenda. Indeed, the Punta del Este Ministerial Declaration explicitly stated that

CONTRACTING PARTIES agree that the principle of differential and more favorable treatment embodied in Part IV and other relevant provisions of the General Agreement . . . applies to the negotiations . . . [D]eveloped countries do not expect reciprocity for commitments made by them in trade negotiations to reduce or remove tariffs and other barriers to trade of developing countries. (GATT, 1986: 7)

S&D remains in the WTO. Special provisions for developing and least developed countries can be grouped under five headings: (1) a lower level of obligations; (2) more flexible implementation timetables; (3) best endeavour commitments by developed countries; (4) more favourable treatment for least-developed countries; and (5) technical assistance and training. The relevance of each of these categories for WTO agreements is summarized on an issue-by-issue basis in Annex 6. Many of the specific provisions have been discussed in earlier chapters. A subsidiary body of the WTO's General Council, the Committee on Trade and Development, is to be a focal point for trade-related concerns of the least-developed countries.

With the exception of the subsidies agreement, no criteria for graduation were agreed to. The Subsidies Agreement stipulates that developing countries that have attained a global market share of 3.5 per cent for a product are required to phase out export subsidies. There is also a per capita GDP criterion (US $1000), under which developing countries' export subsidies will not be countervailed. Disinvocation of Article XVIII remains voluntary, i.e. remains an issue that is effectively negotiated on an *ad hoc* basis. Developing countries blocked significant strengthening of the disciplines of Article XVIII: *b*. At the same time, no additional S&D was sought; the main tactic in this regard was to negotiate longer transition periods and technical assistance to implement negotiated agreements rather than to negotiate substantive exemptions.

In return for participating in the WTO—which includes signing on to the TRIPs Agreement and the GATS, agreeing to the multilateralization of the

Tokyo round codes, the binding of all agricultural tariffs, and a significant increase in binding of industrial tariffs (see Chapter 4)—developing countries obtained a substantial strengthening of the rule-based multilateral trading system. They will benefit from the elimination of VERs and the MFA, and perhaps more importantly from the increased security for trade relations under the WTO agreement. With the inclusion of services and IP in the WTO, unilateral actions in these areas can only be taken by industrialized countries in so far as retaliation has been authorized by the WTO. Liberalization and system strengthening can be expected to boost global growth by providing a more open trading environment for developing countries and additional incentives to invest in developing areas. Finally, membership in the WTO may increase the credibility of domestic economic reforms in developing areas by reducing the uncertainty of trade regimes. This last possibility is of great potential importance, although very much depends on the decisions of governments to exploit the opportunities offered by the WTO by binding tariffs at applied rates, making specific commitments for most of the service sector, and avoiding the pitfalls of AD and balance-of-payments actions (Hoekman, 1995*b*).

As far as developing countries are concerned, key issues for the future include disciplining regional integration, harnessing the threat of contingent protection, and using the WTO to adopt or lock-in more rational trade policies. Much remains to be achieved by developing countries in further liberalization of trade polices and binding tariffs at applied rates. Future progress on the issue of contingent protection is likely to depend in part on more far-reaching integration of developing countries into the WTO—fuller binding of tariffs at rates closer to applied levels, greater commitments in the area of services (see Chapter 5), and continued willingness to play the reciprocal game. With the Uruguay round integration of developing countries into the multilateral trading system, an important step was taken towards ending the dichotomy that has characterized the GATT for several decades. Developing countries are now demonstrably much more committed to the multilateral trading system, and can be expected to play a more active role in the future. One indication of this is the recent use that has been made of dispute-settlement procedures (Box 10.2). As discussed further in Chapter 12, increasing use of WTO dispute-settlement procedures will be one of the challenges confronting the trading system.

Box 10.2. Developing countries and dispute settlement

Developing countries have begun to use multilateral procedures to settle disputes much more than in the past. Three recent cases are illustrative. *Case 1: Malaysia–Singapore.* A dispute between Malaysia and Sin-

gapore concerning Malaysian import procedures introduced in early
1994 for plastic resins—polyethylene and polypropylene—was the
first case to be brought to the WTO. The procedures required that
Malaysian plastic producers should follow a 'buy national' policy, and
that those desiring to import must apply for a special import license. The
new rule was alleged by Singapore to have resulted in a 40 per cent fall
in exports of resin, which argued that the use of GATT-consistent
safeguard actions involving tariffs would have been appropriate. Malaysia argued that its measure was non-discriminatory, limited to two years,
and was consistent with GATT's allowance for measures to promote
infant industries. Reportedly the Malaysian change in rules resulted in
part from lobbying by a Taiwanese-owned industrial group that produced resins (*Financial Times*, 23 February 1995). After consultations,
Malaysia adopted a system of automatic import licensing, and Singapore
refrained from requesting a panel.

Case 2: Brazil–Mexico. In 1991 two Brazilian firms won an international tender for electric power transformers issued by the Federal
Electricity Commission of Mexico. Subsequently, three of the Mexican
firms that lost the tender alleged dumping by the Brazilian firms, and
requested their Ministry of Trade and Industrial Development to initiate
an investigation. Following the investigation, AD duties ranging from 26
to 35 per cent were imposed in September 1993. Brazil believed that the
Mexican decision contravened the Tokyo round Antidumping Agreement and requested the Antidumping Committee to conciliate. It argued
that the AD duty was not based on sufficient evidence—dumping having
been found by comparison of the prices bid by the different firms for the
original tender (i.e. based on price undercutting, not a comparison of
prices charged in the home and the export market)—and that the
Mexican firms had since underbid Brazilian firms in subsequent tenders. This dispute was resolved bilaterally.

Case 3: India–Poland. In November 1994 India brought a complaint
against Poland to the GATT, alleging that an increase in the Polish tariff
on cars from 15 to 35 per cent, and a granting of a duty-free quota of
30,000 to the EU under the provisions of a 1992 bilateral FTA with the
EU, had resulted in a decline in its exports from 4.5 thousand units in
1991–2 to 500 in 1993–4. Bilateral consultations having failed to settle
the matter, India requested a panel, supported by Japan, Korea, the USA,
and a number of other countries.

Sources: *GATT Activities*, various issues; *GATT Focus*, No. 112, November 1994.

10.3. CONCLUSIONS

Developing countries were for a long time effectively second-class members of the GATT-based trading system. The insistence on S&D and the refusal to engage in reciprocal negotiations meant that the benefits of GATT membership were substantially reduced. As argued repeatedly throughout this book, the main value of the WTO is that it can help government's keep their trade policy open, transparent, and on a liberal track. But by excluding themselves from the progressive liberalization induced by the dynamics of reciprocity, developing countries greatly reduced the external pressure that drives liberalization in the MTN-WTO setting. Domestic exporters in developing countries were given fewer incentives to invest resources to support liberalization. The end result was that levels of protection in developing countries remained much higher than in OECD countries, and that the latter kept higher barriers on the goods of primary interest to developing countries than on those largely traded among themselves. The three decades following the creation of UNCTAD demonstrated that the S&D strategy was an ill-advised one. The fundamental dynamic of the GATT was and remains reciprocity. Those not willing to play this game found the benefits of free-riding to be small. Indeed, from an economic perspective, the strategy was counter-productive, as import substitution proved to be a very costly and ineffective development strategy (Bhagwati, 1988).

External events in the 1980s gradually changed the attitude of many countries towards trade policy. The debt crisis induced many nations— especially in Latin America—to change tack, and shift towards a much more liberal policy stance. As important was the demonstration effect of the successful export-based economies of East Asia, and the collapse of communism in Eastern Europe and the former Soviet Union. The internal political balance-of-power changed in many developing countries, with export interests becoming more important. GATT played a role, but it was a minor one. As new centres of economic activity emerged—in South-East Asia in particular—these countries became subject to increasing pressure to graduate. Greater emphasis on graduation can be expected in the WTO-context than under the GATT-1947. But of far greater importance are the unilateral policy choices that are made regarding the extent to which the good and bad options of the WTO are exercised. The management of trade relations between the high-income North and the emerging high-growth centres in the developing world and the economies in transition to a market economy is likely to become an increasingly central issue in the WTO during the coming decades (see Chapter 12).

10.4. FURTHER READING

Much has been written about the role of developing countries in the trading system, and the impact of the free-riding strategy that was pursued. Readers can do no better than to turn to Robert Hudec's excellent and comprehensive analysis of the issue, which includes a review of the relevant GATT history: *Developing Countries in the GATT Legal System* (London: Trade Policy Research Centre, 1987). For a characteristically accessible and very readable account of the effects of inward-looking, import-substituting development strategies of the type popular in the 1960s and 1970s, as well as the shift to more outward-looking policies in the 1980s, see Jagdish Bhagwati, *Protectionism* (Cambridge, Mass.: MIT Press, 1988).

Brian Hindley, 'Different and more Favorable Treatment—and graduation', in J. M. Finger and A. Olechowski (eds.), *The Uruguay Round: A Handbook for the Multilateral Trade Negotiations* (Washington DC: The World Bank, 1987) is a short, perceptive review of S&D-related issues written at the start of the Uruguay round. Rolf Langhammer and Andre Sapir, in *Economic Impact of Generalized Tariff Preferences* (London: Trade Policy Research Centre, 1987), analyse the economic effects of GSP schemes, arguing that these largely benefit those who pursue export-oriented policies—mostly countries that do not need preferences to compete. The contributions in Jagdish Bhagwati and John Ruggie (eds.), *Power, Passions and Purpose: Prospects for North-South Negotiations* (Cambridge: MIT Press, 1984) discuss issues and strategies followed by developing countries regarding international co-operation and global negotiations on economic matters during the 1970s and early 1980s. The contribution by Martin Wolf in that volume ('Two-Edged Sword: Demands of Developing Countries and the Trading System') offers a critical analysis of the impact of developing countries' insistence on non-reciprocity in the GATT.

Stephan Haggard, *Pathways from the Periphery* (Ithaca, NY: Cornell University Press, 1990) and Stephan Haggard and Steven Webb (eds.), *Voting for Reform: The Politics of Adjustment in New Democracies* (New York: Oxford University Press, 1995), contain in-depth discussions of the role of domestic politics and policy choices underlying the adoption of export-oriented development strategies in newly industrializing countries. John Whalley, 'Developing Countries and System Strengthening in the Uruguay Round', in Will Martin and Alan Winters (eds.), *The Uruguay Round and the Developing Economies* (Washington DC: World Bank, forthcoming) summarizes developing-country negotiating stances and objectives during the Uruguay round.

11
Future Challenges

Starting with the Kennedy round, an increasing number of agenda items of MTNs involved the negotiation of rules and disciplines for specific trade-related policies. The trend for MTNs to address domestic policies shows no sign of abating. Likely topics for a post-Uruguay round negotiation include issues such as competition policy, labour standards and regulations, foreign direct investment (FDI) policies, and the interaction between trade and environmental policies (Feketekuty, 1992). Although the negotiating agenda has expanded over time, the focus has largely been on the reduction and abolition of discrimination among products and producers. That is, the approach has been one of negative or shallow integration—agreement not to do something. This contrasts with positive or deep integration, which involves agreement to pursue common policies, to harmonize (Lawrence and Litan, 1991). Under shallow integration governments remain free to decide whether to pursue a given policy, but if they do they are bound by certain rules. The approach has been quite successful in increasing market-access opportunities. The resulting specialization in production, with associated FDI and trade flows, has increased the visibility of differences in national regulatory regimes. Its very success led to calls for deeper integration at the multilateral level, ranging from co-ordinated application of national policies to the harmonization of regulatory regimes. Such harmonization is sometimes held to be necessary to ensure fair trade or an equality of competitive opportunities for foreign and domestic firms.

This chapter discusses the general issue of moving towards deeper integration in the WTO context, and provides an introduction to the main issues that are likely to be prominent on the multilateral negotiating agenda in the coming decade. The key general challenge is to identify the rationale for—and objectives behind—proposals to address a specific issue in the WTO, and to determine what type of co-operation is appropriate. In principle, the test to determine appropriateness should be based on an economic welfare standard: do solutions exist that are a Pareto improvement for all parties concerned? In practice, as discussed in Chapter 3, the Pareto criterion is more realistically framed in terms of the political preferences of incumbent governments, which are in turn dependent on interest-group power and activity. What constitutes an improvement depends not only on the issue under discussion, but also on the linkages that are made with other issues and the threat point that may emerge if discussions break down. Harmonization is rarely first-best, as economic conditions and preferences vary significantly across countries.

11.1. ENHANCING THE CONTESTABILITY OF MARKETS

Sovereign states have traditionally pursued limited economic integration in the multilateral context. The approach has been one of reducing barriers to market access, initially border measures such as tariffs and quotas, later domestic policies with a potential trade impact such as subsidies and standards, and most recently new issue areas such as services. The objectives have always been to enhance the contestability of markets and to determine the conditions of competition facing foreign products. The Uruguay round continued to revolve around shallow integration. However, the Agreement on TRIPs constituted a break in the historical tradition in that it involves some harmonization of policies. Although the TRIPs Agreement illustrates that multilateral agreement on minimum standards for regulatory policies is possible, it should be recalled that over a century of international co-operation existed in the IPR area. There was basic agreement regarding the type of IP protection that was appropriate in principle. The issue was to get many developing countries to grant and enforce patents—which had in the past perceived this not to be in their interests—not to obtain agreement on the modalities of protecting specific types of IP.

Deep integration has so far only occurred in the bilateral or regional context, the primary example being the EU, which involves some harmonization of regulatory regimes with a view to minimizing their impact on internal trade. Despite the fact that the countries involved are relatively similar, harmonization of standards (for products, professions, or regulatory regimes) proved to be a very slow and ineffective process, reflecting the fact that in practice Member States often opposed it. This was recognized in the mid-1980s with the adoption of the Single European Act, which called for a much greater reliance on mutual recognition—a shift back towards competition in rules. The key to mutual recognition is that, subject to the satisfaction of minimum standards, countries accept each others' standards as equivalent. A lesson from the EU experience is that deeper economic integration does not necessarily require complete harmonization. Mutual recognition may be just as good, if not better, as long as agreement exists regarding minimum standards.

Why is deep integration moving on to the multilateral agenda? The RIAs suggest that one answer is that this may be a necessary condition for governments to fully commit themselves not to use trade policy any more—that is, to accept free trade. Another is the globalization of production. Firms are centred less and less on purely national markets. Indeed, it has become almost a platitude that what counts for firms are local, regional, and global markets—

not necessarily the market that is defined by the borders of a nation-state. The managerial and technological innovations of the last decade—such as just-in-time inventory management and the increased tradeability of services resulting from declining transport, telecommunications, and information-technology costs—allowed greater specialization and geographical diversification of production. This in turn made regulations pertaining to services, FDI, the transfer of technology, and the protection of intangible assets more important for both governments and firms. Enterprises consequently seek to minimize regulatory constraints to enter, operate in, and exit from a market.

For the multilateral trading system, the key objective is to move progressively closer to achieving freedom to contest markets, thus supporting the globalization process. An important question then is what type of co-operation or agreement is necessary for enhancing the contestability of markets. Other questions are what policy issues are the most important in terms of enhancing access to markets, and the extent to which agreement on new issues is necessary for further liberalization on old issues. A move towards harmonization—while not in itself first best for many countries—may none the less be necessary as a side-payment to allow further progress on the WTO's more traditional agenda. The basic problem is that further moves to liberalize access to markets may be somewhat constrained by the political need to satisfy influential interest-groups that have different objectives. It is for that reason that side-payments may have to be considered. An important challenge for the WTO in the future is to minimize the need for such side-payments and to convince the key interest-groups involved that greater contestability of markets will usually help, not hinder, the realization of their goals.

However, for many interest-groups enhancing the contestability of markets is not the objective. Thus, environmental groups are concerned with improving and safeguarding the environment, both at home and abroad, and other groups are concerned with social standards, or human and animal rights. These groups are often supported in their efforts to export national standards to other countries by industries who are worried about their competitiveness *vis-à-vis* firms located in countries that have low environmental or labour standards, or are interested in selling their know-how in meeting such standards to foreign enterprises. Such industries may push for import barriers as a way of offsetting the resulting 'unfair' competition or as an instrument to pressure foreign governments to adopt higher standards. As argued further below, trade policy is rarely an appropriate instrument for attaining environmental or other non-economic objectives. Efficiency considerations require that policy instruments are used that target perceived problems at source. Trade policy cannot do this (Bhagwati and Srinivasan, 1994).

There are many policies that may affect the contestability of markets. They include trade policies (tariffs, quotas, contingent protection), restrictions on foreign direct investment (outright prohibitions or non-national treatment), discriminatory public procurement policies, subsidy practices, and regulatory regimes (including competition law and enforcement, product standards, and policies pertaining to the service sector). A first step for policy-makers is to rank these issues in importance in terms of enhancing the contestability of markets, and in terms of the type of co-operation that is required. The more that can be done through shallow integration, the likelier it is that agreement is feasible. Abstracting from the question of contingent protection, it would appear that the major areas where great progress can still be achieved via the traditional GATT approach of mutual disarmament are government procurement, investment policies, and regulatory regimes for services. On these issues there is no need to harmonize. What is needed in the first instance is agreement to allow foreign firms to contest domestic markets and to refrain from discrimination—i.e. to liberalize and apply the principles of national treatment and MFN. Greater efforts to expand market access—contestability—must be complemented by disciplining the scope to impose import barriers to counteract unfair-trade actions. Attempts—whether unilateral or in the context of the WTO—to extend the reach of the concept of unfair trade to include differences in environmental or labour standards should be vigorously resisted. Whether green or blue, to paraphrase Professor Bhagwati (the 'blue' refers to blue-collar workers), all such protectionist actions are some shade of blue, in that the implicit if not explicit objective is to maintain employment in uncompetitive industries. The irony associated with the fact that protected activities are often both low-skilled and relatively pollution-intensive has often been remarked upon (see Low, 1993*b*). The pursuit of common labour standards and environmental policies is clearly not about improving contestability, although dealing with such pressures may be necessary to maintain, let alone enhance, market access.

Fig. 11.1 provides a framework for thinking about the issue of harmonization versus shallow integration. Support for global norms on an issue may be driven by factors such as uniformity of consumer preferences across nations, the desire for transparency and simplicity on the part of traders regarding import–export formalities, realization of economies of scale and scope, or the fact that a particular issue can only be dealt with at the global level (e.g. ozone depletion). Support for norm diversity, on the other hand, will be stronger the greater are national differences in: preferences and willingness to pay for particular standards, endowments, consumption patterns, production methods, and per capita income levels. Moreover, the smaller the physical spill-overs caused by production or consumption in one nation on another are, the lower the support for harmonization. The stronger the political support for global norms, and the lower the strength of forces favouring a national approach to an issue, the more likely multilateral agreement is.

The first and second quadrants of Fig. 11.1 include issues where there is significant support by interest-groups for a global approach. Issues that fall

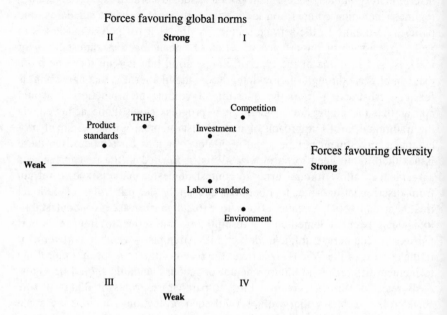

Fig. 11.1 Globalization of norms versus diversity

into quadrant II are the most likely to be addressed successfully in a co-operative fashion, and are also those where harmonization is most feasible. Of the various issues that are—or may be—dealt with under the WTO, IPRs and mandatory product standards or SPMs are examples that fall into this category. While there may be strong forces underlying a common approach, it should be noted that this does not necessarily imply that all nations must implement common standards. In the case of product standards, for example, adoption of the relevant norms is voluntary. Only if a nation desires to adopt mandatory standards do multilateral disciplines apply. This contrasts with the case of TRIPs, where countries have all agreed to adopt common standards.

Matters are more complex with issues located in quadrant I. In this case, strong forces supporting global norms are confronted by strong forces favouring national diversity. In contrast to quadrant II issues, harmonization will be much more controversial, and on most issues will only be possible if issue linkage and/or compensation mechanisms are developed. Examples are competition and investment-related policy. In quadrant IV of the matrix, norm diversity dominates and no global standardization is feasible. Environment and labour standards are likely to be issues that fall into this quadrant. Conditions across countries simply differ too much to allow a common approach. The most that might be feasible are minimum standards: agreement on general principles. Examples in the environmental context might be enforcement of the polluter-pays principle; in the labour context an agreement to make forced labour illegal.

11.2. INVESTMENT POLICIES

GATT disciplines pertain to trade or trade-related policies—they do not extend to the policies used by governments to restrict or attract FDI. Nor does GATT have anything to say about policies that affect the operations of firms that are established in a Member State—such as requirements concerning the employment of nationals, limitations on operations inside the country, restrictions on the number or location of plants or branches, and so forth. As long as they do not lead to discrimination in trade, a WTO Member is free to pursue any policies it pleases.[1]

The rationale for seeking to expand the reach of the WTO to investment policies is that such policies may restrict access to markets, or reduce the contestability of markets. Trade and investment are becoming increasingly complementary—an ever larger share of global trade is intra-firm, involving exchanges between related enterprises (Hipple, 1990). As mentioned earlier, the ongoing globalization of production—with firms sourcing from least-cost producers all over the world—has made investment regulations more important to enterprises because such geographical splintering often requires that the firm establish joint ventures or affiliates in various locations. This may be required to ensure quality, or because technologies are proprietary. At the same time governments seeking to attract FDI may compete with one another—offering subsidies, tax concessions, and so on. Such competition is expensive and inefficient from a world-welfare point of view because the total amount of FDI is not influenced by tax incentives—only its location. In so far as governments are playing a zero-sum game, they have an incentive to agree to mutual disarmament.

As in the case of subsidies affecting trade, obtaining agreement on what type of incentives should be permitted and what types are best constrained is likely to be difficult, however. Even if no financial incentives are granted, a country can offer a regulatory environment that may enhance its attractiveness to investors. Some of those regulatory incentives may in turn be considered to be unfair (e.g. low labour or environmental standards). Any type of industrial policy if applied on a national treatment basis may affect the location decision

---

[1] In practice, many countries have negotiated bilateral investment treaties. OECD countries have also agreed to certain disciplines for specific sectors. To the extent that a government is bound by such agreements, its freedom of action is of course constrained.

of a firm. The empirical literature on this topic suggests that foreign investors give little weight to fiscal incentives; what matters for them are factors such as the quality of infrastructure, political stability, and labour costs and available skills (Wheeler and Mody, 1992). The pressure on rational governments to engage in investment incentive competitions may therefore be lower than is sometimes assumed. In practice, incentives are likely to be most important—and most expensive—for countries that are attempting to offset policy-induced distortions that reduce their attractiveness for FDI. The solution in these cases is to deal with the distortions—bad infrastructure, political instability, etc.—directly. For these reasons, focusing on extending the funda-mental disciplines of the WTO—transparency, national treatment, MFN, and the binding of policies—to the investment policy area may be much more productive than focusing on subsidy issues. A step beyond this could involve agreement not to use specific policies that constrain the operations of firms and reduce the contestability of markets.

One approach to these issues can be found in the NAFTA. The investment disciplines of NAFTA grant investors the right of establishment, and require governments to provide both national treatment and MFN, subject to a negative list of excluded sectors of activity. It covers many types of invest-ment, including various forms of non-equity participation. The security of investments is safeguarded by extensive provisions on the settlement of disputes. The horizontal, negative-list approach taken in the NAFTA is much preferable to that of the GATS, where coverage of disciplines is sector-specific and allowance is made for many exemptions. It is important that any rules that are agreed in the multilateral context apply in principle to all sectors, involving both goods and services. Indeed, maintaining a distinction between investment in goods activities and in services activities makes no economic sense. While this may require a renegotiation of the GATS, as discussed in Chapter 5, this is likely to be beneficial in any event. It would be very unfortunate if the positive-list approach to investment disciplines for services embodied in the GATS were extended to goods as well.

11.3. COMPETITION POLICIES

National competition policy can be defined as the set of rules and disciplines maintained by governments relating either to agreements between firms that restrict competition or to the abuse of a dominant position (including attempts to create a dominant position through merger). The underlying objective of competition policy in most jurisdictions tends to be efficient resource alloca-tion, and thereby the maximization of national welfare. The focus of competi-tion laws is on competition, reflecting the belief—which is extensively supported by empirical evidence—that vigorous competition is frequently the best way to enhance economic efficiency. However, many countries recognize that specific agreements between firms that may reduce competition could be welfare-enhancing, and make allowance for such agreements. As in the case of the environment or labour standards (see below), a nation's choice regarding the existence or severity of its competition laws is its own affair. What matters for the WTO is whether such laws—or their absence, as the case may be—have implications for trade. In the case of competition rules the answer is clearly yes.

Long before it was known whether the Uruguay round would be concluded successfully, commentators were calling for the multilateral trading system to be extended to cover competition (anti-trust) policies. This reflected concerns that competition policies—or the lack of policies—could effectively restrict access to markets, even if overt trade barriers were low, thus granting exporters located in these markets an unfair advantage. For example, if local manufacturers of certain products control distribution channels, they may be able to prevent the sale of imported goods to domestic consumers. The importance attached to competition policy enforcement by the United States as a necessary condition for effective access to the Japanese market figured prominently in bilateral discussions in the 1980s. Competition policy disciplines have always been a key element of the Treaty of Rome establishing the EEC. After bilateral and regional testing of the waters, moving on to the multilateral level appears to be an obvious next step.

Competition policy is already on the agenda. Three WTO agreements contain provisions on or related to competition policy: TRIMs, TRIPs, and the GATS. The TRIMs agreement is limited to a call to consider the need for possible disciplines in this area in the future. The TRIPs Agreement allows governments to take measures to control anti-competitive practices in contractual licenses that adversely affect trade and may impede the transfer and dissemination of technology. The GATS recognizes that the business practices of service suppliers may restrain competition and thus trade in services, but no obligations are imposed on Members regarding either the scope or the enforcement of competition policy. Members are only obliged, on request, to enter into consultations with a view to eliminating business practices that are claimed to restrict trade in services. The Member addressed 'shall accord full and sympathetic consideration to such a request and shall cooperate through the supply of publicly available non-confidential information of relevance to the matter in question' (Article IX). Other information may be provided if permitted under domestic law and upon the conclusion of a satisfactory agreement concerning the safeguarding of confidentiality. There is no requirement to act, only an obligation to provide information. It is therefore unclear how a restrictive practice is to be eliminated, or what constitutes a restrictive business practice. Indeed, Members remain free not to apply competition law and policy to services.

Much of world trade does not occur between independent firms operating in textbook-type perfectly competitive markets. Instead, competition is imperfect in that firms often have some power to influence prices on markets, may pursue collaborative ventures, or engage in intra-firm trade (see Fig. 11.2). Such co-operative or internal interactions are by no means an indication that competition is weak, and that there is a need to apply competition rules. What matters is that markets are contestable. In many of the specific examples mentioned in Fig. 11.2, government policy plays a role in reducing the contestability of the market, either through specific actions (STEs, international cartels, or government procurement) or through more general policy (e.g. agricultural protection). More generally, internalization of exchange—i.e. relying on intra-firm transactions as opposed to contracting with unrelated firms—may be the most efficient method of trade.

Discussions on competition-trade policy linkages often suggest that the perceived problem is one of governments tolerating the fact that firms engage in anti-competitive practices. These practices are held to prevent the realization of 'legitimate expectations' (to use GATT-speak) associated with trade-barrier reductions negotiated in an MTN. There are four holes in the WTO as far as competition policies are concerned (Hoekman and Mavroidis, 1994a). First, purely private business practices restricting access to markets that are not supported by the government cannot be attacked under GATT or GATS. In many circumstances, however, anti-competitive business practices will be supported by the government in some way (e.g. anti-trust exemptions or subsidies). If such support can be identified, a complaint may be possible.

Second, there is no requirement that WTO Members have a competition policy, let alone that it meet certain minimum standards. Many Members have a competition law of some kind; the problem is that there may be significant differences in national laws and in their enforcement. This in turn may affect the international playing-field. But there are myriad policies that do this. Advocates of pursuing multilateral rules on competition policies must produce a convincing argument as to why multilateral disciplines on competition policies should be given priority over other policies that reduce the contestability of markets. As argued by Graham and Richardson (1994), many competition issues are contentious—even within the OECD—suggesting that efforts to harmonize are unlikely to be fruitful.

Third, the WTO pertains to national policies. Some firms may be so large as to have global market power. In such cases, competition rules should in principle also be global, as no single government may be able to control possible anti-competitive behaviour. Although a global competition code with supranational enforcement along the lines of the EU is unlikely to be feasible in the near future, agreement could be sought between the largest traders that competition law enforcement in such cases should be co-ordinated.

Fourth, the reach of the WTO is currently restricted to measures by

Internalization

Arm's length exchange

PERFECT COMPETITION	OLIGOPOLISTIC INTERACTION	TRADE UNDER INTER-FIRM CO-OPERATION ARRANGEMENTS	INTRA-FIRM TRADE
Exchange between unrelated competitive entities	Transactions between state-trading monopolies Transactions between oligopolistic (private) traders International cartels (OPEC, International Air Transport Association (IATA), shipping liners conferences)	Long-term contracts: • Commodity contracts • Countertrade • Industrial co-operation • Bidding consortium • Management contract • Licence • Exploration concession • Joint-venture (minority participation) Centrally planned foreign trade Government procurement contracts	Trade among subsidiaries of multinational corporations

Note: Percentages in brackets refer to the estimated share of world trade.

FIG.. 11.2 Interaction in international trade

governments that affect the conditions of competition in their territory. Practices by firms on export markets or tolerance by governments of anti-competitive behaviour in export markets by firms headquartered in its territory cannot be addressed. Thus the often encountered statement that there are no multilateral disciplines for export cartels. The same applies to actions by governments themselves that have detrimental effects on competition in export markets. It is noteworthy that the regulation of behaviour by firms on export markets and policies by governments affecting exports are not addressed by the WTO. Although export prohibitions or quantitative restrictions and export subsidies are prohibited for industrialized countries (see Chapter 4), current GATT rules basically give Members the freedom to impose tariffs on exports. They also allow for the formation of export monopolies. This implies that Members remain substantially free to attempt to raise the relative price of their exports, to the detriment of the rest of the world. Efforts to agree to multilateral disciplines regarding the treatment of export cartels in domestic competition law, even if successful, will have to be complemented by analogous tightening of the rules regarding the scope that exists for governments to pursue strategic trade policies more generally.

Harmonization does not appear to be the appropriate strategy to deal with these holes. Experience demonstrates that multilateral agreement on the adoption of common competition standards is difficult to achieve. Where it has proved possible, it occurred in a bilateral or regional setting. The two regional arrangements where co-operation on anti-trust proved possible—the EU and the Closer Economic Relations Agreement between Australia and New Zealand (Hoekman and Mavroidis, 1994a)—entail far-reaching liberalization of trade in goods, services, and factors of production, as well as government procurement and subsidies. It is also important to keep in mind that the political economy of co-operation on competition policies—as with NTMs more generally—is different from more traditional trade liberalization. Competition policy does not lend itself very easily to incremental changes (the 'exchange of concessions'). Moreover, specific policies that are pursued by governments may be perceived to be in the national interest. For example, the exertion of market power by firms in a country to reduce prices of imported products may benefit the country as a whole. Exporters may want to see anti-trust rules enforced on such importers, but this will not be in the interest of the government concerned. Incentives may be similarly skewed with respect to the exercise of market power by firms in export markets. Assuming appropriate competition policies are enforced regarding the behaviour of these firms in their home market, the incentives for the exporters' government to regulate behaviour in export markets are small, as such behaviour can be argued to be in the nation's interest.

An example concerns rules regarding mergers in large players such as the EU or the United States. Just as regional integration can be problematical for the multilateral trading system if driven by a desire to raise trade barriers, mergers that occur between large firms may significantly enhance their market power. If the firms sell most of their output on world markets, the national competition authorities are unlikely to object to the merger, even if it reduces competition, as long as the costs of any reduction in competition on domestic or regional consumers is expected to be more than offset by the benefits accruing to the merged firm. If most of the costs are borne by foreign consumers, the home country gains. If competition authorities take a purely selfish point of view, the enforcement of a rational competition policy may therefore be detrimental to the rest of the world (Jacquemin, 1994).

Export cartels and merger policy are areas where multilateral disciplines may be negotiable under WTO auspices, as the potential losers have an incentive to compensate the large traders to enforce competition rules that take their interests into account. While a case can be made that there will be global efficiency gains from some multilateralization of anti-trust, and that each country will share in such gains as long as enough governments co-operate (Caves, 1987), the problem from a practical perspective is that the distribution and magnitude of such gains are uncertain. For GATT's traditional public choice dynamics to work, anti-trust-related market-access barriers affecting a country's exporters must be large enough to offset the gains accruing to industries benefiting from national competition-policy exemptions. Few major trading countries have competition-policy regimes that significantly restrict access to markets. And those that do can be (and have been) subjected to pressure by large trading partners to change their policies (e.g. the application of Section 301 by the USA). This suggests that a linkage strategy may well be necessary to make progress in this area.

11.4. CONTINGENT PROTECTION—COMPETITION POLICY LINKAGES

As noted in Chapter 7, the allowance for anti-dumping policies under the GATT constitutes a major weakness of the multilateral trading system. While the theoretical rationale for AD has always been weak, given current competition on world markets it simply makes no sense to allow price discrimination by domestic firms on national (or in the case of the EU, regional) markets, but to object to it if a foreign firm does so. As important is the increasing globalization of the world economy: with transnational firms sourcing from all over the world and engaging in joint ventures and cross-border strategic alliances, the measurement of dumping and injury becomes an inherently arbitrary and meaningless exercise. Calls for dealing with the anti-dumping problem are likely to proliferate in the coming years.

Advocates of AD policies sometimes argue that it constitutes a justifiable attempt by importing-country governments to offset the market-access restrictions existing in an exporting firm's home country that underlie the ability of such firms to dump. Such restrictions may consist of import barriers preventing arbitrage, but may also reflect the non-existence or non-enforcement of competition law by the exporting country. AD may then be defended as a second-best instrument to offset such government-made competitive differences. While certainly not a compelling argument (see Chapter 7), it does suggest that it might be fruitful to attempt to link AD and competition policy. Replacing AD with competition law enforcement is likely to be impossible in the WTO context in the foreseeable future. A second-best option may be to attempt to apply competition principles to define unfair competition in an economically more sensible way. One possibility explored in this connection by Hoekman and Mavroidis (1994*b*) is that efforts be made to obtain agreement that allegations of dumping are first investigated by the anti-trust authorities of the exporter's home country. These would determine whether the exporting firm or industry engages in anti-competitive practices or benefits from government-created or supported entry barriers. The bench-mark used in such investigations would be the exporting firm's home country competition laws. The importing country's competition authorities would be invited to participate in the investigation, and would be provided with all relevant data collected and used. If anti-competitive behaviour is found to exist, a remedy would be applied that would benefit the foreign import-competing industry. If the importing country's competition authorities disagree with the conclusion of the investigation by the competition offices, it would have the option of invoking WTO-dispute settlement mechanisms or initiating an AD investigation. However, a necessary condition for the latter would be that the importing country's competition authorities have concluded that significant barriers to entry exist in the exporter's home market. If not, AD would be prohibited. Countries would always be free to bring a so-called non-violation complaint, alleging that government measures (in this case lax enforcement of competition policies) nullified or impaired legitimate expectations regarding market-access conditions (see Chapter 2). In this case, multilateral mechanisms are left to determine the facts of the matter.

Suggestions along the foregoing lines will of course be opposed by import-competing industries that have come to rely on the threat of AD to reduce competition. But progress may be possible through a linkage strategy. The large users of AD are *demandeurs* on issues such as liberalization of service markets and the creation of multilateral disciplines on investment. This creates an opportunity to change the political balance in user countries. There are undoubtedly many ways through which attempts can be made to further discipline the use of contingent protection. The point is that creative thought needs to be given to developing practical, politically feasible, strategies. AD has a powerful lobby backing it, and will be very difficult to dislodge through a multilateral process. A necessary condition is that enough is brought to the table to mobilize forces in the domestic political markets of major user countries that are willing to take on the pro-AD lobby.

11.5. ENVIRONMENTAL POLICIES

The impact of environmental regulation on trade became the subject of discussions in the GATT in the late 1960s. This was a period when fears had arisen about the limits to growth and the rapid depletion of global natural resources. Environmental policies began to be pursued with some vigour in OECD countries, leading to complaints by affected industries that the costs of these regulations reduced their ability to compete in world markets. A Working Group on Environmental Measures and International Trade was established by GATT contracting parties in 1971. However, it never met, as interest in the subject waned following the recurrent oil price shocks and the economic turmoil that followed. In 1991, after a period when environmental issues had again attained a high profile on the international policy agenda, the Working Group was re-activated. In the WTO it was transformed into a Committee on Trade and the Environment (see Fig. 2.1, above), with the mandate to investigate various aspects of the relationship between environmental and trade policies.

At least four factors have driven environmental issues on to the agenda. First, production and consumption activities in one country may have detrimental impacts on other countries. Such negative spill-overs or externalities may be physical (air and water pollution, or acid rain) or intangible (animal rights, or the consumption of ivory). In almost all cases trade policy will not be the appropriate instrument to deal with the externality. Standard economic theory requires that externalities be addressed at their source (Bhagwati and Srinivasan, 1994). This requires that either the production or the consumption activity be curtailed directly by confronting the producer or consumer with the real costs of the activity, or that property rights be assigned that give owners an incentive to manage and price resources appropriately. For the externality to arise there must be a market failure, which results in prices for the resources used that are too low. Trade sanctions cannot offset an environmental externality efficiently, because they affect both consumers and producers of a good, and usually impact on only a part of total production or consumption.

While this is often recognized, trade policy is often attractive to environmentalists because it can be used in an attempt to induce countries to apply environmental policies that are in principle targeted at the source of the problem. The issue here is to determine the appropriate standard of protection and the feasibility of enforcing it. Countries may have very different preferences regarding environmental protection, reflecting differences in the absorption capacity of their eco-systems, differences in income levels (wealth), and differences in culture. In so far as there are cross-country spill-overs—physical or psychological—the appropriate policies will need to be negotiated. What matters from a trading-system point of view is that the choice of environmental policy in cases where there are spill-overs is not an issue that is appropriately dealt with in the WTO forum. International agreements on the matter are required, to be negotiated by the relevant authorities (not trade officials). Trade policy might be agreed to be the instrument that may be used to enforce internationally agreed obligations. As long as there is consensus on this between WTO Members, no legal problem arises. There may well be economic problems, however. The effectiveness of trade sanctions will be limited if the targeted nation does not have the resources to enforce appropriate environmental regulations. In such cases the sanction may make it harder for the country to achieve environmental improvements because the trade barriers reduce income.

The same conclusion applies if there are no spill-overs. In that case each country must determine for itself what are appropriate environmental policies. The WTO does not impose any constraints on governments regarding their ability to pursue environmental policies on its territory as long as the national treatment rule is respected. If a government seeks to prevent the consumption of particular products, it may restrict imports, as long as the ban, 'ax, or product standard is also imposed on domestic goods (recall also that GATT Article XX makes allowance for general exceptions under which a government may discriminate if this is a necessary condition to achieve health or safety, or natural-resource conservation objectives—see Chapter 7). However, the GATT does prevent the unilateral imposition of domestic standards relating to production processes. A famous example concerns a US ban on tuna imports from Mexico, justified by the fact that Mexican fishing boats did not use the dolphin-friendly nets required under US regulations. A GATT panel ruled against the USA in this case, greatly enhancing the perception of environmentalists that substantial greening of the GATT was required (Esty, 1994). If environmental degradation does not cross frontiers there is a clear-cut case for compensation if a trading partner seeks to impose standards that are higher and more costly than those it desires to implement.

A second motivation for addressing environmental issues in the WTO is a perception that trade *per se* is bad for the environment. It has been argued that freeing trade will lead to expansion of production and thus pollution; that liberalization will facilitate relocation of firms to countries with laxer regulatory environments; that greater trade implies the need for greater transport, leading to more degradation, and so forth (Low, 1993*b*). All of these arguments are weak at best. While trade and liberalization may give rise to such effects, this is only the case if appropriate environmental policies are not pursued. If such policies are in place, producers and consumers will take into account the cost to the environment, as this will be reflected in the price of goods and services. As greater trade and specialization subsequent to liberalization will lead to greater wealth, the capacity and willingness of voters to devote more resources to the environment will increase. Finally, as noted by Anderson (1992), supporting a sector through trade barriers may have very adverse consequences on the environment in so far as producers are induced to use production methods that are excessively polluting (e.g. agriculture in the EU) or to produce goods whose consumption is much more detrimental to the environment than imports would be. EU coal subsidies are an example of the latter possibility. These stimulate an activity that is environmentally costly. By restricting imports and subsidizing consumption, consumers are prevented from switching towards less polluting types of coal that are mined in other parts of the world—areas where the environmental costs of mining are often much lower, or changing to oil or gas.

A third rationale is the unfairness argument, where the case is made that environmental policies are bad for trade because they reduce the ability of enterprises located in countries with high standards to compete with those that operate in nations with low standards. Even if this is true, if high standards are what a society has decided it wants, then the result should be that the affected activities contract. Restricting imports makes no sense in this connection, as it promotes the activities that the environmental policy is attempting to constrain. This, of course, is one reason why the industries pursue trade policy—it is one way of avoiding part of the impact of environmental regulation. More generally, if there is indeed a preference for more environmentally friendly goods on the part of consumers, there should be a willingness to pay for them, both at home and on export markets. Competitive disadvantage is therefore by no means obvious.

There is great danger in acceding to pressure for protection or an import ban that is ostensibly justified on level playing-field grounds. The prospect of protection may induce import-competing firms to support environmental groups in their pursuit of regulation. This increases the likelihood of inefficient instruments being chosen, as these generate greater rents (Hoekman and Leidy, 1992*b*). An example of possible process standards is illustrative. Suppose that environmentalists are concerned with excessive killing of turtles by shrimp fishermen and have managed to pass legislation requiring that domestic fishermen must use nets that incorporate effective turtle-exclusion devices. The domestic industry may then argue that as a result of this policy they face unfair competition from foreign sources not subject to this regulation. Moreover, environmental groups can be expected to insist that foreign imports of shrimp meet the same standards, not because of any concern for the plight of domestic fishermen, but because of their concern for turtles. A tariff or a quota on imports is unlikely to be acceptable to the environmental group. Instead, they are likely to demand a ban on imports. Although there might be a stated willingness on the part of environmentalists to exempt those foreign sources that can prove they do not kill turtles (perhaps because there are no turtles in their waters), in practice this may be very difficult to establish. It involves not only allowing the inspection of trawlers, but also providing assurance that no mixing of sources occurs. Even if this can be done by foreign suppliers, establishing the turtle-friendliness of their products will take time and be costly, so that the environmental policy will make it more attractive to shift to third markets. Domestic fishermen will not care whether there are turtles in foreign waters. For them what counts is the playing-field—domestic regulations raise costs and they should be compensated for this. The uniform application of the process standard will both have significant trade-distorting effects and is very likely to increase the level of protection.

This brings us to the fourth, and final rationale that will be mentioned for discussing environmental issues in the WTO. Environmental policies may unnecessarily restrict trade. This justification is one that appears to fit best in the WTO context—trade restrictions are after all what the WTO deals with. Environmental polices may be unduly trade-restricting because of the political economy factors noted previously. It is a fact that environmental policies have often been of the command-and-control type rather than more efficient price-based instruments such as taxes (Hoekman and Leidy, 1992*b*; Low, 1993*b*). The reason is that such instruments may create rents that can be captured by the industries that are affected by the environmental regulations. Industry then has an incentive to push for inefficient policies in situations where environmental groups are sufficiently powerful to get environmental standards adopted. Environmental policies that are based on regulation rather than taxation may easily have trade-restricting effects because the trade equivalent may be a ban on imports. The US tuna–dolphin case noted earlier is a case in point.

As with many other areas, much greater transparency and more objective analysis of the impact of environmental policies on trade, and vice versa, is required. This is the mandate that has been given to the Committee on Trade and the Environment. One issue that will have to be addressed by this Committee is the need to expand the coverage of GATT Article XX to include environmental objectives, and if so, how to ensure that such an expansion does not become another loophole in the GATT allowing for discriminatory trade restrictions to be imposed. The question whether CVDs might be used to countervail imports originating in countries with lax standards of environmental protection is also likely to figure on the agenda.

11.6. LABOUR STANDARDS

Discussions relating to workers' rights and trade have a long history. Indeed, they pre-date discussions on IPRs, going back at least 150 years. In the nineteenth century, the question was one of improving working conditions. Trade entered the picture because of concerns expressed by industries that domestic legislation prohibiting child labour or limiting the working week would put them at a competitive disadvantage (Leary, 1994). Recurring international discussions starting in the late nineteenth century led to the creation of the ILO in 1919. The ILO is a unique body, in so far as it is tripartite—bringing together employers, labour unions, and governments. As of 1994, the ILO had passed over 170 conventions dealing with various aspects of working conditions. These are adopted by governments at their discretion; many countries have only adopted a limited number. The United States, for example, had accepted less than two dozen ILO conventions as of 1994. The ILO has no binding enforcement mechanism, although it does monitor compliance by Member States.

Although the fears expressed in the past continue to motivate discussions, an additional source of concern in the current context is that liberalization of trade and closer integration of the world economy may lead to a race to the bottom, with countries that have high standards being forced to lower them if they want their firms to remain competitive with those in industrializing countries. At the insistence of the USA and France, the issue of labour standards was introduced in the final stage of the Uruguay round. The objective of these countries was to initiate discussions on the introduction of a Social Clause specifying minimum standards in this area, presumably as a pre-condition for market access.[2] This was not the first attempt to introduce the issue into the GATT. The USA and other OECD countries had made efforts in this area periodically since the 1950s. Although no agreement was reached that the topic should be on the agenda of the WTO—through the establishment of a committee or working party—calls for linking the benefits of WTO membership, or even membership itself, to the adoption and enforcement of minimum labour standards can be expected to continue to be heard. In March 1995, three months after the creation of the WTO, the Director-General of the International Labour Organization (ILO) wrote to the WTO urging that Members should be required to ratify ILO conventions that prohibit forced labour and grant workers the right to form unions and engage in collective wage-bargaining (*Financial Times*, 9 March 1995, p. 9).

Two issues should be distinguished. The first concerns differences in labour costs across countries; the second relates to differences in labour standards. The debate centres on the second, not the first. The reason is that labour costs are endogenous, and largely reflect a country's comparative advantage. Insisting that further liberalization of trade be made conditional upon convergence in labour costs makes absolutely no sense, and would constitute blatant

---

[2] See Bhagwati (1994*a*) on the issue of harmonization in the trade-policy context generally, and Bhagwati (1994*b*) on the question of labour standards specifically.

protectionism. The gains from trade result precisely from differences in costs, which are a reflection of differences in the endowments and technological capacities of countries. The focus of attention is therefore mostly on labour standards and basic workers' rights. Absolute norms are few in this area. While all will agree that slavery or forced labour is morally abhorrent, and that products so produced should be subjected to import bans, legitimate differences of opinion arise on most of the dimensions of social and labour-related norms. The problem, of course, is that even if the focus of attention is not on relative labour costs *per se*, labour standards may raise costs, and thus reduce the competitiveness of particular firms located in countries that are asked to adopt the standards.

The impact of labour standards on the competitiveness of firms depends on the circumstances (Ehrenberg, 1994). It is not necessarily the case that high standards—with respect to social security, for example—will reduce the ability of firms to compete in world markets. If firms can ensure that the incidence of the implicit tax is borne by workers—that is, that the work force pays for the resulting benefits through lower wages—labour costs may be unaffected. Moreover, in so far as the cost-raising effects of workers' rights cannot be fully shifted to workers, the resulting increase in product prices (due to higher costs) will put pressure on the exchange rate (because foreign demand for exports falls as prices increase, all other things equal). The resulting depreciation will lower the standard of living by raising the cost of imports. While the whole economy thus bears the burden of the higher standards, the exchange-rate adjustment allows firms to continue to compete on world markets. As in the case of environmental policies, if the level of labour standards is desired by voters, the costs of implementation simply reflects the trade-off between monetary and non-monetary wealth that the society has made. However, if standards are unilaterally imposed on a country, it is very unlikely that they will reflect the preferences of the population.

These arguments suggest that imposing a tariff or other trade barriers to offset the cost disadvantage for domestic firms may not be necessary to level the playing-field; it will also distort resource allocation and have a detrimental effect on the realization of the non-economic objectives that are pursued by pro-labour standards groups. Trade policies raise the prices of foreign products, thus imposing a welfare cost at home, while at the same time probably worsening the labour situation in the exporting country. For example, imposing a relatively high minimum wage in a developing country with low per capita income will be akin to a high tax on employment of low-skilled workers. Unemployment will rise, and given the absence or weakness of social safety-nets (unemployment insurance), can be expected to have a very detrimental impact on poverty. It should come as no surprise, therefore, that developing countries oppose any attempt to link market access to labour standards.

As with the other issues discussed in this chapter, the multilateral institutions can play a useful role in this connection by undertaking and supporting the research required to identify appropriate multilateral solutions. It may prove feasible to achieve agreement that all countries adopt minimum standards that are akin to basic human rights. A number of the ILO's conventions may be relevant in this regard (Leary, 1994). As with the environment, however, these are matters that need to be addressed through negotiation. The WTO is not the appropriate place for this, although it could again potentially allow trade sanctions to be used as an enforcement tool, if agreement can be reached on certain basic human-rights-based minimum standards. Realism suggests that if the pressure mounts enough, some concessions may need to be made by developing countries for progress to be feasible on further reductions of market-access restrictions.

11.7. CONCLUSION

The WTO will face a rather daunting agenda in the decades to come. The true test of the intentions of its Members will be the extent to which remaining regulations that limit the contestability of markets can be swept away. There is very much that still needs to be done on services and on agriculture and textiles and clothing (where tariff barriers remain much higher than average—see Chapter 8). There is also much that needs to be done to control the use of contingent protection, especially anti-dumping (see Chapter 7). As far as the new issues that have been discussed briefly in this chapter are concerned, investment policies are perhaps the most important in market-access terms. This is also an issue where a classic GATT approach (shallow integration) can work quite well. Although agreement to harmonize competition policies appears to be highly unlikely, in principle exploring the possibility of linking competition policy with anti-dumping may prove fruitful in moving the trading system in a more liberal direction.

An important challenge will be to contain the threat of protectionist capture of the environment and labour standards issues. This may require some acceptance of harmonization through an agreement to adopt specific minimum labour standards, and making allowance for the use of trade policy to achieve environmental objectives under narrowly specified conditions. Some movement in this direction may be required as a quid pro quo for further market opening in the WTO's traditional areas—goods and service markets. If so, care must be taken to minimize the possibility of capture by industrial or anti-trade lobbies. Transparency will be important here. Moreover, a necessary condition should be that affected countries are compensated for the trade barriers, except if trade sanctions are used to enforce a multilaterally agreed treaty. Protection in such cases should not be allowed to benefit the domestic import-competing industries. As the purported objective is environmental standards or related to labour rights, revenues collected through trade actions should be used to ameliorate the situation in the exporting country.

11.8. FURTHER READING

Jagdish Bhagwati, 'Fair Trade, Reciprocity and Harmonization: The New Challenge to the Theory and Policy of Free Trade', in Alan Deardorff and Robert Stern (eds.), *Analytical and Negotiating Issues in the Global Trading System* (Ann Arbor: University of Michigan Press, 1994) is an excellent discussion of the threat to further progress in liberalizing access to markets that is presented by calls for harmonization. More generally on the theme of deep integration and the problems of dealing with domestic policy differences, see Jagdish Bhagwati and Robert Hudec (eds.), *Harmonization and Fair Trade: Prerequisite for Free Trade?* (Cambridge, Mass.: MIT Press, forthcoming).

See Rachel McCulloch, 'Investment Policy in the GATT', *World Economy*, 13 (1990), 541–53, and DeAnne Julius, 'International Direct Investment: Strengthening the Policy Regime', in *Managing the World Economy: Lessons from the First 50 Years After Bretton Woods* (Washington DC: Institute for International Economics, 1995) for a discussion of the need for—and possible elements of—multilateral rules on investment. Kym Anderson and Richard Blackhurst (eds.), *The Greening of World Trade Issues* (London: Harvester-Wheatsheaf, 1992) and Patrick Low (ed.), *International Trade and the Environment* (Washington DC: World Bank, 1993) are collections of papers written mostly by trade economists exploring the linkages between trade and the environment. Daniel Esty, *Greening the GATT: Trade, Environment and the Future* (Washington DC: Institute for International Economics, 1994) is a balanced and comprehensive treatment of the issues, written more from an environmental perspective. The WTO Secretariat publishes a newsletter devoted exclusively to green issues that have been discussed in the Committee on Trade and Environment, entitled *Trade and the Environment*.

F. M. Sherer, *Competition Policies for an Integrated World Economy* (Washington DC: Brookings Institution, 1994) provides an introduction to the linkages between competition and trade policies. Bernard Hoekman and Petros C. Mavroidis, in 'Competition, Competition Policy, and the GATT', *World Economy*, 17 (1994), 121–50, analyse the scope to bring competition-related complaints to the GATT, and question the need to give priority to attempting to establish global competition rules in the WTO. Ronald Ehrenberg, *Labor Markets and Integrating National Economies* (Washington DC: Brookings Institution, 1994) discusses the economics of labour-market regulation and the need for convergence in labour standards in an integrating world economy.

12
Conclusion

The GATT was created by a group of governments with a clear vision of the co-operation that was needed to foster economic growth and reconstruction. Although the vision called for an ITO, the GATT managed to fulfil the objectives of the original signatories quite well. It proved a very successful trade-liberalizing instrument. The elimination of QRs by industrialized countries in the post-Second World War period was locked in under its auspices, and tariffs were reduced very substantially. As of the 1970s, trade barriers in the form of tariffs and quotas had declined significantly in importance, and governments came to be confronted increasingly with the trade-distorting aspects of other economic policies. To use Robert Baldwin's analogy, trade liberalization can be likened to the draining of a swamp: as the water level (average tariff level) fell due to successful pumping efforts, rocks, stumps, and all manner of other obstacles (NTBs) emerged (Baldwin, 1970). GATT-1947 proved very able to drain the swamp. It was much less successful in clearing the drained land (eliminating NTBs), and keeping the water from flooding back (contingent protection). Dealing with the tree stumps and rocks was difficult in large part because reciprocal exchange became more difficult. Governments sometimes perceived discussions on non-tariff policies as zero-sum games. The issue linkages and side-payments required to make progress in establishing multilateral disciplines on regulatory regimes greatly complicated matters.

The first 50 years of the life of the GATT has a close similarity with the life-cycle of a product. At first market growth is slow, as consumers become acquainted with it. This is followed by a period of rapid expansion of market share and output as the product takes off. In the third or mature stage, growth levels off but sales remain high. In the final stage sales begin to fall. Basic marketing theory teaches that by the time of the third stage a firm had better have a new product ready to introduce in order to survive and prosper. For the GATT, the take-off and maturity stages occurred in the 1950s and 1960s. This was the period when the most progress was made in terms of trade liberalization. By the early 1970s, the demand for the GATT product had levelled off. An attempt was made to diversify into new markets by shifting attention to NTBs, but this did not prove very successful. Tentative steps were taken to address trade-related domestic policies, but progress was slow. With the establishment of the WTO, the GATT-1947 was transformed into an organization, and its reach was substantially broadened. What is the relevance of the WTO as the multilateral trading system moves into the twenty-first century?

Will it be able to revitalize international co-operation and move the multilateral trading system onto a new growth path? What challenges must be confronted to ensure that the relevance of the institution is enhanced and intergovernmental co-operation is bolstered?

In answering these questions it is useful to review briefly some of the fundamental changes that occurred in the world economy in the latter part of the twentieth century. The WTO confronts a very different economic environment than the GATT did when it was created in 1947. The US hegemony that existed in the 1950s has been eroded. The demise of central planning and the adoption of outward-oriented economic development strategies by many countries in the 1980s led to the demise of ideological differences and competition. Given that the rule-oriented multilateral trading system was firmly founded on the existence and superiority of a market-based economy, in some sense this constituted a triumph for the GATT. The institution never really played much of a direct role in these developments, however. Integration of international financial markets, unilaterally implemented regulatory changes, and technological change and managerial innovations fostered what has come to be called the globalization of the world economy. The GATT was a facilitator of this process—having helped to create the necessary pre-conditions by lowering trade barriers—but to a large extent governments did things unilaterally or regionally. In the process they addressed issues such as the taxation of firms, investment policies, foreign-exchange restrictions, intellectual property protection, privacy of data, trade in services, and movement of personnel. Often actions were taken under pressure from the international capital markets or the international financial institutions. The inclusion of many of these issue areas on the agenda of the Uruguay round constituted more a catch-up phenomenon than proactive leadership.

The qualitative change in the nature of cross-border exchange that has occured in recent years is important in understanding the challenges facing the WTO. In the 1950s international trade was relatively simple: a product was made in Country X and shipped to an importer in Country Y. Interactions between producer and buyer were very superficial. Trade was of a ship-and-forget nature (Cooper, 1988). Foreign direct investment was generally a substitute for trade—a way to jump over high tariff walls. Over subsequent years this has changed fundamentally. The service intensity of production and consumption have increased significantly. It is a commonplace that modern economies have become service economies. Many firms now sell intangibles—processes, performance, information, a life-style image—that may or may not be bundled with tangible products. In the current economy, value tends to be closely associated with the performance and utilization of systems composed of material products, services, information of commercial value (trade marks or patents) and client–producer relations. The establishment of a relationship with clients is crucial in today's economy, as is ensuring that customers have access to complementary products, services, upgrades, and maintenance. Clients want open systems: what matters for them are outcomes or results. What counts is performance in meeting the customers' needs. More often than not this implies custom tailoring of solutions. Strategic partnerships and networking are often necessary to provide the solution to a client's problem. Firms increasingly need to enter into *ad hoc* or more formal relationships with other firms. Production and consumption are also more and more a joint process, requiring inputs and feedback from the customer. All of this means that managing the intangible aspects of the production process often requires establishment in a foreign market and access to telecommunications networks and global databases. FDI and trade have become increasingly complementary.

What does all this imply for the WTO? One implication is that the incentive structure of firms regarding the policy stance of governments changes. Firms 'think global and act local' (Levitt, 1983). They have become much more sensitive and averse to regulatory barriers that restrict their ability to interact with complementary suppliers and with customers, and to source from—and sell to—a market. This in turn has implications for the political economy of the trade-policy-setting process in many countries. Transnational enterprises with a customer orientation have a greater incentive to form coalitions with export-oriented interests in host countries to lobby for the opening of local markets and for otherwise creating a more competition-friendly environment. Multinationals need to be able to buy from the lowest-cost source to stay competitive, while local export interests need to ensure that the regulatory regime allows them to compete for contracts with globally diversified firms. These changes in incentives help to explain the trade-policy developments observed in many countries in the 1980s and early 1990s: unilateral liberalization in developing countries; the shift to market-based systems in Eastern Europe and the former Soviet Union; deregulation in many OECD countries; and the expansion of the scope and coverage of RIAs in Europe, North America, and the Pacific.

The foregoing appears to imply that the relevance of reciprocal WTO-type bargaining may be diminished because there is now greater support for open markets. If true, this simply enhances the potential beneficial role of the organization. The WTO is important and remains relevant to firms and consumers in the new world economy for a number of reasons. First, much remains to be done in terms of addressing new issues so as to further the globalization process. Major holes in the trading system include the fact that the GATT pertains to products (goods), not to producers (FDI), and that the GATS is not yet a general agreement given its limited sectoral coverage. As far as FDI in the goods sector is concerned, there is only the TRIMs agreement, which is limited to trade-related policies such as local content requirements, not FDI more generally. GATS does allow Members to make commitments on

FDI, but these are usually limited to specific services, and are often subject to derogations. The sectoral coverage of commitments is limited, with many countries refusing to guarantee national treatment or market access for activities where in practice they actually pursue policies that satisfy these principles. What is needed is a generic approach, with horizontal investment disciplines that apply to economic activity in any sector. More generally, the distinction between goods and services makes very little sense. In principle, a case can be made to undertake an effort to merge the GATT and the GATS, in the sense that general principles such as national treatment and MFN apply across the board, and that generic, horizontal disciplines are negotiated not only for FDI, but for all modes of supply.

Second, powerful protectionist forces still exist in many countries, whether industrialized or developing. Many governments have so far proved unwilling to lock in or bind currently applied trade regimes, and the WTO continues to embody many loopholes, in particular contingent protection. So there are still important battles to be fought. Reciprocal exchange will continue to be the only currency available to governments that seek to close the holes and loopholes in the WTO. Third, even if a government pursues a liberal, non-discriminatory trade and investment policy, the WTO remains of great value as a forum for negotiations on new issues and through its role as a forum for the settlement of disputes relating to alleged violations of negotiated market-access commitments by trading partners. It establishes an upper limit on backsliding and defines the minimum standards regarding the conditions of competition that apply in a market. The WTO's *raison d'être* is to constrain the ongoing civil war in the polity of Members regarding the trade-policy stance that should be pursued. The WTO enters the picture by giving foreign players a voice in domestic political markets—the negotiating leverage of pro-liberal domestic lobbies is enhanced because foreign export lobbies will support them in MTNs, by bringing complaints to the WTO, and by calling for compensation if negotiated market-access conditions are violated.

Perhaps the greatest challenge facing the WTO is the further integration of developing countries. For most of GATT-1947's existence, developing countries basically did not participate in the multilateral system of rules and principles. This has changed. Many are pursuing reform programmes that, if successful, will make them as—if not more—open to trade than high-income countries, and allow them to grow at rates that will far exceed those of the OECD. The competitive pressures that result could lead to demands for protection that exceeds that witnessed in past decades, especially if potential economic giants such as Brazil, China, India, and Russia take off. These countries need the WTO to help keep foreign markets open and in turn need to be as WTO-consistent as possible to reduce the likelihood of being accused of being unfair traders. Key questions facing developing countries are what to do about RIAs, how to go about reducing their vulnerability to unfair-trade actions in export markets, and what to do about calls for harmonization of domestic regulatory regimes (e.g. environmental or labour standards). To some extent calls for harmonization are simply another manifestation of the contingent protection issue. Ultimately, what is at stake is the possibility of being confronted with allegations of social or environmental dumping. As discussed in Chapter 11, fears of unfair competition from developing countries are driven by factors such as the very large nominal wage differences across countries. In 1995 the hourly average cost of unskilled labour in Thailand, Russia, or China was less than $1, as compared to $25 in Germany and $15–17 in France, Japan, and North America. Continued efforts must be made to reduce the scope for protectionist forces to point to such nominal cost differences as a legitimate rationale for seeking to raise trade barriers. After all, nominal wages differences—adjusted for productivity as well as other costs of doing business in a country—are a major source of the gains from international trade.

With the virtual demise of tariffs and the ever greater prominence of non-tariff policies—product standards, investment regulations, environmental or social standards, competition laws—there is a danger of moving away from a positive-sum game and towards a zero-sum game. That is, while tariffs do not make much economic sense, a nation's regulatory regime or lack of one may well be welfare-enhancing. A necessary condition for harmonization efforts in cases where this is zero-sum is that linkages are established across issues or side-payments are made. The goal should be mutual recognition—i.e. negotiation of minimum standards on those issues where this is welfare-improving or where it appears to be necessary to maintain the liberalization momentum. The question to be answered is to what extent countries are willing and able to pursue mutual recognition. Even if willing, decentralized economies with substantially autonomous local and municipal governments may find it difficult to agree to and/or enforce multilaterally negotiated disciplines.

To enhance the relevance of the WTO, greater interest in the institution must be shown by multinational business and domestic consumer organizations. The WTO, as was true of the GATT-1947, represents an opportunity—much depends on the willingness of a government to exploit the opportunities offered. This in turn depends on the pressure that is exerted upon the government to do so. A crucial need as far as business is concerned is to use the WTO more as an insrument of corporate strategy. Changes in trade policy require support in domestic political markets. This is very well known by multinationals. Those that are proactive and attempt to alter the equilibrium in political markets in their favour do not, however, push for the government to lock in trade-policy liberalization by, for example, binding tariffs at applied rates. They also seldom take a general equilibrium view of trade policy, instead being largely concerned with the specific tariffs and other policies that raise their costs or restrict their access to a market. The result is often a pattern of individual tax exemptions or subsidies and a dispersed tariff structure. Long-run sustainable growth will be maximized if policies are liberalized across the board, so that incentives are neutral. To achieve this, institutional solutions need to be found for global firms, to alleviate the free-rider problem that affects efforts to lobby for broad-based liberalization of market access. One option in this regard is to foster further transparency of trade policy.

Great progress has been made in comparison with GATT-1947 in terms of surveillance and collection of basic data on trade policy, but these are not used to estimate the costs of protection and the incidence of these costs. It is a truism that to reduce protection and protectionist pressures those negatively affected need to be aware of the costs of such policies. The clients for the analysis are not governments, but the constituencies in individual countries who are negatively affected by policy. A corollary of this is that the institution(s) that undertake the analysis do not necessarily require public funding. Indeed, such activities should be financed by the parties that have the most to gain: exporters and consumer organizations. It is, however, crucial that the data-collection function of the WTO Secretariat be maintained and enhanced, as this will often require the co-operation of governments. A necessary condition, of course, is that agreement is obtained that these data are made publicly available.

There are a number of other ways to strengthen the constitutional role of the WTO that could be pursued by those favouring stability and liberal trade policies. One would be for governments to allow domestic firms and consumer organizations to invoke WTO rules and principles in domestic courts. This would go a long way in offsetting the weakness of the dispute-settlement mechanism, which ultimately depends on the threat of retaliation—a weak threat at best. WTO rules are generally not self-executing; they do not have direct effect in the domestic legal orders of most Members. This implies that implementing legislation is required, providing scope for lobbies to attempt to renegotiate deals that were made in MTNs. For example, as discussed in Chapter 7, a number of changes were made to the GATT rules on anti-dumping in the Uruguay round that made the instrument somewhat less protectionist. In the context of drafting the required implementing legislation in the United States,

the necessity of making these liberalizing changes provoked opposition from those industries in the United States that see the antidumping law as a source of protection from import competition. The Clinton Administration responded to the pressure by proposing other amendments in the law—amendments permitted but not required by the Code—that frequently are more restrictive than existing law. Whether, on balance, the resulting legislation is more or less restrictive than its predecessor is a subject for debate. (Palmeter, 1995: 1)

Such problems can be avoided if negotiated agreements have direct effect.

The political dynamics in developing countries are similar enough to those in the OECD that mercantilism can continue to work if it is necessary to induce a government to liberalize. Pressure from foreign exporters can be relied upon; but they will increasingly have to form coalitions with internal interest-groups that can be mobilized to fight for liberalization. Education and objective analysis of the various dimensions of the issues at hand must play a major role. One can hope that the WTO Secretariat will be given a mandate to be more proactive in this regard. One problem in terms of marketing the institution in the past has been that a marketing-push strategy has been pursued rather than a marketing-pull approach. That is, the focus has been on governments (the middlemen) not on consumers (the ultimate clients). Although greater emphasis on the economic impact of trade policies—even if WTO-legal—would be very beneficial, many governments are unlikely to support such initiatives without strong domestic political support in favour of this change.

ANNEX 1: GATT/WTO MEMBERSHIP, 1994
(Dates indicate accession to the GATT-1947)

Angola 1994
Antigua and Barbuda 1987
Argentina 1967
Australia 1948
Austria 1951
Bahrain 1993
Bangladesh 1972
Barbados 1967
Belgium 1948
Belize 1983
Benin 1963
Bolivia 1990
Botswana 1987
Brazil 1948
Brunei 1993
Burkina Faso 1963
Burundi 1965
Cameroon 1963
Canada 1948
Central African Republic 1963
Chad 1963
Chile 1949
Colombia 1981
Congo 1963
Costa Rica 1990
Côte d'Ivoire 1963
Cuba 1948
Cyprus 1963
Czech Republic 1993
Denmark 1950
Djibouti 1994
Dominica 1993
Dominican Republic 1950
Egypt 1970
El Salvador 1991
Fiji 1993
Finland 1950
France 1948
Gabon 1963
Gambia 1965
Germany 1951

Ghana 1957
Greece 1950
Grenada 1994
Guatemala 1991
Guinea, Republic of 1994
Guinea-Bissau 1994
Guyana 1966
Haiti 1950
Honduras 1994
Hong Kong 1986
Hungary 1973
Iceland 1968
India 1948
Indonesia 1950
Ireland 1967
Israel 1962
Italy 1950
Jamaica 1963
Japan 1955
Kenya 1964
Korea, Republic of 1967
Kuwait 1963
Lesotho 1988
Liechtenstein 1994
Luxembourg 1948
Macao 1991
Madagascar 1963
Malawi 1964
Malaysia 1957
Maldives 1983
Mali 1993
Malta 1964
Mauritania 1963
Mauritius 1970
Mexico 1986
Morocco 1987
Mozambique 1992
Myanmar 1948
Namibia 1992
Netherlands 1948
New Zealand 1948

Nicaragua   1950
Niger   1963
Nigeria   1960
Norway   1948
Papua New Guinea   1994
Pakistan   1948
Paraguay   1993
Peru   1951
Philippines   1979
Poland   1967
Portugal   1962
Qatar   1994
Romania   1971
Rwanda   1966
St Kitts and Nevis   1994
St Lucia   1993
St Vincent and   Grenadines 1993
Senegal   1963
Sierra Leone   1961
Singapore   1973
Slovak Republic   1993
Slovenia   1994
Solomon Islands   1994

South Africa   1948
Spain   1963
Sri Lanka   1948
Surinam   1978
Swaziland   1993
Sweden   1950
Switzerland   1966
Tanzania   1961
Thailand   1982
Togo   1964
Trinidad and Tobago   1962
Tunisia   1990
Turkey   1951
Uganda   1962
United Arab Emirates   1994
United Kingdom   1948
USA   1948
Uruguay   1953
Venezuela   1990
Yugoslavia   1966
Zaire   1971
Zambia   1982
Zimbabwe   1948

ANNEX 2: MEMBERSHIP OF PLURILATERAL TRADE AGREEMENTS (March 1995)

Agreement on Civil Aircraft	Agreement on Government Procurement	International Dairy Arrangement	International Bovine Meat Arrangement
Austria	Austria	Argentina	Argentina
Belgium	Canada	Australia	Australia
Canada	European Union	Bulgaria	Austria
Denmark	Israel	Egypt	Belize (provisional)
Egypt	Japan	European Union	Brazil
European Union	South Korea	Finland	Bulgaria
France	Norway	Hungary	Canada
Germany	Sweden	Japan	Colombia
Greece (signed)	Switzerland	New Zealand	Egypt
Ireland	United Kingdom	Norway	European Union
Italy	United States	Poland	Finland
Japan		Romania	Guatemala
Luxembourg		South Africa	Hungary
Netherlands		Sweden	Japan
Norway		Switzerland	New Zealand
Portugal		Uruguay	Nigeria
Romania			Norway
Spain			Paraguay
Sweden			Poland
Switzerland			Romania
United Kingdom			South Africa
United States			Sweden
			Switzerland
			Tunisia
			United States
			Uruguay

ANNEX 3: GENERAL DISPUTE SETTLEMENT PANELS (1984–1994)

(excluding antidumping and countervail-related cases)

Requesting Country	Date	Issue
	1983	
United States	February	Treatment of value-added tax in EC government procurement contracts
United States	April	Japanese restraints on leather imports
EC	April	'Manufacturing Clause' in US copyright legislation
EC	May	US subsidies on exports of wheat-flour to Egypt
Nicaragua	July	US decision to reduce Nicaragua's sugar import quota
	1984	
Canada	March	EC reduction of its duty-free newsprint quota
Finland	October	Imposition of anti-dumping duties by New Zealand on electrical transformers from Finland
South Africa	November	Discriminatory application of retail sales tax on gold coins in Canada (Ontario)
	1985	
EC	February	Definition of industry concerning wine and grape products contained in the US Trade and Tariff Act of 1984
EC	March	Import distribution and sale of alcoholic drinks by provincial market agencies in Canada
Canada	March	US restrictions on imports of certain products containing sugar
Nicaragua	October	US trade measures affecting Nicaragua
	1986	
Canada	August	Initiation by the United States of a countervailing duty investigation into softwood lumber products from Canada
United States	October	Japanese restrictions on imports of certain agricultural products
EC	October	Canada's countervailing duty investigation into processed beef from the EC
	1987	
Canada, EC, Mexico	February	US taxes on petroleum and certain imported substances
EC	February	Japanese customs duties, taxes, and labelling practices on imported wines and alcoholic beverages

Requesting Country	Date	Issue
Canada, EC	March	US customs user fee
United States	March	Canada's restrictions on exports of unprocessed salmon and herring
EC	April	Japan's trade in semiconductors
EC	October	Section 337 of the US Tariff Act of 1930
United States	November	India's import restrictions on almonds
	1988	
United States	March	Norway's restrictions on imports of apples and pears
Canada	March	Japanese imports of spruce-pine-fir lumber
Chile	May	EC's restrictions on imports of apples
Australia	May	Korea's restrictions on imports of beef
United States	May	Korea's restrictions on imports of beef
Australia	May	Japanese import restrictions on beef
United States	May	Japanese import restrictions on beef and citrus
United States	June	EC payments and subsidies on oil-seeds and related animal feed proteins
Chile	June	EC restrictions on imports of dessert apples
United States	September	EC restrictions on imports of apples
Australia	September	US restrictions on imports of sugar
New Zealand	September	Korean restrictions on imports of beef
Japan	October	EC regulations on imports of car parts and components
United States	December	Canada import restrictions on ice cream and yoghurt
	1989	
Brazil	February	US import restrictions on certain products from Brazil
EC	June	US restrictions on imports of sugar and sugar-containing products applied under the 1955 waiver and under the headnote to the schedule of tariff concessions
United States	July	EC restraints on export of copper scrap
Canada	December	US countervailing duties on fresh, chilled, and frozen pork from Canada
	1990	
United States	April	Thailand's restrictions on importation of and internal taxes on cigarettes
	1991	
United States	February	Canada's import distribution and sale of certain alcoholic drinks by provincial marketing agencies
Mexico	February	US restrictions on imports of tuna

Requesting Country	Date	Issue
Brazil	April	US denial of MFN treatment to imports of non-rubber footwear from Brazil
Canada	May	US measures affecting alcoholic and malt beverages
	1992	
Yugoslavia	March	EC trade measures taken for non-economic reasons
EC	July	US restrictions on imports of tuna
	1993	
Colombia, Costa Rica, Guatemala, Nicaragua, Venezuela	February	EC member states' import regimes for bananas
EC	May	US taxes affecting imported automobiles
Colombia, Costa Rica, Guatemala, Nicaragua	June	EC import regime for bananas
Chile	September	EC restrictions on imports of apples
	1994	
Argentina, Brazil, Colombia, El Salvador, Guatemala, Thailand, Zimbabwe	January	US measures affecting the importation and internal sale of tobacco
EU	October	US standards for reformulated gasoline
India	November	Poland's import regime for automobiles

ANNEX 4: A COMPILATION OF POLICIES AFFECTING TRADE

(Information drawn in part from Deardoff and Stern, 1985)

Quantitative Restrictions and Similar Measures

1. *Import/export quotas.* Restrictions on quantity and/or value of imports or exports of specific products for a given time-period; may be in absolute terms or relative to domestic output (i.e. market share); apply to all countries or just a subset. May be administered on a first-come first-served basis, or allocated to specific suppliers. If allocated, may be free of charge or auctioned to the highest bidders. Quota rights may or may not be tradeable (transferable).

2. *Voluntary export restraints.* Quantitative restrictions imposed by an importing country but administered by the exporting country or countries. In GATT jargon, these have often been referred to as 'grey-area measures'.

3. *Prohibitions.* May be selective in respect of commodities or activities and countries of origin or destination; includes embargoes on exports and imports; and may carry legal sanctions.

4. *Domestic content and purchase requirements.* Requires that an industry use a certain proportion of domestically produced components and/or materials in producing its products.

5. *Discriminatory trade agreements.* Preferential trading arrangements that may be selective by commodity and country; includes free-trade agreements and unilateral preferences. Requires rules of origin.

6. *Offsets and counter-purchase requirements.* Arrangements whereby imports or market access is conditional on agreements to counter-purchase a given value or quantity of goods and services (including offset requirements).

7. *Exchange and other financial controls.* Restrictions on receipts and/or payments of foreign exchange designed to control international trade and capital flows; will generally require some system of licensing.

8. *Transfer-of-technology requirements.* Imports (market access) conditional on associated transfer of technology.

9. *Licensing, rules of origin, and import surveillance.* Required to administer quotas on imports or exports. May be subject to specific conditions (e.g. export performance requirements). Licensing may also be automatic, used for statistical purposes, or to monitor import penetration trends for individual products. Rules to determine the origin of products are required if trade policies discriminate across foreign sources of supply.

Charges, Taxes, and Related Policies

1. *Tariffs (customs duties).* Taxes imposed on imports or exports at the frontier when entering or leaving the country. May be specific (per unit of quantity) or *ad valorem* (percentage of the value).

2. *Variable levies.* Based on a target domestic price for imports, a levy is imposed so

that the price of imports reaches the target price whatever the cost of imports. Equivalent to the imposition of a minimum price requirement for products sold on the domestic market.

3. *Advance deposit requirements.* Some proportion of the value of imports must be deposited in advance of the payment, often with no allowance for interest accrued on the deposit.

4. *Anti-dumping duties.* Imposition of a special import duty when the price of imports is alleged to be less than what is charged by the producer on its home market or to be below some measure of costs of production; GATT rules require that dumped imports be shown to materially injure domestic producers of the like product.

5. *Countervailing duties.* Imposition of a special import duty to counteract an alleged foreign government subsidy to output or exports that materially injures domestic producers of the like product.

6. *Price undertakings and price surveillance.* Commitment by exporters, accepted by the authorities of the importing country, to increase export prices in instances where dumping or subsidization has been deemed to occur.

7. *Border tax adjustments and duty drawbacks.* Border tax adjustments arise when indirect (e.g. sales or value-added) taxes are levied on the basis of the so-called destination principle. Imports are then subject to indirect taxes but production for export is exempt. Duty drawbacks are repayments of tariffs on imported inputs that are embodied in products that are exported.

8. *Tariff-quotas.* A system under which a low tariff is imposed on imports up to a certain limit (which may be in quantity or value terms); once this limit has been reached a higher tariff is imposed on additional imports.

9. *Price ceilings and minimum prices.* Imposition of upper or lower limits on prices for certain imported goods.

10. *Subsidies.* Government-financed aid to particular factors of production, firms, industries, regions, or activities. May be direct or indirect, and does not necessarily have implications for the government budget.

11. *Customs valuation, classification, and clearance procedures.* Valuation or classification practices may inflate value for tariff-collection purposes. Clearance procedures relate to documentation requirements. May include pre-shipment inspection policies whereby products are inspected at the point of origin rather than at the point of importation.

Policies with an Indirect Impact of Quantities and/or Prices

1. *Health and product standards.* Mandatory product standards are technical specifications for products to ensure compatibility with standards of public and animal health, safety, and protection of the environment.

2. *Application of domestic norms to production for export.* E.g. policies designed to prohibit or restrict bribes and related practices in connection with foreign trade and investment.

3. *Standards of competition.* Anti-trust and related policies designed to foster or restrict competition may have an impact on foreign trade.

4. *Copyrights, patents trade-marks, brand-names, and franchises.* Instruments to

determine property rights to intangible assets. Differences across countries in the recognition and enforcement of such rights may distort trade and may effectively restrict imports or exports.

5. *Immigration policies.* General or selective policies designed to limit or encourage international movement of labour may have an impact on foreign trade.

6. *Government procurement.* Preferences are often given to domestic over foreign firms in bidding on public-procurement contracts.

7. *State trading, monopolies, and exclusive franchises.* May result in protection, effective export subsidization, or discrimination across suppliers or countries.

ANNEX 5: Major GATT Articles

I	General MFN requirement.
II	Tariff schedules and bindings.
III	National treatment.
V	Freedom of transit of goods.
VI	Allows anti-dumping and countervailing duties. Superseded by the GATT-1994 Agreement on Anti-dumping, and the Agreement on Subsidies and Countervailing Duties.
VII	Requires that valuation for customs purposes be based on a good's 'actual' value; superseded by the GATT-1994 Agreement on the Implementation of Article VII.
VIII	Requires that fees connected with import or export formalities be cost-based.
IX	Reaffirms MFN for labelling requirements and calls for co-operation to prevent abuse of trade names.
X	Obligation to publish trade laws and regulations; complemented by the WTO's Trade Policy Review Mechanism and various notification requirements.
XI	Requires the general elimination of quantitative restrictions.
XII	Allows for trade restrictions to safeguard the balance of payments.
XIII	Requires that quotas be administered in a non-discriminatory manner.
XVI	Establishes GATT-1947 rules on subsidies: complemented in GATT-1994 by the Agreement on Subsidies and Countervailing Measures.
XVII	Requires that state-trading enterprises follow MFN.
XVIII	Allows developing countries to restrict trade to promote infant industries, protect the balance of payments, or maintain a certain level of reserves.
XIX	Allows for emergency action to restrict imports of particular products. Superseded by the GATT-1994 Agreement on Safeguards.
XX	Sets out general exceptions to the disciplines of the GATT.
XXI	Allows for national security exceptions.
XXII	Provides for consultations between parties that have a trade dispute; necessary condition for invoking Article XXIII.
XXIII	GATT's dispute-settlement provision, allowing parties to address actions that are perceived to nullify or impair a concession. Complemented by the WTO Understanding on Rules and Procedures Governing the Settlement of Disputes.
XXIV	Sets out the conditions under which the formation of free-trade areas or customs unions is permitted.
XXVIII	Allows for renegotiation of tariff concessions; modification of schedules.
XXVIIIbis	Calls for periodic MTNs.
XXXIII	Allows for accession.
Part IV	Calls for more favourable and differential treatment of developing countries.

ANNEX 6: REFERENCES TO DEVELOPING AND LEAST-DEVELOPED COUNTRIES IN THE WTO

Subject	Concession			
	Lower level of obligation	Best-endeavour commitment	Longer time-frame[a]	Technical assistance
WTO	—	LDCs	LDCs	DCs
Balance of payments	LDCs and DCs	—	—	DCs
Safeguards	DCs	DCs	—	—
Anti-dumping	—	DCs	—	—
Subsidies	DCs and LDCs	DCs	DCs and LDCs	—
TRIMs	DCs	DCs and LDCs	DCs and LDCs	—
Import licensing	DCs	DCs and LDCs	DCs	—
Customs valuation	DCs	DCs	DCs	DCs
Preshipment inspection	—	—	—	DCs
Rules of origin	—	—	—	—
Technical barriers	DCs	DCs	DCs and LDCs	DCs and LDCs
Sanitary/phyto-sanitary	—	DCs and LDCs	DCs and LDCs	DCs
Agriculture	DCs and LDCs	DCs and LDCs	DCs	LDCs
Textiles and clothing	—	LDCs	LDCs	—
Services	DCs	DCs and LDCs	DCs and LDCs	DCs and LDCs
TRIPs	—	LDCs	DCs and LDCs	DCs and LDCs
Dispute settlement	—	DCs and LDCs	—	DCs
Trade policy review	DCs and LDCs	—	—	DCs and LDCs

[a] Longer time-frame refers to longer transitional periods for implementing negotiated disciplines.
Note: DCs = Developing countries; LDCs = Least-developed countries.
Source: GATT (1994a); Weston (1994).

REFERENCES

Allen, D. (1979), 'Tariff Games', in S. Brams, A. Schotter, and G. Schwoediauer (eds.), *Applied Game Theory* (Wuerzburg: Physica-Verlag).

Anderson, K. (1992), 'Effects on the Environment and Welfare of Liberalizing World Trade: The Cases of Coal and Food', in K. Anderson and R. Blackhurst (eds.), *The Greening of World Trade Issues* (London: Harvester-Wheatsheaf).

—— (1993*a*), 'Lobbying Incentives and the Pattern of Protection in Rich and Poor Countries', Discussion Paper no. 789 (London: Centre for Economic Policy Research).

—— (1993*b*), 'US-EC Farm Trade Confrontation: An Outsider's View', Discussion Paper no. 849 (London: Centre for Economic Policy Research).

—— and Norheim, H. (1993), 'History, Geography and Regional Integration', in K. Anderson and R. Blackhurst (eds.), *Regional Integration and the Global Trading System*. (London: Harvester-Wheatsheaf).

Baldwin, R. (1970), *Non-Tariff Distortions in International Trade* (Washington DC: Brookings Institution).

—— (1986), 'Toward More Efficient Procedures for Multilateral Trade Negotiations', *Aussenwirtschaft*, 41: 379–94.

—— and Clarke, R. (1987), 'Game Modelling the Tokyo Round of Tariff Negotiations', *Journal of Policy Modeling*, 9: 257–84.

Banks, G. (1983), 'The Economics and Politics of Countertrade', *World Economy*, 6: 159–82.

Bhagwati, J. (1971), 'The Generalized Theory of Distortions and Welfare', in J. N. Bhagwati, R. Mundell, R. Jones, and J. Vanek (eds.), *Trade, Balance of Payments and Growth* (Amsterdam: North Holland).

—— (1984), 'Splintering and Disembodiment of Services and Developing Nations', *World Economy*, 7: 133–44.

—— (1987), 'Trade in Services and the Multilateral Trade Negotiations', *World Bank Economic Review*, 1: 549–69.

—— (1988), *Protectionism* (Cambridge, Mass: MIT Press).

—— (1991), *The World Trading System at Risk* (Princeton, NJ: Princeton University Press).

—— (1993), 'Regionalism and Multilateralism: An Overview', in J. de Melo and A. Panagariya (eds.), *New Dimensions in Regional Integration* (Cambridge: Cambridge University Press).

—— (1994*a*), 'Fair Trade, Reciprocity and Harmonization: The New Challenge to the Theory and Policy of Free Trade', in A. Deardorff and R. Stern (eds.), *Analytical and Negotiating Issues in the Global Trading System* (Ann Arbor: University of Michigan Press).

—— (1994*b*), 'Labor Standards, Social Clause, and the WTO', (New York: Columbia University, mimeo).

—— and Irwin, D. (1987), 'The Return of the Reciprocitarians: US Trade Policy Today', *World Economy*, 10: 109–30.

―― and Patrick, H. (eds.) (1990), *Aggressive Unilateralism: America's 301 Trade Policy and the World Trading System* (Ann Arbor: University of Michigan Press).

―― and Srinivasan, T. N. (1994), 'Trade and the Environment: Does Environmental Diversity Detract From the Case for Free Trade?', in J. Bhagwati and R. Hudec (eds.), *Harmonization and Fair Trade: Prerequisite for Free Trade?* (Cambridge, Mass.: MIT Press, forthcoming).

Bovard, J. (1991), *The Fair Trade Fraud* (New York: St Martins Press).

Braga, C. P. (1995), 'Trade-Related Intellectual Property Issues', in W. Martin and A. Winters (eds.), *The Uruguay Round and the Developing Economies* (Washington DC: World Bank, forthcoming).

Caves, R. (1987), 'Industrial Policy and Trade Policy: The Connections', in H. Kierzkowski (ed.), *Protection and Competition in International Trade* (London: Basil Blackwell).

―― and Jones, R. (1985), *World Trade and Payments: An Introduction* (Boston: Little, Brown).

Chan, K. (1985), 'The International Negotiation Game: Some Evidence from the Tokyo Round', *Review of Economics and Statistics*, 67: 456–64.

Conybeare, J. (1987), *Trade Wars* (Princeton, NJ: Princeton University Press).

Cooper, R. (1988), 'Comment' in L. Castle and C. Findlay (eds.), *Pacific Trade in Services* (London: Allen and Unwin).

Corden, W. M. (1974), *Trade Policy and Economic Welfare* (Oxford: Clarendon Press).

Curzon, G. (1965), *Multilateral Commercial Diplomacy* (London: Michael-Joseph).

―― and Curzon, V. (1973), 'GATT: Traders' Club', in R. Cox and H. Jacobson (eds.), *The Anatomy of Influence: Decision Making in International Organizations* (New Haven, Conn.: Yale University Press).

―― ―― (1976), 'The Management of Trade Relations in the GATT', in A. Schonfield (ed.), *International Economic Relations of the Western World, 1959–71* (London: Random House).

Curzon-Price, V. (1991), 'GATT's New Trade Policy Review Mechanism', *World Economy*, 14: 227–38.

Dam, K. (1970), *The GATT: Law and International Economic Organization* (Chicago: University of Chicago Press).

Davies, S. and McGuiness, A. (1982), 'Dumping at less than Marginal Cost', *Journal of International Economics*, 12: 169–82.

Deardorff, A. (1987), 'Safeguards Policy and the Conservative Social Welfare Function', in H. Kierzkowski (ed.) *Protection and Competition in International Trade*. (Oxford: Basil Blackwell).

―― (1992), 'Third-Country Effects of a Nondiscriminatory Tariff', Research Forum in International Economics Discussion Paper no. 306 (Ann Arbor: University of Michigan).

―― and Stern, R. (1985), *Methods of Measurement of Non-Tariff Barriers* (Geneva: UNCTAD).

―― ―― (1987), 'Current Issues in Trade Policy: An Overview', in R. Stern (ed.), *US Trade Polices in a Changing World Economy* (Cambridge, Mass.: MIT Press).

De Jong, H. (1968), 'The Significance of Dumping in International Trade', *Journal of World Trade Law*, 2: 162–88.

De Melo, J., Panagariya, A. and Rodrik, D. (1992), 'Regional Integration: An Analytical and Empirical Overview', in J. de Melo and A. Panagariya (eds.), *New Dimensions in Regional Integration* (Cambridge: Cambridge University Press).

Downs, A. (1954), *An Economic Theory of Democracy* (New York: Harper & Row).

Edwards, S. and Savastano, M. (1989), 'Latin America's Intra-Regional Trade: Evolution and Future', in D. T. Greenaway, T. Hyclak, and R. Thornton (eds.), *Economic Aspects of Regional Trading Arrangements* (New York: New York University Press).

Eglin, R. (1987), 'Surveillance of Balance-of-Payments Measures in the GATT', *World Economy*, 10: 1–26.

Ehrenberg, R. (1994), *Labor Markets and Integrating National Economies* (Washington DC: Brookings Institution).

Esty, D. (1994), *Greening the GATT: Trade, Environment and the Future* (Washington DC: Institute for International Economics).

Ethier, W. (1982), 'Dumping', *Journal of Political Economy*, 90: 487–506.

Evans, J. W. (1972), *The Kennedy Round in American Trade Policy* (Cambridge: Harvard University Press).

Feinberg, R. and Kaplan, S. (1993), 'Fishing Downstream: The Political Economy of Effective Protection', *Canadian Journal of Economics*, 26: 150–58.

Feketekuty, G. (1988), *International Trade in Services: An Overview and Blueprint for Negotiations* (Cambridge Mass.: Ballinger Publications).

—— (1992), 'The New Trade Agenda', Occasional Paper no. 40 (Washington DC: Group of Thirty).

Finch, D, and Michalopoulos, C. (1988), 'Development, Trade, and International Organizations', in A. Krueger (ed.), *Development with Trade: LDCs and the International Economy* (San Francisco: Institute for Contemporary Studies).

Finger, J. M. (1974), 'Tariff Concessions and the Exports of Developing Countries', *Economic Journal*, 335: 566–75.

—— (1979), 'Trade Liberalization: A Public Choice Perspective', in R. Amacher, G. Haberler, and T. Willett (eds.), *Challenges to a Liberal International Economic Order* (Washington DC: American Enterprise Institute).

—— (1982), 'Incorporating the Gains from Trade into Policy', *World Economy*, 5: 367–77.Finger,

—— (1991), 'The GATT as International Discipline Over Trade Restrictions: A Public Choice Approach', in R. Vaubel and T. Willett (eds.), *The Political Economy of International Organizations: A Public Choice Approach* (Boulder, Colo.: Westview Press).

—— (ed.) (1993*a*), *Antidumping: How it Works and Who Gets Hurt* (Ann Arbor: University of Michigan Press).

—— (1993*b*), 'GATT's Influence on Regional Agreements', in J. de Melo and A. Panagariya (eds.), *New Dimensions in Regional Integration* Cambridge: Cambridge University Press).

—— (1994), 'Subsidies and Countervailing Measures and Anti-Dumping Agreements', in *The New World Trading System: Readings* (Paris: OECD).

—— (1995), 'Legalized Backsliding: Safeguard Provisions in the GATT', in W. Martin and A. Winters (eds.), *The Uruguay Round and the Developing Economies* (Washington DC: The World Bank, forthcoming).

―――― and Murray, T. (1990), 'Policing Unfair Imports: The United States Example', *Journal of World Trade*, 24: 39–55.

―――― and Olechowski, A. (eds.) (1987), *The Uruguay Round: A Handbook for the Multilateral Trade Negotiations* (Washington DC: The World Bank).

――――, Hall, H.K., and Nelson, D. (1982), 'The Political Economy of Administered Protection', *American Economic Review*, 72: 452–66.

Fitchett, D. (1987), 'Agriculture', in J. M. Finger and A. Olechowski (eds.), *The Uruguay Round: A Handbook on the Multilateral Trade Negotiations* (Washington DC: The World Bank).

Garrett, G. (1992), 'International Cooperation and Institutional Choice: The European Community's Internal Market', *International Organization*, 46: 543–60.

Garten, J. (1994), 'New Challenges in the World Economy: The Antidumping Law and US Trade Policy', speech presented at the US Chamber of Commerce, Washington DC, 7 Apr.

GATT (General Agreement on Tariffs and Trade) (1985), *Trade Policies for a Better Future: Proposals for Action*, Leutwiler Report (Geneva: GATT).

―――― (1986), *The Text of the General Agreement* (Geneva: GATT).

―――― (1988), *GATT Activities, 1987* (Geneva: GATT).

―――― (1989), *GATT Activities, 1988* (Geneva: GATT).

―――― (1994*a*), *The Results of the Uruguay Round of Multilateral Trade Negotiations: The Legal Texts* (Geneva: GATT Secretariat).

―――― (1994*b*), *Analytical Index* (Geneva: GATT Secretariat).

―――― (1994*c*), 'The Results of the Uruguay Round: Market Access for Goods and Services' (Geneva: GATT Secretariat).

―――― (1995), *International Trade: Trends and Statistics* (Geneva: GATT).

Globerman, S. (1992), 'North American Trade Liberalization and Intra Industry Trade', *Weltwirtschaftliches Archiv*, 128: 487–97.

Graham, E. M. and Richardson, J.D. (1994), Summary of the Institute for International Economics Project on International Competition Policies (Paris: OECD).

Greenaway, D. (1987), 'Intra-Industry Trade, Intra-Firm Trade and European Integration: Evidence, Gains and Policy Analysis', *Journal of Common Market Studies*, 26: 153–72.

Groupe MAC (1988), *Technical Barriers in the EC: An Illustration by Six Industries*, Research on the Costs of Non-Europe, vol. vi (Brussels: Commission of the European Communities).

Hamilton, C. and Whalley, J.. (1989), 'Coalitions in the Uruguay Round', *Weltwirtschaftliches Archiv*, 125: 547–62.

Herin, J. (1986), 'Rules of Origin and Differences between Tariff Levels in EFTA and in the EC', Occasional Paper no. 13 (Geneva: EFTA).

Hillman, A. and Moser, P. (1995), 'Trade Liberalization as Politically Optimal Exchange of Market Access', in M. Canzoneri, W. Ethier, and V. Grilli (eds.), *The New Transatlantic Economy* (New York: Cambridge University Press).

Hindley, B. (1987), 'Different and more Favorable Treatment — and Graduation', in J. M. Finger and A. Olechowski (eds.), *The Uruguay Round: A Handbook for the Multilateral Trade Negotiations* (Washington DC: The World Bank).

—— (1994), 'Safeguards, VERs and Anti-Dumping Action', in OECD, *The New World Trading System: Readings* (Paris: OECD).

—— and Messerlin, P. (1993) 'Guarantees of Market Access and Regionalism', in K. Anderson and R. Blackhurst (eds.), *Regionalism and the Global Trading System* (London: Harvester-Wheatsheaf).

Hipple, F. S. (1990), 'The Measurement of International Trade Related to Multinational Companies', *American Economic Review*, 80: 1263–70.

Hirschman, A. (1981), 'Three Uses of Political Economy in Analyzing European Integration', ch. 12 of id., *Essays in Trespassing* (London: Cambridge University Press).

—— (1969), *National Power and the Structure of Foreign Trade* (Berkeley: University of California Press).

Hoekman, B. (1993), 'Multilateral Trade Negotiations and Coordination of Commercial Policies', in R. Stern (ed.), *The Multilateral Trading System: Analysis and Options for Change* (Ann Arbor: University of Michigan Press).

—— (1995*a*), 'Tentative First Steps: An Assessment of the Uruguay Round Agreement on Services', in W. Martin and A. Winters (eds.), *The Uruguay Round and the Developing Economies* (Washington DC: World Bank, forthcoming).

—— (1995*b*), *Trade Laws and Institutions: Good Practices and the World Trade Organization* (Washington DC: World Bank).

—— and Crémoux, P. (1993), 'Perspectives for Multilateral Reductions in Agricultural Support Policies', in R. Stern (ed.), *The Multilateral Trading System* (Ann Arbor: University of Michigan Press).

—— and Leidy, M. (1990), 'Policy Responses to Shifting Comparative Advantage: Designing a System of Emergency Protection,' *Kyklos*, 43: 25–51.

—— —— (1992*a*), 'Cascading Contingent Protection', *European Economic Review*, 36: 883–92.

—— —— (1992*b*), 'Environmental Policy Formation in a Trading Economy: A Public Choice Perspective', in K. Anderson and R. Blackhurst (eds.), *The Greening of World Trade Issues* (London: Harvester-Wheatsheaf).

—— —— (1993), 'Holes and Loopholes in Integration Agreements: History and Prospects', in K. Anderson and R. Blackhurst (eds.), *Regional Integration and the Global Trading System* (London: Harvester-Wheatsheaf).

—— and Mavroidis, P. C. (1994*a*), 'Competition, Competition Policy and the GATT', *World Economy*, 17: 121–50.

—— —— (1994*b*), 'Antitrust-based Remedies and Dumping in International Trade', Discussion Paper no. 1010 (London: Centre for Economic Policy Research).

—— —— (1995), 'The WTO's Government Procurement Agreement', *Public Procurement Law Review*, 4: 63–79.

Hudec, R. (1987), *GATT and the Developing Countries* (Aldershot: Gower, for the Trade Policy Research Centre).

—— (1993), *Enforcing International Trade Law: The Evolution of the Modern GATT Legal System* (New York: Butterworth).

Jackson, J. H. (1969), *World Trade and the Law of GATT* (Indianapolis: Bobbs-Merrill).

—— (1989), *The World Trading System: Law and Policy of International Economic Relations* (Cambridge, Mass.: MIT Press).

—— (1990), *Restructuring the GATT System* (London: Pinter Publishers).

—— (1994), 'The World Trade Organization, Dispute Settlement, and Codes of Conduct', in B. Bosworth and S. Collins (eds.), *The New GATT: Implications for the United States* (Washington DC: Brookings Institution).

Jacquemin, A. (1994), 'Goals and Means of European Antitrust Policy After 1992', in H. Demsetz and A. Jacquemin (eds.), *Antitrust Economics: New Challenges for Competition Policy* (Lund: Lund University Press).

Josling, T. (1977), *Agriculture in the Tokyo Round Negotiations* Thames Essay no. 10 (Ashford: Headly Brothers for the Trade Policy Research Centre).

—— (1994), 'Agriculture and Natural Resources', in S. Collins and B. Bosworth (eds.), *The New GATT* (Washington DC: Brookings Institution).

Kemp, M. and Wan, H. (1976), 'An Elementary Proposition Concerning the Formation of Customs Unions', *Journal of International Economics*, 6: 95–7.

Kindleberger, C. (1983), 'Standards as Public, Collective and Private Goods', *Kyklos*, 36: 377–96.

Kostecki, M. (1979), *East-West Trade and the GATT System* (London: Macmillan Press for the Trade Policy Research Centre).

—— (1982), *State Trading in International Markets* (New York: St Martin's Press).

—— (1983), 'Trade Control Measures and Decision Making', *Economia Internazionale*, 36: 1–20.

—— (1987), 'Export Restraint Agreements and Trade Liberalization', *World Economy*, 10: 425–53.

—— (1991), 'Marketing Strategies Between Dumping and Anti-Dumping Action', *European Journal of Marketing*, 25: 7–19.

—— and Tymowski, M. J. (1985), 'Customs Duties versus Other Import Charges in the Developing Countries', *Journal of World Trade Law*, 19: 269–86.

Kotler, P. Fahey, L., and Jatusripitak, S. (1987), *La Concurrence Total* (Paris: Les Editions d'Organisations).

Kowalczyk, C. (1990), 'Welfare and Customs Unions', NBER Working Paper no. 3476, (Cambridge, Mass.: NBER)..

Krasner, S. D. (1983), 'Structural Causes and Regime Consequences: Regimes as Intervening Variables', in S. Krasner (ed.), *International Regimes* (Ithaca, NY: Cornell University Press).

Krueger, A. (1992), 'Free Trade Agreements as Protectionist Devices: Rules of Origin', (Durham, NC: Duke University, mimeo).

Lawrence, R. and Litan, R. (1991), 'The World Trading System After the Uruguay Round', *Boston University International Law Journal*, 8: 247–76.

Leary, V. (1994), 'Worker's Rights and International Trade: The Social Clause', in J. Bhagwati and R. Hudec (eds.), *Harmonization and Fair Trade: Prerequisite for Free Trade?* (Cambridge, Mass.: MIT Press, forthcoming).

Leidy, M. (1994a), 'Trade Policy and Indirect Rent-Seeking: A Synthesis of Recent Work', *Economics and Politics*, 6: 97–118.

—— (1994b), 'Quid Pro Quo Restraint and Spurious Injury: Subsidies and the Prospect of CVDs', in A. Deardorff and R. Stern (eds.), *Analytical and Negotiating Issues in the Global Trading System* (Ann Arbor: University of Michigan Press).

—— and Hoekman, B. (1993), 'What to Expect from Regional and Multilateral

Trade Negotiations: A Public Choice Perspective', in K. Anderson and R. Blackhurst (eds.), *Regional Integration and the Global Trading System* (New York: Harvester-Wheatsheaf).

Levitt, T. (1983), 'The Globalization of Markets,' *Harvard Business Review*, May–June, 92–102.

Low, P. (1993a), *Trading Free: The GATT and US Trade Policy* (New York: Twentieth Century Fund).

—— (1993b) (ed.), *International Trade and the Environment* (Washington DC: World Bank.

—— (1995), *Preshipment Inspection Services* (Washington DC: World Bank).

—— and Subramanian, A. (1995), 'TRIMs in the Uruguay Round: An Unfinished Business?', in W. Martin and A. Winters (eds.), *The Uruguay Round and the Developing Economies* (Washington DC: World Bank, forthcoming).

McCloskey, D. (1982), *The Applied Theory of Price* (New York: Macmillan).

McMillan, J. (1993), 'Does Regional Integration Foster Open Trade? Economic Theory and GATT's Article XXIV', in K. Anderson and R. Blackhurst (eds.), *Regional Integration and the Global Trading System* (London: Harvester-Wheatsheaf).

Mansfield, E. (1994), 'Intellectual Property Protection, Foreign Direct Investment, and Technology Transfer', IFC Discussion Paper no. 19 (Washington DC: World Bank).

Maskus, K. and Eby-Konan, D. (1994), 'Trade-Related Intellectual Property Rights: Issues and Exploratory Results', in A. Deardorff and R. Stern (eds.), *Analytical and Negotiating Issues in the Global Trading System* (Ann Arbor: University of Michigan Press).

Mavroidis, P. C. (1992), 'Surveillance Schemes: The GATT's New Trade Policy Review Mechanism', *Michigan Journal of International Law*, 13: 374–414.

Messerlin, P. (1989), 'The EC Antidumping Regulations: A First Economic Appraisal, 1980–85', *Weltwirtschaftliches Archiv*, 125: 563–87.

—— (1990a), 'Antidumping Regulations or Procartel Law? The EC Chemical Cases', *World Economy*, 13: 465–92.

—— (1990b), 'The Antidumping Regulations of the European Community: The "Privatization" of Administered Protection', in M. Trebilcock and R. York (eds.), *Fair Exchange: Reforming Trade Remedy Laws* (Toronto: C. D. Howe Institute).

—— and Noguchi, Y. (1991), 'The EC Antidumping and Anticircumvention Regulations: A Costly Exercise in Futility' (Paris: Institut d'Etudes Politiques), mimeo.

Olson, M. (1965), *The Logic of Collective Action: Public Goods and the Theory of Groups*, Harvard Economic Studies (Cambridge, Mass.: Harvard University Press).

OECD (Organization for Economic Cooperation and Development) (1993), *Industrial Policy in OECD Countries, Annual Review 1992* (Paris: OECD).

Palmeter, N. D. (1995), 'US Implementation of the Uruguay Round Antidumping Code', *Journal of World Trade*, June.

Patterson, G. (1966), *Discrimination in International Trade: The Policy Issues, 1945–1965* (Princeton, NJ: Princeton University Press).

Penrose, E. (1953), *Economic Planning for the Peace* (Princeton, NJ: Princeton Unversity Press).

Petersmann, E.-U. (1994), 'The Dispute Settlement System of the World Trade

Organization and the Evolution of the GATT Dispute Settlement System Since 1948', *Common Market Law Review*, 31: 1157–1244.

Prebisch, R. (1952), 'The Economic Development of Latin America and its Principal Problems', *Economic Bulletin for Latin America*, 7: 1–22.

Preeg, E. (1970), *Traders and Diplomats* (Washington DC: Brookings Institution).

Primo-Braga, C., Safadi, R., and Yeats, A. (1994), 'Regional Integration in the Americas: *Déjà-Vu* all over Again?', *World Economy*, 17: 577–601.

Rodrik, D. (1994*a*), 'What Does the Political Economy Literature on Trade Policy (Not) Tell Us That We Ought to Know?', Discussion Paper no. 1039 (London: Centre for Economic Policy Research).

—— (1994*b*), 'Comments on Maskus and Eby-Konan', in A. Deardorff and R. Stern (eds.), *Analytical and Negotiating Issues in the Global Trading System* (Ann Arbor: University of Michigan Press).

Roessler, F. (1978), 'The Rationale for Reciprocity in Trade Negotiations', *Kyklos*, 31: 258–74.

—— (1980), 'The GATT Declaration on Trade Measures taken for Balance-of-Payments', *Case Western Reserve Journal of International Law*, 12: 383–403.

—— (1982), 'State Trading and Trade Liberalization', in M. Kostecki (ed.), *State Trading in International Markets* (London: Macmillan).

—— (1985), 'The Scope, Limits and Function of the GATT Legal System', *World Economy*, 8: 289–98.

Sampson, G. (1987), 'Safeguards', in J. M. Finger and A. Olechowski (eds.), *The Uruguay Round: A Handbook for the Multilateral Trade Negotiations* (Washington DC: World Bank).

—— and Snape, R. (1985), 'Identifying the Issues in Trade in Services', *World Economy*, 8: 171–81.

Samuelson, W. (1985), 'A Comment on the Coase Theorem', in A. Roth (ed.), *Game Theoretic Models of Bargaining* (Cambridge: Cambridge University Press).

Schott, J. (1989) (ed.), *Free Trade Areas and US Trade Policy* (Washington D.C: Institute for International Economics).

—— and Buurman, J. (1994), *The Uruguay Round: An Assessment* (Washington DC: Institute for International Economics).

Sherwood, R. (1990), *Intellectual Property and Economic Development* (Boulder, Colo.: Westview Press).

Snape, R. (1987), 'The Importance of Frontier Barriers', in H. Kierzkowski (ed.), *Protection and Competition in International Trade* (London: Basil Blackwell).

—— (1993), 'History and Economics of GATT's Article XXIV', in K. Anderson and R. Blackhurst (eds.), *Regional Integration and the Global Trading System* (London: Harvester-Wheatsheaf).

—— Adams, J., and Morgan, D. (1993), *Regional Trading Arrangements: Implications and Options for Australia* (Canberra: Australian Government Publishing Service).

Tollison, R. and Willett, T. (1979), 'An Economic Theory of Mutually Advantageous Issue Linkages in International Negotiations', *International Organization*, 33: 425–49.

Tumlir, J. (1983), 'Strong and Weak Elements in the Concept of European Integration', in F. Machlup, G. Fels and H. Müller-Groeling (eds.), *Reflections on a Troubled World Economy* (London: Macmillan).

—— (1985), *Protectionism: Trade Policy in Democratic Societies* (Washington DC: American Enterprise Institute).

UNCTAD, (1985), 'Services and the Development Process', TD/B/1008/Rev. 1 (Geneva: United Nations).

—— (1994), *The Outcome of the Uruguay Round—Supporting Papers to the Trade and Development Report, 1994* (Geneva: United Nations).

—— and World Bank (1994), *Liberalizing International Transactions in Services: A Handbook* (Geneva: United Nations).

Vaubel, R. (1986), 'A Public Choice Approach to International Organization', *Public Choice*, 51: 39–57.

Vousden, N. (1990), *The Economics of Trade Protection* (Cambridge: Cambridge University Press).

Wheeler, D. and Mody, A. (1992), 'International Investment Location Decisions: The Case of US Firms', *Journal of International Economics*, 33: 57–76.

Weston, A. (1994), 'The Uruguay Round: Unraveling the Implications for the Least-Developed and Low-Income Countries' (Geneva: UNCTAD).

Winham, G. (1986), *International Trade and the Tokyo Round Negotiation* (Princeton, NJ: Princeton University Press).

Winters, L. A. (1987*a*), 'Reciprocity', in J. M. Finger and A. Olechowski (eds.), *The Uruguay Round: A Handbook for the Multilateral Trade Negotiations* (Washington DC: World Bank).

—— (1987*b*), 'The Political Economy of the Agricultural Policy of Industrialized Countries', *European Review of Agricultural Economics*, 14: 285–304.

—— (1994*a*), 'Subsidies', in *The New World Trading System: Readings*. (Paris: OECD).

—— (1994*b*), 'The EC and World Protectionism: Dimensions of the Political Economy', Discussion Paper no. 897 (London: Centre for Economic Policy Research).

—— (1995) (ed.), *Foundations of an Open Economy: Trade Laws and Institutions for Eastern Europe* (London: Centre for Economic Policy Research).

Wonnacott, R. (1991), *The Economics of Overlapping Free Trade Areas and the Mexican Challenge* (Toranto: C.D. Howe Institute).

World Bank (1986), *World Development Report* (Washington DC: World Bank).

——(1995), *Global Economic Prospects and the Developing Economies* (Washington DC: World Bank).

Xafa, M., Kronenberg, R., and Landell-Mills, J. (1992), 'The European Community's Trade and Trade-Related Industrial Policies', Working Paper no. 92/94 (Washington DC: International Monetary Fund).

Yang, Y. (1994), 'The Impact of Phasing out the MFA on World Clothing and Textile Markets', *Journal of Development Studies*, 30: 892–915.

INDEX